New NF/NF JUN 4 2004

917.75
B57w
2004

A TRAILS BOOKS GUIDE

WISCONSIN'S OUTDOOR TREASURES

A Guide to 150 Natural Destinations

TIM BEWER

TRAILS BOOKS
Black Earth, Wisconsin

Library of Congress Control Number: 2003105893
ISBN: 1-931599-29-7

Editor: Jerry Minnich
Project Manager: Michael Martin
Assistant Project Manager: Erika Reise
Designer: Denise Sauter
Cover and Text Photos: Wisconsin Department of Tourism
Author Photo: Candice Bartholomew

Printed in the United States of America

08 07 06 05 04   6 5 4 3 2 1

Trails Books, a division of Trails Media Group, Inc.
P.O. Box 317 • Black Earth, WI 53515
(800) 236-8088 • e-mail: info@wistrails.com
www.wistrails.com

THANKS TO...

everyone who sent me information or took the time to answer my questions. Special thanks to Kirsten Frickle for all her helpful advice and for introducing me to piping plovers.

Contents

NORTHWEST

SOUTHWEST

SOUTHEAST

Baby black bear.

Introduction

WISCONSIN IS THE LAND that inspired John Muir, one of America's early leaders in the effort to preserve the natural world; Aldo Leopold, a pioneer in the study of ecology, and Frank Lloyd Wright, whose prairie style of architecture was derived from nature. Wisconsin may not have mountains or oceans, but those of us who know the state well would never trade its subtle but fantastic scenery. I have traveled throughout the world and am still routinely awed by the natural beauty of my home state. From the Mississippi River bluffs, to the forests of the Northwoods, to the glacial topography covering most of the state, there is a world of undiscovered and underappreciated beauty here. This book will lead you to some of Wisconsin's best and hopefully create a greater appreciation for the land that makes this state such a wonderful place.

In the two years that went into researching and writing this book I visited well-known places including all of the state and national parks and forests, but I also searched out lesser-known areas including county parks, state wildlife areas, state natural areas, and private reserves. I personally visited nearly 500 properties in search of Wisconsin's best and, as you will see, not only are these little-known places often just as beautiful as the well-known parks, but often visitors will have the entire areas to themselves.

This is a guide for nature lovers and so it emphasizes the natural aspects of each area and offers practical advice for visitors such as detailed trail information, where to go to avoid the crowds, and where to view wildlife. Information about campgrounds and other facilities is also provided—it is just not the main focus. I hope you find this guide both useful and enjoyable.

Wisconsin's unique glacial legacy.

Planning Your Trip

WHEN TO GO

Summer and weekends are by far the busiest times to visit any of these sites; put them together and some of the more popular areas can be downright crowded. Naturally, holiday weekends are the worst. Still, even at the most popular properties such as Devil's Lake or Peninsula state parks, hiking trails remain an underappreciated commodity and you should find sufficient solitude if you get out and walk. Two other events to keep in mind are the opening weekend of Wisconsin's fishing season, held annually the first weekend in May, and the deer-gun hunting season which always begins the weekend before Thanksgiving. Large bodies of water such as the Chippewa Flowage will be nearly covered with boats during the former, and it's just too dangerous to be out hiking in most places during the nine days of the latter.

While summer is by far the most popular time to get outdoors, the other seasons have much to offer, including more solitude. In the off-season it is possible that you could find yourself all alone at some places. Fall is the perfect outdoors time. Not only do you get the short-lived beauty of the changing colors, but the cooler climate is nearly perfect, mosquitoes and flies are gone, and wildlife becomes more active in preparation for the coming winter. In winter, frozen waterfalls and ice-sculpted shorelines can be truly spectacular, and a fresh snowfall has a beauty all its own. Tracking animals in the snow is rewarding, even if you never do see your prey. Like fall, spring offers cooler temperatures and the lack of mosquitoes and flies, and wildflowers explode on the forest floor before the leaves on the trees come out and steal all the sunlight. Young animals can be a thrilling sight, and the birds that flew south for the winter are returning.

WILDLIFE WATCHING

Wisconsin is home to a wide variety of wildlife, and watching these creatures is one of the fastest-growing outdoor activities in Wisconsin and across the country. Well over 400 bird species have been recorded in Wisconsin, along with 75 mammals, 20 amphibians, and 35 reptiles. To increase your chances of seeing wildlife, move slowly since sudden movements will startle animals. Animals are most active in the early morning and late afternoon to early evening, so these are the best times to look. Lists of birds and sometimes other animals that have been seen at a particular place are often available—just ask. Also, field guides, binoculars, hand lenses, and similar items may be borrowed from many state parks, although you can never be sure what they will have or even if the office will be open, so it is best to bring your own if you have them.

Many places, especially state wildlife areas, have closed areas (always clearly marked) which prohibit hunting at certain times. Even though these areas may not prohibit entry, they should be avoided during the times posted to protect nesting or migrating birds.

STATE PARK STICKER AND STATE TRAIL PASS

All motor vehicles stopping in state parks, forests, and recreation areas must have a state park sticker. The admission sticker allows unlimited visits to all properties within the state park system for the year in which it was purchased and, considering just how good the system is, the sticker is one of the greatest bargains available anywhere. Visitors may also purchase a daily sticker (valid for two days if you are camping) or even a one-hour pass at some properties. Stickers are available for purchase at all properties where they are required.

The state trail pass, also available in a daily or annual variety, is required for all people age 16 or older on most long-distance state recreation trails (it is not required for hikers) as well as some off-road bike, horse, and cross-country ski trails in state parks and forests. Like the park sticker, a trail pass is valid at all locations. They can be bought at self-registration stations at major trail access points, and at area businesses and DNR offices.

CAMPING RESERVATIONS

Though not always necessary, it would be wise to make reservations for summer weekends. And while you can usually get by without them during the week at all but the most popular parks, reservations are still a good idea. Reserve America handles reservations for both Wisconsin's state park system and the Chequamegon-Nicolet National Forest, though policies and procedures differ for each. Although their fees are outrageous, Reserve America is your only reservation option, so do not call the campground to make a reservation. However, park or forest staff will be happy to answer all other camping-related questions, including telling you whether you really need a reservation for the particular time that you will be there. For all other properties, including the Apostle Islands National Lakeshore, call the office directly.

The number for the state park system is (888) 947-2757—or (800) 274-7275 for TTY service; you can also book on-line at www.reserveamerica.com. Sites are available 11 months in advance and, if you pay with a credit card, as late as two days before arrival. The non-refundable reservation fee is $9.50, and they charge another $8.50 to make any changes or $5 to cancel.

For National Forest campgrounds, you need to call (877) 444-6777 or log on to www.reserveusa.com. Campsites may be booked anytime between eight months and four days in advance, and the non-refundable reservation fee is $9, while a change or cancellation will cost you $10.

MAPS

With the exception of most state wildlife areas, maps for just about every property detailed in this book are available on site. You can get wildlife area maps through the appropriate DNR offices or use DeLorme Publishing's *Wisconsin Atlas and Gazetteer*, which shows most trails, dikes, and service roads. Even without one of these maps, the trail descriptions in the text provide sufficient information to hike without getting lost.

Though the company does a poor job keeping it current, the *Wisconsin Atlas and Gazetteer* remains the best map available for touring the state. The Official State Highway Map, available free from the Wisconsin Department of Tourism—(800) 432-8747, www.travelwisconsin.com—is good enough to get you to all the places covered by this book.

RUSTIC ROADS

Created in 1973, the Rustic Road System helps to preserve scenic, lightly traveled, and largely undisturbed country roads. Brown and yellow signs mark the routes, and if any pass through a property included in this book, they are listed under the AUTO TOUR section. To obtain a free booklet with maps and information about all of Wisconsin's Rustic Roads, or to suggest a new road for inclusion, call the Wisconsin Department of Transportation at (608) 266-8108 or access www.dot.wisconsin.gov/travel/scenic/rusticroads.htm

THE NATURE CONSERVANCY

The Nature Conservancy, an international nonprofit organization, works to protect some of the most ecologically-sensitive areas in the state, mostly through outright purchase of land. They also obtain conservation easements and work with private landowners toward effective land management. The Wisconsin Chapter has protected over 62,000 acres across the state, and seven of their properties are detailed in this book: the Catherine Wolter Wilderness Area, Mink River Estuary, Page Creek Marsh, Quincy Bluff and Wetlands Preserve, and Hemlock Draw, Baxter's Hollow, and Honey Creek in the Baraboo Hills.

To become a member, send a donation, get information, or report vandalism and other problems, contact them at (608) 251-8140. http://nature.org/wisconsin; Email: wmail@tnc.org

Please observe the following guidelines when visiting a Nature Conservancy preserve.

— DO NOT pick flowers, berries, nuts, mushrooms, shells, rocks, or other parts of the natural landscape. Collecting plants, animals, and minerals is allowed for scientific research ONLY and requires a permit from the Wisconsin Conservancy office.

Respect these restrictions; the following are NOT ALLOWED on Conservancy preserves:

— Pets (even on a leash, with the exception of seeing-eye dogs).

— Horseback riding.

— Bicycles or other off-road vehicles.

— Ice skating.

— Fires.

— Rock climbing, rappelling, ice climbing, or spelunking.

— Camping.

— Fishing or trapping.

— Hunting (except by permit on preserves where deer damage is excessive).

— Also, please do not trespass on private property adjacent to Conservancy preserves.

DONALD S. ABRAMS

The Ice Age Trail, a Wisconsin original.

Ice Age National
Scenic Trail and Scientific Reserve

APPROXIMATELY 100,000 years ago, near the beginning of the last Ice Age, or more properly the Pleistocene Epoch, the Wisconsin glacier began its slow crawl south through North America. Around 25,000 years ago the massive ice sheet hit Wisconsin and spent nearly 15,000 years advancing and retreating across the state, carving up much of the land as it moved forward and dropping tons of sand, silt, and rock as it melted back. The Wisconsin, the last of the four stages of the great glacier to cover most of northern North America, stretched from the Atlantic coast to the Rocky Mountains, but nowhere did it leave behind such outstanding examples of glacial landforms as it did in the Badger State.

The glacier, up to a mile thick in some places, formed such remarkable features as eskers, kames, and potholes, and even land not buried by the glaciers was sculpted by rushing meltwater and the enormous temporary rivers and lakes it filled. Even more amazing, though less obvious to the naked eye, is that the land once under the glaciers has rebounded as much as 160 feet since the glaciers left and is still rising about half an inch per year, a process known as isostatic uplift.

The Ice Age National Scientific Reserve, established in 1971, covers 40,000 acres in nine units and is a cooperative effort between the National Park Service and the Wisconsin Department of Natural Resources. It protects some of the world's most significant glacial landforms, though it is a far cry from the 800-mile Ice Age Glacier National Forest Park proposed by Milwaukee attorney Ray Zillmer in the 1950s. Unfortunately, at that time the National Park Service could not imagine a long and narrow park like this, and they dismissed the idea. Local citizens, however, had bigger dreams than the bureaucrats, and decided to push forward with the trail that Zillmer had envisioned, traversing the length of the park. Volunteers began building the trail through the Kettle Moraine State Forest in the 1950s, and it was designated a National Scenic Trail in 1980.

The 1,200-mile trail roughly follows the moraine of the Wisconsin Glacier. From Potawatomi State Park in Door County, the trail heads south through the Kettle Moraine and on over to Green County, where it swings north to Langlade County and then turns west, ending on a steep vertical bluff high above the St. Croix River in Interstate State Park, in Polk County. So far, approximately 600 miles of trail are completed and open to hiking, though only about half have been officially certified by the National Park Service.

The reserve units with developed facilities include the Kettle Moraine State Forest-Northern Unit, Horicon Marsh State Wildlife Area, Devil's Lake State Park, Mill Bluff State Park, Chippewa Moraine Ice Age State Recreation Area, and Interstate State Park. Each is detailed individually in its own section of this book. The three other units are the Campbellsport Drumlins, Cross Plains, and Two Creeks Buried Forest. The Campbellsport Drumlins Unit covers 3,600 acres in Fond du Lac County and is impressive for the abundance of its namesake geologic feature. The area lies near the town of Campbellsport, just west of the Northern Kettle Moraine State Forest, and is best viewed from Scenic Drive, which forms the unit's northern border. The 160-acre Cross Plains Unit is located at the edge of the glacial advance in Dane County, and features a subglacial gorge carved by the rushing meltwaters. At just 25 acres, the world-famous (among geologists, that is) Two Creeks Buried Forest Unit in Manitowoc County is by far the smallest unit. The trees discovered here are about 12,000 years old, and because they were buried under soil and rock, they were not destroyed when the glaciers last advanced over them. The site provides evidence that the periods between glacial advances were long enough for forests to take hold. In order to protect the site, entry is discouraged; besides, there is really nothing of interest to see.

WILDLIFE—Most animals native to Wisconsin may be seen along the various segments of the trail.

HIKING—The Ice Age Trail connects five of the reserve units: Kettle Moraine, Devil's Lake, Chippewa Moraine, Interstate, and eventually Cross Plains. There might also be a connector trail to the Two Creeks Buried Forest some day. An icon marks properties detailed in this book that have trail segments ![icon] or are Ice Age Reserve units ![icon]. Some of the most outstanding trail segments are in the Chequamegon-Nicolet National Forest, the northern and southern units of the Kettle Moraine State Forest, Hartman Creek State Park and Emmons Creek Fishery Area, and the Chippewa Moraine Ice Age State Recreation Area. Much of the trail is on private land so please be extra courteous on these segments. Disrespectful hikers littering and straying from the trail have forced landowners to close a few routes.

For the full scoop on the trail, pick up detailed maps or the *Ice Age Trail Companion Guide* from the Ice Age Park & Trail Foundation. The DNR's interactive Ice Age Trail Map Buffet (www.dnr.state.wi.us/org/at/et/geo/iceage) is another helpful resource.

CANOEING—The Horicon Marsh, Chippewa Moraine, and Interstate State Park reserve units offer good canoeing.

BIKING—The trail follows portions of the Ahnapee, Glacial Drumlin, Sugar

River, Military Ridge, Tuscobia, and Gandy Dancer state trails which are all open to bikes. A few other segments are also open to off-road bikes, but for the most part the trail is hiking only and will remain so.

WINTER—Several segments are groomed for cross-country skiing or have ad-joining trails that are. All units of the Kettle Moraine State Forest (Lapham Peak is the only place along the trail lit for night skiing), Indian Lake County Park, Devil's Lake State Park, the Rib Lake Trails, and Hartman Creek State Park are some of the most popular. All are detailed elsewhere in this book.

OTHER—Horses are allowed on the Ahnapee, Tuscobia, and Gandy Dancer state trails, and the Ice Age Trail through the Chequamegon-Nicolet National Forest.

COUNTIES—There are trail segments in Door, Kewaunee, Manitowoc, She-boygan, Fond du Lac, Washington, Waukesha, Jefferson, Walworth, Rock, Green, Dane, Columbia, Sauk, Marquette, Waushara, Portage, Waupaca, Marathon, Langlade, Lincoln, Taylor, Price, Chippewa, Rusk, Barron, Wash-burn, Burnett, and Polk counties. Eventually the trail will also pass through Adams and maybe Juneau counties. Dodge and Monroe counties have reserve units, but not trail segments.

DIRECTIONS—Campbellsport Drumlins Unit is one mile north of Camp-bellsport (in Fond du Lac County) on County V, then one mile west on County Y. Cross Plains Unit is three miles east of Cross Plains (in Dane County) on Highway 14, then half a mile south on Cleveland Rd. All other reserve units are described in their own sections elsewhere in this book.

FACILITIES—Ice Age Interpretive Centers are found at the Chippewa Mor-aine, Northern Kettle Moraine, and Interstate units.

CAMPING—Camping ranges from backpacking to Adirondack-style shel-ters to family campgrounds, depending on the unit or trail segment.

ENTRY—Open year-round. Many trail segments are closed during deer-gun hunting season. State park sticker or daily fee required for entry to state parks and forests. State trail pass required for use of bikes on state trails.

ON THE WEB—www.iceagetrail.org; www.aqd.nps.gov/grd/parks/icag; www.nps.gov/iatr

CONTACT—Ice Age Park & Trail Foundation, 207 E. Buffalo St., Suite 515, Milwaukee, WI 53202. Phone (414) 278-8518 or (800) 227-0046; National Park Service, 700 Rayovac Dr., Suite 100, Madison, WI 53711. Phone (608) 264-5610.

Ice Age Topography:
A Glossary

Drift—Rock material transported and deposited by glaciers.

Drumlin—A long, narrow hill of glacial drift facing the direction of glacial movement that formed under the glacial ice.

Erratic—A large rock picked up by the advancing glacier and deposited far from its source or in an unusual position.

Esker—A long, narrow ridge of glacial drift deposited in a subglacial stream.

Ice-Walled Lake Plain—A plateau formed by glacial drift first settling on the bottom of a lake formed by walls of ice in stagnating glaciers and then deposited on the ground when the glaciers melted.

Kame—A conical hill formed by glacial drift deposited down a hole in the glacier.

Kettle—A depression in the ground, usually circular and often filled with water, formed by a block of ice getting buried by glacial drift and then melting.

Moraine—A ridge of glacial drift deposited along the edge of a glacier. A "terminal moraine" marks the furthest extent of glacial advance while an "interlobate moraine" forms between two glacial lobes.

Outwash—Glacial drift carried beyond the edge of the glacier by meltwater, often forming an "outwash plain."

Pothole—Circular depression carved into rock by sand and gravel caught in a strong, persistent whirlpool.

White-tailed deer.

NORTHWEST

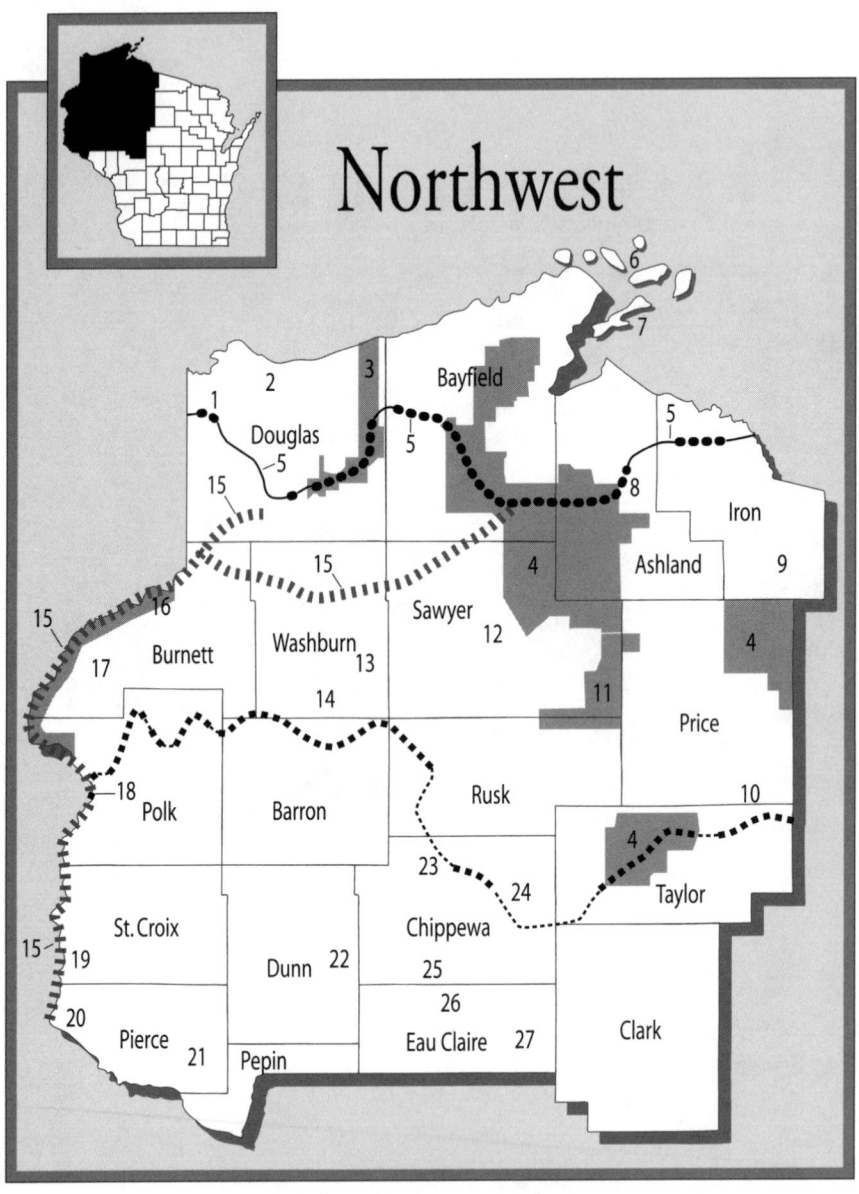

Northwest

Bayfield

Douglas

Iron

Ashland

Sawyer

Washburn

Burnett

Price

Polk

Barron

Rusk

Taylor

St. Croix

Dunn

Chippewa

Clark

Pierce

Pepin

Eau Claire

····················· *Proposed* Ice Age National Scenic Trail

■■■■■■■■■■■■■■■■ *Existing* Ice Age National Scenic Trail

8

1. Pattison State Park
2. Amnicon Falls State Park
3. Brule River State Forest
4. Chequamegon-Nicolet National Forest
5. North Country National Scenic Trail
6. Apostle Islands National Lakeshore
7. Big Bay State Park
8. Copper Falls State Park
9. Turtle-Flambeau Scenic Waters Area
10. Timm's Hill National Trail and Timm's Hill County Park
11. Flambeau River State Forest
12. Chippewa Flowage
13. Sawmill Lake and Loyhead Lake Primitive Canoe Routes
14. Hunt Hill Audobon Sanctuary
15. St. Croix National Scenic Riverway
16. Governor Knowles State Forest
17. Glacial Lake Grantsburg Wildlife Complex
18. Interstate State Park
19. Willow River State Park
20. Kinnickinnic State Park
21. Nugget Lake County Park
22. Hoffman Hills State Recreation Area
23. Chippewa Moraine Ice Age State Recreation Area and Townline-Knickerbocker Canoe Trail
24. Brunet Island State Park
25. Lake Wissota State Park
26. Beaver Creek Reserve
27. Augusta Wildlife Area

Pattison State Park

PATTISON STATE PARK is home to 165-foot Big Manitou Falls, Wisconsin's highest waterfall and the fourth highest east of the Rocky Mountains. Little Manitou Falls, in the southern end of the park, is no slouch either; at 31 feet it is the state's eighth tallest. Both drop over ancient lava deposited a billion years ago. At each of the falls is a picnic area and numerous overlooks, some of which are wheelchair accessible. The best waterfall viewing, especially for Little Manitou, is in spring when the river is running high, though they are worth a look at any time of the year. Scenic rapids are found along the rest of the Black River within the park, except at Interfalls Lake between the two falls.

Big Manitou Falls was an important gathering site for the Ojibwe, who were here when the first Europeans arrived. Not only was it a prominent landmark, but they believed that the voice of the Great Spirit Gitchi Monido could be heard here. Long before the Ojibwe, early Copper Culture tribes mined and shaped the metal they found in the area. In the mid-1800s miners again came looking for copper, and this was the site of the first known copper exploration in northwest Wisconsin, though prospectors had minimal success. Two more attempts were made at copper mining in the region before the turn of the 20th century, but they proved equally unsuccessful. Evidence of these attempts is scattered about the park. The most significant mining remnants are below each of the falls—look for a triangular opening below Big Manitou Falls and a shallow cave dug to the left of Little Manitou Falls.

Big Manitou Falls was almost destroyed by a hydroelectric dam planned for the Black River. Martin Pattison, a wealthy Superior businessman who loved the falls and surrounding area, secretly purchased 660 acres along the river in 1917, and the next year donated the land to the state for use as a park. He died later that year after having successfully thwarted the dam. The park opened in 1920 and today contains nearly 1,500 acres. Ironically, Pattison's appreciation for the area came from the time he spent logging along the Black River in and around what is now the park. While he made his vast fortune as a lumber baron, he later became successful in mining and banking and served as both mayor and sheriff of Superior. His 42-room Fairlawn Mansion in Superior is now a museum.

WILDLIFE—Some of Wisconsin's most fascinating wildlife can be found at Pattison. Moose, bobcat, fisher, and timber wolf are rare, but might be sighted. Other more common park mammals include bear, coyote, fox, deer, mink, beaver, and otter.

Over the course of a year, 180 species of birds pass through Pattison (half of those nest here) including ruffed grouse, common loon, ducks, bald eagle, and osprey. Migrating hawks congregate around Lake Superior in the fall and are frequent guests in the park; mid-September is generally the best time to see them.

HIKING—There are four trails totaling nearly nine miles winding through the wooded park. The Big Falls Trail is a steep half-mile descent to the bottom of the gorge, a very scenic destination even without the views of the falls along the way. The easy, two-mile Beaver Slide Nature Trail (also known as Interfalls Trail and likely to be renamed the Traces of the Boreal Forest Trail) circles Interfalls Lake and interpretive panels discussing the park's ecology are planned for the near future. Branching off the back end of Beaver Slide is the mostly level Little Falls Trail which follows the river for just over half a mile to Little Manitou Falls; a round trip from the main use area to the falls and back around the lake is about three miles. The Big Manitou Geology Walk combines these three trails and has eight interpretive stops corresponding to a detailed brochure (available at the park office) which explains the formation of the falls and other landforms in the park.

The 4.7-mile Logging Camp Trail leads to the quiet back end of the park following the river much of the way. There are some hills along this trail, but none is very steep and they offer some great views. The remains of Pattison's logging camp are found along this trail, hence the name.

Though it does not yet lead beyond the park, the North Country National Scenic Trail (p. 24) follows some of the trails through the park.

In the fall, the park naturalist sometimes leads hikes to Copper Creek Falls, an unpublicized waterfall in the far north end of the park that tumbles about twenty feet over twin ledges. Reaching it requires a wet and wild bushwhack with poison ivy and abandoned mine pits as some of the potential hazards, but if you want to try and reach it on your own, ask at the park office and someone can direct you there.

PADDLING—Canoeists can paddle around 27-acre Interfalls Lake, though the best option is along the Black River south of Little Manitou Falls. The recommended run is to start at Milchesky Road and canoe back to the park. There are rapids on this stretch of the river and even in spring when the water is higher there are rocky areas that may have to be portaged.

WINTER—The main winter activity is cross-country skiing. A groomed 4.5-mile trail follows the same path as the Logging Camp Trail. The backpack sites remain open and the family campground becomes a ski-in campground.

COUNTY—Douglas.

DIRECTIONS—12 miles south of Superior on Highway 35.

FACILITIES—Water, toilets, nature center, nature programs, picnic area, grills, picnic shelter, beach, playground, fitness course, volleyball, horseshoes.

CAMPING—59 sites, 18 electric, three backpack sites, open year-round, reservations accepted, showers.

ENTRY—Open year-round. State park sticker or daily fee required.

ON THE WEB—www.wiparks.net

CONTACT—Pattison State Park, 6294 Highway 35, Superior, WI 54880. Phone (715) 399-3111.

Amnicon Falls State Park

ON ITS 30-MILE journey north to Lake Superior, the Amnicon River drops 640 feet. Nearly a third of that drop occurs on the less than two miles of river within this park. This rapid tumble is caused by the Douglas Fault, which stretches between Ashland, Wisconsin, and St. Paul, Minnesota. The Douglas Fault is unique in that the rock did not drop down but was forced up, a process called thrust faulting.

The river splits just before hitting the actual fault line, and alongside the small island are three large waterfalls—Upper, Lower, and Snake Pit—each dropping about twenty feet. Another small waterfall—appropriately named Now and Then Falls, since it runs in a third river channel that fills only when water levels are very high—is located across the main picnic area from Upper Falls. This park receives only a fourth as many visitors as each of the two other waterfall-based state parks in the area (Pattison and Copper Falls), but it is no less beautiful.

The Ojibwe lived in this area when the first French voyageurs arrived, and the river's name comes from their term for "where fish spawn." Settlers in the 1850s tried mining copper here but found their efforts unprofitable, as was the case in most of Douglas County. Loggers arrived in the 1880s and an old sandstone quarry, now a scenic pond, was worked at the end of the 19th century. The rock taken from this and other area quarries was used to build the cities of Superior and Duluth.

In 1932 Douglas County purchased 60 acres from James Bardon who owned land around the falls. He donated an additional 65 acres and this became Bardon Park. Over the years the park was transferred to the town of Amnicon, then back to the county before the state took over in 1961. It has grown to 850 acres since then, though the only development occurs right around the falls, leaving the rest of the park wild.

The 55-foot covered bridge spanning the river near Lower Falls is almost as popular an attraction as the falls themselves. The uniquely designed bridge,

RJ & LINDA MILLER

Snake Pit Falls, Amnicon Falls State Park.

then uncovered, originally crossed the river along a county road nearby and was moved here in 1930. Rivets and bolts were replaced by hook clips which the inventor Charles Horton claimed made the bridge stronger, cheaper, and faster to build. Only seven other bridges of this type remain, including five in the Van Loon Wildlife Area in La Crosse County (p. 203). In the past, many dances and other special events were held on the picturesque span, and it was illuminated at night. Today it is occasionally used for weddings.

WILDLIFE—The park is home to otter, beaver, mink, porcupine, fox, coyote, and bear. Lucky visitors might even see a moose or a timber wolf. Some 140 species of birds have been recorded in the surrounding forest, and over half of those nest here. Look for ruffed grouse, turkey vulture, ducks, bald eagle, and osprey.

HIKING—There are only two short trails in the park but both are very beautiful. The best views of the waterfalls are from the island and the two bridges that lead to it. A half-mile trail wraps around the island and then continues south along the river, though most people just wander randomly around here. Pick up a Geology Walk brochure at the park office for a detailed description of the forces that shaped this area. The Douglas Fault is visible at Upper Falls behind the stairs.

The seldom-used 0.75-mile Thimbleberry Nature Trail follows the river west before looping back; the route is mostly wooded and somewhat hilly. A guide available at the trailhead discusses the plants found along the trail as well as their uses by Native Americans. Do not miss the short spur near the trailhead that drops down to Snake Pit Falls, or the overlook of the scenic sandstone quarry at the far end.

WINTER—There are no designated winter trails though cross-country skiing and snowshoeing are both allowed throughout the park.

COUNTY—Douglas.

DIRECTIONS—Nine miles southeast of Superior on Highway 53, then one mile east on Highway 2, and a quarter mile north on County U.

FACILITIES—Water, toilets, picnic area, grills, playground, volleyball.

CAMPING—36 sites, two walk-in sites, open year-round, reservations accepted.

ENTRY—Open year-round. State park sticker or daily fee required.

ON THE WEB—www.wiparks.net

CONTACT—Amnicon Falls State Park, 6294 S. State Rd. 35, Superior, WI 54880. Phone (715) 398-3000 or (715) 399-3111 (off-season).

Brule River State Forest

THE BRULE RIVER begins and ends within this narrow 40,882-acre state forest. Known as the "River of Presidents," thanks to fishing trips by Grant, Cleveland, Coolidge, Hoover, and Eisenhower, this famous waterway draws visitors from across the nation for canoeing and trout fishing. While commonly referred to as just "the Brule," it's actually the Bois Brule, French for "burnt wood" and a variant of the Ojibwe name *Misacoda* or "burnt pine." It is so named because the pine barrens through which it flowed frequently caught fire. Forest has replaced most of the barrens, though some still remain. Boreal forest, which typifies Wisconsin's Lake Superior coast, dominates the northern end.

The river does a Jekyll-and-Hyde act. The upper river flows rather gently through a vast undisturbed bog, dropping just 3.5 feet per mile for the first 26 miles. Then the river meets the Copper Range, a drastic upthrust of volcanic rock, and it drops sharply—328 feet in the final 18 miles, with a hundred-foot drop occurring in just the three miles downstream from the Copper Range Campground—over rocky ledges. The lower river is lined by scenic bluffs much of the way.

The St. Croix River originates half a mile southwest of the Brule's headwaters and the two are separated by the continental divide, which causes the rivers' respective southern and northern flows. These two rivers, linked by a two-mile portage trail, formed an important trade route between Lake

Superior and the Mississippi River for Native Americans and, later, trappers, traders, and missionaries. French explorer Daniel Greysolon Sieur duLhut, namesake of the city of Duluth, made the first record of the portage in 1680, and it soon became so important to the French that they built forts at both ends. The portage trail, which still exists today, is now listed on the National Register of Historic Places.

Logging eventually replaced trapping, and much of the timber was floated down the Brule to Lake Superior and on to sawmills in nearby towns. Frederick Weyerhauser, who had previously logged the area, donated the initial 4,320 acres to the state in 1907. The forest was established in 1932, and by 1959 it encompassed the entire river. Land acquisition continues, and though there is still considerable private property within the forest boundaries, most landholders along the river have joined together to prevent future development.

WILDLIFE—Deer, coyote, fox, fisher, bear, bobcat, moose, and the endangered timber wolf are found in the forest (though you'd be extremely lucky to spot any of the last three), while beaver and otter frequent the river.

Generally the calm upper river has the best bird-watching; pick up the *Brule River State Forest Birdwatcher's Guide* at the office for some suggested locations. Some of the just over 200 species of birds recorded in the forest include bald eagle and osprey (both nest along the river); ruffed and sharp-tailed grouse; Canada goose; great blue heron; kingfisher; pileated, black-backed, and three-toed woodpeckers; red-breasted nuthatch; winter wren; golden-crowned and ruby-crowned kinglet; and oven bird. Northern parula, golden-winged, Nashville, Blackburnian, and chestnut-sided are some of the warblers that nest here, and just about every bird common to the area passes through during migration. In winter, ravens perform a staging ritual of aerial displays and calls before roosting for the night. The site changes each year, though you can ask at the office if you want to see it.

A sea lamprey barrier at the north end of the Brule, 6.5 miles from its confluence with Lake Superior, includes a fish ladder and is a good place to watch spawning salmon and trout. An underwater viewing window, used by fishery managers to monitor the health of the river's fish, offers a unique perspective on the migrations; call (715) 392-7988 to find out when it is open. It's a mile-long walk to the barrier from the end of Loveland Road.

HIKING—There is some excellent hiking in the forest. The best-known path is the centuries-old Historic Portage Trail between the St. Croix and Brule rivers. The narrow, two-mile path starts on County A across from the St. Croix Lake Picnic Area, and heads right up the steep hill forming the continental divide; the rest of the route is mostly level. The final portion of the trail, which leads to the Brule River, is through bog and can be wet. Unfortunately, a section in the middle was recently logged, but overall it's a beautiful walk. The Historic Portage Trail is the southern end of the North Country National Scenic Trail (p. 24) which continues for more than another 20 miles through the forest over rolling terrain, and features some wonderful valley vistas. Backpacker campsites, complete with latrine, have been constructed at Winneboujou Bluff and on the bluff just east of lovely Jerseth Creek. The trail continues to the Chequamegon-Nicolet National Forest. The formal trailhead on Highway 27 includes a massive granite stone dedicated to former governor and senator Gaylord Nelson, a major trail supporter.

The southern half of the two-mile Old Bayfield Road Trail follows the route of the first road between Superior and Bayfield (1870–1885) which was then replaced by the railroad. The trail also passes a fire tower and an old mine. There are a few hills along the thickly wooded path, but overall it is a pretty easy walk.

The narrow 1.7-mile Stoney Hill Nature Trail, beginning at the Bois Brule Campground, has interpretive signs discussing the trees found along its steep hills. Atop Stoney Hill is an overlook with views of the Brule River valley, and despite a radio antenna disrupting the natural setting on the hill, and a few pine plantations along the route, it is not a bad trail overall.

The Afterhours Trail is primarily a cross-country ski trail and not maintained during the summer (thus much of it will be overgrown), but it is otherwise a nice destination. The River Loop has many hills and good river views.

Arguably the best hiking in the forest is not on a trail; it is the nine miles of Lake Superior shoreline that top the forest. Here hikers can wander the sandy coast between the cliffs and the world's largest lake, or head out along the top of the cliffs. Several streams have to be crossed and, if taking the cliff-top option, there are a few quarter-mile stretches of private property that must be avoided by walking south through paper company land. The best lakeshore access is at the mouth of the Brule River or at Beck's Road at the far west end of the forest. Several other roads approach the shore but end atop the cliffs. There are also unmarked but well-worn trails leading along the river from just about all of the angler parking areas.

PADDLING—The upper stretches of the Brule offer easy canoeing with just a few small rapids, while the whitewater on the lower stretches will challenge even experienced paddlers. The abrupt change in water flow takes place just below the Copper Range Campground, three miles north of the village of Brule. Many of the river's nearly one hundred rapids (including some Class IV) should be portaged by all but experts.

With ten canoe landings (you can also put in or take out at County FF), trips of anywhere from an hour to three days are possible. Stone's Bridge Landing at County S in the south end of the forest to Highway 2 makes an easy one day trip covering 12 miles. Whitewater enthusiasts will want to start at Pine Tree Landing. The Copper Range Campground is the obvious place to break up a two-day trip though using both campgrounds to make a three-day journey is the more relaxing way to do it. Those planning to camp should consider getting a site before setting out on the water, since reservations are not accepted. Many private landowners along the river have built picnic areas for river users, though camping is not allowed at these spots.

BIKING—Off-road bikers will find some challenges along the Afterhours Trail. Another option is the Tri-County Corridor which parallels Highway 2 through the forest, though it is also used by ATVs and motorcycles.

WINTER—The Afterhours Trail has a countless variety of loops totaling 14 miles that are groomed for traditional and skate skiing. The main grade was once a railway and is very level, though some paths are quite challenging. A warming shelter is available. The trailhead is one mile west of the village of Brule on Highway 2. The Old Bayfield Road Trail is dedicated to snowshoers.

The 23-mile Brule-St. Croix Snowmobile trail connects to both the Douglas and Bayfield county trail systems. It also connects to the Tri-County Corridor which is open to snowmobiles.

OTHER—The fish hatchery between the forest headquarters and Highway 27 on Fish Hatchery Road is open to the public. ATVs and motorcycles are allowed on the Tri-County Corridor.

COUNTY—Douglas.

DIRECTIONS—The headquarters is half a mile west of Brule on Highway 2, then 0.75 mile south on Anderson Rd.

FACILITIES—Water, toilets, boat launch, picnic area, grills.

CAMPING—Two campgrounds, 40 sites, four walk-in sites, open late March to late November, backpacking permitted throughout forest (except right along the river) with free permit.

ENTRY—Open year-round. State park sticker or daily fee required at campgrounds. State trail pass required for skiing on the Afterhours Trail.

ON THE WEB—www.wiparks.net

CONTACT—Brule River State Forest, 6250 S. Ranger Rd., Box 125, Brule, WI 54820. Phone (715) 372-8539.

Chequamegon-Nicolet
National Forest

THE CHEQUAMEGON (shuh-WAH-muh-gun) is the larger half of Wisconsin's only national forest. Established in 1933, the national forest initially included both the Chequamegon and Nicolet sides, though they were separated later that year. To save money, the forests were administratively rejoined in 1998, though most people still think of the two separately and for convenience sake they are discussed as individual forests in this book. The Chequamegon side's three separate sections cover nearly 860,000 acres of forest, lakes, and wetlands. Chequamegon is an Ojibwe word for "place of shallow waters," an appropriate name since the last glaciers to cross Wisconsin left behind abundant wetlands and more than 800 lakes in the forest's boundaries.

The Chequamegon has two designated wilderness areas, both in Bayfield County. The 4,446-acre Porcupine Lake Wilderness Area can be reached from Forest Road 213, six miles southeast of Drummond, and the 6,583-acre Rainbow Lake Wilderness Area can be reached by Forest Highway 35, four miles to the north of Drummond. The latter was designated in 1975 and was one of the first wilderness areas east of the Mississippi. Another 52,000 acres of semi-primitive, non-motorized areas have also been set aside for silent sports and nature lovers.

Dozens of archeological sites have been found in the forest from the Ojibwe, who were here when the French first arrived, and many earlier Native American cultures. Several more recent historic sites of interest include the Round Lake Logging Dam, built in 1876 and restored in 1995. At one time, the water stored behind this log-driving dam was released in spring to send the winter timber harvest down the South Fork Flambeau River to sawmills. The dam, located in Price County, 17 miles east of Fifield on Highway 70 then two miles north on Forest Road 144, is one of the last of its kind in the state and is listed on the National Register of Historic Places.

Also on the National Register of Historic Places is the Mondeaux Dam Recreation Area, whose lake and surrounding facilities were constructed by the CCC and WPA during the Great Depression. The main picnic and swimming area is located next to the dam at the north end of the lake, and the restored concession area has some interesting historical displays as well as a small restaurant. It is located in Taylor County, nine miles west of Westboro on County D, then 1.5 miles south on County E, then 1.5 miles east on Park Road.

The Smith Rapids Covered Bridge looks historic, but it was actually built in 1991, the first of its kind erected in Wisconsin in over a century. It spans

JEFF MILLER

High above the Chequamegon-Nicolet National Forest at St. Peter's Dome.

the South Fork Flambeau River along Forest Road 148 in Price County. Take Highway 70 east from Fifield for 12 miles, then head two miles north to the bridge. Naturally, this is a popular spot for photos.

WILDLIFE—With its large size and variety of habitats, it is no surprise that wildlife abounds in the forest. More than 225 species of birds are found here, including bald eagle, osprey, red-shouldered hawk, common loon, sandhill crane, tundra swans, turkey vulture, ruffed and sharp-tailed grouse, pheasant, and an abundance of songbirds. Forest mammals include beaver, otter, mink, pine marten, fisher, porcupine, badger, deer, fox, coyote, bear, bobcat, moose, and timber wolf. Lucky visitors might even catch sight of an elk. Hunted to extinction in Wisconsin by the mid-1800s, 25 were released near Clam Lake in 1995 as part of a reintroduction study, and the population has grown to over a hundred since then. Elk-viewing observation areas and an auto tour are currently under development; check with the Great Divide Ranger Station in Clam Lake for details.

While wildlife can be seen nearly anywhere, the Forest Service has five recommended wildlife-viewing areas, each with interpretive exhibits. The Day Lake Recreation Area and Campground sits alongside this bog-encircled, 640-acre lake, a quiet nesting area for bald eagle and common loon. There is a barrier-free viewing platform and a half-mile interpretive trail along the lake, though the best viewing is by canoe. Day Lake is located in Ashland County, one mile north of Clam Lake on County GG.

Like Day Lake, the Chequamegon Waters Recreation Area also has nesting eagles and loons, and is best explored by canoe. The 2,730-acre flowage on the Yellow River is in Taylor County, 3.5 miles west of Perkinstown on County M.

There is a half-mile interpretive trail with panels discussing the surrounding wetlands, and an important waterfowl haven, at the remote Popple Creek/Wilson Flowage site in Price County. Part of the trail follows an esker. Take Highway 70 east from Fifield for 13 miles, then go six miles south on Forest Road 137.

There are two short trails at Lynch Creek. North of the small impoundment, a quarter-mile, wheelchair-accessible path leads to a viewing platform, while a less-often-used trail leads along the south side of the flowage for close to half a mile. Lynch Creek is located in Sawyer County, 10 miles east of Cable on County M, then 4.5 miles south on Forest Road 203, and then 0.3 mile south on Forest Road 622.

The Moquah Pine Barrens is a 7,200-acre restoration area in the far north end of the forest. This large, sandy outwash plain left over from the last Ice Age is a National Natural Landmark and an unusual habitat for this part of the state. Visitors can follow the 20-mile marked auto tour or get out and walk the many side roads. The easiest access is 15 miles west of Ashland on Highway 2; the auto tour begins on Forest Road 236.

HIKING—The North Country (p. 24) and Ice Age (p. 1) national scenic trails are hiking highlights that account for about half of the forest's nearly 200 miles of non-motorized trails. The 61-mile stretch of the North Country Trail, which crosses both of the forest's wilderness areas, offers one of the best long hikes in the state. The west trailhead is in Bayfield County, five miles south of Iron River on County A, and the east end is in Ashland County, 2.5 miles west of Mellen on Forest Road 390. The thickly wooded Anderson Grade is another good route through the Rainbow Lake Wilderness—the relatively level four-mile trail stretches between the Perch Lake Campground (on Forest Highway 35, six miles north of Drummond) and Forest Road 228. Between the wilderness areas, the North Country Trail shares a path with the Drummond Woods Interpretive Trail through an old-growth white pine forest. The North Country Trail also shares a part of its path with the 7.6-mile Penokee Mountain Trail. The longest of the Penokee's three hilly loops is 5.3 miles. The Penokee Overlook near the trailhead offers great views of the surrounding Penokee-Gogebic Range. The overlook and trailhead are three miles west of Mellen on County GG. The trail continues west of the forest and should be connected to the Brule River State Forest (p. 14) in the near future. There is a formal trailhead for this section on County A just south of Iron River.

A 42-mile section of the Ice Age Trail crosses the Taylor County section of the forest, traversing the terminal moraine from the last glacial advance on the west side. The trail has some rolling hills and passes many wetlands. The ends of the trail are 18 miles west of Medford on Highway 64, and 15 miles north of Medford on Forest Road 101.

Price County's Round Lake Trail winds through the 3,600-acre Round Lake Semi-Primitive Non-Motorized Area. The hilly, 10.8-mile trail has several loops along the northern half of Round Lake. Between Round Lake and Tucker Lake to the northeast is a stand of old-growth forest. The main trailhead is at the Round Lake Logging Dam, 17 miles east of Fifield on Highway 70 then two miles north on Forest Road 144. The trail can also be accessed at the Twin Lakes Campground.

One of the most scenic hikes in the forest is the two-mile St. Peter's Dome Trail in Ashland County. This steep, 3.6-mile hike leads to the highest point in the forest, 1,600 feet above sea level. From the top of this granite monadnock, Michigan, Minnesota, and the Apostle Islands are all visible on clear days. A short spur half a mile into the trail leads to the spectacular Morgan Falls, which drops 70 feet, making it the second highest waterfall in the state. There are many rare flowers and ferns along the trail, especially on the cliffs adjoining the falls, so do not stray from the trail for any reason. The trailhead is seven miles west of Mellen on County GG, then four miles northwest on Forest Road 187, and four miles northwest on Forest Road 199.

The four-mile Black Lake Trail loops around Black Lake right on the northeast corner of Sawyer County. An interpretive brochure discussing the logging history of the area corresponds to numbered posts along the mostly level trail, though the forest has been recovering since the 1930s. It's a very beautiful walk. The trail begins at the Black Lake Campground, which is nine miles south of Clam Lake on County GG, then goes four miles west on Forest Road 164, and three miles south on Forest Road 173.

Also beautiful is the easy three-mile Namekagon Trail. The one-mile East Loop has a bogwalk, old growth hemlock, and an interpretive brochure discussing it all. It begins just north of the Namekagon Campground (11 miles east of Cable on County M, then 5.5 miles north on County D, and 0.3 mile east on Forest Road 209) in Sawyer County.

Several short nature trails are described above in the Wildlife section.

PADDLING—The Namekagon, Chippewa, and Flambeau rivers all originate in the Chequamegon, though the upper stretches of each tend to have low water levels in the summer. Check with forest personnel before planning to paddle them.

The 98-mile Namekagon River, part of the St. Croix National Scenic

Riverway, starts at Namekagon Lake in Bayfield County. There are some Class I rapids in the forest and beyond. See the St. Croix National Scenic Riverway (p. 48) for more details.

The East Fork Chippewa and South Fork Flambeau rivers are both under consideration for National Scenic River status. The Chippewa flows for 27 miles through the forest in Ashland and Sawyer counties from the Stockfarm Bridge Campground (5.5 miles west of Glidden on County D, then four miles west on Forest Road 167, then four miles south on Forest Road 166, and two miles east Forest Road 164) to the Winter Dam at the Chippewa Flowage (p. 43). It is a scenic, wooded route with several lakes and many rapids, including a few Class II and III. The 15,300-acre Chippewa Flowage, a popular canoeing destination often combined with trips on the Chippewa River, lies along the southwest end of the forest. Of course there are also hundreds of other lakes throughout the forest for scenic and quiet paddling.

The Flambeau starts at Round Lake (17 miles east of Fifield on Highway 70, then two miles north on Forest Road 144) and flows for 20 miles through the Price County section of the forest with many Class II and III rapids. Many paddlers begin their trips at the Smith Rapids Campground (12.5 miles east of Fifield on Highway 70, then two miles north on Forest Road 148) seven miles downstream from Round Lake. The last landing within the forest is at Forest Road 152.

The Yellow River through Taylor County is a less common destination. It has only a few Class I rapids.

BIKING—The Chequamegon Area Mountain Bike Association (CAMBA) maintains 300 miles of marked trails, mostly on forest roads, through the forest and adjacent county and private lands. This is arguably the Midwest's best trail system, drawing riders from across the region.

The six trail clusters (near the towns of Cable, Delta, Drummond, Hayward, Namekagon, and Seeley, all in the northern section of the forest) range from 40 to 100 miles and offer a wide variety of conditions. Some of the most challenging trails are the Delta Hills Loop and Rock Lake Loop in the Namekagon Cluster, the Seeley Firetower Loop in the Seeley Cluster, and the Esker Trail in the Cable Cluster. The Chequamegon Fat Tire Festival, one of the country's largest off-road bike races, is held annually on the Cable Cluster. The Namekagon and Patsy Lake loops in the Namekagon Cluster and the Northern Lights Loop in the Seeley Cluster are among the easiest trails. The Drummond Cluster is the easiest cluster overall.

Elsewhere in the forest, mountain bikes are allowed on any road or trail that does not run through a wilderness area and is not posted against bikes.

WINTER—Over 120 miles of trails are groomed for cross-country skiing, including the Penokee Mountain and Namekagon trails described above under Hiking, plus the 10.3-mile Valkyrie and eight-mile Teuton trails (collectively known as Valhalla) near Washburn; the 5.6-mile Drummond, 26.3-mile Rock Lake, 11.1-mile West Torch, and 17.2-mile Mukwonago trails in the general vicinity of Cable; the 7.2-mile Newman Springs and 7.9-mile Wintergreen trails near Park Falls in the Price County section; and the 13-mile Perkinstown (AKA Sitzmark) Trail in Taylor County. All trails are a series of interconnected loops, allowing skiers to choose the length and difficulty of the trip. Rock Lake is rightly the most popular and, along with the Valkyrie and Mukwonago, the most challenging trail. The latter two also have beginner loops, while overall the Namekagon and West Torch River trails are the easiest. The Mukwonago and Valkyrie trails can accommodate skate-skiers, and there are warming shelters at the Penokee Mountain, Valkyrie, Teuton, and Perkinstown trails. Perkinstown also has rentals available on-site.

Snowmobilers have well over 300 miles of groomed trails to ride.

AUTO TOUR—The Great Divide National Forest Scenic Byway roughly follows the north-south continental divide separating the watersheds of the Great Lakes and the Mississippi River. The divide is formed by the rugged Penokee Range rising to the north of the road. The route stretches 29 miles along Highway 77 between Glidden and Lost Lake, near Hayward.

An auto tour through the Moquah Barrens is described in the Wildlife section above.

OTHER—Over 200 miles of trails are open to ATVs and motorcycles. Horseback riders commonly follow the ATV trails though they prefer a 15-mile trail where motors are prohibited, starting at the Smith Rapids Campground.

COUNTIES—Bayfield, Ashland, Sawyer, Price, Vilas, and Taylor.

DIRECTIONS—Ranger stations are located in Medford, Park Falls, Glidden, Hayward, and Washburn. Information for the entire forest is available at the Northern Great Lakes Visitor Center, a regional museum/tourism office 2.5 miles west of Ashland on Highway 2.

FACILITIES—Water, toilets, boat launch, picnic area, grills, picnic shelter, beach, playground, horseshoes.

CAMPING—25 campgrounds, 550 sites, 16 walk-in sites, most campgrounds are open May through October though you are welcome to walk or ski into them the rest of the year, reservations accepted, showers, group camp, backpacking permitted throughout the forest.

ENTRY—Open year-round. Some developed facilities are free though most require a $3 daily or $10 annual parking permit—only the daily permits are available at the specific sites; you must purchase annual permits at Forest Service offices or area businesses.

ON THE WEB—www.fs.fed.us/r9/cnnf and www.cambatrails.org

CONTACT—Forest Supervisor, 1170 4th Ave. S., Park Falls, WI 54552. Phone (715) 762-2461 or (715) 762-5701 (TTY). Chequamegon Area Mountain Bike Association, PO Box 141, Cable, WI 54821. Phone (800) 533-7454. E-mail: camba@cheqnet.net

North County
National Scenic Trail

THE NORTH COUNTRY TRAIL stretches 4,200 miles across seven states from Lake Sakakawea on the Missouri River in central North Dakota to Crown Point State Historic Site on Lake Champlain in eastern New York. When completed it will be the longest continuous trail in the nation. Currently over 1,700 miles have been certified by the National Park Service since the trail's inception in 1980, and another 800 miles are completed but not yet certified. Wisconsin's 220-mile slice of the trail crosses the northern tip of Wisconsin; 102 miles are completed and certified thus far. Both the trail's concept and name originated in the Chequamegon-Nicolet National Forest in the mid-1960s. The 61-mile section through the forest ranks among the entire trail's most scenic segments.

WILDLIFE—Though what you might see largely depends on where you are, the North Country Trail traverses some of the most remote parts of the state, and consequently you stand a good chance of spotting wildlife—particularly in the Chequamegon-Nicolet National Forest, because it passes through two relatively undisturbed wilderness areas.

HIKING—The trail enters Wisconsin from Upper Michigan near Hurley, possibly coming down historic and notorious Silver Street, though a final decision on the route across the state line has yet to be made. The first certified segment is a seven-mile path through Iron County Forest lands known as the Uller Trail, and more uncertified trail continues in both directions, allowing a 17-mile hike. This segment is hilly with many scenic overlooks and passes a balanced rock near the Uller Trail's midpoint. The trail route continues west along the Penokee-Gogebic Iron Range, ancient mountains worn away by glaciers and Father Time, picking up the next completed segment at gorgeous Copper Falls State Park. The trail runs south through the park, down to the city of Mellen, and over to the Chequamegon-Nicolet National Forest, which begins just two miles west of town.

The 61-mile segment through the Chequamegon is among the best long-distance hikes in the state. There are many wetlands, streams, and glacial lakes on the route, and though the wettest sections are bridged, expect to get wet feet in the spring—but do not expect any crowds. The eastern end of the trail continues along the Penokee-Gogebic Range, and there are many rock out-croppings and scenic overlooks here. At the far east end of the forest, the North Country shares a path with part of the 7.6-mile Penokee Mountain Trail, passing the well-known Penokee Overlook. Further west down the trail by the Marengo River and the old Swedish homestead, are some of the most beautiful views in the forest. As the trail moves to the west the hills become gentler and the lakes more prevalent. Before exiting the forest it crosses both the 4,450-acre Porcupine Lake and 6,600-acre Rainbow Lake wilderness areas.

For years, the completed trail stopped at the edge of the Chequamegon, but no longer. Some of the best designed and maintained portions of the trail con-tinue west through the Bayfield County Forest and on through the Brule River State Forest. Though a short gap remains between the county and state forests, the dedicated volunteers building trail in this section should have it bridged in the near future. Including the current two-mile walk along Troy Pit Road, there is another 30 miles of wonderful trail west of the Chequamegon. In the Bayfield County Forest portion the trail passes several remote kettle lakes. Two designated backpacker campsites, complete with a wilderness-style latrine,

DAVID W. HERRICK

Marigolds along the North Country National Scenic Trail.

overlook Erick Lake. Turning south from Troy Pit Road through the Brule River State Forest, significant portions of the trail follow the rim of steep hillsides and serve up a series of expansive vistas overlooking the Bois Brule River Valley. More backpacker campsites, complete with latrine, have been constructed at Winneboujou Bluff and on the bluff just east of lovely Jerseth Creek. The last 2.5 miles running south though the Brule River State Forest follow the historic Brule-St. Croix Portage. Once used by Native Americans, early European explorers, and fur traders, this ancient path crosses the continental divide and connects these two famous rivers, thus linking Lake Superior with the Mississippi River. Along the way, eight stones with brass plates commemorate some of the early users of the portage such as Daniel Greysolon Sieur duLhut and Henry Schoolcraft.

Just to the south of the Historic Portage are another three miles of certified trail leading right through the village of Solon Springs and Lucius Woods County Park. Here the trail turns northwest toward Jay Cooke State Park in Minnesota. Though currently there is no trail, certified or otherwise, west of Highway 53, except for 2.6 miles through Pattison State Park, construction should proceed rapidly through the Douglas County Wildlife Area, more commonly known as the Bird Sanctuary, with 4,000 acres of brush prairie.

The trail in Wisconsin is constantly expanding and evolving, so the usually up-to-date maps showing completed sections, as well as some recommended road routes between them posted on the North Country Trail Association's website are a very handy resource. You can also buy numerous maps and guides directly from the association online, and thus let your money assist in their work on the trail. If you would like to help build or maintain any of the trail in Wisconsin contact either the North Country Trail Association or the National Park Service; information is provided below.

WINTER—Cross-country skiing and snowshoeing are fantastic on the trail in the Chequamegon-Nicolet National Forest (the Penokee Mountain and Drummond trail systems, both groomed, intersect with the North Country Trail) and Brule River State Forest though the North County Trail is not groomed. The Uller Trail is part of a heralded 19-mile groomed trail system; short portions of the trail serve as part of the groomed trail systems at Pattison and Copper Falls state parks.

COUNTIES—Douglas, Bayfield, Ashland, and Iron.

DIRECTIONS—The Uller Trail segment can be accessed at the Weber Lake Campground off County E three miles west of Iron Belt. All other parks and forests with completed trail segments are detailed elsewhere in this book.

FACILITIES—Other than what is available at the parks and forests along the trail there are few trailhead facilities so come with your water bottles full.

CAMPING—Backpacking is permitted along the trail in the Chequamegon-Nicolet National Forest (including two Adirondack-style shelters), Brule River State Forest, Bayfield County Forest, and Iron County Forest—permits (free) are required in all but the National Forest. There are also designated backpack sites along the trail in Pattison and Copper Falls state parks. Developed campgrounds are located in each of the parks and forests with trail segments.

ENTRY—Open year-round. Free.

ON THE WEB—www.nps.gov/noco and www.northcountrytrail.org

CONTACT—National Park Service, 700 Rayovac Dr., Suite 100, Madison, WI 53711. Phone (608) 441-5610. E-mail: IATR_Information@nps.gov North Country Trail Association, 229 E. Main St., Lowell, MI 49331. Phone (888) 454-6282. E-mail: HQ@northcountrytrail.org

Apostle Islands
National Lakeshore

THE 22 APOSTLE ISLANDS dot Wisconsin's northern tip. Though the real reason for the name is lost in time, apparently some early explorers counted only a dozen, and therefore conferred the name Apostle, after Jesus' followers. All of the islands but Madeline, the largest, plus a 12-mile stretch of shoreline on the Bayfield Peninsula, make up the National Lakeshore. Ranging from three-acre Gull to 10,054-acre Stockton (over 42,000 acres total), the islands offer sandstone cliffs, sea caves, sandy beaches, old-growth forests, pristine wetlands, and a rich, well-preserved history.

Because these are islands, visiting them does require a little extra effort. For visitors without their own boats, the easiest way to enjoy the scenery is on one of the excursion boat trips, which can be used to take a short sight-seeing tour or as inter-island transportation. Boats stop on Stockton, Oak, Sand, Raspberry, and Manitou islands during the summer months. A water taxi can also take up to six people from Bayfield to most of the islands, though this can be very expensive.

Lake Superior is deserving of its name; it is the largest body of fresh water in the world, holding an eighth of the world's entire supply. Both the lake and the islands are products of the Ice Age. As the glaciers moved south, they carved the lake basin, and meltwater filled it. These islands are chunks of bedrock that weren't completely worn away by the glaciers. Wind, waves, and ice later sculpted the park's famous shoreline cliffs, as well as the caves on Mawikwe Bay (formerly called Squaw Bay) on the mainland, Swallow Point on

ANDY KRAUSHAAR

Sea kayaks let you get up close and personal with the Apostle Islands' sea caves.

the east shore of Sand Island, and the northern tip of Devils Island. The latter are the most impressive. Also on the north end of Oak Island is an impressive arch known as the Hole-in-the-Wall.

Ecologically, the Apostles lie in the transitional zone between northern hardwood and boreal forests, both of which are common here. Though the islands were logged, old-growth areas still exist. Among these are Raspberry and Devils Islands, which were completely spared, and large blocks around the lighthouses (to allow lighthouse keepers access to firewood) on Outer and Sand islands. These four areas comprise the Apostle Islands Maritime Forest State Natural Area.

Humans have resided on the islands for at least a thousand years. Many early Woodland peoples made seasonal camps on the islands to be close to fish spawning areas. Because they offered bountiful resources and shelter from Lake Superior storms, the French made the islands a center of their fur trading activities, and this attracted Huron, Dakota, Fox, Iroquois, and other trading partners. The Ojibwe were living on Madeline Island when the French arrived, and today the Red Cliff Reservation includes much of the tip of the Bayfield Peninsula and a small part of Madeline. The first fur traders were here in 1659, and the enterprise thrived for nearly two centuries before dying out. Commercial fishing, mostly for lake trout, whitefish, and lake herring, slowly replaced the fur trade and continues today, though on a much smaller scale. The fishing industry declined because of severe overfishing and the invasion of sea lampreys. Two restored fish camps provide a look at the industry. The Manitou Fish Camp on Manitou Island operated into the 1970s and now has been restored as it was during the 1930s to 1950s, reflecting the hard life of winter fishing. At Little Sand Bay on the mainland you'll find the Hokenson Brothers Fishery, which operated from the 1920s to the 1960s. Both fish camps are on the National Register of Historic Places and offer guided tours in the summer.

Quarrying was another important island industry. The first rock was cut in 1869 and the work lasted until the turn of the 20th century. Brownstone, a very popular building material, was taken from Basswood, Stockton, and Hermit islands, where the pits may still be seen. Brownstone, a hard, red sandstone, was used in many cities, including Chicago when it was rebuilt after the great fire of 1871. Detroit, St. Paul, Omaha, Cincinnati, and many others also have prominent Apostle Island brownstone buildings. The old brownstone county courthouse in Bayfield, which now houses the National Lakeshore Visitor Center, is on the National Register of Historic Places. Farming began around the same time though it was much less successful than other industries. The difficulty of clearing the land, the short growing season, and the isolation drove settlers away. Sand Island was the only island other than Madeline to have a year-round community.

From the first canoes of the voyageurs to the giant freighters of today, shipping has been important to the area as evidenced by the six lighthouses located on the islands—more than in any other National Park unit. These popular attractions, now on the National Register of Historic Places, were all built in the latter half of the 19th century and are still in operation. The Raspberry Island lighthouse and gardens have been restored as they were in the 1920s when the keepers and their families lived there. Summer tours are offered by the park staff. Volunteers lead tours of the lighthouses on Sand, Devils, Outer, and Michigan islands.

The national lakeshore was officially established in 1970, though Apostle Island tourism began long before this. Wealthy Eastern families began spending summers here in the late 1800s, and the railroad also brought many more shorter-term visitors. A local newspaper first proposed this as a national park in 1891, and in 1930 the National Park Service considered but rejected the idea, primarily because of the devastation wrought by the timber companies. Decades later the land has recovered and the islands have been rediscovered. The islands will likely receive an official wilderness designation in coming years—a routine wilderness study began in 2001—though this will bring few, if any, noticeable changes since they have been managed as such since the 1980s.

WILDLIFE—Bears, excellent swimmers, are found on several islands, but are most common on Oak, Sand, and Stockton; the last, with as many as two dozen, has the world's greatest concentration of black bears. As forests mature, deer and beaver are becoming less common, but they are still found on many of the islands. Otter, mink, red fox, and coyote are also island dwellers, while fisher, bobcat, porcupine, and the endangered pine marten reside only on the mainland.

Named a Globally Important Bird Area by the American Bird Conservancy, the Apostles host more than 240 species during the course of a year and roughly 110 nest here, including the very rare piping plover. The forests are also an important habitat for Neotropical migrants such as bay-breasted, Blackburnian, Cape May, Connecticut, and Wilson's warblers. Other park birds include bald eagle, merlin, northern goshawk, sandhill crane, common loon, wood duck, pileated woodpecker, yellow-bellied sapsucker, yellow-bellied fly-catcher, white-breasted nuthatch, winter wren, and pine siskin. The largest concentrations of birds are on Gull and Eagle islands, which are covered with cormorants, gulls, and great blue heron in spring and summer. Both are bird sanctuaries and entry is prohibited. Many migrating birds stop here in the spring before heading north across the lake. Long Island—which is currently connected to the mainland—is a great place to spot waterfowl throughout the year, but especially during migration. Impressive numbers of hawks can be seen from Outer Island early in the year.

HIKING—There are nearly 60 miles of trails on 12 of the islands and the mainland. These range from just a quarter-mile path on South Twin to a 14.5-mile system on Stockton. Old logging roads are still passable on some islands, offering even more routes to follow. While for the most part the trails cross through deep forest, some also lead along sandpits and through bogs.

Because they were not logged, Devils and Raspberry islands are good choices for hikers, though the trails are short. Devils Island has the park's most impressive sea caves and these can be seen from the north end of the trail.

With 12 miles of trail, Oak Island is an excellent destination for hikers seeking seclusion and scenery. The overlook at the north end of the island is atop a 200-foot cliff, with views of the Hole-in-the-Wall sea arch and ten other islands. Trails also lead to a beach at the southern end of the island and across the highest point in the Apostles.

Stockton is the most visited island, but with 14.5 miles of trails on 10,504 acres, there is plenty of room to get away. One of the most popular trails is the Julian Bay Nature Trail, which has a guide booklet discussing the several environments it crosses in its 0.4-mile path. It starts at the visitor center and leads to the "Singing Sands" on Julian Bay. The 4.7-mile Trout Point Trail crosses the interior of the island out to its northern tip. Other trails follow the shore.

Sand Island has a great two-mile trail leading from the dock to the lighthouse. The trail offers views of the island's sea caves and passes through an old-growth white pine forest.

The 2,500-acre, 12-mile-long mainland section is the most readily accessible area and should not be overlooked, especially by visitors with limited time. The Lakeshore Trail, beginning at Meyers Beach (just off Highway 13, four miles northeast of Cornucopia), currently extends a couple of miles atop the shoreline cliffs and caves, though they are not readily visible from the trail. Eventually the trail will be completed all the way (another ten or so miles) to the Little Sand Bay Visitor Center. The rugged, often steep path crosses several streams, so expect to get a little wet. For an easier walk, hikers could just follow Meyers Beach, which extends north for a mile. Visitors may also take short beach strolls at Little Sand Bay.

PADDLING—Sea kayaks have become the travel mode of choice since they offer unlimited access to the islands; and with kayaking, getting there is half the fun. From a kayak you can get great views of the rocky cliffs and, when the lake is calm, enter and explore the sea caves. The Mawikwe Bay sea caves begin just a mile from the nearest landing, so it is a pretty easy trip. While Lake Superior is generally calm in summer, storms can approach quickly. Because of the lake's unpredictability, canoes are not recommended.

Kayaks can be put in at Little Sand Bay and Meyers Beach within the park. Bayfield and Red Cliff are good launching spots nearby. Kayaks can also be transported to the islands on the excursion boats. Rentals, instruction, and guided trips are available from several companies in Bayfield and other area towns.

WINTER—Snowshoeing, skiing, and other winter activities are becoming increasingly popular. Very few people camp here in winter because of the severe weather, but it is allowed. The sea caves are fantastic in the winter when frozen waterfalls form giant pillars and ice crystals grow into needlelike icicles. The Mawikwe Bay sea caves can be accessible as early as late December, though generally the ice is safe only from late January until early March. For short periods, most years (usually by February) an ice bridge connects the mainland to many of the islands. Winter visitors should ALWAYS check with the park office (or at least call the automated Ice Line at (715) 779-3398, ex. 499) before heading out, since ice conditions are highly unpredictable, especially in recent years with global warming.

OTHER—The Apostle Islands Cruise Service (715) 779-3925 or (800)

323-7619 offers many excursion trips out of Bayfield, including several that stop at the islands. Their most popular trip is the three-hour Grand Tour which operates from mid-May to mid-October. It passes most of the islands, including the Devils Island sea caves and several lighthouses, but makes no stops. Other trips feature the lighthouses, sea caves, sunsets, and sailing on a classic schooner.

Sailors and boaters have long been drawn to the islands for the wonderful scenery. Access is easy, with docks at half of the islands and many protected bays to anchor in. Boats can be launched at Little Sand Bay on the mainland or at several nearby places outside the lakeshore boundaries. Many local marinas offer rentals and mooring, and the park office can give you a current list.

The area around the Apostles is littered with shipwrecks, about a hundred in all, which are well preserved by the cold water. These wrecks are good scuba diving destinations, though several partially exposed above water are easily viewed by anyone in a boat. Divers will also enjoy the sea caves and cliffs, all made even better by Superior's exceptionally clear water. One popular site is "The Wall" on the southwest side of Stockton Island, with a sheer drop of more than a hundred feet below the surface. Diving permits are available at the headquarters in Bayfield.

COUNTIES—Bayfield and Ashland.

DIRECTIONS—The main Visitor Center is in Bayfield at 4th Ave. and Washington Ave. The Little Sand Bay Visitor Center is 13 miles northwest of Bayfield via Highway 13, County K, and Park Road. There is also a visitor center on Stockton Island.

FACILITIES—Water, toilets, boat launch, nature center, nature programs, picnic area.

CAMPING—53 walk-in/backpack sites on 13 islands and one on the mainland (free, permit required), open year-round, reservations accepted, group camp, backpacking permitted with free permit on all but Eagle, Gull, and North Twin islands. The town-owned Little Sand Bay Campground (20 sites, open May 1 to October 15) across from the Little Sand Bay Visitor Center is not scenic, but very convenient.

ENTRY—Open year-round. The Little Sand Bay and Stockton Island Visitor Centers are open only during the summer. Free. Excursion boats are privately operated and charge a fee.

ON THE WEB—www.nps.gov/apis and www.apostleisland.com

CONTACT—Apostle Islands National Lakeshore, Rt. 1, Box 4, Bayfield, WI 54814. Phone (715) 779-3397. E-mail: APIS_Webmaster@nps.gov

Big Bay State Park

L ARGEST OF THE 22 Apostle Islands, Madeline Island is the only one with commercial development and thus the only one not a part of the Apostle Islands National Lakeshore (p. 27), though the natural scenery at the 2,418-acre Big Bay State Park is equally stunning and much more easily accessed. The jagged shoreline cliffs and caves, sculpted by Lake Superior's waves, freezes, and thaws, should not be missed. Best viewed by boat, they are also easily visible from park trails. An overlook at the end of Hagen Road, just beyond the park entrance, is the most convenient viewing point.

While the cliffs are the most spectacular sight, there is much more to see at Wisconsin's northernmost state park. Lake Superior has constructed a 1.5-mile barrier beach at the back end of Big Bay. The 200-acre Big Bay Lagoon sitting behind the beach is surrounded by one of the richest floating bogs in the Lake Superior region. The bog harbors numerous rare plants and is the core of the 440-acre Big Bay Sand Spit and Bog State Natural Area. Because of the cool climate created by Lake Superior, the park's 100-plus species of wildflower bloom up to two weeks later than on the mainland.

French explorers, traders, and missionaries first came here in the 17th century, and the island hosted the first European settlement in what is now Wisconsin. The Ojibwe had settled on Madeline Island sometime in the 15th century and part of the Bad River Reservation now lies at the island's east end.

WILDLIFE—More than 240 species of birds can be spotted throughout the Apostles, including common loon, herons, sandhill crane, ducks, bald eagle, numerous hawks, and turkey vulture, plus the occasional common and Caspian terns, osprey, and peregrine falcon; all threatened or endangered in Wisconsin. Naturally, since it sits on an island, mammals are generally rare, though those in the park include deer, beaver, and bear.

HIKING—There are eight miles of trails in the park, all of which are worth a stroll. Two level paths lead along the edge of Big Bay Point and have great views of the cliffs and caves. The 1.3-mile Bay View Trail and the Point Trail, a 1.5-mile loop, are both wooded. The short cut-off which completes the Point Trail loop has interpretive markers discussing the surrounding forest. An excellent overlook between the two trails is just a short walk from the picnic area.

A 0.75-mile boardwalk Nature Trail parallels the bay through the unique vegetation along the barrier beach and leads to a wildlife observation deck. Interpretive panels along the path discuss the formation of the lagoon and beach. The beach is also great for walking and is connected to the trail at several points allowing the two to be combined into a loop.

The least-used trail is the 2.5-mile Lagoon Ridge Trail, which leads through

33

the moss and fern-covered boreal forest floor between the main picnic area and the indoor group camp. This narrow trail has many small hills and is not as easy a hike as the others though it is not difficult. Small logs, boardwalks, and bridges surface many spots, though parts may still be wet early in the season or after rains. As the name implies, the trail leads along a ridge above the lagoon which is visible at times through a thin line of trees. A bench cut into a large fallen tree can be found near the midpoint of the trail.

PADDLING—The lagoon can be reached from a narrow inlet at the north end of Big Bay. Canoeing is not recommended on Lake Superior outside of Big Bay because of the likelihood of large waves and potential for sudden changes in weather, but sea kayaks are a great way to see the park's spectacular shore.

WINTER—The Bayview and Point trails as well as the beach offer over five miles of easy, groomed, cross-country skiing trails. During especially cold winters, the shoreline cliffs and ice caves can be explored up close from the frozen lake.

The Madeline Island ferry normally does not run January through March, but visitors can still get to the island. When the passage is frozen, an ice road lined with discarded Christmas trees connects La Pointe to the mainland, and visitors can simply drive over to the island. A passenger-only wind sled makes the trip during freeze-up and thaw.

COUNTY—Ashland.

DIRECTIONS—A 20-minute ferry ride takes visitors (and their cars) from Bayfield to La Pointe on Madeline Island. The park is then four miles east of La Pointe on County H and two miles east on Hagen Rd.

FACILITIES—Water, toilets, nature programs, picnic area, grills, beach.

CAMPING—60 sites, seven walk-in sites, open year-round, reservations accepted, showers, group camp.

ENTRY—Open year-round. State park sticker or daily fee required.

ON THE WEB—www.wiparks.net and www.madferry.com (Madeline Island Ferry)

CONTACT—Big Bay State Park, PO Box 589, 141 S. 3rd St., Bayfield, WI 54814. Phone (715) 747-6425.

Copper Falls State Park

TOURISM BROCHURES from the mid-20th century called Copper Falls State Park "Wisconsin's Most Beautiful Possession," and many visitors today might still agree. Opened in 1929, the park contains nearly 2,700 acres of wooded hills, but most people come just to see a half-mile section of the

Bad River (so named by the French because of their difficulties navigating it) and its tributary, Tyler's Forks, where the two rivers drop over a pair of large waterfalls and cut through narrow, vertical gorges up to a hundred feet deep. Copper Falls is a double falls that drops 29 feet before entering the narrow gorge. Below the namesake falls, the Tyler's Forks River plunges rapidly over a beautiful series of cascades and then drops 40 feet over Brownstone Falls before joining the main river. Both Copper and Brownstone are among Wisconsin's ten tallest waterfalls.

The park lies along the ancient Penokee mountain range that has long since eroded away into nothing more than a stretch of steep hills. The gorge along the Bad River is cut through an exposed chunk of lava that flowed to the earth's surface a billion years ago, and the various colors of rock and irregular erosion patterns form a striking backdrop to the river. Much of the rest of the river above and below the falls is a series of rapids caused partly by the abundance of boulders deposited by the retreating glaciers. Many thousands of years ago, Lake Superior, filled by glacial meltwater, stretched all the way up to the park.

The name Copper Falls comes from the area's long mining history. Prehistoric Copper Culture Native Americans likely lived here and molded weapons and tools out of the copper they mined. In the early 1860s, miners searched the canyon between Copper and Brownstone falls for copper to help supply northern troops during the Civil War. Prospectors returned at the end of the century and actually rerouted the Bad River. Not enough metal was found, however, to make the venture worthwhile.

WILDLIFE—A wide variety of wildlife is found in the park. More than 200 species of birds can be spotted throughout the year, including common loon, herons, ducks, pileated woodpecker, ruffed grouse, bald eagle, and many songbirds. Beaver, otter, mink, fisher, porcupine, fox, coyote, deer, bear, bobcat, and the endangered timber wolf are some of Copper Falls' many mammals.

HIKING - Four hiking trails, totaling about nine miles, lead through the park. The Three Bridges Trail, by far the most popular, winds around the falls and gorge area with numerous overlooks and geological interpretive markers explaining the area's formation. The trail is an easy 1.7 miles, but allow plenty of time because there is so much to see. A wheelchair-accessible section of the trail begins at a disabled access parking area. Joining the Three Bridges Trail is the mile-long Valley Trail. The wooded and hilly path leads up a steep hill to an observation tower from which Lake Superior and the Apostle Islands are visible. Much less used is the 2.5-mile Red Granite Falls Trail in the southern part of the park. It is also wooded and crosses many hills, and the back half leads up to the Bad River and a series of scenic rapids, making this the most interesting of the two loops.

A five-mile segment of the North Country National Scenic Trail (p. 24) runs through the park, encompassing a portion of the Three Bridges Trail. The segment north of the falls is a scenic and very peaceful trek. The North Country Trail continues south out of the park for three miles to Mellen, and then it's another two miles along Kornstead Road (follow River Street west from Highway 13 in town) to the Chequamegon-Nicolet National Forest.

PADDLING—Thirty-four-acre Loon Lake provides easy canoeing; however, it lies along the park road and has a swimming beach, so it's not always peaceful.

BIKING—The off-road bike trail has two separate sections, and both the three-mile Western and two-mile Eastern trail loops are wooded and hilly. Bikes are also allowed on the section of the North Country Trail running south out of the park to Mellen.

WINTER—In winter the biking, most of the hiking, and a few additional winter-only trails combine for 14 miles of groomed cross-country ski trails that can accommodate beginners and challenge experts.

COUNTY—Ashland.

DIRECTIONS—Two miles north of Mellen on Highway 169.

FACILITIES—Water, toilets, canoe launch, picnic area, grills, playground,

DOUG ALFT

Copper Falls.

picnic shelter, beach, ball field.

CAMPING—Two campgrounds, 55 sites, 13 electric, four walk-in sites, one backpack site, barrier-free cabin, open year-round, reservations accepted, showers, group camp.

ENTRY—Open year-round. State park sticker or daily fee required.

ON THE WEB—www.wiparks.net

CONTACT—Copper Falls State Park, Rt. 1, Box 17AA, Mellen, WI 54546. Phone (715) 274-5123.

Turtle-Flambeau
Scenic Waters Area

THE TURTLE-FLAMBEAU FLOWAGE is known locally as the "Crown Jewel of Wisconsin," a title that is hard to dispute. The 14,000-acre Rorschach test splattered across southern Iron County has 114 miles of virtually untouched mainland shore and nearly 200 islands scattered about. While there are a few resorts at the far north and west ends, over 95 percent of the shoreline remains wild. Isolated island and shore camping let you truly appreciate the splendor of the area.

The vast undeveloped area around the lake is thickly wooded with abundant wetlands, most notable are the extensive patches of patterned bog. In 1990 the state bought most of the flowage to preserve its wilderness character. Current state ownership covers nearly 32,000 acres on and around the lake, and over time the state plans to acquire another 15,000 acres. The flowage itself was created in 1926 by a dam on the North Fork Flambeau River, which combined 16 lakes. The flowage, also fed by the Turtle and Manitowish rivers and many creeks, ensures a steady water supply for several hydroelectric dams downstream on the Flambeau.

WILDLIFE—The flowage is an excellent place to view wildlife, with the east end of the flowage featuring Wisconsin's greatest concentration of nesting bald eagle, osprey, and common loon. More than 160 species of birds can be seen here throughout the year: hooded merganser, great blue heron, Canada goose, common raven, ruffed grouse, black-capped chickadee, and white-throated sparrow are likely to be spotted, while black tern, horned grebe, northern goshawk, merlin, and snowy owl are some notable rare species. Also of interest to bird-watchers is the bountiful spring warbler migration which includes Nashville and Magnolia warblers.

Mammals found here include otter, beaver, mink, porcupine, fisher, fox, coyote, bear, and deer. Lucky visitors might even catch a glimpse of a bobcat, moose, or the endangered timber wolf.

HIKING—A two-mile, self-guided nature trail at Fisherman's Landing off Popko Circle East should be completed by the time this book is published. The trail heads east through the forest, ending at a hilltop overlook of the lake on a small peninsula. Portions are surfaced with gravel and thus are wheelchair accessible. There are also roughly four miles of hunter walking trails off Popko Circle West in the north end of the area and these may be used for hiking.

PADDLING—This is one of the best open-water canoeing areas in the state, especially the eastern fifth, which is a "voluntary quiet area" in the summer. A proposed wilderness designation for this quiet section was scrapped, due to opposition from horsepower addicts, though the quiet/no wake requests are generally respected. Whether this is out of courtesy or because this area has many stumps and rock bars is unclear, though the latter is probably the principal factor. The abundance of underwater hazards actually spreads across the majority of the flowage and keeps pleasure motor-boaters to a relative minimum elsewhere, too, so paddling and peaceful fishing can be good all over.

Murray's Landing, the only boat launch in the quiet area, is the main starting point for paddlers. Two miles to the west is Bonies Mound, one of the highest points on the flowage and a prominent landmark. There are six other landings on the flowage, including one at Lake of the Falls County Park.

AUTO TOUR—The 24-mile Turtle-Flambeau Scenic Waters Area Auto Tour follows Popko Circle Drive along the northern end of the area. A guide booklet available from the DNR office in Mercer describes the area and points out interesting sites on the route, including several osprey nests. Despite its one-sided view of forest management, there are many interesting facts in the booklet.

COUNTY—Iron.

DIRECTIONS—Murray's Landing is three miles southeast of Mercer on Hwy. 51, then six miles southwest on Murray's Landing Rd.

Lake of the Falls County Park is 0.75 mile northwest of Mercer on Highway 51, then five miles west on County FF.

FACILITIES—Boat launch, water, and toilets available at Springstead Landing. Lake of the Falls County Park has water, toilets, boat launch, picnic area, grills, shelter.

CAMPING—60 first-come, first-served sites (free) are accessible by water only, and one is designed to be wheelchair accessible; open year-round (expect to find all sites occupied during the fishing opener the first weekend in May and holiday weekends during the summer); group camp. Lake of the Falls County Park has 30 sites, five electric, open early May to late September.

ENTRY—Open year-round. Free.

ON THE WEB—www.turtleflambeauflowage.com

CONTACT—DNR, 5291 N. Statehouse Circle, Mercer, WI 54547. Phone (715) 476-7846. Iron County Parks Dept., 300 Taconite, Hurley, WI 54534. Phone (715) 561-2697.

Timm's Hill National Trail
and Timm's Hill County Park

FEW PEOPLE outside the Rib Lake area know about the gorgeous Timm's Hill National Trail, despite its designation as an official National Scenic Trail. The ten-mile path connects the Ice Age National Scenic Trail (p. 1) with Timm's Hill, Wisconsin's highest point at 1,951.5 feet above sea level. The trail was built in 1986 and received its national status four years later, becoming the first side trail to earn such recognition.

The 220-acre park at the trail's north end lies between two of the highest lakes in the state—Bass to the south and Timm's to the north. An observation tower at the top of the hill offers expansive views which are most impressive during the peak of fall color.

WILDLIFE—The area is home to deer, fox, coyote, porcupine, bear, hawks, ruffed grouse, great blue heron, ducks, and many songbirds.

HIKING—Wandering past many glacially formed hills and lakes, the thickly wooded Timm's Hill National Trail offers a very scenic and peaceful hike. There are also several historic sites along the trail. The first quarter-mile of the trail is wheelchair accessible and leads past interpretive markers discussing the history of, and pointing out the scant remains of, the Rib Lake Lumber Company's Camp 6. The southern end is also the main access point for the Rib Lake Trail System—over 12.5 miles of hilly paths that branch off the Ice Age Trail between the village of Rib Lake and County C in Taylor County. A detailed guide booklet available at the parking lot on County C provides much more historical and geological background.

Five wooded trails cross Timm's Hill County Park. A pair of fairly level, 1.25-mile loops are named for each of the park's lakes. The mostly level Bass Lake Trail circles that lake while the quieter Timm's Lake Trail leads around Timm's Hill just briefly, passing its namesake body of water. Less interesting are the Pearson Lake Trail, which descends for 1.25 miles toward (but does not actually reach) its namesake lake sitting across the road from the park, and the mile-long Hardwoods Trail; both are a bit hilly. It is a quarter-mile climb up the Tower Trail to the observation town.

BIKING—Off-road bikes are allowed on Timm's Hill National Trail.

WINTER—Timm's Hill National Trail and the Rib Lake Trails are both groomed for cross-country skiing and have easy sections for beginners, though for the most part these are challenging trips. The trails around Timm's Hill County Park are a part of the Highpoint Ski Trails. These groomed loops between the park and County C total 7.5 miles and include a mile-long section that is periodically lit for night skiing. They are very hilly overall, but have one easy segment. The Highpoint Trails can accommodate skate skiing and have a warming shelter.

AUTO TOUR—County RR in Price County which leads along the southern border of Timm's Hill County Park is Rustic Road #62. Rustic Road #1 crosses County C and Timm's Hill National Trail just north of Rib Lake.

OTHER—Horses are allowed on Timm's Hill National Trail, but not in the park. There is a hitching post at the park entrance if you want to hike up the hill.

COUNTIES—Price and Taylor.

DIRECTIONS—The southern trailhead is two miles east of Rib Lake on Highway 102, then three miles north on County C. The park itself is another seven miles north on County C, then half a mile east on County RR.

FACILITIES—Water, toilets, boat launch, picnic area, grills, picnic shelter, playground.

CAMPING—Three walk-in sites at south end of Timm's Hill National Trail.

ENTRY—Open year-round. Free.

CONTACT—Price County Tourism Department, 126 Cherry St., Phillips, WI 54555. Phone (715) 339-4505 or (800) 269-4505.

Flambeau River State Forest

COVERING WELL OVER 90,000 acres, this is Wisconsin's second largest state forest. The forest protects 60 miles of the Flambeau River whose north and south forks merge at the southern end. It is no surprise that paddling is the most popular activity here, since the boulder-strewn Flambeau churns up some of the Midwest's premiere whitewater. There are also quiet stretches of river for those who prefer to avoid whitewater.

The forest was officially established in 1930, but efforts to preserve this area date back to the beginning of the 20th century when local conservationists worked to protect land along the river. By 1913, 3,600 acres, much of it old-growth forest, were under public ownership, and wilderness protection along the Flambeau River continues to the present day. In the 1980s the state purchased a 16-mile-long, 300-foot-wide stretch of land along each side of the Flambeau's upper stretches. The Upper North Fork Flambeau Natural Area, as the newly purchased area is generally known, was originally preserved by The Nature Conservancy and is now an adjunct unit of the state forest. Largely untouched by loggers, this section of river beginning below the Turtle-Flambeau Dam features a nearly pristine boreal forest and has virtually no development.

Lake of the Pines (273 acres) and Connors Lake (429 acres), at the heart of the forest on opposite sides of County W, are focal points of other forest activities; each has a campground, beach, boat launch, and nature trail.

WILDLIFE—Although you would be lucky to see a timber wolf, three packs are known to roam within the forest boundaries. Other forest residents include deer, bear, coyote, fox, fisher, porcupine, bear, bobcat, ruffed grouse, many songbirds, and the state-threatened osprey and red-shouldered hawk. Also look for beaver, otter, mink, herons, bald eagle, ducks, and geese along the river and in the creeks and lakes.

HIKING—Three short but scenic trails offer easy hikes. Each of the campgrounds has a 0.7-mile nature trail with interpretive signs; both are wooded and have some small hills along their paths. The lovely Little Falls-Slough Gundy Scenic Area Trail is a mostly level half-mile loop leading through the forest to Little Falls and the surrounding rapids on the South Fork Flambeau

Flambeau River rapids.

River. This very scenic area is nine miles north of Hawkins on County M.

There are two thickly wooded options for longer hikes. The eight-mile Oxbo Trail, in the northern end of the forest, 8.5 miles east of Draper on Highway 70, is situated between a large bend in the river, and although used principally by skiers offers some decent hiking. There are five loops branching off one another allowing hikers to choose trips of various lengths. Loop #1 at the southern end of the trail is the shortest hike at 2.4 miles, and it is about seven miles around the perimeter of all the loops. Each numbered loop gets a little hillier, with the 1.2-mile Loop #5 at the north end being quite strenuous.

The 14-mile Flambeau Hills Trail has three principal loops stacked on top of one another, and affords frequent views of the river to the west. The shortest route is the 1.1-mile Short Swing, while it is an almost five-mile walk around the Rim Creek Loop in the middle and an 8.5-mile hike around all three loops. The terrain is comprised of rolling hills except for the 1.4-mile Squirrel Tail Trail and 0.6-mile Ridge Run, which together form most of the northernmost loop; these two trails are both quite steep. Branching off the back loop is the 4.6-mile Snuss Trail, which leads north to Highway 70, connecting the Flambeau Hills Trail to the Oxbo Trail. The Mason Creek Bridge near the southern end of the Snuss Trail is an especially scenic spot. The main Flambeau Hills trailhead is on County W, just east of the river.

PADDLING—The Flambeau River offers canoeing for both beginners and experts. Though there are still some cabins and resorts on private land along the river, overall this is a wild and a scenic trip. The North Fork is the easier and most popular branch. The northern half of the trip through the forest offers easy paddling, with just one set of rapids along the 17 miles between Nine Mile Landing and the County W Bridge Landing. There are a few small rapids on the next 10 miles down to the Camp 41 Landing, but the real excitement begins along the final ten miles to the Beaver Dam Landing (the last one within the forest) since there are numerous Class II rapids along this stretch. The South Fork is a less-traveled route, partly because summer water levels aren't very reliable. From County W, five miles outside the forest in Price County, to its confluence with the North Fork, there are numerous Class III rapids, many of which should be portaged by all but experts.

The 16-mile long Upper North Fork Natural Area lies northeast of the main forest. Starting at the Turtle-Flambeau Flowage (p. 37), where the river originates, and the Agenda Landing on Flambeau Lane four miles north of Park Falls, there are many rapids, including some Class III; this section is definitely not for beginners. The final four miles to the City of Park Falls is a calm run on a narrow flowage. It is another 14 miles from Park Falls to the Nine Mile Landing, the first within the forest. This stretch is almost all flat water with several dams to portage.

Several lakes in the forest offer relaxed paddling. The two largest are Connors Lake and Lake of the Pines, though they are also, by far, the busiest. The best bet is to carry your boat to Bass Lake, a 94-acre designated wilderness lake not far from the campgrounds.

BIKING—Off-road bikes are allowed on the 14-mile Flambeau Hills Trail. The Tuscobia State Trail, following an abandoned railroad right-of-way, cuts across the far north end of the forest and is another biking option, though ATV riders also use it.

WINTER—The Flambeau Hills and Oxbo trails, both groomed, offer 22 miles of excellent cross-country skiing. Skate skiers may use the Flambeau Hills Trail which also has a warming shelter.

Snowmobilers have 44 miles of trails that connect to the Tuscobia State Trail and to the Sawyer, Rusk, and Price trail systems.

OTHER—A 40-mile ATV trail leads along forest roads and the snowmobile trail, from Fisherman's Landing off County M in the south, connecting to the Tuscobia State Trail (also open to ATVs) in the north.

COUNTIES—The main forest is spread across Sawyer, Rusk, and Price, while the Upper North Fork Natural Area is in Iron and Ashland.

DIRECTIONS—The headquarters is 13 miles east of Winter on County W.

FACILITIES—Water, toilets, boat launch, nature programs, picnic area, grills, picnic shelter, beach.

CAMPING—Two campgrounds, 60 sites, 14 canoe camps on the North Fork with two or three sites at each (free), open year-round; canoe camping along river is allowed in Upper North Fork Natural Area; backpacking permitted throughout forest with free permit (backpackers may not use the canoe sites).

ENTRY—Open year-round. State park sticker or daily fee required. State trail pass required for cross-country skiing.

ON THE WEB —www.wiparks.net

CONTACT—Flambeau River State Forest, W1613 County Highway W, Winter, WI 54896. Phone (715) 332-5271.

Chippewa Flowage

Known locally as the Big Chip, this is a sprawling 15,300-acre maze of winding channels and deep bays dotted with more than 200 islands. Two dozen resorts are spread out around Wisconsin's third largest lake, but almost all of the rest of the densely wooded 233 miles of shoreline remain undeveloped, and all future management must "perpetuate the undeveloped shoreline character."

The Northern States Power Company (now Xcel Energy) created the flowage on the Chippewa River with the installation of the Winter Dam in 1923. The Chequamegon-Nicolet National Forest covers part of the lake's eastern shore, while the Lac Courte Oreilles Ojibwe reservation forms much of the southern and western borders. The state bought most of the rest of the land to ensure the area's preservation, and today the DNR manages the area jointly with the U.S. Forest Service and the Lac Courte Oreilles band.

For most visitors, the Big Chip is all about fishing (the world-record muskie, 69 pounds, 11 ounces, was hooked here) but paddling the scenic bays and pitching a tent on a remote island offers the ultimate Chippewa experience. And, even though it receives twice the number of users as the similar Turtle-Flambeau Scenic Waters Area (p. 37), this is still a worthy wilderness getaway.

WILDLIFE—Among the wildlife that can be observed on the flowage and its wooded shores are beaver, otter, mink, porcupine, deer, and bear. If you are very lucky you will hear the howl of a wolf—not to be confused with the coyotes, which howl all the time. More than 130 species of birds have been recorded on and around the Big Chip, most notably the oft-sighted bald eagle as well as osprey, red-shouldered hawk, common loon, wood duck, great blue heron, and kingfisher. Large numbers of waterfowl stop on the lake during the spring and fall migrations.

HIKING—Between the two boat landings on County CC is a sign commemorating the state's land purchase. Here, a short unmarked trail, about a quarter-mile loop, leads out along the shore and offers some good views. Some real hiking trails may be built in the future, but there is little inclination to do so at the present time.

BOATING—The Chippewa Flowage is primarily a fishing lake, but it is also a good place for canoeing. All boaters are required to follow a "speed that is no greater than reasonable or prudent," and if that is not enough to keep pleasure boaters away, the abundance of submerged logs and rock bars is.

There are six public boat launches located around the flowage. Most paddlers stick to the east end of the lake and often combine trips on the flowage with paddling on the Chippewa River. Canoe rentals are available at several places around the lake as are maps.

WINTER—The lake is closed to ice fishing except for tribal members.

OTHER—The Chippewa Queen scenic boat tours, based at the Treeland Resort (715) 462-3874, motor around the lake from Memorial Day weekend to the first weekend in October.

COUNTY—Sawyer.

DIRECTIONS—The boat launch closest to Hayward is 14 miles east of the city on County B, then two miles south on County CC.

FACILITIES—Boat launch.

CAMPING—Allowed only at the 11 free, first-come, first-served, state-owned, island campsites (camp only at marked sites, since there are some tribal sites that are not open to the general public—the DNR has maps of the sites available) that come with picnic tables, fire rings, and pit toilets; open year-round (they fill up fast in the summer). Many of the surrounding resorts also have RV campgrounds.

ENTRY—Open year-round. Free.

ON THE WEB—www.chippewaflowage.com

CONTACT—Chippewa Flowage Manager, DNR, 10220 N. Highway 27, Hayward, WI 54843. Phone (715) 634-2688.

Sawmill Lake and Loyhead Lake
Primitive Canoe Routes

COLLECTIVELY CALLED the Birchwood Canoe Trails, these paddle-and-portage routes offer a sense of adventure and solitude with very little effort required. Wisconsin's own mini-Boundary Waters Canoe Area sits within a 5,000-acre Washburn County Forest Primitive Management Area, home to a high concentration of small lakes. These lakes and their steep banks were formed during the last Ice Age and except for where the routes begin, there is no development along any of their wooded shores.

The pier at the campground on Sawmill Lake is a great place to take in the scenery, swim, or fish. In addition to the largemouth bass and panfish found in most of the lakes, Sawmill Lake is regularly stocked with trout.

WILDLIFE—On the lakes and in the forest, osprey, common loon, ducks, beaver, mink, deer, and maybe even a curious bear may all be sighted.

HIKING—Canoeing is not the only activity here. A narrow 0.75-mile trail starts at the campground and loops through the forest along three of the lakes. Several service roads open to hiking branch off Birchwood Fire Lane within the primitive area, including one just north of the campground.

PADDLING—Paddle around for an hour or a day. The portages, clearly marked by white-topped posts, are pretty much short and easy, and journeys of any length are possible as neither route is completely circular—several lakes have only one portage into them. Maps of both routes are available at the campground.

DAVID W. HERRICK

Taking a break at Sawmill Lake.

The Sawmill Lake route starts at the campground and connects nine lakes, none of which is larger than 29 acres. This route could also be started at the boat launch on the west side of Sawmill Lake, or northeast of the campground on Otter Lake. Of the seven lakes on the Loyhead Lake route, Loyhead is by far the largest at 74 acres. There are two launches for this route, both onto Loyhead Lake from Birchwood Fire Lane. Other lakes in the forest may also be explored.

COUNTY—Washburn.

DIRECTIONS—Sawmill Lake is six miles north of Birchwood on County T, then two miles north on Birchwood Fire Lane. Loyhead Lake is another 0.75 mile north.

FACILITIES—Water, toilets, boat launch, picnic area, grills, picnic shelter.

CAMPING—25 sites, check with county for exact open dates.

ENTRY—Open year-round. Free.

ON THE WEB—www.co.washburn.wi.us/departments/forestry

CONTACT—Washburn County Forest, 850 W. Beaverbrook Ave., Spooner, WI 54801. Phone (715) 635-4490. E-mail: forestry@co.washburn.wi.us

Hunt Hill Audubon Sanctuary

H UNT HILL, owned by the National Audubon Society but operated by the local group Friends of Hunt Hill, is an environmental education center offering classes in outdoor skills and nature appreciation for organized groups such as schools and scouts. However, the general public is welcome to explore the forest, prairie, tamarack bog, and lakes spread out over this exceptionally scenic 500-acre reserve. The entire shores of three spring-fed glacial lakes are protected within the reserve, and there is extensive frontage on Big Devil's Lake. The reserve also owns the land around the Dory's Bog State Natural Area to the east of the main reserve. This natural area protects numerous rare plants, including the insectivorous sundew and pitcher plants, as well as several bog orchids.

The reserve began on land donated to the Audubon Society in 1954 by Frances Hunt Andrews, who wanted to ensure its preservation. The Audubon Society operated an environmental education center here until 1986, when they closed it due to budget problems. The Friends of Hunt Hill reopened the facility in 1990 and have had a successful run ever since.

WILDLIFE—Abundant wildlife can be seen at Hunt Hill including fox, deer, beaver, otter, fisher, and bear. Hunt Hill is a fantastic bird-watching area with more than 240 species having been recorded over the years. Look for common loon, wood duck, green-backed heron, sandhill crane, pheasant, ruffed grouse, wild turkey, bald eagle, pileated woodpecker, red owl, Eastern meadowlark, rose-breasted grosbeak, veery, bobolink, and a multitude of warblers. State-threatened species sometimes seen here include osprey, red-shouldered hawk, and great egret.

HIKING—Most of the eight miles of trails are generally level, though an exception is the half-mile Frances Andrews' Trail which climbs a steep wooded hill before passing along the shore of Big Devil's Lake and looping back. The trail also provides overlooks of Upper Twin Lake. Continuing along the shore of Big Devil's Lake is the 2.7-mile Bear Trail which crosses the eastern half of the reserve. One-quarter mile beyond where it branches off from the Frances Andrews' Trail, the Bear Trail crosses a knee-deep stream (there is no bridge) that flows between Big Devil's and Upper Twin lakes. Across the stream, the trail continues through thick forest between Twin and Reed lakes and around to a bridge at the end of Lower Twin Lake, where a bridge connects it to the mile-long Vole Trail, completing an excellent loop around the lakes.

The Vole Trail, usually accessed at the main center, loops through a prairie that teems with wildflowers. If you want to see more of the prairie, use the adjoining, half-mile Deer Trail to make a longer loop. Do not skip either the tiny Bog or Beaver trails that branch off the Vole Trail. The Bog Trail leads down to a boardwalk that cuts through the tamarack bog ringing Lower Twin Lake, and this is one of the most beautiful spots in the preserve, especially when fall color has kicked in. This path is a bit rough in places and can be wet at times. The hard-to-find Beaver Trail drops down to the back end of Lower Twin Lake where you can see a beaver lodge and, if lucky, some of the home-makers. An interpretive brochure available at the Vole trailhead tells about many of the plants found along these trails.

The 1.75-mile Red Oak Trail rolls over the hills and through the large oaks and white pines away from the lakes. These lovely woods are an adjunct unit of the Dory's Bog State Natural Area. The quarter-mile Barred Owl Trail continues through the woods, connecting the Red Oak Trail to the prairie.

PADDLING—Canoeists can paddle along the shore of Big Devil's Lake and into the undeveloped Upper and Lower Twin lakes.

COUNTY—Washburn.

DIRECTIONS—Three-quarters of a mile east of Sarona on County D, then 0.2 mile north on County P, and 3.5 miles east on Audubon Rd.

FACILITIES—Water, toilets, nature center, nature programs, picnic area, and many facilities for program participants like dormitories and a library.

CAMPING—Two group camps.

ENTRY—Open year-round. Visitors are asked to check in at the office. $2 suggested donation.

ON THE WEB—www.audubon.org/local/sanctuary/hunthill

CONTACT—The Friends of Hunt Hill, N2384 Hunt Hill Rd., Sarona, WI 54870. Phone (715) 635-6543. E-mail: hunthill@spacestar.net

St. Croix National
Scenic Riverway

THE 252-MILE St. Croix Riverway preserves two of the most pristine rivers in the country, the St. Croix and the Namekagon. Established in 1968 as one of the original projects in the National Wild and Scenic Rivers System, the riverway is one of the Midwest's most popular canoeing destinations, but it is long enough to allow canoeists to revel in the wilderness without any crowds, often without any other people at all.

The riverway is managed by the National Park Service except for the final 25 miles between Stillwater, Minnesota, and the Mississippi River, known as Lake St. Croix, which is administered jointly by Wisconsin and Minnesota. This section is very wide, has little current, and is used primarily by motorboaters. It is not recommended for canoes, kayaks, or small boats.

The 154 miles of the St. Croix within the national riverway start below the St. Croix Flowage at Gordon Dam Park in Douglas County. The upper stretch of the river is narrow and shallow in places, but eventually becomes wide and deep where it serves as the Wisconsin-Minnesota border. The Namekagon, which is entirely in Wisconsin, begins as a small trout stream below Namekagon Lake in the Chequamegon-Nicolet National Forest (p. 18) in Bayfield County, and is mostly narrow and winding along its 98-mile path. Most of the land along both rivers is thickly forested, though occasionally the Namekagon and the St. Croix above its junction with the Namekagon widen as they pass through extensive wetlands. Scenic cliffs line the St. Croix in many places—the most spectacular are the 200-foot-high Dalles of the St. Croix, between Wisconsin and Minnesota's Interstate state parks (p. 60), which have been a major tourist attraction since the mid-1800s.

Along with the Brule River, the St. Croix formed an important trading route between Lake Superior and the Mississippi River, used by Native Americans for centuries and later by fur traders. When the fur trade declined, logging became the main industry in this part of the state, and the St. Croix became an important river for transporting logs to sawmills. In 1886, the Dalles was the site of the largest logjam on record, requiring 200 men six weeks to break it up. The St. Croix was also a major commercial shipping corridor as far north as St. Croix Falls. Steamboats could not travel beyond there because of the steep, cascading rapids (it is not really a waterfall), which are now submerged below the dam.

WILDLIFE—While wolves are very shy and rarely seen, the upper half of the St. Croix Valley has one of the densest wolf concentrations in the state. Three to four packs have territories along the rivers, and the St. Croix is an important travel corridor, so you could get lucky and see one along the shore. Other mammals that make the river valleys their home include bobcat, bear, fox, coyote, deer, fisher, porcupine, badger, mink, otter, and beaver.

Birds are especially abundant along the riverway; bald eagle and osprey are frequently seen here. Also look for wood duck, trumpeter swan, sandhill crane, great blue heron, and belted kingfisher along the rivers, especially when they pass through wetlands. Red-shouldered hawks, peregrine falcon, turkey vulture, wild turkey, ruffed and sharp-tailed grouse, pileated woodpecker, great crested flycatcher, white-breasted nuthatch, veery, winter wren, rose-breasted grosbeak, and scarlet tanager may also be seen.

Because it has little pollution, the St. Croix hosts one of the most diverse populations of freshwater mussels in the country. Of the 40 species, two—the Higgins Eye and Winged Maple Leaf—are federally endangered. The state threatened Blanding's and wood turtles are also found here, generally north of Highway 70.

HIKING—Canoeing is not the only way to explore the riverway; the park service maintains six trails in Wisconsin. Polk County's Ridge View Trail is a three-mile loop located two miles north of Osceola on County S, right by the Riverway maintenance facility. This mostly-level path leads past many narrow valleys and rock outcroppings along the Chisago Loop. There are views of the St. Croix bottomlands along the bluff side of the Osceola Loop; though distinct, both loops are very scenic. A few miles north, the wooded, wheelchair-accessible, Indianhead Flowage Trail crosses several streams on small bridges as it follows the St. Croix River for three quarters of a mile. The trailhead is just a mile north of the St. Croix Visitor Center on Highway 87 and is usually accessed at Lions Park.

The mostly wooded Sandrock Cliffs Trail in Burnett County is a five-mile loop along the river with several short loops branching off the north end. There are some hills on the trail, but it is not an overly difficult walk. The trail begins at Highway 70 and can also be accessed at the Sandrock Cliffs Campground at the north end of the trail. The scenic, namesake cliffs are located near the campground.

Two trails are located in Washburn County near the village of Trego: the Trego Nature Trail and the Trego Lake Trail. The Nature Trail starts just a quarter mile east of the Namekagon Visitor Center on Highway 63 and leads along the high banks above the Namekagon River. The hilly, wooded, 2.8-mile trail is arguably the most scenic in the riverway and an excellent wildlife-watching spot. The 3.6-mile Trego Lake Trail has three wooded loops along this narrow flowage on the Namekagon River. The beginner loop is level, while the intermediate and advanced loops have many hills. It begins north of Trego, two miles west of Highway 53 on North River Road.

The wooded Namekagon-Court Oreilles Portage Trail is located south of Hayward in Sawyer County. Take Highway 27 to Rainbow Road, turn west to Rolf Road, then head north for a quarter-mile to the trailhead. The generally level 0.8-mile loop leads through a rich, diverse forest to a wetland boardwalk heading out to the river. The trail is named for, but does not follow the actual path of, an ancient portage route.

There is also excellent hiking in the adjacent state parks and forests, especially Governor Knowles State Forest (p. 53) and Interstate State Park (p. 60).

PADDLING—The riverway can accommodate trips of a few hours to more than a week. And, with only Class I rapids—except below the St. Croix Falls Dam and in a few other places during high water periods—both the Namekagon and the St. Croix are ideal for beginning paddlers. Canoe rentals and shuttle service can be found all along the riverway; the park office can provide you with a current list of service providers.

The Namekagon and the St. Croix above Riverside Landing are narrow, winding routes with many easy rapids. After the spring, water levels are sometimes too low for canoeing on the St. Croix above the CCC Bridge Landing (a few miles upstream from its confluence with the Namekagon) and the Namekagon above Hayward; check the Riverway website for river levels and canoeing conditions. A very popular and highly recommended trip is from the Namekagon's County K Landing, just below the Trego Dam, to Riverside Landing on the St. Croix. This 35-mile section is one of the least developed stretches of the riverway.

Below Riverside Landing, the 30 miles to Nelson's Landing is an easy and popular route with only a few scattered rapids. The next 11 miles to Highway 70 offer spectacular scenery with tall cliffs, and have some of the river's fastest water, though it is not difficult canoeing. The river widens in the final 35 miles above St. Croix Falls, affording a slow and easy trip. Some small fishing boats do navigate this part of the river. The dam at St. Croix Falls forms ten-mile-long Indianhead Flowage, which many canoeists choose to skip because of frequent motorboat use and reduced current. There is a 1.25-mile portage around the St. Croix Falls dam on the Minnesota side.

Canoeing is also good on the 22 miles of the Lower St. Croix from Interstate State Park downstream to the Apple River, though most people end this trip at Marine on St. Croix, Minnesota. The many tall bluffs lining this route compensate for the increased development and there are many side channels to explore; also, with no rapids, this stretch is ideal for beginners. The scenery, easy paddling, and proximity to the Twin Cities make this the riverway's most popular paddling destination. Motorboaters do use this part of the river, but it is a slow-speed zone. Canoeing is not recommended on the final 30 miles of the St. Croix, a stretch extremely popular with motorboaters.

WINTER—The Sandrock Cliffs and Trego Lake trails are groomed for cross-country skiing. Additional ski trails are found in Kinnickinnic (p. 65), Willow River (p. 63), and Interstate (p. 60) state parks, and in the Governor Knowles State Forest (p. 53).

OTHER—Motorboaters and sailors are the main users of the St. Croix below its confluence with the Apple River, just south of Marine on St. Croix, Minnesota. Motorboaters also frequently use the Indianhead Flowage above the dam at St. Croix Falls. To prevent the spread of zebra mussels, there are restrictions on motorboat travel upstream past the High Bridge just north of Stillwater, Minnesota—a floating ranger station is staffed here. Check with one of the visitor centers for details. Due to heavy boat traffic, water-skiing is prohibited after noon on weekends and holidays above Stillwater. Personal watercraft are prohibited at all times on the St. Croix above Stillwater and on the entire length of the Namekagon.

Boat tours of the Dalles are offered from Taylors Falls, Minnesota (651) 465-6315 or (800) 447-4958 and a steam train ride follows the St. Croix between the historic depot in Osceola, Wisconsin, and Marine on St. Croix, Minnesota (715) 755-3570 or (800) 711-2591. Both run from May through October.

COUNTIES—Bayfield, Douglas, Sawyer, Washburn, Burnett, Polk, St. Croix, and Pierce.

DIRECTIONS—Access sites are found all along the rivers. The St. Croix Visitor Center is in St. Croix Falls, Wisconsin. The Namekagon Visitor Center is in Trego, Wisconsin. The Marshland Center is on Highway 70 on the Minnesota side of river, four miles west of Grantsburg, and is no longer staffed but information racks are kept full. Many state park visitor centers along the St. Croix have riverway information.

FACILITIES—Water, toilets, boat launch, nature center, nature programs, picnic area, grills, picnic shelter.

CAMPING—135 free, first-come, first-served campsites are stretched out along the Riverway, available year-round. All sites are marked by signs and have fire rings and pit toilets, and most also have a picnic table. Individual campsites allow up to three tents and eight people, though a few group sites can accommodate twice as many. Campers can walk in from parking lots to sites at the following landings: Phipps, Earl Park, Howell, and West Howell on the Namekagon and Riverside; Old Railroad Bridge, County O, Sunrise Ferry, Nelson's, Norway Point, and Sandrock Cliffs on the St. Croix. Strict regulations have been enacted to protect the fragile river environment, and as these are always subject to change, it is a good idea to get current information before heading out. Currently, campers must use designated sites above St. Croix Falls. There is a one-night limit above the Nevers Dam Landing (13 miles upstream from St. Croix Falls) and a three-night limit on the remaining stretch. There are few campsites below St. Croix Falls, but camping is allowed for up to seven nights anywhere on federal land except the areas immediately south of Interstate State Park and around the towns of Osceola, and Marine on the St. Croix. Another exception to this rule is that camping is restricted to islands between Stillwater and the High Bridge. There are no designated Riverway campsites below Stillwater. Camping is also available at many adjacent state forests and parks.

ENTRY—Open year-round. The St. Croix Visitor Center is open year-round, the Namekagon Visitor Center is open late May through September.

Free.

ON THE WEB—www.nps.gov/sacn

CONTACT—St. Croix National Scenic Riverway, 401 Hamilton St., PO Box 708, Saint Croix Falls, WI 54024. Phone (715) 483-3284. E-mail: SACN_Interpretation@nps.gov

Governor Knowles State Forest

Governor Knowles is the least developed and least visited of Wisconsin's state forests, and thus a great place to find solitude. Governor Knowles was established in 1970 as an extended resource protection zone for the St. Croix National Scenic Riverway and was originally christened the St. Croix River State Forest. It was renamed in 1981 after former Wisconsin Governor Warren Knowles, an avid conservationist who was in office when the forest was established. The nearly 20,000 acres of forest stretches in a narrow band for 55 miles along the St. Croix River, ranging from a half to two miles in width.

As the last glacier retreated from Wisconsin, the St. Croix River was blocked by an ice dam forming Glacial Lake Grantsburg, which left behind the sandy soil found throughout the area. Sand barrens, which once dominated this region, are still scattered throughout the forest. Large wetlands, low-lying remnants of the lake, remain in the region, some within the forest, though these are far more prevalent in the nearby Glacial Lake Grantsburg Wildlife Complex (p. 56). Much of the river along the forest is bordered by a high ridge which makes for scenic trips by land or water. The easily accessible sandstone cliffs just north of Highway 70 are the most spectacular.

The St. Croix was once part of an important trade route between Lake Superior and the Mississippi, plied by Native Americans and later by French voyageurs. The Fox, Dakota, and Ojibwe were some of the more recent tribes to have lived here. The Dakota and Ojibwe often battled over access to the area's abundant resources, including the wild-rice-producing lakes. Eventually the Dakota were driven westward, but the battles did not end until well into the 19th century. The Sioux Portage Group Camp at the northern tip of the forest is located at one end of a shortcut used by Native Americans between the St. Croix and Yellow rivers.

WILDLIFE—One of the more thrilling sights at Governor Knowles are the bald eagles that frequently soar along the St. Croix River; osprey and peregrine falcon might also be seen along the shoreline. Wild turkey, ruffed and sharp-tailed grouse, pileated and three-toed woodpeckers, and winter wren reside in the forest, while sandhill cranes and ducks are common along the river. Bird-watchers will appreciate the concentration of warblers during the spring migration and should combine the search for forest dwellers at Governor Knowles with the grassland and wetland species at the adjoining Glacial Lake Grantsburg Wildlife Complex (p. 56).

Area mammals include bear, deer, fox, coyote, porcupine, fisher, badger, beaver, otter, mink, plus the occasional moose, bobcat, and timber wolf.

HIKING—Two long trails roughly parallel the St. Croix, passing primarily along the tops of the ridge but occasionally dropping down to the river. There are generally just rolling hills along these wooded routes, though there are some steep climbs where the trails lead up and down the escarpment. The 16-mile southern trail (stretching from Evergreen Avenue in Polk County at the south end to West River Road in Burnett County at the north end) is closer to the river overall than the 22-mile northern trail (stretching from Gile Road at the south end to the Sioux Portage Group Camp on North River Road at the north end; both trailheads are in Burnett County) but both routes are very scenic. As more land is acquired for the forest, the two trails will eventually be joined into one. Both sections cross several roads, allowing access for shorter hikes.

Starting at the Norway Point Landing (at the end of Norway Point Road, almost directly north of Grantsburg) the level Cedar Interpretive Trail shares a path with the northern hiking trail for half a mile through the 330-acre Norway Point Bottomlands State Natural Area, one of six natural areas in the forest, and passes through a lovely stand of cedar. There are many boardwalks along this section, but it can still be quite wet. The wetlands, cedar forest, and boardwalks continue beyond the Cedar Trail. Overall, this is one of the most scenic sections of the forest. A few miles to the east, the trail hits the 690-acre Kohler-Peet Barrens and Cedar Swamp State Natural Area, which is a very interesting area both ecologically and visually.

At its south end, the northern trail joins the Brandt Pines Trails, which consist of four hilly trails totaling 8.5 miles. The Ravine and Ridge Line trails, each 1.5 miles, comprise the Brandt Pines Interpretive Trail which loops through the 190-acre Brandt Brook Pines and Hardwoods State Natural Area. This area features an old-growth forest dominated by red pines and has interpretive panels discussing the forest. The two-mile River View Trail, also within the natural area, leads down the steep escarpment to the river. The Oak Hills Trail is a 3.5-mile loop branching off the north end of the other three.

The beautiful Wood River Interpretive Trail starting at the campground drops down into the Wood River Valley. Interpretive panels lining the mile-long loop discuss the natural history of the river and forest. You can appreciate some of the scenery without climbing the long hills from the viewing platform on the east side of the trail. Across Highway 70 from the campground is the Sandrock Cliffs Trail, a five-mile loop along the river that is officially a part of the St. Croix National Scenic Riverway (p. 48).

PADDLING—Canoeing on the St. Croix River is fantastic, and though there are some stretches of whitewater north of Highway 70 (some of the fastest water along the entire St. Croix is found along the five-mile stretch below Nelson's Landing and during high water a few of these rapids can run as Class II) it is generally suitable for those of limited ability. The river widens below Highway 70, offering all gentle canoeing, perfect for families. Plan on three days to paddle the length of the forest from the Highway 77 bridge to the Never's Dam Landing (eight miles north of St. Croix Falls on Highway 87, then 3.5 miles west on 230th Ave., then a few hundred yards south on Old River Road). See the St. Croix National Scenic Riverway section for more information.

WINTER—The 8.5-mile Brandt Pines Trails are groomed for cross-country skiing and offer a warming shelter at the midpoint. The St. Croix Riverway's Sandrock Cliffs Trail is also groomed. Snowmobilers have 32.5 miles of trails in the forest which connect to the trail systems in both Burnett and Polk counties.

OTHER—The Trade River Horse Trails, starting on Evergreen Avenue at the south end of the forest, have three loops totaling 35 miles that pass through Governor Knowles and the adjacent Polk County Forest. An additional 18-mile horse trail connects the Trade River Trails to the village of Grantsburg.

COUNTIES—Burnett and Polk.

DIRECTIONS—The forest headquarters is on Highway 70 in Grantsburg.

FACILITIES—Water, toilets, boat launch, nature programs, picnic area, grills, picnic shelter.

CAMPING—31 sites, open May through October; separate horserider campground (free, may be used by anyone), group camp, backpacking permitted at designated sites along hiking trails with free permit. Several St. Croix Riverway sites are located along the forest; Nelson's Landing, Norway Point, and Sand Rock Cliffs offer walk-in camping.

ENTRY—Open year-round. State park sticker or daily fee required. State trail pass required for cross-country skiing and horseback riding.

ON THE WEB—www.wiparks.net

CONTACT—Governor Knowles State Forest, 325 Highway 70, PO Box 367, Grantsburg, WI 54840. Phone (715) 463-2898.

Glacial Lake Grantsburg
Wildlife Complex
CREX MEADOWS, FISH LAKE, AMSTERDAM SLOUGHS, and
DANBURY WILDLIFE AREAS

THIS EXPANSIVE COMPLEX covers 70 square miles and is quite possibly the state's top overall wildlife-watching spot. The centerpiece is the
29,000-acre Crex Meadows Wildlife Area, Wisconsin's largest state-owned
wildlife area. Since Crex has the most to offer visitors, it is the most visited
area in the complex, though the other seldom-visited areas are also scenic
and one could easily spend several days exploring here.

Glacial Lake Grantsburg was formed 10,000 years ago during the last Ice
Age, as the melting glaciers retreated north. When the ice dam that blocked
the St. Croix River and created the lake melted, the lake drained, but the deep-
est parts remained, leaving behind several small shallow lakes, although
through natural succession most became the extensive sedge marshes found
here today. The legacy of the glacial lake also includes the sandy soil found all
across the region. Forests took hold in some places, but most of the area has
become jack pine-scrub oak prairie savanna, more commonly referred to as
brush-prairie. The brush-prairie covered 1,500 square miles in a long strip
stretching from northern Polk to northern Bayfield counties before European
settlers arrived in the mid-1800s and created major changes to the landscape.

The area's vast marshes were drained in an attempt to create productive
farmland, though half a century of effort failed to establish agriculture here. In
1912 the Crex Carpet Company purchased much of the area and harvested the
native wire grass (*Carex stricta*) for which Crex Meadows is named. The grass
was shipped to St. Paul where it was made into carpets. The company eventually went bankrupt, in large part due to the advent of linoleum. Wildfire sup-
pression also affected the landscape. Fire had been an important part of the
natural ecology of the region, maintaining the balance of prairie/savanna vegetation. Without the fire, the barrens were replaced by forest.

The state began purchasing the mostly tax-delinquent lands in 1945 and
has since managed the area to recreate the pre-European settlement prairie
and wetland communities. The prairie plants had lain dormant under the
emerging forest and reappeared only when restoration began. Today, Crex,
with its diverse and extensive plant communities, is as important ecologically
for its vegetation as it is for its more popular wildlife. Crex now has the largest
barrens community in Wisconsin.

Many Native American groups, such as Fox, Ojibwe, and Dakota, attracted by the excellent hunting opportunities and bountiful wild rice beds, lived in the area, and it is known that frequent battles took place among them in the 17th century. Today, through cooperative efforts with the Great Lakes Indian Fish and Wildlife Commission, wild rice has been successfully reintroduced in several of the flowages, including Phantom and North Fork at Crex.

About half of Crex Meadows, the core property, is wetlands and flowages, while much of the rest has been restored to brush-prairie, though some forest still remains. At the northwest corner of the wildlife refuge (which sits in the middle of the property), is the 79-acre Crex Sand Prairie State Natural Area, a prime example of the native prairie recovery. The Friends of Crex, a local non-profit group, provided funding for the construction of the Crex Meadows Wildlife Education & Visitor Center in the southwest corner. A rest area with picnic facilities is in the center of the property; camping is allowed here in the fall.

While significantly smaller than Crex Meadows, at 13,197 acres, Fish Lake Wildlife Area is still among Wisconsin's largest. Restoration efforts are only in their early stages, but it is still a very scenic property. A hilltop parking area along Highway 48 on the eastern border offers good, though distant, views of Grettum Flowage which is part of a 1,200-acre wildlife refuge. Maps and brochures may be picked up here. There are better views of the flowage along Grettum Dike Road to the south. Another elevated viewing area is located on Stolte Road, at the north end of Dueholm Flowage.

Overall the 6,138-acre Amsterdam Sloughs Wildlife Area is not as interesting as Crex Meadows or Fish Lake, but its 500-acre Black Brook Flowage in the northwest corner should not be missed. The many dead trees here support a large great blue heron colony, as well as nesting bald eagle and osprey. Parking areas along County D provide both good views and access to the dike. The brush-prairie habitat will be restored here as well, but it is currently mostly wooded.

By far the smallest area, at 2,245 acres, Danbury Wildlife Area is also the least interesting. It is mostly wooded with some brush-prairie and marsh in the center, and currently there are no plans to restore the brush-prairie here.

WILDLIFE—Most of the 100,000-plus yearly visitors come to watch wildlife, particularly birds. More than 270 species of birds have been recorded in the area, with half nesting locally. The diversity and multitude of threatened and endangered species prospering here has prompted the American Bird Conservancy to name Crex Meadows as a Globally Important Bird Area. Crex is the center of a trumpeter swan release program and the federally endangered bird is now often sighted on the flowages here. Other threatened or endangered birds that may be viewed include osprey, loggerhead shrike,

Caspian tern, common tern, yellow rail, and red-necked grebe which nest here, as well as great egret and peregrine falcon. In 1957 a captive flock of Canada geese, which were extirpated from the area by 1912, were released at Crex, and their numbers slowly increased. Today the local flock numbers over 3,000 and is still rising. Crex is also a major staging area for sandhill cranes, with more than 7,000 passing through in October and November. As many as 10,000 geese and 7,000 ducks also gather here during the fall migration. One of the more fascinating birds in the area is the sharp-tailed grouse; Crex has the largest flock east of the Mississippi. They perform their mating display from late March to early June, and you can watch the ritual up close from one of the reservable viewing blinds.

At least two timber wolf packs use the area. At Crex Meadows, wolves spend most of their time in the northern part of the refuge, and though sightings are rare, you have as good a chance of spying one here as you do anywhere else in Wisconsin. Other resident mammals include bear, bobcat, badger, coyote, deer, otter, mink, and beaver. The rare Karner Blue butterfly and Blanding's turtle also make their homes here.

HIKING—Driving is the easiest way to see the area, but the best way is to get out and walk, and, since there are hardly any hills here, hiking is easy wherever you go. Dikes and seldom-used dirt service roads lead along the flowages into the prairie, or through wooded areas, and all can be hiked unless posted otherwise. Two good options at Crex are east of the Phantom Lake overlook, which is stop number two on the auto tour, or west from Phantom Lake Road past the small Whiskey Creek Flowage.

Crex also has three hiking trails. The 3.7-mile Upper Phantom Trail, usually accessed from East Refuge Road (where there is a map posted) contains three wooded loops and a linear section that leads along the edge of Upper Phantom Flowage. The Hay Creek Trail is a 1.5-mile loop starting at the maintenance shed, just east of the visitor center. The path is largely wooded and there is an observation platform overlooking Hay Creek Flowage at the far end. The three-quarter-mile WCC Wildlife Trail at the Rest Area circles the southern end of the shallow Rest Area Flowage, and though notoriously wet and mosquito infested, it is arguably the most scenic trail at Crex. None of the trails get heavy use, and so they can be a little overgrown at times, but are still very easy to follow. Though not a designated hiking trail, the half-mile dike creating the shallow Zulliger Flowage is restricted to foot travel only and is an excellent wildlife watching spot. Though it can be completely overgrown with grass over your head in a few sunny spots, the path is discernible and worth the hassle.

One of the best places to hike at Fish Lake Wildlife Area is along the dike on the southern end of Dueholm Flowage. Another good hike is the Southwest

Dike, accessible from County O or Shogren Road. There are also service roads branching off Hickerson Road. At Amsterdam Sloughs Wildlife Area, the dike along Black Brook Flowage can easily be walked, while some of the smaller flowages can be reached from the many service roads leading north of Olson Road. There are also many service roads leading south from County D. If you want to explore the Danbury Wildlife Area, a few dirt roads enter the area from Broeffle Road, which bisects the area, and from County F along the southern border.

PADDLING—Canoeing the many flowages is a great way to see the area and its wildlife up close. At Crex, almost any flowage will do. Black Brook Flowage at Amsterdam Sloughs is perhaps the most scenic anywhere in the complex. Here and elsewhere, do not canoe too close to heron rookeries. Dueholm Flowage at Fish Lake Wildlife Area has many small islands, making this a good destination, and Fish Lake is a good choice because it is set back from the main road.

WINTER—The Upper Phanton Trails at Crex are groomed for cross-country skiing.

AUTO TOUR—A 24-mile self-guided auto tour of Crex Meadows begins at the nature center. The guide booklet points out many excellent wildlife viewing areas, including four hilltop observation areas, and several minor historic sites.

COUNTY—Burnett.

DIRECTIONS—Crex Meadows, the nature center, and the headquarters for all the properties are one mile north of Grantsburg on County F. Fish Lake, three miles south of Grantsburg on Highway 48. Amsterdam Sloughs, nine miles west of the headquarters on County D. Danbury, half a mile south of the village of Danbury on County F then half a mile west on Broeffle Road.

FACILITIES—Water, toilets, boat launch, nature center, nature programs, picnic area, grills.

CAMPING—Camping is allowed at the Crex Meadows rest area (no individual sites, but tents can be set up on the grass and there is room for a few trailers in the parking area, free), open September 1 to December 31, group camp.

ENTRY—Open year-round. Free.

ON THE WEB—www.crexmeadows.org

CONTACT—DNR, PO Box 367, Grantsburg, WI 54840. Phone (715) 463-2896.

Interstate State Park

CREATED IN 1900, Interstate was Wisconsin's first state park and is still one of the most beautiful. The park's famed cliffs, known as the Dalles of the St. Croix, rise 200 feet straight out of the St. Croix River and run for over half a mile right around a sharp bend in the river. Though best known for its famed cliffs, Interstate's beauty spreads across all of its 1,330 acres.

By the mid-1800s, the Dalles had become a popular tourist destination and thousands of visitors traveled upriver by steamboat and railroad to see them. Just as tourism became a major economic asset to the communities of St. Croix Falls, Wisconsin, and Taylors Falls, Minnesota, plans were being made to blast the Dalles into gravel for use as road-surfacing material. Local citizens in both states were outraged and pushed for the creation of a national park to ensure the area's protection. The National Park Service was not interested, but both Wisconsin and Minnesota stepped in to create their own parks alongside the river. Park stickers from either state are valid in both parks during non-holiday weekdays.

Long before the first tourists, French voyageurs, who arrived in the late 17th century, traded furs with the Dakota and Ojibwe here. The St. Croix River later served as the prime route for floating logs to sawmills downstream. In June of 1886, the Dalles was the site of the largest logjam ever. More than 150 million board feet were backed up along three miles of the river. It took 200 men six weeks to clear the river.

While the park has surpassed the century mark, the spectacular rock formations along the St. Croix River were first formed a billion years ago by molten lava seeping up from below the earth's crust. The river's erosion shaped the rocks as we know them today, including the obligatory tourist-pleasing formations such as Devils Chair and the Old Man of the Dalles. Rushing glacial meltwaters from an overflowing Lake Superior poured through 10,000 years ago with such force that huge boulders were carried away. As these boulders rushed downstream, they too helped shape the Dalles. Sand and gravel caught up in these same torrents cut the most spectacular glacial formations in the park, the potholes. Trapped in whirlpools, they carved circular pits deep into the rock: the largest in the park are six feet across and 12 feet deep. Across the river in Minnesota's smaller park, some stretch 25 feet across and 80 feet deep. Over 200 are found in the two parks.

Because of its unique examples of glacial action, the park is a unit of the Ice Age National Scientific Reserve (p. 1) and it is also the western terminus of the Ice Age Trail (p. 1). The Ice Age Interpretive Center contains displays on

A pothole at the Dalles of the St. Croix in Interstate State Park.

the human and geological history, fossils, and a short video display on the process which created the gorge and the potholes. Another film discusses the process of glaciation throughout Wisconsin.

WILDLIFE—Deer, fox, and an occasional bear roam the wooded uplands, while beaver, otter, and mink may be spotted along the river and its side channels, primarily in the southern end of the park. Nearly 200 species of birds have been documented over the course of a year at Interstate. Well over half of those nest here, including green-backed heron, wood duck, bald eagle, Cooper's hawk, Northern harrier, turkey vulture, pileated woodpecker, ruffed grouse, belted kingfisher, least flycatcher, red-breasted nuthatch, pine and Cerulean warbler, Eastern and Western meadowlark, and bobolink. Common loon, tundra swan, osprey, Caspian tern, pine siskin, and a profusion of warblers all pass through during migration.

HIKING—Nearly nine miles of trails wind through the park. Four loops cross the 48-acre Dalles of the St. Croix River State Natural Area which contains the Dalles, potholes, and other unique geological features. Naturally these are the most spectacular destinations, but they are also the busiest paths. The relatively flat 0.4-mile Pothole Trail leads past the best examples of those formations and offers arguably the best river views as well. The River Bluff and Echo Canyon trails, both 0.7-mile long, and the half-mile Summit Rock

Trail, all lead along rock-strewn paths and have short but steep climbs. Like the Pothole Trail, these three paths also have great river views, but are very beautiful inland as well. It is worth spending a lot of time strolling this area.

Not as striking as those in the natural area, the trails through the south and east ends of the park are nevertheless very scenic. They offer the best examples of the rich forest flora—nearly 400 species of fern and flowering plants are found within the park—and are never crowded. The 0.8-mile Eagle Peak Trail leads to the top of a rock-strewn mound, offering unspoiled valley views. The Silverbrook Trail, named for a mansion which once stood here (the ruined building resting along the trails is not the mansion, but a copper mine office), follows an old wagon road south for 1.2 miles. The generally level path primarily leads through forest, although some open field and wetlands add variety and make it excellent for wildlife viewing. A small waterfall hidden by a stand of trees is located at the end of the trail. The 1.6-mile Skyline Trail leads along the thickly wooded east ridge of the park. It has steep climbs and can be wet in some places due to several small streams that race down the hillside. The level north end of the Skyline Trail is known as the Skyline Nature Trail, a 0.75-mile loop with interpretive signs along its path discussing forest ecology. The Skyline Trail also joins the half-mile Ravine Trail, which leads up a steep hill along the path of a small stream. There are steps and stairs at the steepest parts, but this trail is quite rough in places.

Three other short trails are found within the park. The half-mile Horizon Rock Trail connects the Pothole Trail with the Ice Age Interpretive Center and offers some river views, though it largely leads along the main park road. Both it and the 0.3-mile Meadow Valley Trail are wooded and have short but steep climbs on rocky hills. The partially wooded Lake O' the Dalles Trail is an easy one-mile loop around the lake.

The Ice Age Trail (p. 1) comes into the park along the Skyline Trail, follows the Horizon Rock Trail down to the Pothole Trail, and ends at a fantastic overlook of the Dalles.

PADDLING—Canoes are a great way to see the Dalles. The river is part of the St. Croix National Scenic Riverway (p. 48) and even though there is quite a bit of development along the way, trips below the park are quite scenic. Popular day-trips include the seven-mile float to Osceola and the 17-mile trip to Minnesota's William O'Brien State Park. Canoe rental and shuttle service are available at Minnesota's park, (651) 257-3550 or (800) 447-4958, from May to early-October. You can get additional information at the National Park Service's Riverway headquarters in downtown St. Croix Falls.

WINTER—The Skyline and Silverbrook trails are part of an 11-mile system of groomed cross-country ski trails with paths available for all abilities. A warming shelter is available. At the southwestern end of the park is the Interstate Lowland Forest State Natural Area. This 90-acre wet forest lies on a stretch of land that is an island in the warmer months when water levels are high. It is accessible only during the winter when the level, two-mile Point Trail loops through it.

OTHER—The steep cliffs are one of the Midwest's best rock-climbing destinations, though its proximity to the Twin Cities also makes it one of the busiest. Bordering the park to the north, just a short walk from the campground, is the St. Croix Falls State Fish Hatchery, where nearly a million trout are raised each year to be stocked in lakes and rivers across the state. Paddleboat excursions through the Dalles are offered from the Minnesota side, May through October.

COUNTY—Polk.

DIRECTIONS—The entrance is just a quarter mile south of St. Croix Falls on Highway 35.

FACILITIES—Water, toilets, boat launch, nature center, nature programs, picnic area, grills, picnic shelter, beach, playground, horseshoes, ball field.

CAMPING—Two campgrounds, 85 sites, open year-round, reservations accepted, showers, group camp.

ENTRY—Open year-round. State park sticker or daily fee required.

ON THE WEB—www.wiparks.net

CONTACT—Interstate State Park, PO Box 703, St. Croix Falls, WI 54024. Phone (715) 483-3747.

Willow River State Park

THE WILLOW RIVER flows for six miles through the middle of this large park, rushing through a rocky gorge before making an 11-foot drop over Willow Falls. This beautiful spot had been buried behind a dam until 1992, when it was removed and the water flowed freely again. Most park facilities are on the southern shore of the man-made Little Falls Lake, downstream from the falls, though you will find some quiet meadow and prairie—good wildlife viewing areas—in the less-visited north end of the park. Willow River covers more than 3,000 acres and the adjacent wildlife management land creates a 5,000-acre preserve. Its proximity to Minneapolis/St. Paul makes this one of Wisconsin's most visited parks.

WILDLIFE—More than 220 species of birds can be seen during the course of a year: great blue and green-backed herons, ruffed grouse, wild turkey, upland sandpiper, Cooper's hawk, chestnut-sided warbler, white-breasted nuthatch, savannah sparrow, yellow-billed cuckoo, and Western meadowlark are all common, while tundra swan, American white pelican, snowy owl, prothonotary warbler, and pine grosbeak are rare summer visitors. Ducks and geese are especially abundant during migration, and bald eagles are most likely to be seen in the winter months. Some state threatened and endangered species that may be spotted include great egret, red-necked grebe, osprey, red-shouldered hawk, and Cerulean warbler. Also keep your eyes peeled for deer, fox, badger, mink, beaver, and otter.

HIKING—There are nearly ten miles of trails in the park, most with just small rolling hills. Combining the trails south of the river forms a recommended six-mile loop. Beautiful Willow Falls is reached by the mile-long Willow Falls Trail. Even without the falls as a destination, this wooded route along the lake and river is the park's most scenic hike. It is relatively level, though the quarter-mile Willow Falls Hill Trail at the end climbs a steep hill near the falls, connecting it to the 0.85-mile Pioneer Trail which makes a loop almost back to the campground. The Pioneer Trail leads past the gravesite of the Scott family, whose homestead was here in the early 1800s. The graves are not very interesting, but there is a nice lake view near the burial plot.

Three scenic overlooks above Willow Falls offer breathtaking views of the valley below the falls and the rocky cliffs along the river above them. One overlook is south of the river, and the path leading to it can be reached either from the Pioneer Trail or from a parking lot on County A. The others, north of the river, are accessed by the Burkhardt Trail. This mostly wooded path is quite hilly, and while the overlooks are just above the falls, it is about a mile hike to reach them. The rest of the 3.4-mile trail generally follows the fast-moving river through the forest and then meadow at the back end.

The Knapweed, White Tail, Oak Ridge, and Little Falls trails are each about a mile long. Knapweed is level and primarily leads through open field. The White Tail Trail, one of the least used in the park, is also mostly open, though the forest edge makes it ideal for seeing deer. The paved Little Falls Trail generally follows the park road and has some steep hills. Despite its name, the trail does not pass by any waterfalls. The wooded Oak Ridge Trail connects these three trails as it runs up and down the park's glacial hills.

The half-mile Hidden Pond Nature Trail starts at the nature center and has several interpretive signs along it discussing park ecology. This trail is also paved. Nearby, the easy Trout Brook Trail leads for just over a mile through a mix of open and wooded terrain along the river in the southwest corner of the park.

The Mound Trail, the park's newest, follows the river around a big bend at the easternmost end of the park. A dam was removed here around the turn of the century, and the old lake bed where the trail runs is being restored to prairie. It is an easy, level path offering good bird-watching.

PADDLING—Little Falls Lake, 172 acres, provides some nice, easy paddling, particularly on the quieter north end. No motors of any kind are allowed on the lake. Canoe rentals are available.

BIKING—Bikes are allowed only on the Little Falls Trail, a mile-long, paved route along the lake.

WINTER—Most of the trails are groomed for cross-country skiing and some can accommodate skate skiers. A warming shelter is available and the campground offers ski-in camping. The Burkhardt Trail is packed for winter hiking.

AUTO TOUR—Trout Brook Road along the park's west end is Rustic Road #13. It runs for three miles between River Road in the north and County A in the south.

OTHER—Trout fishing is good in the eastern end of the park and several parking areas provide anglers with river access.

COUNTY—St. Croix.

DIRECTIONS—Five miles northeast of Hudson on County A.

FACILITIES—Water, toilets, boat launch, nature center, nature programs, picnic area, grills, beach, playground, ball field, disc golf course.

CAMPING—78 sites, 25 electric, showers, open year-round, reservations accepted.

ENTRY—Open year-round. State park sticker or daily fee required.

ON THE WEB—www.wiparks.net

CONTACT—Willow River State Park, 1034 County Highway A, Hudson, WI 54016. Phone (715) 386-5931.

Kinnickinnic State Park

THIS 1,242-ACRE state park at the confluence of the St. Croix and the Kinnickinnic rivers is one of Wisconsin's newest, having opened in 1972. The hub of activity is a 70-acre sand delta at the mouth of the Kinnickinnic River which flows through the park for over two miles before emptying into the St. Croix. While the delta is mostly wooded, its open, sandy areas are popular places for boaters to picnic or camp. There is a developed picnic area on the delta and another on the hill above it. The latter features a wheelchair-accessible overlook of the St. Croix and Kinnickinnic river valleys.

Before it reaches the St. Croix, the Kinnickinnic passes through a deep, narrow gorge with tall, vertical cliffs at many points. The last mile of the gorge along with the delta comprises the 100-acre Kinnickinnic River Gorge and Delta State Natural Area. It was designated a natural area due to the gorge's undisturbed nature as well as the fact that this is one of the best examples of a river delta in the state. While the gorge is mostly forested, except for small prairie openings on some south facing slopes, most of the rest of the park is grassland; much of it is being restored to prairie. Though all development, including the trails, is in the northern half of the park, the south is the most fascinating part.

WILDLIFE—Herons and ducks are abundant on the river lowlands and the delta, especially during migration. Hawks commonly soar along the Kinnickinnic River gorge and bald eagles congregate here in winter because the delta narrows the St. Croix to a quarter of its normal width, speeding up the current and keeping the water open. Also look for pheasant, ruffed grouse, wild turkey, plenty of warblers, mink, beaver, badger, fox, and deer. Timber rattlesnakes live in the gorge, though it is extremely unlikely that you will encounter one—if you do, just give it a wide berth and there is nothing to worry about.

HIKING—There are seven interconnected trails totaling just over six miles at Kinnickinnic. The level Purple and Green trails are both a mile long. The former is wooded while the latter leads through a large prairie restoration. The mostly level, 1.2-mile Yellow Trail also passes through the prairie restoration, though it has a few small wooded segments. The 0.6-mile Orange Trail generally follows the same path as the southern part of Yellow Trail, but takes some hilly bypasses into the forest and offers some limited views of the gorge. Combining these four trails makes a recommended three-mile loop.

Less interesting are the Blue, Brown, and Red trails. The 0.7-mile Blue Trail extends into the rolling east end of the park through a mix of open and wooded terrain. The 0.2-mile Brown Trail branches off the Blue and leads up a steep hill, but the forest blocks views of the gorge. The level 1.6-mile Red Trail loops through the prairie surrounding the park office.

Though the trails are fine, the most scenic hiking is found elsewhere in the park. The wild and phenomenally beautiful gorge—known variously as the Devil's Den, Devil's Mixing Bowl, and Devil's Punch Bowl—opens up to the south side of the Kinnickinnic River gorge and is rimmed by many old-growth white pines. Spring-fed streams drop as small waterfalls during the warmer months and make free-form ice sculptures in winter. The unmarked, though well-worn, trail starts near the west end of 770th Ave. just past the bridge—ask for directions at the park office. It is a fairly easy half-mile hike to the top of the stout valley, and you can scramble down and explore the interior if you want to, though be very careful out here; someone gets seriously hurt just about every year and rattlesnakes do reside here. The Kinnickinnic River gorge offers a much wilder hike. A narrow, unmaintained trail begins at the angler's parking lot and follows the river for a quarter of a mile out to a small island. Traveling beyond this requires some bushwhacking and river wading, though if you are an adventurous sort, it is well worth the effort. It is about a three-mile hike back to the park's beach.

PADDLING—The Lower St. Croix between the Apple and the Mississippi rivers is very popular with motorboaters and thus not recommended for paddlers. It is a very scenic trip through the Kinnickinnic River gorge, though the lack of boat landings on the St. Croix below the park dissuades most from trying it—it is a very long climb up from the delta to the nearest parking area. Even if this does not stop you, water levels are generally only sufficiently high enough to make the run during the spring. If you really want to dip your oar, then consider the peaceful but shallow 3.5-hour run from Glen Park in River Falls to the Anglers Parking Lot at the edge of the park, just before the gorge.

WINTER—All trails are open for cross-country skiing, except the Brown Trail, which becomes a sledding hill. They are not groomed.

COUNTY—Pierce.

DIRECTIONS—Five miles north of Prescott on County F, then a quarter mile west on 820th Ave.

FACILITIES—Water, toilets, picnic area, grills, beach.

CAMPING—Boat camping only (fee, must have toilet on board).

ENTRY—Open year-round. State park sticker or daily fee required.

ON THE WEB—www.wiparks.net

CONTACT—Kinnickinnic State Park, W11983 820th Ave., River Falls, WI 54022. Phone (715) 425-1129.

Nugget Lake County Park

This largely undeveloped 752-acre park lies in a geologically unique area known as the Rock Elm Disturbance. Likely an ancient meteor crater, the circular area spans four miles and features an erratic geology that is totally different from the rest of the region. Many of the rocks found here exist nowhere else in western Wisconsin. It is also significantly lower than the surrounding land and much of the bedrock is faulted, folded, or even gone. The differences in geological features are best exemplified at Blue Rock, an exposed rock face along Plum Creek.

The name of this park stems from gold mining that took place in the area around the turn of the 20th century. At the time it was suspected that this might become the largest diamond-producing area in the world. Despite some small successes, the grand plans never panned out. In addition to gold and diamonds, topaz, garnets, and platinum were found in significant quantities.

WILDLIFE—Along the park's forests and creeks, visitors might spot beaver, mink, deer, ducks, great blue heron, wild turkey, and ruffed grouse. Bald eagles nest on the lake and osprey are frequent visitors.

HIKING—Seven interconnected trails totaling six miles wind through the park's mostly wooded terrain, and numerous benches along the trails allow quiet contemplation. Just a short walk down the mile-long Orange Trail is the Blue Rock overlook. The trail serves up several nice views along the top of Blue Rock, as well as a scenic "underlook" from below. This trail has a few hills along it.

Also starting at the Blue Rock Trail entrance is the 1.3-mile Black Trail. This level path follows Plum and Rock Elm creeks with bridges spanning the waterways at several points. Three lesser-used trails branch off the Orange and Black trails. The 0.7-mile Green Trail is generally level, while the 0.2-mile Red and 0.7-mile Brown trails have some steep hills.

The level, mile-long loop comprising the Yellow Trail has interpretive stops, which correspond to a pamphlet available at the trailhead or the office, while the half-mile Blue Trail has some of the steepest climbs in the park. Both trails start at the campground.

A short but steep path starting at the beach leads to a scenic overlook of the lake. There is also a small, secluded picnic area along the lake accessed from the southern end of this same narrow trail.

PADDLING—The park lies at the northern end of 116-acre Nugget Lake which offers scenic, quiet paddling. This narrow, man-made lake stretches south for nearly two miles. Only electric motors are allowed on the lake; canoes and rowboats may be rented at the park.

WINTER—The trails are groomed for cross-country skiing.

COUNTY—Pierce.

DIRECTIONS—Four miles west of Plum City on Highway 10, then three miles north on County CC, and two miles east on County HH.

FACILITIES—Water, toilets, boat launch, nature programs, beach, picnic area, grills, picnic shelter, beach, playground, ball field, horseshoes.

CAMPING—55 sites, 42 electric, open year-round, reservations accepted, showers.

ENTRY—Open year-round. Daily fee or annual pass required.

ON THE WEB—www.co.pierce.wi.us/nugget_lake/nl_main.htm

CONTACT—Nugget Lake County Park, N4351 County Rd. HH, Plum City, WI 54761. Phone (715) 639-5611. E-mail: nugget@svtel.net

Hoffman Hills
State Recreation Area

QUIET HIKING and skiing are the main draws to the wooded hills of this 707-acre park, and though not spectacular, the trails are certainly scenic. The best thing about this often overlooked park, however, is that it is one of the least visited in the state park system, so it's a great place to avoid crowds, even on weekends.

As the name implies, the park is covered by hills. The last glacier to cross Wisconsin did not reach Dunn County—though earlier glaciers shaped the area—so the hills are generally tall and steep. Forest covers most of the park, though for a bit of variety the west end is a mix of wetlands and grasslands, including a small prairie restoration. The initial 281 acres for the park were donated to the state in 1980 by the Hoffman family, hence the name.

WILDLIFE—Deer, fox, coyote, Cooper's and sharp-shinned hawks, bald eagle, osprey, pileated woodpecker, ruffed grouse, pheasant, wild turkey, Acadian and great-crested flycatcher, red-breasted nuthatch, chestnut-sided and palm warbler, scarlet tanager, rose-breasted grosbeak, and green-backed heron are all common inhabitants. Bear and even the endangered timber wolf have been reported in the area, but are very unlikely to be seen.

HIKING—The nine miles of mostly wooded trail generally go over rather than around the hills. There are some pine plantations along the trails, but they mostly cross a mixed hardwood forest. Benches are located along all the trails, mostly at spots that offer good views.

The main trails have four color-coded loops to follow, but the interconnected trails offer countless possibilities. The 3.5-mile Red Trail is the most difficult; the Blue and Yellow trails, at 2.6 and 3.8 miles respectively, are less hilly; and the 1.7-mile Green Trail is considered the easiest of the three, although it also has many climbs.

Interpretive panels discussing the park's trees line the steep, two-mile Tower Nature Trail. It leads to the 60-foot observation tower perched atop one of the highest points in the county, and naturally the view of the surrounding area from the tower is superb. The "point of interest" marker just east of the group camp merely marks the intersection of four townships.

The newest trail is the one-mile, wheelchair-accessible, Catherine Hoffman Hartl Memorial Wetland Trail, which leads through meadow, wetlands, and around two ponds. It starts at a second parking area just beyond the main one.

WINTER—The trails are groomed for cross-country skiing and can accommodate skate skiers. There is also a sledding hill and a 160-acre snowshoe area west of the park road.

COUNTY—Dunn.

DIRECTIONS—Five miles east of Menomonie on Highway 12/29, then three miles north on Ney Rd., then a quarter mile east on Swamp Rd., and 1.5 miles north on Cedar Valley Rd.

FACILITIES—Water, toilets, picnic area, grills, picnic shelter.

CAMPING—Group camp.

ENTRY—Open year-round. Free, though donations are encouraged. State trail pass required for cross-country skiing.

ON THE WEB—www.wiparks.net

CONTACT—Hoffman Hills Recreation Area, 921 Brickyard Rd., Menomonie, WI 54751. Phone (715) 232-1242.

Chippewa Moraine Ice Age 🍃 🏕
State Recreation Area and
Townline-Knickerbocker Canoe Trail

CHIPPEWA MORAINE, chock-full of steep glacial hills and deep glacial lakes, is one of the most beautiful properties in the state park system, yet somehow it remains one of the least visited. This Ice Age Reserve (p. 1) unit was named after the Chippewa Lobe of the last glacier to cross Wisconsin which stopped here and formed this striking and rare landscape. Known as an ice-core moraine, it differs from the typical terminal moraine because it was formed by the slow disintegration of large masses of ice that broke off the main glacier and were buried by sand and rock still being pushed south by the glaciers. The dozens of kettle lakes scattered across the 3,855-acre reserve are tucked in between the moraine, hummocks, ice-walled-lake plains, eskers, and kames, while a flat outwash plain in the southwest corner of the reserve marks the glacier's farthest advance.

The Chippewa Moraine Interpretive Center, developed by the National Park Service and featuring displays and films about the Ice Age, as well as the area's natural and human history, sits a hundred feet above the surrounding land atop a unique glacial feature called an ice-walled-lake plain. These flat-topped mounds were once the bottoms of lakes that lay in pits in the ice sheet; when the ice melted, the accumulated debris formed the mounds. The Ice Age Trail (p. 1) passes over another of these plains at the easternmost section of the reserve.

WILDLIFE—Look for deer, bear, coyote, porcupine, fisher, pheasant, and ruffed grouse in the forest and prairie restorations, while beaver, otter, mink, ducks, and great blue heron may be seen in the lakes. Bald eagle, osprey, and red-shouldered hawk are also spotted here occasionally.

HIKING—The Mammoth Nature Trail, beginning at the interpretive center, offers a quick glimpse of the gorgeous scenery and has several interpretive panels along it discussing the geology and ecology of this unique area. The 0.7-mile trail leads down a steep hill, passing three lakes before looping back. There are more (and arguably even more beautiful) lake views along the hilly, 1.8-mile Dry Lake Trail that follows the west end of the Mammoth Trail and adds a long stretch of prairie to the hike. Pick up the trail brochure at the interpretive center if you are going to hike this trail.

To really explore the area, follow the nine miles of the Ice Age Trail. The narrow and wooded path is quite hilly, and passes dozens of lakes with bridges over a few wet areas. There are two parts to the trail. A 4.5-mile loop circles the interpretive center in the west end of the reserve, and another 4.5-mile stretch heads east from this loop to Plummer Lake Road at the edge of the reserve. Beyond the border, the trail continues for another 14 miles to County CC, across the Chippewa River from Brunet Island State Park (p. 72). The trail crosses several roads along the way, allowing easy access for shorter hikes. A geology brochure discussing the formation of various glacial landforms found along the Ice Age Trail is available at the interpretive center.

PADDLING—A block of county forest within the reserve contains the Townline-Knickerbocker Canoe Trail which connects nine lakes. Forty-eight-acre Townline Lake at the east end is the largest, while six others are each under five acres. The longest of the easy portages between the lakes is just 650 feet. Though the trail may be started at either Townline or Knickerbocker lakes, the former is the more common starting point because it has the easier access. As with the rest of the county forest, camping is allowed here. The largest lakes in the reserve, including South Shattuck and Plummer, have boat ramps that allow easy access for paddlers.

WINTER—Cross-country skiing is allowed on the trails, but they are better suited to snowshoes, which may be borrowed from the interpretive center. Call (715) 967-2800 before your visit to reserve a pair.

COUNTY—Chippewa.

DIRECTIONS—Seven miles east of New Auburn on County M.

FACILITIES—Water, toilets, nature center, boat launch, picnic area.

CAMPING—Three backpack campsites. Backpacking is also permitted in the Chippewa County Forest (both along the Ice Age Trail and the canoe trail) and a primitive site is maintained along the Ice Age Trail at Harwood Lake #1.

ENTRY— Open year-round.

ON THE WEB—www.wiparks.net

CONTACT—Chippewa Moraine State Recreation Area, 13394 County Highway M, New Auburn, WI 54757. Phone (715) 967-2800. Chippewa County Forest and Parks Department, 711 N. Bridge St., Chippewa Falls, WI 54729. Phone (715) 726-7880.

Brunet Island State Park

THIS 1,225-ACRE park lies at the confluence of the Chippewa and Fisher rivers. Most facilities are found on the 169-acre namesake island: swimming, boating, and fishing are all popular activities in the park. The French-born Jean Brunet was one of the first settlers in the area and founder of the adjacent city of Cornell (formerly known as Brunet Falls). The foundation of Brunet's log home and trading post still exists on the river's west shore, about a mile below the dam.

Nature lovers will notice two unique natural features on the island, hemlocks and hummocks. More common in the northeast part of the state, the large hemlocks covering much of the island are well over a hundred years old. Unfortunately, they are not regenerating as the sprouts are a favorite food of the white-tailed deer. The small lumps—known as hummocks—blanketing the forest floor are formed when a fallen tree rots and the soil caught in its roots creates a small mound. While both are also found on the quieter mainland section, the most noteworthy features here are the glacial hills and kettles created during the last Ice Age. The Chippewa River valley was carved by the rushing meltwater of the same glaciers that formed these hills.

WILDLIFE—It is all but guaranteed that you will spot some of the park's famously tame deer, and they will often go on about their business as you walk close by. Other animals residing in the forest include fox, badger, porcupine, and ruffed grouse. Bald eagle and osprey are often seen soaring along the rivers, while beaver, otter, mink, ducks, and great blue heron may also be sighted along the park's waterways.

HIKING—The park offers about six miles of scenic trails. The four narrow trails through the island's forest are each level and easy. The 0.75-mile Jean Brunet Nature Trail on the northern tip of the island has interpretive panels discussing the forest. The half-mile Spruce Trail leads along the Fisher River, while the 0.75-mile Timber Trail runs right through the center of the island. A young aspen grove at the northern end of the Timber Trail marks the site of a 1977 tornado that downed 12 acres of the native hemlock. The Pine Trail, also 0.75-mile long, connects the other three trails.

A quieter and more secluded experience is available on the mainland along the 4.3-mile Nordic Trail which leads away from park roads and facilities. Both the 1.7-mile northern and the 1.3-mile southern loops are entirely wooded and cross rolling hills, the main difference being that the northern loop passes within sight of the Fisher River. Several benches provide quiet rest stops.

A 20-mile stretch of the Ice Age Trail (p. 1) begins just west of the park along County CC, two miles north of Highway 64. It leads west mostly through county forestlands, ending at the Chippewa Moraine Ice Age Center. It crosses several roads on the way, allowing access for shorter hikes.

PADDLING—The park owns undeveloped land on both shores of the Chippewa and Fisher rivers, creating a relatively unspoiled setting for paddlers, especially on the smaller Fisher River. Poking around the park's islands, bays, and rivers can provide an enjoyable couple of hours. Longer trips upstream from the park are possible on either river. Most campsites in the wooded North Campground lie along the river or bay, allowing canoes or boats to be brought right up to the campsite.

BIKING—A paved, mile-long link connects the park to the Old Abe State Trail trailhead in Cornell. Old Abe leads 19.5 miles south to near Lake Wissota State Park. To reach that park, follow the wide shoulder along County O for two miles.

WINTER—The Nordic Trail is groomed for cross-country skiing.

OTHER—The Cornell Bowmen Archery Club maintains a field archery range just before the park entrance. It is open to the public.

COUNTY—Chippewa.

DIRECTIONS—One mile northwest of Cornell on Park Road.

FACILITIES—Water, toilets, boat launch, nature programs, picnic area, grills, picnic shelter, beach, playground, ball field.

CAMPING—Two campgrounds, 69 sites, 24 electric, open as long as there is no snow, reservations accepted, showers.

ENTRY—Open year-round. State park sticker or daily fee required. State trail pass required for riding the Old Abe Trail.

ON THE WEB—www.wiparks.net

CONTACT—Brunet Island State Park, 23125 255th St., Cornell, WI 54732. Phone (715) 239-6888.

Lake Wissota State Park

LAKE WISSOTA is one of Wisconsin's newest state parks. Land acquisition began in 1961 and the park opened a decade later, after facilities were constructed and work began to restore the old farm fields to forest and prairie. Today, the park covers over a thousand acres along its namesake lake, a 6,300-acre flowage on the Chippewa River. Complementing the young forest and large prairie restoration—south of the campground entrance are two interesting display panels discussing the prairie—is a small marsh along the southern edge of the property.

While the last glacier to cross Wisconsin stopped about six miles to the northeast of the park, it still had a major effect on shaping this land. The lakeshore's high steep bank is the edge of a 12-mile-wide outwash plain, and glacial meltwaters also carved the Chippewa River Valley.

WILDLIFE—Deer, fox, beaver, mink, weasel, and porcupine all reside within the park; lucky visitors might even catch sight of an otter or badger. The 200-plus species of birds recorded here include red-necked grebe, peregrine falcon, and osprey—all threatened or endangered species—plus bald eagle, ruffed grouse, sandhill crane, great blue heron, Canada goose, and many ducks.

HIKING—The park is almost entirely flat, making for easy hiking along the nearly eight miles of trails. The trails are all short, but can easily be combined for longer hikes. The 1.4-mile Lake Trail that leads along the ridge above the lake is the most popular path, and with good reason, since it offers so much. The southern, wooded half climbs a long hill from the beach up the lakeshore ridge, where it continues through mostly open terrain, offering good lake views and passing two long panther effigy mounds. At the far end at the campground, near the trail's halfway point, stairs lead down to the shore.

In the southeast corner of the park, the mile-long Beaver Meadow Nature Trail and the two-mile Staghorn Trail loop through a mature mixed forest and are arguably the park's most scenic trails. The Beaver Meadow Nature Trail has boardwalks that lead along a spring-fed stream and marsh; interpretive panels line its path. Also in the southern part of the park are the 0.75-mile Jack Pine Trail and the half-mile Eagle Prairie and Fox trails; all are loops. The Jack Pine Trail leads through a young mixed woodlot, while the Eagle Prairie and Fox trails cross the park's prairie restoration. The southern section of the 1.5-mile Red Pine Trail leads through more prairie, while the northern part passes through a pine plantation, as does the 0.7-mile Plantation Trail.

PADDLING—The lake is heavily developed and is often crowded with motorboats, so it does not offer a good natural experience. If you really want to get out and paddle, you can poke around the narrow bays just south of the park or take a look at the sandstone cliffs below the main picnic area. Those looking for a longer trip can continue up the Yellow River. Canoe and rowboat rentals are available.

BIKING—The Lake, Beaver Meadow, and Staghorn trails are closed to bicycles, but bikes are allowed on all other park trails, including the horse trail—a total of 11 miles. Bicyclists can also ride the Old Abe State Trail, a 19.5-mile paved path along a former railroad grade, north to Brunet Island State Park. It starts two miles west of the park and you can ride the wide shoulder along County O between Lake Wissota and the trailhead.

WINTER—The Red Pine, Jack Pine, Plantation, and Staghorn trails and the southern part of the Lake Trail are groomed for cross-country skiing, a total of 7.5 easy miles. All but the Staghorn Trail can accommodate skate skiing. Snowshoes are available for rent from the park office if you want to explore the rest of the park. A five-mile stretch of the county snowmobile trail system also passes along the east end of the park.

OTHER—There is a level 6.5-mile horse trail in the park. It runs primarily through open field along the north and east ends of the park.

COUNTY—Chippewa.

DIRECTIONS—3.5 miles northeast of Chippewa Falls on County S, then two miles east on County O.

FACILITIES—Water, toilets, boat launch, nature center, nature programs, picnic area, grills, picnic shelter, beach, playground, ball field.

CAMPING—81 sites, 17 electric, open year-round, reservations accepted, showers, group camp.

ENTRY—Open year-round. State park sticker or daily fee required. State trail pass required for horse trails and riding on the Old Abe Trail.

ON THE WEB—www.wiparks.net

CONTACT—Lake Wissota State Park, 18127 County O, Chippewa Falls, WI 54729. Phone (715) 382-4574.

Beaver Creek Reserve

THE COUNTY-OWNED Beaver Creek Reserve, 360 acres of forest, wetlands, prairie, and oak savanna, is located in the Eau Claire River Valley, and this large river forms the reserve's southern and western boundaries. The namesake waterway flows through the reserve's south end and several other smaller streams also pass through before emptying into the river. The Ralph H. Wise Nature Center, sitting atop a ridge overlooking the Beaver Creek bottoms, houses displays relating to the area's plants, animals, and ecology. Nature programs for all ages are offered to school groups and the public throughout the year. The building itself was built using renewable energy resources and energy conservation methods. The Eau Claire County Youth Camp and Hobbs Observatory round out the reserve.

WILDLIFE—The reserve, which lies adjacent to a large expanse of county forest, is home to abundant wildlife. Look for deer, fox, coyote, porcupine, beaver, otter, mink, bear, bald eagle, wild turkey, ruffed grouse, herons, ducks, and many songbirds. Blanding's and wood turtles, both threatened species, are found along the waterways, and a butterfly garden is located near the nature center.

HIKING—About seven miles of trails wind through the reserve's wooded hills and valleys. South of the nature center the trails are narrow and generally flat (the few hills are made easy by steps) and except where noted are primarily wooded. Bridges and boardwalks lead over streams and wet areas, and benches allow quiet observation. The mile-long Marsh Loop leads along a small marsh to the west, while the rest of the trail is a mix of wooded and open terrain. The half-mile Interpretive Trail has several signs discussing the area's ecology and runs past Beaver Creek and a small prairie restoration. South of the Marsh Loop is the quarter-mile Savannah Cutoff which, naturally, leads through an oak savanna. There is an elevated photography/ wildlife viewing blind here. The short All Accessible Trail east of the nature center offers views of some of the valley below. South of Beaver Creek are the 0.75-mile Thicket Loop and the mile-long River Ridge Trail which is the reserve's least followed trail. It leads up a ridge above the creek and then heads south, where it follows the Eau Claire River back to the trailhead. It can be somewhat overgrown, but is generally very easy to follow.

A paved underpass connects the Wise Nature Center with the Eau Claire County Youth Camp, where the rest of the reserve's trails are located. Just north of the camp area is the Cycle of Life Nature Trail, with more interpretive panels along its path. This wooded, quarter-mile path leads down to Deinhammer Creek before looping back. The 1.25-mile Fitness Trail leads along the creek and provides access to the trails on the other side of Deinhammer Creek; despite having exercise stations along it, it is a nice walk, particularly along the creek. Deinhammer Creek flows through a steep, narrow valley northwest of the camp area, and the level, half-mile Pine Loop follows the ridge overlooking the creek. It shares part of its path with the mile-long Oak Loop, which has several steep hills. A half-mile path branching off from the two loops leads along the ridge above the creek. A mile-long trail branching off the Oak Loop leads through the county forest to Big Falls County Park, where the featured attraction is a drop of 15 feet over a large granite outcropping. The water is not deep enough for swimming here, but the sandy-bottomed river is a popular place to cool off, and it makes a great spot for a picnic.

PADDLING—The Eau Claire River is popular for canoeing. Much of the river both upstream and downstream from the reserve passes through undeveloped county forestlands, making this a scenic trip. Except for Little Falls at the reserve and Big Falls, just to the west, that must be portaged, the river is calm and ideal for family outings. There are several put-ins and take-outs above and below the reserve, so you can plan trips of just about any length.

WINTER—The trails are groomed for cross-country skiing and there is a warming shelter. Skis and snowshoes are available for rent.

OTHER—The Hobbs Observatory is a joint project between the reserve, the UW–Eau Claire physics department, and the Chippewa Valley Astronomical Society. There are two separate domes with telescopes and several smaller telescopes are set up outside during public viewing sessions.

COUNTY—Eau Claire.

DIRECTIONS—Four miles north of Fall Creek on County K.

FACILITIES—Water, toilets, nature center, nature programs, picnic area, fitness trail, many other facilities for group camp users.

CAMPING—Two canoe sites (free), group camp.

ENTRY—The reserve and youth camp are open year-round. The Hobbs Observatory is open for public viewing May–October on clear Saturday nights, one hour after sunset, and special programs are held every third Saturday of the month except December. Entrance to all facilities is free.

ON THE WEB—www.beavercreekreserve.org

CONTACT—Beaver Creek Reserve, S1 County Highway K, Fall Creek, WI 54742. Phone (715) 877-2212. E-mail: bcr@beavercreekreserve.org. Hobbs Observatory, phone (715) 877-2787.

Augusta Wildlife Area

WHILE OVER HALF of Augusta's 2,100 acres consists of upland forest, the wetlands are the main draw for visitors and the principal reason for its existence as a wildlife area. Land acquisition began in the 1940s in an effort to stem the region's rapid loss of waterfowl habitat, and to further that goal four flowages were constructed in the northwest part of the property along Browns Creek. These lakes are surrounded by extensive marshes.

WILDLIFE—The wetlands attract large numbers of birds, including ducks, geese, herons, tundra swan, and sandhill crane. Beaver, otter, and mink are also found here. The upland areas are managed primarily for deer and ruffed grouse, but bear, fox, coyote, hawks, and wild turkey can also be seen.

HIKING—There are two parking areas—one in the north along County G, a half mile east of County GG, and the other in the east off Kelly Road, a mile south of County G—and the principal hiking trails connect them. The

Kelly Road parking area is generally the best entrance. From here, a gravel service road heads west on a dike out to the south flowage. After about half a mile, a road turns north through a small wooded area, then continues along a dike through the marsh. Eventually this road turns west along the middle flowage and zig-zags north and west through a mostly wooded area before following the west edge of the northern flowage up to the other parking area. Though overall it is a less scenic option, if you do not want to retrace your steps, another path (starting between the northern and middle flowage) leads south through the forest back to the south flowage. Either way, it is about a four-mile round-trip. The forested sections in the middle of both trails can be a bit overgrown, though still easily passable, while the sections through marsh and along the flowages are clear and easy to hike.

Several other trails pass mostly through the wooded uplands to the north and east, but these are generally overgrown and not as interesting as the other trails.

PADDLING—Canoeists can paddle around the flowages, which are easily reached from both the County G and Kelly Road parking areas.

COUNTY—Eau Claire.

DIRECTIONS—1.5 miles east of Augusta on Highway 12, then 0.75 mile east on Coon Fork Rd., and three miles north on Kelly Rd.

FACILITIES—None.

CAMPING—None.

ENTRY—Open year-round. Free.

CONTACT—DNR, PO Box 4001, 1300 W. Clairemont Ave., Eau Claire, WI 54702. Phone (715) 839-3771.

Mawikwe Bay, Apostle Islands.

NORTHEAST

RUFFED GROUSE, RJ & LINDA MILLER

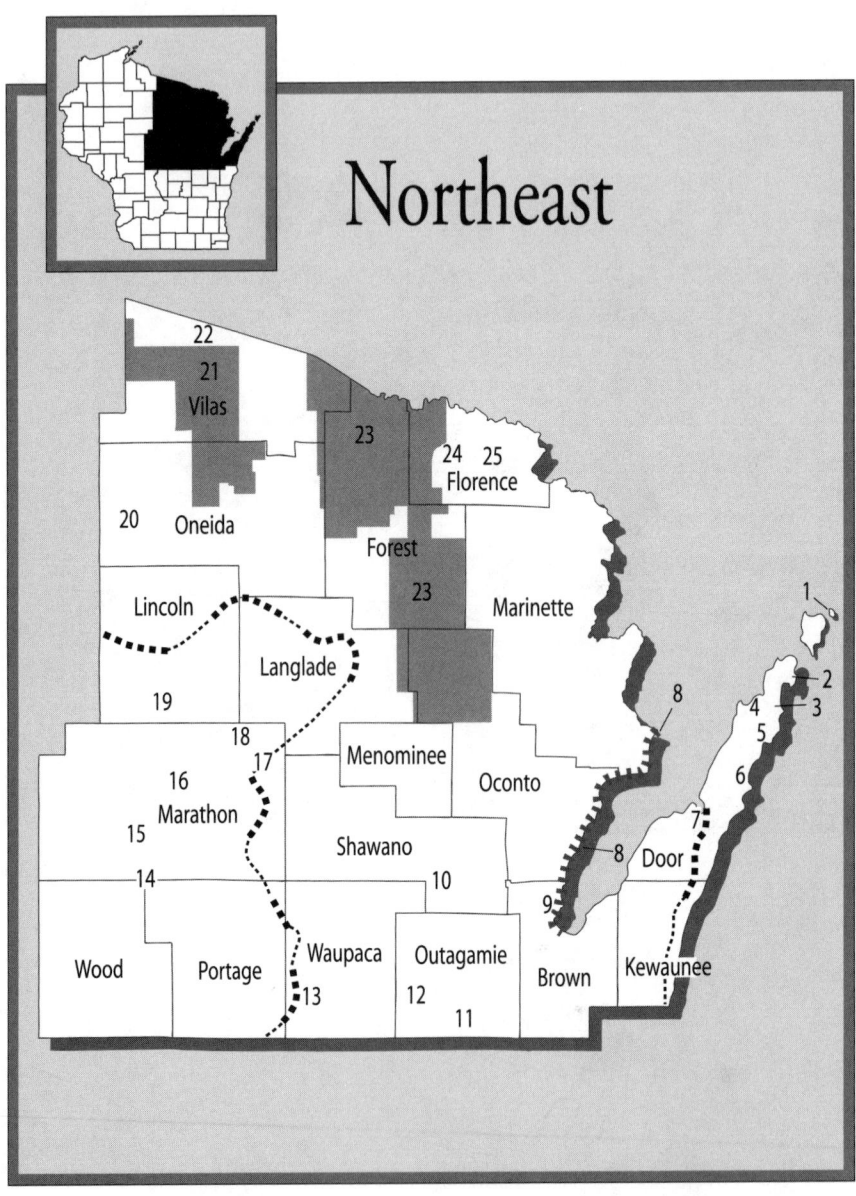

Northeast

22
21
Vilas
23
24 25
Florence
20 Oneida
Forest
Lincoln
23
Marinette
Langlade
19
18
17
Menominee
16
Marathon
Oconto
15
Shawano
14
10
Wood
Portage
Waupaca
Outagamie
13
12
11
Brown
Kewaunee
Door
1
2
3
4
5
6
7
8
8
9

┄┄┄┄┄┄┄┄┄┄┄ *Proposed* Ice Age National Scenic Trail

■■■■■■■■■■■■ *Existing* Ice Age National Scenic Trail

1. Rock Island State Park

2. Newport State Park

3. Mink River Estuary

4. Peninsula State Park

5. The Ridges Sanctuary, Toft Point Natural Area, and Mud Lake Wildlife Area

6. Whitefish Dunes State Park and Cave Point County Park

7. Potawatomi State Park

8. Green Bay West Shores Wildlife Area

9. L. H. Barkhausen Waterfowl Preserve and Fort Howard Paper Foundation Wildlife Area

10. Navarino Wildlife Area

11. Gordon Bubolz Nature Preserve

12. Mosquito Hill Nature Center

13. Hartman Creek State Park and Emmons Creek Fishery Area

14. George W. Mead Wildlife Area

15. Big Eau Pleine County Park

16. Rib Mountain State Park

17. Dells of the Eau Claire County Park

18. Bitzke Bird Walk

19. Council Grounds State Park

20. Willow Flowage Scenic Waters Area

21. Northern Highland-American Legion State Forest

22. Catherine Wolter Wilderness Area

23. Chequamegon-Nicolet National Forest

24. Pine and Popple Wild Rivers

25. LaSalle Falls Trail

Rock Island State Park

ROCK ISLAND, Wisconsin's second least-visited state park, offers one of Wisconsin's most isolated natural experiences. The high cliffs and rocky shore surrounding the 912-acre island make it quite beautiful, too. All vehicles, even bikes, are prohibited, greatly enhancing its natural splendor, and the limited development found on the island is of great historical interest. Most visitors arrive on the *Karfi* passenger ferry from Washington Island, though there is also mooring for private boats.

The state acquired the island at the tip of Door County in 1964 from the estate of Chester H. Thordarson, one of America's greatest electrical inventors—he built the first million-volt transformer, among other things. Born in Iceland, Thordarson moved to Milwaukee in 1873 at the age of five, and he purchased the island (for under $6,000) as a summer retreat in 1910. Nearby Washington Island has the oldest Icelandic community in the U.S., and this likely piqued his interest in the area. Thordarson left an indelible mark on Rock Island during the 1920s. The massive Viking Hall and boathouse, constructed of local limestone and topped with a red tile roof, is the most striking site on the island. Several other buildings fashioned in the same Icelandic style make up the rest of the historic estate, though the mansion he planned was never built. Viking Hall now houses a museum with natural history displays, as well as archaeological finds from the island and displays about Thordarson, most notably his intricately carved furniture.

The Potawatomi Light House, Wisconsin's oldest, holds fort on the northwest corner of the island. The present two-story stone building was constructed in 1858, replacing the original 1836 structure, and is occasionally open for public tours during the summer. Other historic spots on the island include a stone water tower built by Thordarson on the site of a former fishing village (only scattered foundations remain) and three old cemeteries—one located near the lighthouse, another at the island's eastern end, and the last just southeast of the estate area. Silver Band, the last Ojibwe chief from the area, is buried in the last plot.

The island had a storied history before Thordarson purchased it. Native Americans routinely followed the Grand Traverse island chain, first coming to Rock Island about 600 BC, and as many as 12 different nations have lived on the island since then. Among the most recent were the Ottawa, Huron, Ojibwe, and Potawatomi. The remains of numerous native villages have been found here, including one from about 1650 that was surrounded by a stockade, a rarity for Wisconsin. Famed explorer Sieur de LaSalle landed on the island in 1679 and for many years after that, Europeans and Ojibwe lived here together. At its peak in the middle of the 19th century, the island was home to about 200 people, though the main pursuits of fishing and agriculture were not well suited to the remote island. Lake Michigan fishing was very productive, but boats could not readily dock here, and poor soils meant poor yields. Thordarson, for example, cleared an area on the south shore for a vegetable garden, but all that he could grow were rutabagas.

WILDLIFE—Because this is an island, wildlife is not overly abundant and mammals are especially rare. The only mammals found here are deer, coyote, red and gray fox, red squirrel, lemming, muskrat, four species of bats, and, on very rare occasions, bear, which are excellent swimmers. Among the more than 120 species of birds that may be sighted are ducks, geese, great blue heron, common and Caspian tern, spotted sandpiper, bald eagle, turkey vulture, and Canada and Blackburnian warblers.

HIKING—Rock Island has over nine miles of wonderful trails, and though all are generally hilly, none are difficult. The main path is the 5.2-mile Thordarson Loop which circles the entire island. The trail features great views of the steep cliffs and the historic sites beyond the estate area, including the lighthouse, which is the most popular hiking destination—it is about a two-mile round-trip from Viking Hall. You can explore the rocky shore below the lighthouse by following the stairs just to the east. A scenic overlook along the northeast end of the trail offers views of other islands across the state line in Michigan. The narrow, less-used portion of the Thordarson Trail between the water tower and the eastern end of the Fernwood Trail has the best views of the cliffs and is arguably the most scenic segment. The Fernwood and Hauamal trails, both a mile and a half long, cross the island, allowing shorter loops from the Thordarson Trail, while the short Blueberry Trail allows hikers to bypass the beach area. The Algonquin Nature Trail, starting just behind the boathouse, is a narrow, mile-long loop with interpretive signs discussing the natural history of the island, including the old sand dunes now solidified by vegetation.

PADDLING—The park is just a mile from Jackson Harbor and so it is fairly easy to paddle across the channel, though it is best to go by sea kayak instead of canoe, since waves can become fairly large. Kayaks are also an excellent way to see the island's shoreline cliffs.

BICYCLING—Although bike riding is prohibited on the island, visitors who plan to ride on Washington Island may keep their bikes with them at their campsites.

WINTER—In winter, the channel between the islands freezes, allowing foot access, though it is important to check locally on ice conditions. Cross-country skiing, snowshoeing, and snowmobiling are allowed, though no trails are maintained. Planning is especially important when visiting the island

January through March, as there are infrequent ferry crossings between Washington Island and the mainland—and no services to Rock Island itself.

COUNTY—Door.

DIRECTIONS—The *Karfi* ferry docks at Jackson Harbor on the northwest end of Washington Island and the last departure from Rock Island always leaves enough time to catch the last ferry from Washington Island back to the mainland. Ferry service from the mainland to Washington Island runs year-round, though winter service is very limited and reservations, (920) 847-2546 or (800) 223-2094, are required for vehicles.

FACILITIES—Water, toilets, boat launch, nature center, nature programs, picnic area, grills, picnic shelter, beach.

CAMPING—35 walk-in sites, five backpack sites, open year-round, reservations accepted, group camp.

ENTRY—Open year-round, though there is no staff person on the island during winter. The passenger ferry runs late May to mid-October. Fee for ferry and boat mooring.

ON THE WEB—www.wiparks.net

CONTACT—Rock Island State Park, RR 1, Box 118A, Washington Island, WI 54246. Phone (920) 847-2235 or (920) 746-2890 (off-season).

Newport State Park

THIS 2,440-ACRE PARK, one of Wisconsin's best, is managed with a wilderness philosophy that keeps development to a bare minimum. A picnic area along the beach on Newport Bay and the hiking trails are the only significant facilities. Camping is allowed only at designated backpack sites, most of which are spread out along the 11 miles of Lake Michigan shoreline. The lakeshore, lined by small coves, rocky points, and sandy beaches, is the park's most outstanding feature, though the forest covering most of the interior is quite scenic, too. The 140-acre Newport Conifer Hardwoods State Natural Area in the southern end includes diverse northern and boreal forests and protects many rare plants. Within the natural area, and elsewhere, exposed ridges of dolomite bedrock mark the extent of the lake some 10,000 years ago. Except for these ridges, some of which rise eight feet high, Newport is almost completely flat.

The park was established in 1964 and received official wilderness designation a decade later. It is a drastic change from the late 1800s when what is now the picnic area was a thriving logging village, also named Newport. Lumber was shipped from here to mills all along Wisconsin's eastern shore.

DEBORAH PROCTOR

Newport State Park has some of the lovliest shoreline on all of Lake Michigan.

WILDLIFE—Deer, fox, coyote, fisher, porcupine, and the occasional bear may be seen in the park along with 175 species of birds, including northern harrier, ruffed grouse, pileated woodpecker, white-breasted nuthatch, and indigo bunting. Plus, if you are lucky you will spy a merlin, green-winged teal, or Caspian tern. Snowy owl and white-winged crossbill come down for the winter. Warblers are abundant in May and monarch butterflies migrate through the area in late August and September.

HIKING—The park's 22 miles of trail offer exceptionally scenic hiking. The trails are almost completely level, and though there are some rough spots because of the abundant rocks, particularly along the Rowleys Bay Trail, none are difficult. All trails run through forest except the Upland Nature and Monarch. The *Newport-Out of Wilderness into Wilderness* brochure, available at the nature center, highlights historic spots along each of the trails.

The trails through the south end of the park are arguably the best. The Newport Trail, a five-mile loop, is adjoined by the 1.2-mile Ridge and the two-mile Rowleys Bay trails. Together these trails offer several hiking options. The Newport and Rowleys Bay trails both follow the shore, though the Ridge Trail, which does not, should not be overlooked. It leads through the natural area and is named for the scenic dolomite ridge, formerly the lakeshore, that it passes. Sand Cove's rocky shore, at the northeast end of the Newport Trail, is a fantastic destination. The rocks extending out from the shore form hundreds of miniature islands that you can roam at will. For something different, take the Monarch Trail, a 1.8-mile loop through the open field southwest of the park entrance where these butterflies are likely to be seen.

The 1.4-mile Lynd Point Trail leads along the shore north of the picnic area and beach. Lynd Point is a scenic spot in which to relax, or you can scramble over the rocks jutting out into the lake. The 0.7-mile Fern Trail heading west from Lynd Point passes another part of the ancient shoreline ridge. The Europe Bay Trail, which heads to the far north end of the park, also follows the ridge in many places. The trail is seven miles round-trip with a short but especially scenic loop at the end. The 1.3-mile Hotz Trail at the north end of the Europe Bay Trail passes along Europe Lake and has several small hills.

The two-mile Upland Nature Trail primarily leads through a meadow that junipers are now overtaking in many places. A guide booklet available at the trailhead near the park entrance (the trail can also be started at the beach) discusses the natural and human history of the area. The old building foundation just east of the start of the loop is worth a look.

The 1.5-mile Sugarbush Trail, the newest in the park, runs through an old sugar mapling area with a cool, mature pine forest at the back end. The generally level path also has a few rock outcroppings, part of an even older ancient shore than you pass along the other trails. Because it starts well away from the main park entrance it gets relatively few hikers.

PADDLING—The undeveloped shore offers good scenery, but large waves can be a problem for canoeists. Most of the campsites lie along the lake, so you can reach them by water. Europe Lake has some development, but is still not a bad destination for easy, quiet paddling; boats can be launched outside the park at the end of Europe Lake Road.

BIKING—Off-road bikes are allowed on most of the trails, about 15 miles in total. Like all the others, the Rowleys Bay Trail is almost completely level, but it is rated advanced because the many exposed rocks make it quite rough. All campsites are accessible by bike.

WINTER—The Europe Bay, Newport, Hotz, Fern, and Monarch trails provide over 12 miles of groomed cross-country ski trail: the last is flattened for skate skiers. The rest of the trails are ideal for snowshoers. A warming shelter is available by the beach.

COUNTY—Door.

DIRECTIONS—Two miles east of Ellison Bay on Highway 42 then 2.5 miles southeast on Newport Dr.

FACILITIES—Water, toilets, nature center, nature programs, picnic area, grills, picnic shelter, beach, playground.

CAMPING—17 backpack sites, open year-round (except deer-gun hunting season), reservations accepted, group camp.

ENTRY—Open year-round. State park sticker or daily fee required.
ON THE WEB—www.wiparks.net and www.dcty.com/newport
CONTACT—Newport State Park, 475 County Highway NP, Ellison Bay, WI 54210. Phone (920) 854-2500.

Mink River Estuary

The Mink River Estuary is one of the most pristine estuaries on Lake Michigan and one of the last undeveloped estuaries in the country. Because of its natural character and the abundance of rare and threatened plants, it has been designated the Mink River Estuary State Natural Area. The spring-fed river flows just 1.5 miles before emptying into the lake and The Nature Conservancy owns most of the land surrounding it. They stepped in in 1976 after several plans to create a park or refuge here failed due to lack of public funding. Since that time, The Nature Conservancy has expanded its holdings from an initial 60 acres to over 1,500.

The mixing of the Mink River-Rowleys Bay wetland system is unique because the winds on Lake Michigan cause a seiche, a regular reversal of the river's flow. Depending on the intensity of this seichal activity, the water level in the estuary can fluctuate vertically from four to twelve inches in cycles that range from hourly to considerably longer periods. When the water flows in from the lake, the marsh floods, while some ground is exposed as the water flows out. In addition to this local seiche phenomenon, the dynamics of the Mink River hydrologic cycle are affected from year to year by the changing water levels of Lake Michigan. The constant changes create a variety of habitats because no single plant community can dominate.

WILDLIFE—Over 200 species of birds have been recorded here throughout the course of a year. Some of the many endangered, threatened, and locally rare species that might be seen include American black duck, black tern, black-crowned night heron, yellow rail, bobolink, sedge wren, Blackburnian warbler, Cooper's hawk, osprey, and a pair of nesting bald eagles. Beaver, otter, mink, deer, coyote, porcupine, and the occasional bear are some of the preserve's mammals, and the Mink River is an especially important area for spawning fish.

HIKING—There are roughly 3.5 miles of marked trails leading through the northern mesic forest around the river, all level and easy to follow. To the east, off Newport Drive (a sign marks this entrance as the Shoenbrunn Nature Conservancy in honor of the family which once owned the land), is the 0.75-mile Hemlock Trail which leads up to the river where benches provide a scenic spot to relax. The trail shown on some maps leading south along the river is no longer maintained. On the opposite shore the half-mile Fern Trail leads toward the river from the main parking area on Mink River Road, meeting the 1.5-mile Maple Ridge Trail. The short Mink River Trail connecting the Maple Ridge Trail to the river can be quite wet.

PADDLING—The best way to see the area is from the water; canoes may be launched at the mouth of the river at Rowleys Bay. Paddlers are urged to stay away from the tall grasses lining the shore from May through July, since many birds nest there. The Wagon Trail Resort, (920) 854-2385, (888) 559-2466, on the bay rents canoes.

WINTER—The trails are open to cross-country skiing though they are not groomed.

COUNTY—Door.

DIRECTIONS—1.5 miles south of Ellison Bay on Mink River Rd.

FACILITIES—None.

CAMPING—None.

ENTRY—Open year-round. Free.

ON THE WEB—http://nature.org/wisconsin

CONTACT—The Nature Conservancy. Phone (608) 251-8140. E-mail: wmail@tnc.org

Peninsula State Park

PENINSULA STATE PARK is one of Wisconsin's busiest state parks, but it is also one of the largest (3,776 acres), so there is plenty of room to escape the Door County masses. The cliffs, reaching nearly 200 feet tall at some points, lining most of the park's seven miles of Lake Michigan shoreline, are part of the Niagara Escarpment which stretches all the way across Canada to Niagara Falls. Picnic areas and overlooks line Shore Road which follows the park's perimeter. The 75-foot Eagle Tower (its top platform is 250 feet above the lake) stands atop Eagle Bluff, once an island when Lake Michigan was at a much higher level. Many more overlooks, including Sven's Bluff Overlook with arguably the best views in the park, are found along Skyline Road in the northern end of the park.

Many of Door County's earliest European settlers made their homes in what is now the park, including Door County's first settlers, Increase and Mary Clafin. They arrived at Sturgeon Bay in 1835, and seven years later moved to Weborg Point near the southwest corner of the park, where they are buried. The earliest inhabitants arrived on the peninsula about 9,000 years ago and the Menominee, Fox, Ho-Chunk, Iroquois, and Potawatomi were among the more recent Native American tribes to live here.

WILDLIFE—As many as 200 species of resident and migrating birds can be seen throughout the year at Peninsula. Some of the many nesting warblers include Nashville, black-throated green, chestnut-sided, and Blackburnian. Also look for common loon, ducks, herons, ruffed grouse, wild turkey, pileated woodpecker, winter wren, red-breasted nuthatch, and red-shouldered hawk. Park mammals include deer, fox, coyote, porcupine, and an occasional bear.

HIKING—There are 13 miles of interconnected hiking trails in the park. All are wooded with just a few small scattered grassy openings.

The two-mile Eagle Trail loops above and below the most spectacular cliffs. The most scenic section is not atop the bluff, but rather below, where you can get some spectacular up-close views of the cliffs and their many small, cave-like openings. The trail is steep up and down the cliffs, with steps at the roughest spots, and while it is level at the bottom it is a bit rough where it follows the shore. The Minnehaha Trail continues along the shore for another 0.7 mile and has some good views of Eagle Bluff. It is level but also a little rough in spots. The Sentinel Trail, a level two-mile loop, has a guide to the trees and flowers found along the trail, and the 0.6-mile section east of Highland Road is wheelchair accessible. It passes along the 80-acre Peninsula Park Beech Forest State Natural Area that was protected as an excellent example of Northern Mesic Forest and exposed Niagara Escarpment. The 0.6-mile Lone Pine Trail is a scenic path leading down the steep bluff which, combined with the three previously mentioned trails, makes an excellent 3.5-mile loop.

The rolling, 1.8-mile Hemlock Trail offers the most variety of the park's trails. At its southern end it passes the cemetery where Door County's earliest settlers are buried, continues along Weborg Marsh, and enters the 53-acre Peninsula Park White Cedar Forest State Natural Area. This natural area exemplifies the continuum of plant communities from open marsh to upland forest. The Hemlock Trail shares part of its path with the Skyline Trail, a 2.5-mile loop. Both have long climbs at the end with rolling hills along the rest of their routes. A half-mile loop off the Skyline Trail leads to the spectacular Sven's Bluff Overlook.

The 2.2-mile Nicolet Bay Trail also has rolling hills. The section south of the beach follows the Hidden Bluff Bike Trail through a heavily used section of the park and really is not all that worthwhile, though the rest is not bad. The 0.6-mile Trail Tramper's Delight is a level path used as far back as the 1920s that connects Nicolet Bay with the Eagle Bluff Lighthouse. Finally, the White Cedar Nature Trail, a half-mile loop with some hills, has display panels discussing white-tailed deer.

The off-road bike trails get fairly heavy use, but they also allow scenic hikes. Just keep your eyes peeled for oncoming bikes.

PADDLING—Canoes and sea kayaks are a good way to see the cliffs, though there are usually lots of boats, and waves on Green Bay can be quite large. Horseshoe Island, a quarter-mile offshore at its nearest point, is part of the park and can be explored during the day, but no camping or fires are allowed. Canoe, kayak, paddleboat, and sailboat rentals (plus sailing lessons) are available at Nicolet Bay.

BIKING—The park's nearly six miles of surfaced bike trails are very popular. They are mostly level with only a few small hills and are connected to a three-mile marked route following lesser-used park roads. The main path is the gravel-surfaced, 5.1-mile Sunset Trail which leads along the western end of the park. The 0.75-mile Hidden Bluff Trail forms a loop at the northern end of the Sunset Trail and shortens the route to Nicolet Beach. The park's roughly nine miles of off-road bike trails are quite hilly and very popular. Bikes may be rented at Nicolet Bay in the park or just outside the Fish Creek entrance.

WINTER—The park has 18 miles of groomed cross-country ski trails, most of which follow the off-road bike trails and the hiking trails south of Shore Road. Unfortunately, they intersect with snowmobile trails quite often. Most trails are hilly, though there are a few miles suitable for beginners and portions of the Purple, Red, and Blue Loops can accommodate skate skiing. There is a warming shelter available.

The Minnehaha Trail and parts of the Eagle and Sentinel trails are designated a two-mile snowshoeing trail. The steep 17th fairway of the golf course becomes a popular sledding and tubing hill.

OTHER—The 1868 Eagle Bluff Lighthouse has been restored by the Door County Historical Society. Guided tours are offered from late-May to mid-October for a small fee. The popular American Folklore Theater offers performances at the amphitheater during the summer.

COUNTY—Door.

DIRECTIONS—The main entrance is half a mile east of Fish Creek on Highway 42.

FACILITIES—Water, toilets, boat launch, nature center, nature programs, picnic area, grills, picnic shelter, beach, playground, fitness course, volleyball, tennis, golf course.

CAMPING—Five campgrounds, 472 sites, 102 electric, open year-round, reservations accepted, showers, group camp.

ENTRY—Open year-round. State park sticker or daily fee required. State trail pass required for off-road bikers.

ON THE WEB—www.wiparks.net

CONTACT—Peninsula State Park, 9462 Shore Road, PO Box 218, Fish Creek, WI 54212. Phone (920) 868-3258.

The Ridges Sanctuary, Toft Point
Natural Area, and Mud Lake Wildlife Area

THESE THREE adjoining properties comprise one of Wisconsin's most important natural preserves. Each has been designated a state natural area and the complex is collectively a National Natural Landmark. Together they cover nearly 4,000 acres and comprise Door County's largest patch of wilderness. An exceptional variety of natural wonders are protected here, most notably the abundance of rare wildflowers. The principal reason behind the rare plant bounty is the cooling effect of Lake Michigan during spring and summer. The latter allows a diversity of unusual habitats that are normally found much farther north to exist here. One of these, boreal forest, is found in far northern Wisconsin along Lake Superior, but is more typical of Canada.

The Ridges Sanctuary, at the heart of this complex, is the largest, most accessible, and most visited of the three areas—many visitors are not even aware that the other two exist. The Ridges' 1,200-plus acres contain one of the greatest concentrations of rare plants in the Midwest, including more than a dozen state-endangered or threatened species and the federally-endangered Dwarf Lake Iris. In total, more than 500 different plant species, including over two dozen native orchids, have been identified here.

The namesake beach ridges are as fascinating as the rich flora. They began to form about 1,200 years ago when a much higher Lake Michigan covered this area. The 30 or so slightly curved crests that roughly parallel the shore of Baileys Harbor Bay were formed by the wind and waves as the lake level rose and fell over decades; vegetation eventually stabilized the ridges, resulting in the landscape you see today. What makes the ridges so interesting, beside their relative uniformity, are the long and narrow wetlands (called swales) between them. This ridge-swale topography features extremely varied plant communities—ranging from forest to open water and also featuring marsh, bog, and swamp—all within a few meters of each other. Among the most interesting plants found in the swales are the insectivorous round-leaved sundew and pitcher plant.

The Ridges Sanctuary began with just 40 acres set aside in 1937 to protect the native orchids. The initial acquisition was a most important conservation battle. The land was owned by the U.S. Lighthouse Service but leased to the county which planned to develop a trailer park. Concerned individuals, led by Albert Fuller, botanist at the Milwaukee Public Museum, formed a private, non-profit group and successfully prevented the development. The group continues to manage and expand the area today. The unique range lights, built in 1869 to guide ships into shallow Baileys Harbor, remain within the sanctuary and are now listed on the National Register of Historic Places.

They operated for a hundred years until a single light replaced them. A long boardwalk at the west end of the trail system passes the lights.

East of the Ridges Sanctuary, the Toft Point Natural Area protrudes more than a mile into Lake Michigan between Baileys Harbor and Moonlight Bay. The 740-acre preserve spans almost the entire peninsula, including some four miles of uninterrupted shoreline; only the west side (not a part of the natural area) is developed. The mostly rocky shore provides a significantly different outdoor experience from that of the Ridges. It is very easy to visit, but with no facilities or marked trails, few people come here. The Toft family operated a small resort on the site—some cabins still remain—and were actively involved with the original effort to preserve the Ridges. They sold their land to The Nature Conservancy in order to preserve the area. It was eventually transferred to the University of Wisconsin–Green Bay, which maintains it now.

Most of the nearly 2,000-acre Mud Lake Wildlife Area consists of white cedar swamp and is generally inaccessible. The completely undeveloped namesake lake (a trail reaches its shore) is the main destination for visitors. The shallow drainage lake covers about 155 acres, but its size varies considerably with the rainfall. Reibolts Creek, a popular trout stream, connects Mud Lake to Lake Michigan. Management here is minimal, with resource protection being the main goal, as was the desire of Leland Thorp when he donated 1,040 acres around the lake to the state.

WILDLIFE—This large area is home to an abundance of wildlife, with bear, deer, fox, coyote, porcupine, beaver, otter, mink, and fisher being some of the mammalian residents. Bird-watchers flock here in part because of the numerous area-sensitive species, including 17 species of nesting warblers—black-throated green, northern parula, and northern waterthrush are some of the most sought after. Other nesting birds that you might spot include merlin, northern harrier, osprey, bald eagle (which nest nearby), ruffed grouse, pied-billed grebe, American bittern, common golden eye, pintail, blue-winged teal, wood duck, Caspian tern, Virginia rail, and winter wren.

The area has the largest remaining population of the federally endangered Hine's emerald dragonfly which is found in just three locations in all of the world—the others being small sites in Illinois and Upper Michigan.

HIKING—Most people hike on the Ridges' five miles of narrow, level trails, most of which follow the ridges and are connected by more than a dozen boardwalks through the swales. There are many benches to rest or relax on along the way. Because of the fragile environment here, it is very important not to stray from the designated paths. The trails are laid out in such a way as to allow endless combinations. Walking with no destination is a great way to see the area, though most people take a guided tour (available May through October) or follow one of three loops recommended in the guide booklet. The 1.4-mile Blue Loop follows numbered posts which correspond to explanations of the area's unique ecology in the booklet, while the 0.8-mile Green Loop is a shortened version of the Blue. The 1.2-mile Red Loop has two observation decks extending into a large open swale north of the trail, but has no interpretive stops of its own. Whether you follow the recommended loops or not, the Mountain Maple Trail is a must. The quarter-mile path leads over five boardwalks between the ridges and contains a wide variety of plant communities. The Pine and Wintergreen trails are not significantly different from any of the others, but since they are not a part of the recommended loops you will encounter fewer people.

The undeveloped rocky shore at Toft Point is a great place for a hike. Access is easy from a parking area at the end of Ridges Road or from three short paths off Point Drive, which leads for one mile into the area. Virtually nothing man-made is visible on the opposite shore, providing a great wilderness experience. One building that adds to the scenery is the Cana Island Lighthouse, several miles away across Moonlight Bay. An unmarked dirt road off Ridges Road (just before it turns south) is a less used but highly recommended entrance. The road, open to walking only, continues through the forest for about 0.75 mile beyond the gate to the old resort area. Between the gate and the buildings, a short, quarter-mile path branches off to the west. This narrow trail passes through a mostly open area before rejoining the road. Past the buildings, another narrow trail leads along the rocky shore for less than a mile, eventually leading out of the forest to an open area along a small, beautiful cove. There are several rock outcroppings inland along this path, marking where the shoreline existed shortly after the last Ice Age.

Mud Lake has very limited land access. The best is at the end of Birch Road on the eastern border; from here, a level road, less than half a mile long, leads out toward the lake and a narrow path continues the rest of the way. Though this route can be quite wet, it is usually possible to stay dry by walking on pieces of wood lying in the wettest areas. There is also limited access at the north end from Lime Kiln Road—a service road leads south for half a mile through mostly open field before becoming very wet—though this part is not all that interesting.

PADDLING—Canoeists can paddle a mile up Reibolts Creek to Mud Lake, while Moonlight Bay is the best canoeing area along this part of the Lake Michigan shoreline. A parking area on County Q provides access to both.

WINTER—The boreal forest makes this an especially scenic area in winter. The Ridges' trails are open for cross-country skiing but are not groomed.

AUTO TOUR—Ridges Road, which follows the shore of Baileys Harbor, is Rustic Road #39.

COUNTY—Door.

DIRECTIONS—Ridges, half a mile north of Baileys Harbor on Highway 57 then 0.1 mile east on County Q. Toft Point, 1.5 miles east of Baileys Harbor on Ridges Rd. Mud Lake, half a mile north of Baileys Harbor on Highway 57, then three miles east on County Q, then 1.25 miles north on Sunset Dr., and a quarter mile west on Birch Rd.

FACILITIES—Water, toilets, nature center, nature programs.

CAMPING—None.

ENTRY—Open year-round. Modest trail fee at Ridges.

ON THE WEB—www.ridgesanctuary.org

CONTACT—The Ridges Sanctuary, PO Box 152, Baileys Harbor, WI 54202. Phone (920) 839-2802. E-mail: ridges@itol.com
Toft Point, UW–Green Bay, Dept. of Natural and Applied Sciences, Green Bay, WI 54311. Phone (920) 465-2371.
Mud Lake Wildlife Area, Manitowoc DNR, 1314 Highway 310, Manitowoc, WI 54220. Phone (920) 683-4926.

Whitefish Dunes State Park
and Cave Point County Park

THE BEAUTIFUL and impressive dunes at the heart of this 863-acre park are the largest along the entire western shore of Lake Michigan. Old Baldy, the park's tallest, towers 93 feet above the lake. Though best known for its sand piles, the rocky cliffs along the northern half of the park's two-mile shoreline provide a striking contrast. The cliffs at Cave Point County Park, a 19-acre property nestled entirely within Whitefish Dunes, are actually the most popular sight here. When the winds are strong, they send large waves crashing well over the top—a spectacular sight in all seasons—and small caves have been worn into the cliffs by the repeated pounding.

Thousands of years ago, Clark Lake, forming the park's western border, was part of Whitefish Bay and most of the land that now makes up the park did not exist. Known as a baymouth bar lake, Clark was separated from Lake Michigan by the formation of the dunes. Today, most of the dunes have stabilized and are forested, but the wind continues to shape many of them. The 230-acre Whitefish Dunes State Natural Area, a diverse domain stretching between Lake Michigan and Clark Lake, contains all successional dune stages from open beach through forest. Five endangered or threatened species and many other rare plants uniquely adapted to this environment survive here, including the extremely rare dune thistle which is the first plant to take root in the dunes, setting

Cave Point.

the stage for all others. The thistle and its pinkish blossoms can be seen in several places in the park including on Old Baldy. Wildflowers are also abundant
here, and because of Lake Michigan's cooling effect they generally bloom two to
four weeks later than the same plants on Door County's Green Bay shore.

Archaeological surveys in the park have uncovered over 35,000 Native
American artifacts, providing evidence of seven separate occupations by four
distinct cultures, the North Bay (the earliest known settlers dating back to 100
BC), Heins Creek, Late Woodland, and Oneota. Remains of a commercial fishing operation from the mid-1800s were also found. Good fishing and canoe
access are likely the main reasons they settled here. Simulated villages from the
various Native American tribes that lived here have been erected just west of
the interpretive center.

Despite having no camping and few other developed facilities, Whitefish
Dunes is a very popular park. The primary reasons are the scenery and the
6,600-foot-long sandy beach. Strong rip currents can form here, so the first 225
yards of beach is closed to swimming; be sure to heed the posted warnings. A
specially designed wheelchair, available at the park office, allows disabled access to the beach and lake.

WILDLIFE—Well over 120 species of birds have been recorded at Whitefish Dunes, including ruffed grouse, pheasant, wood duck, black-crowned

night heron, sandhill crane, pileated woodpecker, 16 warbler species including Canada and Blackburnian, Eastern wood pewee, winter wren, white-breasted nuthatch, and osprey—the latter a threatened species in Wisconsin. Park mammals include beaver, mink, fox, coyote, deer, fisher, porcupine, and the occasional bear.

HIKING—There are nine miles of trails in the park, all interconnecting loops and all virtually flat except for the 2.8-mile Red Trail. This, the park's most popular hiking route, passes through the largest dunes and there are some small rolling hills, especially on the narrow northern half. The best dune views are along the southern half of this trail where a wooden walkway leads to the top of Old Baldy; both Lake Michigan and Clark Lake are visible from the summit. Because of their fragile nature and the concentration of rare plants, access to the dunes is restricted to this trail. Climbing on them can cause long term damage, so please resist the urge.

Branching off the Red Trail are the narrow 1.8-mile Green and the 4.2-mile Yellow trails. The sections of these trails north of Clark Lake Road are wooded, while south of the road they are more open. The 0.7-mile Clark Lake Spur branches off the Green Trail right up to that lake's sandy shore. The Yellow Trail leads to the less visited western side of the park, where the wooded half-mile Whitefish Creek Spur leads to that small creek; a bench here provides a quiet, secluded place to relax. The southeast end of this trail has some small hills.

The wooded 2.5-mile White Trail leads to the east side of the park where it connects with Cave Point County Park's cliffs via the short Contemplation Walk. Finally, the 1.5-mile wheelchair-accessible Brachiopod Nature Trail begins at a fossil rock display and has an interpretive guide that explains the park's natural history as it leads through the forest.

BIKING—The southern half of the Red Trail and a branch connecting it to Clark Lake Road, 1.5 miles total, are surfaced with crushed gravel; bikes are allowed.

WINTER—Six miles of trails, the Red, Yellow, and Green are groomed for cross-country skiing, and a warming shelter is available. The ice formations at Cave Point are an especially beautiful sight.

COUNTY—Door.

DIRECTIONS—Nine miles northeast of Sturgeon Bay on Highway 57, then 2.5 miles east on Clark Lake Road.

FACILITIES—Water, toilets, nature center, nature programs, picnic area, grills, picnic shelter, beach.

CAMPING—None.

ENTRY—Open year-round. State park sticker or daily fee required. Cave

Point is free and can be accessed separately—follow the signs.

ON THE WEB—www.wiparks.net

CONTACT—Whitefish Dunes State Park, 3275 Clark Lake Rd., Sturgeon Bay, WI 54235. Phone (920) 823-2400.

Potawatomi State Park

THIS 1,225-ACRE park sits on a wooded plateau overlooking Sturgeon Bay—the body of water, not the city—though the urban version is just a stone's throw away. Steep, rocky cliffs parallel the more than two-mile shoreline, then curve inland around the park's northwest border; the tallest cliffs are best viewed from the road leading down to the boat launch. These scenic limestone cliffs sit back from the water now, but 8,500 years ago they *were* the shore. They are part of the Niagara Escarpment, a ridge of rock which forms the Door County Peninsula and arcs all the way to New York, where it creates Niagara Falls. A 75-foot observation tower sits atop the park's highest bluff looking out over Lake Michigan, and from the top, 225 feet above the lake, it is possible to see Menominee, Michigan, across the waters of Green Bay.

This area was once known as Government Bluff and was under the ownership of the U.S. War Department before being transferred to the state in 1928 for use as a park. It was originally named Nicolet State Park after the first European to enter what would become Wisconsin. He likely stopped at what is now the park in 1634. When the park opened in 1929, the name was changed to honor the Native Americans who last lived here.

WILDLIFE—More than 200 species of birds have been recorded here and at least 50 species of songbirds nest in the park's forest. Look for ducks, geese, pileated woodpecker, Blackburnian warbler, and pine siskin. Mammalian residents include deer, porcupine, fox, and even the occasional bear.

HIKING—The park's three trails total 6.5 miles. They are thickly wooded except along Sturgeon Bay and are generally level except where they cross the cliffs; the steepest parts have steps. The narrow and easy half-mile Ancient Shores Nature Trail, beginning west of the campground, has an interpretive guide (available at the trailhead) to explain the natural history of the area.

A better place to explore the moss-covered "ancient shore" is along the north end of the 2.5-mile Hemlock Trail which follows the cliff for close to a mile. This trail is best accessed at the picnic areas along Sturgeon Bay in the south end of the park; this part is paved. The trail's west side is less interesting, since it passes right next to the park's busy main road.

The 3.5-mile Tower Trail winds through the northern half of the park and offers the most solitude. The eastern end leads along Sturgeon Bay before the trail crosses Shore Road and returns through the forest. An extra loop continues along the shore and returns through the north end of the campground. A short section by the ski hill is paved.

Potawatomi is the eastern terminus of the Ice Age Trail (p. 1). It begins at the observation tower and follows the Tower Trail east to Sturgeon Bay and then continues along the shore to the southeast corner of the park, where it exits along Duluth Ave. The marked route continues right through the city of Sturgeon Bay to the Ahnapee State Trail, which it follows south out of Door County.

PADDLING—Dedicated canoeists can paddle around Sturgeon Bay and Sawyer Harbor, though there is much development here and boat traffic can be quite heavy. Canoes and paddleboats may be rented at the park.

BIKING—A four-mile off-road bike trail with some small hills winds around the park, pretty much paralleling the Hemlock Trail and looping inside the Tower Trail. Work is currently under way to expand the trail by a mile and a half. Several short gravel bike trails connect the park roads with little-used country roads outside the park. Bike rentals are available at the park.

WINTER—The Tower and Hemlock trails plus some short additions are groomed for cross-country skiing, eight miles total, and half of these miles accommodate skate skiing. There is a warming shelter and a small sledding hill. Most of the eight miles of snowmobile trail follow park roads, though they unfortunately intersect with the ski trails quite frequently.

Potawatomi contains Door County's only downhill ski area, and though it has not been operated for several years it could open again if enough volunteers are wrangled up to run it.

COUNTY—Door.

DIRECTIONS—Two miles west of Sturgeon Bay on Highway 42/57, then 2.5 miles north on County PD.

FACILITIES—Water, toilets, boat launch, nature programs, picnic area, grills, picnic shelter, playground.

CAMPING—123 sites, 25 electric, barrier-free cabin, open year-round, reservations accepted, showers.

ENTRY—Open year-round. State park sticker or daily fee required.

ON THE WEB—www.wiparks.net

CONTACT—Potawatomi State Park, 3740 County Rd. PD, Sturgeon Bay, WI 54235. Phone (920) 746-2890.

Green Bay West Shores
Wildlife Area

THIS AMBITIOUS project stretches for 42 miles between the cities of Green Bay and Marinette. Historically, this area has been a major waterfowl feeding and breeding area, but in recent decades pollution and urban sprawl have threatened the land and its natural residents. Green Bay West Shores was established to maintain the ecological integrity of the shore zone as a vital aspect of the Green Bay ecosystem. The 11 units currently encompass about 7,700 acres, and if all goes according to plan most of the units will be greatly expanded—the overall ownership goal is 14,000 acres.

The first preservation efforts began in 1936 when Long Tail Point became a federal waterfowl refuge; the land was given to the state in 1961. The first state-acquired land, beginning in 1948, came in the Sensiba Unit. Six years later, four miles of shoreline were purchased at Peshtigo Harbor and other areas were added throughout the 1950s. In 1965 the state Department of Natural Resources decided to actively pursue most of the remaining undeveloped land on the west shore in Oconto and Marinette Counties, and Brown County was added to the project in the 1970s.

Each of the units, from the south to the north, is described in detail below. Most have limited access, but all are very scenic and ideal for roadside wildlife viewing. Ideally, a visit to the wildlife area should be combined with a stop at the L. H. Barkhausen Waterfowl Preserve and Fort Howard Paper Foundation Wildlife Area (p. 104), a Brown County park that lies between the Long Tail and Peats Lake Units. The West Shores Interpretive Center at the park provides a great deal of information about the human and natural history of this entire area.

The 385-acre **Peats Lake Unit** lies just one mile north of Green Bay along Highway 41. East Deerfield Road, which runs parallel to the highway, provides good views of the marsh. At the end of the road, a short gravel path heads east, allowing views of Peats Lake (which is really a small bay).

The 350-acre **Long Tail Unit** includes a narrow, wooded peninsula jutting into Green Bay south of the Suamico River. It can be seen from several points along the shore. Currently very little land has been acquired along the shore here.

The **Sensiba Unit** covers 620 acres of marsh as well as upland and lowland forest. Most of the unit lies north of the Suamico River between Sunset Beach Road to the south and Resort Road to the north. A mile-long dike, constructed to prevent erosion, can be reached from the end of Sunset Beach Road. Though often overgrown, it is still possible to walk along it for good

101

views of the marsh. From a parking area off Sunset Beach Road, a level wooded trail leads north for about three-quarters of a mile, ending where the marsh begins. Another trail goes south through the area from Resort Road, but it is generally wet and overgrown. Cottage Row, a short road at the end of Resort Road, also provides good views of the marsh and bay.

The **Little Tail Unit,** situated just south of the Brown-Oconto county line, consists of 270 acres of mostly marsh. It is bisected by Hook Road and the best viewing is along the bay at the end of the road. The **Tibbet-Suamico Unit** is 263 acres of bottomland forest and marsh just north of the Brown-Oconto county line, and is best seen from Lade Beach Road. The **Charles Pond Unit,** a 110-acre State Natural Area used for monitoring long-term changes in the region, lies midway between the Tibbet-Suamico and Pensaukee Units. None of the three units has significant foot access.

The 406-acre **Pensaukee Unit** begins at the village of Pensaukee and continues south for about two miles: it is bisected by County S. Near the southern end, a quarter-mile gravel service road leads to the lake through a mix of open fields and woods. This is the best entry point, although a few overgrown trails lead east and west of the highway, too.

The **Pecor Point Unit,** the smallest at 87 acres, is one of the most scenic spots in the entire wildlife area. Pecor Point Road passes through marsh and extends out to the bay, allowing great lakeshore views. At the corner of Pecor Point Road and County S is a Department of Transportation wetland mitigation project with a small hill providing good views of the marsh and its wildlife. While not a part of the wildlife area, this viewing venue is a worthwhile stop for bird-watchers.

The **Oconto Marsh Unit,** currently the second largest unit at 924 acres, is popular for bird-watching. The unit extends for about four miles along County Y to northeast of the city of Oconto. The southern part of the area consists of a large flowage surrounded by marsh, while the north is mostly forest. For the best views of marsh wildlife follow the dike along the flowage. It begins off County Y, one mile north of Harbor Road. The path becomes increasingly overgrown the farther you go, but the beginning is always easily passable.

The 183-acre **Rush Point Unit** extends to the north of the Oconto Marsh Unit. It can be seen from County Y north of County A, but there is no good access.

By far the largest of the eleven units, the **Peshtigo Harbor Unit** encompasses 4,015 acres of marsh and lowland forest, more than half of the land currently in the entire wildlife area. Not surprising, this unit offers visitors the most to see and do. The winding Peshtigo River which divides the property empties into Lake Michigan in the eastern half of the property. In 1867 a sawmill was established at the mouth of the river and lumber was shipped south along the shore, primarily to Chicago. At the peak of the logging era, a town of 500 people stood here, but the mill burned in 1895 and the town quickly faded; the pillars still standing in the bay are the only remaining traces. Most of the land in the unit is west of the river, but both sides offer great scenery. The western portion is accessed by Harbor Road, which runs southeast through the unit, and by Hale School Road towards the north. Several mostly wooded service roads branch off the pair and can be hiked. Harbor Road ends at the mouth of the river and has good lakeshore and marsh views and a historical marker commemorates the town and mill which once stood here. The eastern side of the Peshtigo Harbor unit has two noteworthy scenic vistas. There are sweeping views of the marsh from the end of an unnamed gravel road (marked with a large "Road Closed" sign) that leads south from County BB into the wildlife area and up to a small branch of the river. At the very east end of the property, Pond Road runs south from County BB up to the shore of Green Bay, offering nice marsh and shoreline views from the road.

WILDLIFE—A remarkable 350 species of birds have been recorded here over the years, with nearly half of them nesting. Look for ducks, geese, tundra swans (several thousand stop during migration), sandhill crane, black-crowned night heron, common loon, white pelican, pheasant, ruffed grouse, turkey vulture, Cooper's hawk, and bald eagle. Threatened and endangered species include peregrine falcon, red-shouldered hawk, northern harrier, great egret, Forster's and common tern, upland sandpiper, and an impressive number of songbirds. Blanding's and wood turtles are also threatened species found here. Mammals include deer, coyote, fox, bear, beaver, mink, and otter, while bobcat and fisher have been spotted in the northern units.

HIKING—Hiking opportunities are detailed in the individual unit descriptions. The Peshtigo Harbor, Sensiba, and Oconto Marsh units offer the best foot access. There are also over nine miles of trails at the Barkhausen Preserve.

PADDLING—The Peshtigo River is an easy paddle that offers a great way to view the marsh and its wildlife. Canoes can be launched from the end of Harbor Road. The city of Peshtigo is about 15 miles upstream for those who want to make a longer trip. Long Tail Point and Peshtigo Harbor are two good spots on the shore of Green Bay, though if you canoe here be cautious of large waves.

COUNTIES—Brown (Peats Lake, Long Tail, Sensiba, Little Tail), Oconto (Tibbet-Suamico, Charles Pond, Pensaukee, Pecor Point, Oconto Marsh, Rush Point), and Marinette (Peshtigo Harbor).

DIRECTIONS—See individual unit descriptions above.

FACILITIES—Boat launches line the shore.

CAMPING—None.

ENTRY—Open year-round. Free.

CONTACT—DNR, 1125 N. Military Ave., PO Box 10448, Green Bay, WI 54307. Phone (920) 492-5800.

L. H. Barkhausen
Waterfowl Preserve and Fort Howard Paper Foundation Wildlife Area

GREEN BAY'S west shore is one of Wisconsin's most important rest stops for migrating waterfowl. This 920-acre county park preserve rests between the Long Tail and Peats Lake Units of the Green Bay West Shores Wildlife Area (p. 101) which protects a 42-mile stretch of this vital habitat from development. Conservationist Louis Henry Barkhausen bought land here in 1926 and created one of Wisconsin's first waterfowl preserves. In 1955 he donated his private preserve to the county and the local paper company's charitable foundation added 446 acres in 1976. Lineville Road bisects the park, with the Barkhausen section to the north and the Fort Howard section to the south, though they are managed as a single unit.

The Fort Howard section has well over a mile of Green Bay shoreline, though no trails approach the lake. The shore is dominated by marsh, and besides hosting many birds this is an important spawning area for northern pike. The rest of the Fort Howard lands contain a mix of meadow and mostly young forest. The southwest corner of this section, as well as the northeast corner of the Barkhausen section, contains the most mature and thus the most interesting forest. The Barkhausen section is comprised of meadow, forest, marsh, and a large prairie restoration across the north end. The West Shores Interpretive Center at the heart of it all houses natural and historical displays; it is a good place to stop for those visiting nearby units of the Wildlife Area. Nature programs for school groups and the public are held throughout the year.

WILDLIFE—Louis Barkhausen reintroduced the giant Canada goose (the largest subspecies), which by the 1930s was presumed extinct in Wisconsin, to his preserve, and today the resident flock is a major attraction. They like to waddle around the interpretive center and may easily be viewed up close. Migration brings thousands more geese to the area.

Because of its location and varied habitats, Barkhausen is a great spot for bird-watching; more than 175 species have been recorded here. Throughout the year, visitors might spot bald eagle, ducks, yellow-headed blackbird, sandhill crane, herons, and various other shorebirds along the bay and in the wetlands, plus ruffed grouse, and a variety of warblers in the forest and field. Threatened and endangered species include great and snowy egrets, common and Forster's terns, and the occasional migrating osprey. Fox, coyote, otter, and deer might be seen here as well.

HIKING—There are over nine miles of level trail crisscrossing the preserve. All trails start and end at the nature center, though a parking lot on Lineville Road allows direct access to the less used Fort Howard section. The principal path is the five-mile Shores Trail which loops around the entire park encompassing a little of all the area has to offer. All other trails follow the Shores Trail before branching off at various points and, except for the Mosquito Creek Trail, are essentially just Shore Trail shortcuts.

The wheelchair-accessible Woodcock Trail is the shortest at 0.8 mile, but it still offers views of all the park's primary habitats. This mostly wooded path passes several small ponds and wetlands as well as the large prairie restoration to the north, where a wildlife observation blind is located. The narrow path in the middle of the loop leading to the marsh study area is also a nice walk. Only half of the 2.3-mile Mosquito Creek Trail shares the path with the Shores Trail; at its far end it returns along the edge of the marsh, making it a good choice for birders. The Meadow Ridge Trail is 3.25 miles; its short cut-off bypasses the Fort Howard section. The wooded 3.5-mile Birches Trail can be used to make loops from the Lineville Road parking area for those hiking only in the Fort Howard section. The 4.25-mile Pot Hole Trail, named for numerous small ponds dug for waterfowl habitat, cuts off the far end of the Shores Trail. The 0.75-mile section of the Shores Trail beyond the Pot Hole Trail is particularly nice because it passes through more mature forest.

WINTER—All trails are groomed for cross-country skiing, while snowshoeing is encouraged on the rest of the property. Rental snowshoes and a warming shelter are available.

COUNTY—Brown.

DIRECTIONS—Four miles north of Green Bay on Highway 41/141, then half a mile east on Lineville Rd., and a quarter mile north on County J.

FACILITIES—Water, toilets, nature center, nature programs, picnic area.

CAMPING—Group camp.

ENTRY—Open-year-round. Free. County trail pass or daily fee for cross-country skiing.

ON THE WEB—www.co.brown.wi.us/parks/parks/barkhausen

CONTACT—West Shores Interpretive Center, 2024 Lakeview Dr., PO Box 187, Suamico, WI 54173. Phone (920) 448-6242.

Navarino Wildlife Area

NESTLED IN A former glacial lake bed between the Wolf and Shioc Rivers, Navarino contains the largest publicly owned wetland in northeastern Wisconsin, but water covers only about half of the 14,581 acres. The marsh, brush swamp, bog, bottomland forest, and 15 flowages (totaling 1,415 acres) are intermixed with extensive forests and nearly a thousand acres of restored prairie, making this a bustling wildlife haven. Plans drawn up in the 1960s called for managing this as an additional stopping area for the migrating Horicon Marsh goose flock, but the project was shelved because it would have required clearing most of the forest.

The Navarino Nature Center, located at the southeast end of the wildlife area, is run by a local non-profit group. Wildflower, butterfly, and backyard habitat gardens plus tree and prairie plant identification paths are maintained around the education center, and there is a large prairie restoration immediately to the west. Naturalist-led classes and tours are offered throughout the year.

WILDLIFE—Navarino is a very popular and productive bird-watching destination with more than 175 species of regular residents or short-term visitors—in total nearly 240 species have been documented. Canada goose, wood duck, green heron, sandhill crane, bald eagle, Cooper's hawk, wild turkey, ruffed grouse, common moorhen, pileated woodpecker, red-breasted nuthatch, veery, chestnut-sided and pine warblers, scarlet tanager, and swamp sparrow are some of the 100-plus species that nest on or near Navarino, while great egret, trumpeter swan, Caspian and Forster's Tern, and Cerulean warbler, each state endangered or threatened species, might be seen during migration. Deer, bear, bobcat, fox, coyote, fisher, porcupine, badger, otter, mink, and beaver are among Navarino's many mammals.

An elevated viewing site on Lindsten Road is ideal for watching migrating waterfowl and sandhill cranes. MacDonald Road is another good viewing area, and there is a wheelchair-accessible viewing blind on the MacDonald Flowage.

HIKING—Five marked trails totaling nine miles begin at the nature center. The mostly wooded and generally level loops branch off each other so you can combine them into your ideal hiking route. In addition to the forest, the mile-long Blue Trail passes a large prairie restoration and has a boardwalk through a small bog; a guide pamphlet discussing the various habitats the trail traverses is available. The 1.4-mile Green Trail continues off the Blue Trail through the forest back toward the flowages, and you can return through the prairie via the 0.7-mile Birding Trail which skirts between the prairie and the forest. The two longest trails, the 2.2-mile Red and 3.8-mile

Yellow, lead around and across Pikes Peak Flowage, one of Navarino's largest. There is a large prairie restoration on the north side of the flowage. The Yellow Trail crosses MacDonald Road and can also be accessed there.

The marked hiking trails are just a small fraction of the hiking available. Another 56 miles of service roads are maintained throughout the property, offering great hiking and wildlife viewing. The most frequently followed are those that run between MacDonald Road and County K.

PADDLING—The best canoeing option is the Wolf River, which flows for 9.5 scenic miles along the western edge of Navarino. Unlike the famous rapids further north, the river here is calm and relaxing. There are two boat launches onto the river in the wildlife area, one on Highway 156 and another to the north on River Road off County C. Several of the flowages are easily accessible and also offer quiet paddling.

WINTER—The marked trails are groomed for cross-country skiing and many of the ungroomed service roads also make good ski routes. Snowshoes, available for rent at the nature center when it is open (primarily weekends, but there are some weekday hours, too), are a great way to explore the area; there is a 1.4-mile winter-only trail set aside for their use.

COUNTIES—Shawano and Waupaca.

DIRECTIONS—2.5 miles northwest of Navarino on Navarino Rd., then half a mile north on Birr Rd., and a quarter mile east on Lindsten Rd.

FACILITIES—Water, toilets, boat launch, nature center, nature programs, picnic area, picnic shelter, playground.

CAMPING—Group camp.

ENTRY—Open year-round. Free.

ON THE WEB—www.navarino.org

CONTACT—DNR, 647 Lakeland Rd., Shawano, WI 54166. Phone (715) 524-2183. Navarino Nature Center, PO Box 606, Shawano, WI 54166. Phone (715) 758-6999. E-mail: nnc1@tds.net

Gordon Bubolz Nature Preserve

DESPITE BEING so close to Appleton, this preserve can be a fantastic getaway. The 200-acre white cedar swamp, one of the southernmost in the nation, is the highlight, although the wet forest floor, dominated by ferns and mosses covering much of the rest of the 775-acre preserve, is also very scenic. There is also meadow, prairie restoration, and lowland hardwood forest. Attempts at agriculture here failed due to the wet soils, and the area, previously known as Center Swamp, was purchased by Natural Areas Preservation Inc., formed by noted conservationist Gordon Bubolz. Bubolz was also instrumental in establishing High Cliff State Park, Mosquito Hill Nature Center, and Woodland Dunes Nature Center. Displays about the area are located in the earth-sheltered nature center, where a wide variety of programs are offered throughout the year for school groups and the general public.

WILDLIFE—More than 150 species of birds can be seen here throughout the year, including hawks, pheasant, ruffed grouse, blue winged teal, Canada goose, sandhill crane, and many songbirds. Also look for beaver, otter, fox, coyote, and deer; the last are especially abundant. There is a butterfly garden near the nature center.

HIKING—There are eight miles of level trails through the preserve and an excellent interpretive guide booklet discusses the area in detail. The 1.5-mile White Cedar Trail, an extremely scenic path leading through the cedar swamp, should not be missed. The half-mile Four Seasons Trail primarily passes through the prairie restoration, although a short stretch also hits the cedar forest. The 0.4-mile Esker Trail—so named because there is an esker near the start of the trail—leads around the ponds just north of the nature center. Each of these trails is wheelchair accessible.

Two longer trails lead to the more remote back ends of the preserve; both are a mix of open field and forest with portions through the cedar swamp. Almost half of the two-mile Deer Run Trail follows Bear Creek, and there is an elevated viewing blind overlooking Black Acres Pond along this segment. The 4.5-mile Wilderness Trail can be wet at times and is closed to entry in the spring so that newborn animals and nesting birds will not be disturbed. Both of these trails have shortcut loops, helpful if you do not want to hike the whole way around.

WINTER—The trails are groomed for cross-country skiers and snowshoers; winter hikers have their own loops to follow. Skis and snowshoes are available for rent; there is a warming shelter for those using them.

COUNTY—Outagamie.

DIRECTIONS—One mile north of Appleton on Lynndale Dr. (County A).

FACILITIES—Water, toilets, nature center, nature programs, picnic area.

CAMPING—Group camp.

ENTRY—Open year-round. Free admission, fee for use of ski trails.

ON THE WEB—http://my.athenet.net/~bubolz

CONTACT—Gordon Bubolz Nature Preserve, 4815 N. Lynndale Dr., Appleton, WI 54913. Phone (920) 731-6041. E-mail: bubolz@dataex.com

Mosquito Hill Nature Center

MOSQUITO HILL, the highest point in the area, rises 200 feet above the surrounding plain. Though the dolomite-capped sandstone mound resisted glacial erosion, the mountains of ice did leave their mark here. The glacier approached from the northeast, carving a gradual slope up that side of the hill and leaving a nearly vertical southwest face.

Several different ecological communities are found on the center's 430 acres. The preserve lies in the ecological "tension zone" where northern and southern plant communities come together, and each type of forest is found on its respective side of Mosquito Hill—southern forest dominates the top. While the mound itself is wooded, it is surrounded mostly by grasslands, mostly old farm fields slowly returning to forest through natural succession. A 13-acre prairie planting begun in 1975 is found near the interpretive building. The majority, nearly three quarters of the area, is swamp forest in the flood plain of the Wolf River which forms the southern boundary. Though the origin of the hill's name is unknown, it was likely bestowed by loggers working in these mosquito-ridden bottomlands.

Opened in 1974, the center is run by Outagamie County and used by numerous school groups, but displays and programs are designed for all ages. Archaeological finds, some of which are displayed in the interpretive center, show that Native Americans hunted and fished here at least 7,000 years ago.

WILDLIFE—Beaver, otter, and mink are found in the swamp, as are sandhill cranes, ducks, and Canada goose. Cooper's hawk and turkey vultures often soar around the hill, while deer, fox, and a multitude of warblers are commonly seen in the forest. Bobolink, Eastern meadowlark, and grasshopper sparrow are some of the birds residing in the reserve's grasslands. State-threatened species that might be spotted include osprey, red-shouldered hawk, yellow-crowned night heron, and great egret. In total, over 200 species of birds have been recorded here over the course of a year. During the warmer months there is a 30 x 50-foot mesh covered butterfly house near the interpretive center.

HIKING—All but one of the center's six trails (4.5 miles total) are limited to the upland areas. Despite being mostly inaccessible, the swamp forest is still a highlight, especially along the 0.4-mile Waterthrush Walkway, a gravel path that leads into the edge of the swamp. The wetlands can also be experienced up close from platforms along other trails. All of the trails have benches along them, allowing for quiet viewing.

A guidebook discussing the ecology of the area is available for three connected trails: Deer Path, Overlook, and Wet Meadow. The 0.75-mile Deer Path

Trail loops through the prairie and has a floating platform on a pond at its far end. From here the oxbow pond still appears to be a bend of the Wolf River. It is kept filled by frequent floods. Because of the level terrain in this area, the Wolf changes course and floods often. The wheelchair-accessible Wet Meadow Trail is just a quarter mile long and has a few boardwalks within a small wetland area. The mile-long Overlook Trail leads up and around the top of Mosquito Hill. This loop trail has wooded paths along the north and south sides, passing several exposed rock ledges. It is a long, steep climb, but definitely worthwhile, more for the scenery along the trail itself than for the views from the top, which consist mostly of New London and surrounding farms.

The Grass Path and Succession Loop, each a mile long, connect to form a loop around Mosquito Hill. The Grass Path leads through open field along the edge of the swamp forest and has two platforms extending into the wetlands. The Succession Loop passes through old fields that are slowly returning to forest. It is a little hilly and not very scenic because of the views of adjacent farms, especially to the north of Mosquito Hill. It is, however, lightly used and is a good bird-watching spot.

WINTER—In winter, a five-mile snowshoe trail (there are several cut-offs allowing shorter hikes) leads deep into the swamp forest, which is essentially inaccessible the rest of the year. Snowshoes are available for rent. Cross-country skiing is allowed here, but conditions are not very good and no trails are groomed.

COUNTY—Outagamie.

DIRECTIONS—1.5 miles east of New London on County S, then half a mile south on Rogers Rd.

FACILITIES—Water, toilets, nature center, nature programs, picnic area.

CAMPING—None.

ENTRY—Open year-round. Free.

ON THE WEB—www.co.outagamie.wi.us/Parks/MH_home.htm

CONTACT—Mosquito Hill Nature Center, N3880 Rogers Rd., New London, WI 54961. Phone (920) 779-6433.

Hartman Creek State Park
and Emmons Creek Fishery Area

THIS POPULAR PARK rests at the west end of the busy Upper Waupaca Chain O' Lakes, and six of the 22 lakes in the chain are contained within the park. Hartman Lake, with its beach and picnic area, is the heart of the park, while Allen Lake, adjacent to the campground, is the site of the Spring

Hill Trout Farm, operated in the 1930s by George W. Allen. It failed after just a few years and the state took over the land which, with considerable expansion, would later become the park. When the dam creating Allen Lake was built, it flooded the original site of the farm. The birch bark fish cribs still lie at the bottom of the lake. A dozen "history" signs throughout the park identify this and other historical sites. Rolling glacial hills cover much of the park's 1,417-acres beyond the lakes.

The mostly wooded 1,470-acre Emmons Creek Fishery Area, connected to the southwestern corner of the park, more than doubles the protected lands here. Fountain Lake Road, named after the lake in the northwest corner, forms much of the northern border of the area.

The 30-acre Whispering Pines Picnic Area is nestled between three lakes at the far east end of the park. It was operated as a free public park for 46 years by the family which lived there and in 1975, they donated the land to the state. This wooded area is not accessible from the main park entrance and is thus usually very peaceful.

WILDLIFE—The park and wildlife area are home to deer, fox, mink, beaver, otter, Cooper's hawk, turkey vulture, ruffed grouse, wild turkey, pileated woodpecker, ducks, green-backed heron, sandhill crane, belted kingfisher, yellow-billed cuckoo, rose-breasted grosbeak, indigo bunting, scarlet tanager, white-breasted nuthatch, bobolink, and grasshopper sparrow. Some rarer animals that may also be seen include black bears which pass through on occasion, the state-threatened red-shouldered hawk, and the federally endangered Karner Blue butterfly. Many other butterfly species can be seen in the park, especially in the butterfly garden next to the park office. A wildlife viewing blind near the beginning of the Coach Road Trail provides a wetland overlook.

HIKING—There are nearly 15 miles of trails within the park. Pine plantations surround most of the main use areas, but the outlying areas have beautiful scenery highlighted by thick hardwood forests and rolling, open fields. The Oak Ridge Trail in the northwest corner of the park leads for 4.5 miles with several intersecting paths: the perimeter totals three miles. A 0.4-mile segment of this path to the north is called the Glacial Trail because it has the best examples of glacial hills. The northeast end of this trail leads through pine plantation; section C-G of the trail divides the natural forest from the plantation, so try to stick to the south of it.

The 15-mile long Waupaca-Portage County segment of the Ice Age Trail (p. 1) passes through the west end of the park, crossing over the rolling hills of the Oak Ridge Trail as it enters from the north. After 2.5 miles it enters the fishery area where the mostly wooded and hilly path meets some large meadows and a bridge spans Emmons Creek. The 1.75-mile Far Away Valley Loop, which

111

is very scenic, leads west from the main trail to 3rd Avenue, where it also crosses Emmons Creek before turning back. The main trail continues south of the wildlife area to 2nd Avenue. There is no parking area at the 2nd Avenue trailhead, though there is one along the trail on Stratton Lake Road. You can get information about this segment of the Ice Age Trail at the park office.

Connected to the Ice Age Trail in the southern part of the park is the 1.5-mile Windfeldt Trail. It loops through an open field, formerly an orchard, passing a few wooded sections. Along the trail is the park's highest point. While not high enough to offer distant views, the benches there are a nice place to relax and the scenery is wonderful.

Trails lead along both Allen and Hartman lakes. The northern part of the mile-long Deer Path Trail around Allen Lake is mostly through pine plantation, but the west and south ends feature naturally forested hills and make the path worthwhile. The level, wooded Dike Trail, also a mile long, loops along the northern end of Hartman Lake. With the views of the developed lake, the noise of people at the beach, and the extensive pine plantation, the trail is not very interesting.

The level 1.5-mile Pope Lake Trail loops entirely through or along the edge of pine plantation and is also not very interesting, though at the back end it does offer views of Pope and Marl Lakes and leads through the southwest corner of the 80-acre Pope Lake State Natural Area, which surrounds 14-acre Pope Lake and includes a tamarack bog to the north. Rich in aquatic life, Pope Lake is the only entirely undeveloped lake in the chain. The lake views are just as beautiful from the Whispering Pines Picnic Area on the opposite shore.

PADDLING—Canoeing is ideal on all the lakes in the park because only electric motors are allowed on each of them. A canoe rack for campers is located on Allen Lake north of the campground, below site #25. Undeveloped Pope Lake at the east end of the park is a good destination, and the adjoining Manomin and Marl lakes are quite nice, too. The nearest public boat launch to these lakes is at the end of Knight Lane.

BIKING—The Coach Road Trail, so named because in the late 1800s this was part of a stagecoach route between Oshkosh and Stevens Point, is a level, mile-long bike trail surfaced with crushed stone. Off-road biking is also allowed on another five miles of trails in the park, including the Windfeldt Trail, which adjoins the Coach Road Trail and the outer loop of the Oak Ridge Trail. Road biking in this area is excellent.

WINTER—All trails are groomed for cross-country skiing except the Windfeldt Trail and most of the Ice Age Trail, about 10 miles total. North of Hartman Lake is a two-mile designated winter hiking trail. The Windfeldt Trail is part of four miles of snowmobile trails through the park. A warming shelter is available.

AUTO TOUR—Rural Road, which passes through the east end of the park, is Rustic Road #23 and the adjoining Emmons Creek Road, which continues on into the wildlife area, is Rustic Road #24.

OTHER—A 6.5-mile horse trail runs through the park. Its three loops are level and mostly open, though the middle loop passes through a pine plantation.

COUNTIES—Waupaca and Portage.

DIRECTIONS—Six miles west of Waupaca on Highway 54, then 1.5 miles south on Hartman Creek Rd.

FACILITIES—Water, toilets, boat launch, nature programs, picnic area, grills, picnic shelter, beach, playground.

CAMPING—101 sites, tipi rental, open year-round, reservations accepted, showers, group camp.

ENTRY—Open year-round. State park sticker or daily fee required. State trail pass required for off-road bikers and horseback riders.

ON THE WEB—www.wiparks.net

CONTACT—Hartman Creek State Park, N2480 Hartman Creek Rd., Waupaca, WI 54981. Phone (715) 258-2372. Emmons Creek Wildlife Area, DNR, 473 Griffith Ave., Wisconsin Rapids, WI 54494. Phone (715) 421-7800.

George W. Mead Wildlife Area

MEAD, the third largest state-owned wildlife area in the state, encompasses 28,208 acres. Early in the 20th century, like many wetlands, the swamps here were drained. The Little Eau Pleine River, which bisects the property west to east, was even straightened and made into a canal. Despite all this misdirected effort, farming failed and much of the area returned naturally to wetlands. In the mid-1930s, the Consolidated Paper Company began buying land in the valley to create a reservoir to supplement power production on the Wisconsin River during periods of low water, but because they were unable to acquire all the necessary land the plan was eventually abandoned. The property is named in honor of the company's founder, since his son Stanton donated to the state, for conservation purposes, the 20,000 acres of land the company had managed to acquire.

Today the area is managed primarily for its wetlands, though there are significant areas of wooded and open uplands. Nineteen large flowages have been constructed, mostly in the northern half of the property. There is a large prairie restoration around Smoky Hill, just south of the river on Smoky Hill Road.

Not only is Smoky Hill scenic, it is also historic. Before settlers altered the land, it was a wooded island surrounded by marsh, and was home to a band of Ojibwe. In 1755 the Ho-Chunk captured the island, but were soon forced out by the Ojibwe with French army assistance. Several former villages and campsites as well as mounds and burial sites have been found at Mead, and many artifacts have been recovered. Some are on display at the headquarters, where there is also information on plants and animals common to the area.

WILDLIFE—Mead is a popular bird-watching destination because of the variety and abundance of birds found here; more than 250 species have been recorded. Mead is one of the few places in the state where prairie chickens still exist, though their numbers have declined. You are more likely to see the endangered trumpeter swan, which has been reintroduced in this area as part of a larger project to restore the species to the state. Wisconsin's largest inland double-crested cormorant rookery is located on the east end of the Berkhahn Flowage, and great blue heron and black-crowned night heron also nest in these trees. State-threatened species found here include yellow-crowned night heron, great egret, and osprey, while Canada geese, many ducks, sandhill crane, bald eagle, and ruffed grouse are more common residents. Great-crested flycatcher, Eastern wood pewee, marsh wren, red- and white-eyed vireos, chestnut-sided warbler, ovenbird, bobolink, scarlet tanager, and savannah sparrow are some of the property's many songbirds. Beaver, mink, otter, coyote, fox, badger, deer, bear, and bobcat are among the many mammals you might spot.

HIKING—Over 70 miles of level trails and dikes are open to hiking. One of the most popular routes leads east from the headquarters along Townline and Berkhahn reservoirs—the large cormorant and heron rookery is visible along this trail. Hikers can continue south along Townline Reservoir and into the wooded area beyond it, or north along the river and around Berkhahn Flowage. This second path leads back to the office, making a 6.5-mile loop. The north end of this loop can also be reached from a parking area on County S along the river. Two short walks nearby follow Fisher and Teal flowages just north of the river and west of County S. Good trails follow most of the southern bank of the river to the west of County S as well. A scenic, seldom used section is between Rangeline and Smoky Hill roads.

There are also a number of trails in Mead's wooded eastern section. Two good starting points are at the end of the first gravel road north of the river off County O, and at the end of Plum Lane off County H. Both pass through forest before ending along flowages. The Plum Lane trail leads to Townline Reservoir and is connected to the path leading east from the office. A picnic area is located at the County O entrance.

PADDLING—Boat launches for the Little Eau Pleine River are located on County S and County O, though canoes can be launched from other roads as well. Canoeing on the river is easy, though the high banks reduce the scenery in some areas. Paddling the flowages is a good way to get up close to wildlife.

BIKING—From May 15 through August 31, bikes are allowed on the 6.5-mile loop that heads east from the headquarters and along the Townline Reservoir.

COUNTIES—Marathon, Portage, and Wood.

DIRECTIONS—Twelve miles east of Marshfield on County H then three miles north on County S.

FACILITIES—Water, toilets, boat launch, picnic area, grills, picnic shelter.

CAMPING—None.

ENTRY—Open year-round. Free.

CONTACT—George W. Mead Wildlife Area, S2148 County S, Milladore, WI 54454. Phone (715) 457-6771.

Big Eau Pleine County Park

IN FRENCH, *eau pleine* means plenty of water, and it is certainly an appropriate name. Marathon County's largest park covers a wide peninsula that juts over two miles down into the 7,000-acre Big Eau Pleine Reservoir, Marathon County's largest lake. The flowage provides water for electric power production on the Wisconsin River during periods of low flow. Less than half of the 72-mile lakeshore is developed, greatly adding to the park's scenery. While many visitors come here for boating and fishing, those looking for nothing more than natural attractions and solitude will find them on the wooded, 1,450-acre park's trails.

WILDLIFE—The extensive forest and shoreline provide a home for deer, coyote, bear, ruffed grouse, wild turkey, ducks, herons, egrets, common loon, and many songbirds.

HIKING—Eleven miles of level trail lead through the park. The main trail loops around the park for seven miles, roughly following the shoreline, though the path is in the woods, allowing only limited views of the lake. Two cut-offs across the middle of the park create three connected loops; the northern two are both 2.75 miles, while the southern is five miles long. The northern loops are the farthest away from the park's main use areas and thus are the quietest.

The easy Giant Hardwoods Nature Trail loops for three-quarters of a mile through the 105-acre Big Eau Pleine Woods State Natural Area, which was preserved to protect a stand of old-growth maple basswood forest.

DOUG ALFT

Bird-watching at Big Eau Pleine County Park.

PADDLING—Paddlers will want to avoid the middle of the flowage because of the large numbers of powerboaters, but canoeing can be quite pleasant along the park's shoreline, especially to the east and in the narrow channel leading to Freeman Creek northwest of the park.

BIKING—Off-road bikes are allowed on all the trails.

WINTER—The trails are groomed for cross-country skiing. Though most of the park road is closed during the snowy season, the parking lot across from the ranger station is kept open for skiers.

OTHER—Horseback riders may use the two northern loops, which total just over four miles.

COUNTY—Marathon.

DIRECTIONS—5.5 miles west of Mosinee on Highway 153, then 3.5 miles south on Big Eau Pleine Rd.

FACILITIES—Water, toilets, boat launch, picnic area, grills, picnic shelter, beach, playground, horseshoes.

CAMPING—Two campgrounds, 106 sites, 60 electric, open same as park, reservations accepted.

ENTRY—Open May 1 to October 31, trailhead parking area open year-round. Free.

ON THE WEB—www.co.marathon.wi.us/parks.asp

CONTACT—Wausau and Marathon County Parks, Recreation, and Forestry Dept., 212 River Dr., Suite 2, Wausau, WI 54403. Phone (715) 261-1550.

Rib Mountain State Park

A HISTORICAL MARKER set in the rock atop Rib Mountain proclaims this as the "highest known point in the state." In fact, that honor belongs to Timm's Hill (p. 39) in nearby Price County, which is 1,951.5 feet above sea level. Rib Mountain is 11 and a half feet lower and actually ranks third, but this distinction makes little difference to visitors who enjoy the distant views and cooler temperatures at the top. The long, narrow mound, geologically known as a monadnock, is comprised of quartzite—believed to be 1.7 billion years old—that erodes at a much slower rate than the land around it. Numerous bluffs and rock outcroppings jutting out of the forest floor make the mound extremely beautiful up close.

Reaching 650 feet above the surrounding land and 780 feet above the nearby Wisconsin River, Rib Mountain has been a prominent landmark for centuries. In fact, the name Wausau (the city lies just to the east) is derived from a Native American word for "place from which you can see far." The park opened in 1929 after local residents, recognizing the value of the area, purchased 160 acres and donated it to the state. The park now covers nearly 1,200 acres. Most of Marathon County can be seen from atop the 60-foot observation tower, and those who can not make it up the tower can use the wheelchair-accessible observation decks located on each side of the "mountain." The large, black rectangular structures seen in the distance are sheets of a porous material that provides shade for growing ginseng. Over 90 percent of the ginseng grown in the entire United States comes from Marathon County, and much of this is exported to the Far East where it is considered superior to that which is locally grown.

WILDLIFE—Large numbers of turkey vultures soar along the mound; also look for hawks and an occasional bald eagle. Deer and woodchucks are commonly seen on the ski slopes, while fox and coyote might also be spotted in the park.

HIKING—Five trails totaling over seven miles lead through the park. The Red, Blue, Green, and Gray trails all wind around the top of Rib Mountain, each featuring several overlooks. These narrow trails can be rough, but the rocky terrain makes them strikingly scenic, particularly the 1.4-mile Red Trail, arguably the best path in the park. The 0.4-mile Green and 0.9-mile Blue trails are shorter and not as steep, but no less scenic—they can be more crowded, though. The Green Trail provides a bypass to the steep south side of Red trail, which drops partway down the hill. A number of short paths connect these three trails, allowing for easy rambling and climbing amongst the rocks. Some sections of the Green and Blue trails have steps and an asphalt surface to make them a little smoother.

The 1.6-mile Gray Trail travels a bit further around the top of the hill. East of the observation tower, it leads past the ski hill to the campground and is convenient if you are staying there, but overall this part is not very interesting. The four-mile Yellow Trail leads through the rock-strewn forest on the south slope and has many long and steep hills. While not as spectacular as the other trails, it is still a beautiful hike. Four separate inner loops allow shorter routes.

WINTER—The park's downhill ski area has the longest vertical ski drop in Wisconsin (and the second longest in the Midwest). The Yellow Trail is popular with snowshoers.

COUNTY—Marathon.

DIRECTIONS—A quarter mile south of the Wausau city limits on County N, then one mile west on Park Rd.

FACILITIES—Water, toilets, nature programs, picnic area, grills, picnic shelter, playground, horseshoes.

CAMPING—30 sites, two electric, one walk-in, open April through October, reservations accepted, showers.

ENTRY—Open year-round. State park sticker or daily fee required, fee for downhill skiing.

ON THE WEB—www.wiparks.net

CONTACT—Rib Mountain State Park, 4200 Park Rd., Wausau, WI 54401. Phone (715) 842-2522.

Dells of the Eau Claire
County Park

The dells, a beautiful, rugged gorge carved by the Eau Claire River, lie at the heart of this 194-acre park. As the river enters the gorge, it drops over a stretch of exposed bedrock, forming several small waterfalls and islands, and then continues in a fit of whitewater bounded by tall vertical cliffs. Many thousands of visitors come to this popular park each year to climb on or just view these rocks, though few hike the trails away from the river.

The ancient rock, known as Eau Claire River Mylonite, was formed two billion years ago by lava flowing to the earth's crust, and over that time the rock tilted to its present near-vertical position. The dells were formed largely by the rushing meltwater of the last glacier, which stopped its advance just to the east of the park. The river, which drops 65 feet in just a mile and a half here, continues to carve the exposed rocks, though to a much lesser degree. The great force of the glacial river formed several potholes in the dells. These round depressions were created by sand and rock caught in a strong cylindrical water flow.

The dells and the forest to the south of it are part of the 40-acre Dells of the Eau Claire State Natural Area, which in addition to the unique rock formations contains several rare plants that are more commonly found further north in Canada. Because the bedrock remains close to the surface, rocks jut out of the moist forest floor and water commonly pools after rains, making this area very scenic. This pocket of forest alone makes the park worth a visit.

WILDLIFE—Deer, fox, coyote, porcupine, ducks, herons, and ruffed grouse are all common in the park, and you might just see a bald eagle or osprey soar overhead, or a bear lumber through the forest.

HIKING—About five miles of trails wind along the river and through the adjacent forest. The two most popular trails in the park follow the river, passing the dells along the way. Both are about half a mile long and rough in spots because of the many rocks, but overall not difficult. The River Trail hugs the south side of the river, while the Bluff Trail follows the north side, passing along the top of the highest cliffs. These trails connect at the west end of the park at High Bridge and also across County Y where a small dam can be crossed to complete a loop.

The forest in the natural area is actually almost as interesting as the dells. The narrow, mile-long Forest Preserve Trail circles the area from High Bridge to the parking lot south of the river and continues across County Y to the dam. The 0.75-mile Story of the Soil Trail connects the picnic area, High Bridge, and a shelter at the southwest corner of the Forest Preserve Trail. There are many hills along these two trails, but few are steep, and, like the trails along the river, exposed rocks can make them a bit rough in places.

The level, half-mile Hardwood Trail north of the river does not offer spectacular scenery, but it is still a nice walk, especially in the spring when wildflowers blanket the ground.

The Eau Claire Dells Segment of the Ice Age Trail (p. 1) passes through the park, exiting at the southwest corner—currently the trail does not continue north from the park. Just south of the large island, about half a mile beyond the park, the trail crosses the 45th parallel exactly halfway between the North Pole and the Equator.

COUNTY—Marathon.

DIRECTIONS—15 miles east of Wausau on County Z, then 1.5 miles north on County Y.

FACILITIES—Water, toilets, picnic area, grills, picnic shelter, beach, playground, horseshoes.

CAMPING—26 sites, 16 electric, open same as park, reservations accepted, group camp.

Dalles of the Eau Claire River.

ENTRY—Open May 1 to October 31. Free.

ON THE WEB—www.co.marathon.wi.us/parks.asp

CONTACT—Wausau and Marathon County Parks, Recreation, and Forestry Dept., 212 River Dr., Suite 2, Wausau, WI 54403. Phone (715) 261-1550.

Bitzke Bird Walk

THIS LOCALLY POPULAR trail winds through the Bitzke Wildlife Refuge in the northern unit of the 9,115-acre Harrison-Hewitt County Forest. Most of the 280-acre refuge consists of marsh and open water flowages, though scattered woodland and grassland areas create a wide variety of habitats for birds and birders. Constructed in 1992, the trail through the refuge was a cooperative project between the Marathon County Forestry Department, the state Department of Natural Resources, and several local conservation organizations. Hunting is not allowed here, so you can hike year-round.

WILDLIFE—Ducks, herons, sandhill crane, ruffed and sharp-tailed grouse, hawks, and spotted sandpiper are among the numerous birds that can be seen here. A resident flock of giant Canada geese (the largest subspecies) was established in 1987. Beaver, otter, mink, deer, coyote, and bear also live here and in the surrounding forest.

HIKING—The level, 1.9-mile trail passes right through the wetlands, but since it follows dikes most of the way, your feet will stay dry. Walking slowly and stopping often to observe the flora and fauna is the ideal way to visit

Bitzke. Several benches allow for quiet viewing. At the far end of the trail, an observation tower and a boardwalk with a wetland observation deck provide excellent viewing spots. Interpretive signs along the trail provide information about the wildlife found here. The trail can be extended half a mile by following the two mowed dikes that branch off from it. One is near the trailhead and the other is just past the observation tower. You can also shorten your hike to about three quarters of a mile by skipping the second loop of the main trail, but this bypasses the most scenic and interesting parts of the refuge.

AUTO TOUR—A "Watchable Wildlife Auto Trail" starts at the parking lot. It leads past farm fields where sandhill cranes may be seen from late March to September; deer and geese are common, as well. Small wooden signs mark the 2.8-mile route.

COUNTY—Marathon.

DIRECTIONS—1.5 miles south of Antigo on Highway 45, then 11 miles west on County G.

FACILITIES—Toilets.

CAMPING—Camping is allowed in the surrounding county forest with a permit.

ENTRY—Open year-round. Free.

CONTACT—Wausau and Marathon County Parks, Recreation, and Forestry Dept., 212 River Dr., Suite 2, Wausau, WI 54403. Phone (715) 261-1550.

Council Grounds State Park

COUNCIL GROUNDS, situated on the Wisconsin River just upstream from the city of Merrill, is a popular gathering place today, just as it was hundreds of years ago. Until the area was logged in the late 1800s, the Ojibwe annually traveled here by canoe from across the region for councils and celebrations, hence the name. This was a Merrill City Park until its 278 acres were donated to the state in 1938, but it was another 40 years before it officially became a state park. Today it encompasses 508 acres and plans call for increasing its size. The park features three miles of river frontage, including access to Lake Alexander, created by the Alexander Hydroelectric Dam, south of the park's beach.

During northern Wisconsin's logging era, this was the home of the Merrill Boom Company which gathered and sorted the logs floated downriver and then sent them on to sawmills in Merrill. Reminders of this era can be found near the park. Log pilings from the boom company still stand on the shore, and occasionally century-old branded logs float to the surface.

WILDLIFE—Because of Council Grounds' location near Merrill and its relatively small size, it is not the best place in the North Woods to view wildlife, except for deer which are especially tame here. Other species that might be spotted in the park are fox, badger, the occasional black bear, great blue heron, geese, ducks, and many songbirds such as Eastern wood pewee, red-breasted nuthatch, Blackburnian and pine warblers, and scarlet tanager. Bald eagle and osprey both nest in the area.

HIKING—The park has three level hiking trails totaling about four miles. The longest of these is the two-mile River Run Trail which has several different wooded paths. The eastern end of this trail leads along the 21-acre Krueger Pines State Natural Area. These old-growth white pines were planted just after the area was logged in 1881, and the largest reach 125-feet tall with a three-foot-plus diameter. The 0.75-mile Big Pines Nature Trail also passes several large white pines as it loops through the forest. Bridges span the wettest parts and interpretive panels along the trail discuss the forest community. The mile-long Fitness Trail loops through pine plantations and is of little interest naturally, though it is the place to be if you want a workout.

PADDLING—Canoeists can paddle on the Wisconsin River. Below the Alexander Dam (passable by a marked portage) the river eventually flows into Merrill, but there are several miles of wooded banks between the park and the city, making it a fairly scenic trip. There are some small rapids below the dam, but the river is generally calm. Lake Alexander provides easy canoeing, but can have heavy motorboat traffic, especially on weekends.

BIKING—Bikes are allowed on most of the River Run Trail and the Fitness Trail, 2.5 miles total.

WINTER—Most of the hiking trails, plus some additional trails, are groomed for cross-country skiing, five miles total. There is a warming shelter.

COUNTY—Lincoln.

DIRECTIONS—One mile west of Merrill on Highway 107, then half a mile south on Council Grounds Drive.

FACILITIES—Water, toilets, boat launch, nature programs, picnic area, grills, picnic shelter, beach, playground, fitness course.

CAMPING—55 sites, 19 electric, open May 1 to late October, reservations accepted, showers.

ENTRY—Open year-round. State park sticker or daily fee required.

ON THE WEB—www.wiparks.net

CONTACT—Council Grounds State Park, N1895 Council Grounds Dr., Merrill, WI 54452. Phone (715) 536-8773.

Willow Flowage
Scenic Waters Area

A VISIT TO ANY of Wisconsin's three Scenic Waters Areas can be a special trip, but the newest comes closest to serving up true wilderness, and, as regional promoters like to say, no other place in Wisconsin comes as close to offering a Canadian wilderness experience. The remote lake, Wisconsin's 16th largest, sprawls over 6,400 acres and encompasses 93 miles of undeveloped shoreline and 117 islands. There is endless beauty and bounteous wildlife by day, but a night under the stars—quite possibly more than you have ever seen before—might just be the best part of a Willow Flowage trip.

The Wisconsin Valley Improvement Company (WVIC) built the 35-foot tall Willow Dam in 1926 at the confluence of the Tomahawk, Squirrel, and Willow rivers. It serves as a storage reservoir, guaranteeing a steady flow of water to their hydroelectric dams down on the Wisconsin River. Soon after the reservoir filled, the WVIC sold the surrounding land to paper companies, but the property came with deed restrictions prohibiting buildings. This kept development off all but 3.5 miles of shoreline, and just about all of that developed land, consisting of four resorts and about 20 homes, is in the southeast near the dam. Buildings are not the only things in short supply; only a handful of roads, none heavily traveled, skirt the edge of the Willow. In the late 1990s the state stepped in to make the Willow's present situation permanent. They purchased over 16,000 acres plus a 100-foot wide scenic easement along ten miles of shore on the far western end where the land remains in private hands. Three quarters of the state-owned land is upland forest—primarily aspen, red and white pine, and red maple—while the swamps, bogs, and other watery lowlands comprising the rest account for the tea-colored water.

While many come for the beauty and solitude, the self-sustaining fishery is actually the top draw. Walleye are the favorite catch, though northern pike, muskie, large and smallmouth bass, and panfish are all prevalent. If you are heading out to land a lunker, be sure to heed the springtime fish refuges where the Tomahawk and Willow rivers enter the lake.

WILDLIFE—Boaters often sight otters swimming along the lakeshore in the early morning hours, while most days close with the maniacal cry of the common loon. Bald eagle sightings are also very common, and the number of nests ringing the shore is currently nine and rising. A similar number of osprey nest here, too, though it appears they are being forced out by the growing number of eagles. Other frequent bird sightings include spotted sandpiper, which frequently dart along the shore, and great blue herons which are seen all over, but are most common on the flowage's north end where there is a large rookery.

Few ducks and Canada geese nest on the flowage, though waterfowl of all sorts are here in large numbers during the spring and fall migrations.

Many more of the flowage's 180 resident and migrant bird species can be seen in the surrounding forests. Northern goshawk, ruffed and spruce grouse, gray jay, boreal chickadee, alder flycatcher, and veery are all typical, while lucky birders just might add a merlin to their life lists. The surrounding forest is an important habitat for Neotropical migrant songbirds; Connecticut, Blackburnian, and black-throated blue are some of the many warblers that nest here.

Although there is almost no chance of seeing one, you might just hear the howl of a wolf. Two packs roam around the flowage, one to the south and another to the north. The best chance of seeing one is along the shore during the winter months. Deer, bear, bobcat, red fox, coyote, fisher, porcupine, beaver, and the odd star-nosed mole are some other resident mammals.

HIKING—Currently there are two designated, though as of yet unnamed, trails through the aspen, pine, and swamp conifer forest surrounding the flowage. Trail options will very likely be expanded in the near future; check with the office for the latest developments. Starting at the small, unmarked parking lot just east of the boat launch is the fairly easy nature trail. During the two-mile round-trip, you will pass a pair of island-studded bays and a large bog. A couple of other paths branch off the main route for additional lake views. Interpretive panels will be added to the trail in the near future.

Despite what you would expect from the first few hundred yards, the hiking trail is a decent destination, and it is only going to get better. The doublewide trail follows 4.5 miles of old logging road through a three-square mile Native Community Management Area, where foresters are working to revive the native white and red pine forest; it also protects many tamarack bogs. Currently, the trail passes near the Willow in a few places, though it does not lead right up to it; however, it is not tough to cut through the forest for some lakeside scenery. Also, half a dozen other paths branch off the back loop all eventually reaching the lakeshore; some narrow paths leading up to and along the lake are among the earliest possibilities for new trail. Though long, the marked trail is virtually level and an easy hike overall.

While none are currently marked or even shown on the free Willow Flowage map, other old logging roads elsewhere around the flowage can also be hiked— the DNR office can make suggestions, and many are shown in DeLorme Publishing's *Wisconsin Atlas and Gazetteer*. For some real off-the-beaten-track hiking, head out to Indian Point, the large peninsula along the Willow's south shore. The peninsula hosts another Native Community Management Area and several of the campsites can be reached by foot. This route, as do all others in the south, starts out at the end of Iron Gate Road, a 2.5-mile service drive closed to vehicles. From the road's end it is another 5.5 miles to the tip of the point, and the path leading out to it is probably the best wildlife watching destination on the property.

PADDLING—The hiking here is pretty good, but the Willow is all about getting out on the water. Despite its large size and top quality fishing spots, paddlers will almost always find solitude and serenity. Wisconsin's general fishing season opener the first weekend of May is by far the Willow's busiest time. Summer holiday weekends also attract good numbers of visitors, but there has never been a night when all campsites have been occupied. Plus, due to the countless submerged rocks, stumps, and snags—made all the more hazardous by the dark water and fluctuating lake levels—boaters have little choice but to keep speeds slow across most of the flowage. As lake levels drop, which they tend to do as the summer rolls on, boat traffic diminishes, and in dry years the lake can be three or four feet below peak by the start of summer and drop to more than ten feet below by the fall.

Regardless of conditions, most paddlers stick to the southeast section of the flowage, which gets the most boat traffic. It is no less scenic and just might be more peaceful to head out and explore the rest of the lake. There is a pair of boat launches by the dam in the southeast, another pair over on the west side, and one more up at the Cedar Falls Campground (it is private so there is a small launching fee) on the north end. The *Fishing Hot Spots* map is the most highly recommended chart available.

Locals in the know also recommend the five-mile trip through the old-growth red and white pines of the 1,040-acre Tomahawk River Pines State Natural Area, just upstream of the flowage. The most popular put-in is at Camp 9 Road, though some go a few miles further north to Blue Lake Road. It is carefree paddling as long as you remember to take out at Cedar Falls Road to avoid the namesake drop. The Tomahawk serves up more beautiful scenery below the dam, too.

BIKING—Currently, mountain bikers can follow the hiking trail. Though unlikely, this situation could change, so it would be best to check with the DNR office before heading out there to ride. The old logging roads branching off the Iron Gate Road are also open to bikes.

WINTER—Though not groomed, the trails make great ski paths, while the rest of the surrounding forest is prime territory for some deep exploration by snowshoers—be sure to bring a compass.

OTHER—If your time or energy is limited, you can still get a good look at the beauty of the Willow with Wilderness Cruises (715) 453-3310 or (800) 472-1516. Their 76-foot *Wilderness Queen* tour boat runs late May through early October from near the dam. The sightseeing cruises run in the middle of day and early afternoon—not prime wildlife viewing times—so you might want to consider a sunset dinner cruise. Either way, reservations are recommended.

To the astonishment of most, the permissible use of ATVs on the lands around the Willow was expanded by the DNR when the state took over, though motorized riders did not get nearly as much access as they had hoped for and are still limited to a small portion of the property. Their non-winter use is limited to an existing trail in the southwest corner, and though they once routinely flouted the rules and ran roughshod all over the trails and even the shoreline, a step-up in DNR patrols and some self-policing by responsible riders has largely ended the transgressions.

COUNTY—Oneida.

DIRECTIONS—The hiking trail is eight miles southwest of Hazelhurst on Cedar Falls Rd. The Willow Dam, nature trail, and Wilderness Cruises are another two miles south on Cedar Falls Road and then about a mile west on Willow Dam Road.

FACILITIES—Boat launches. The toilets, picnic areas, and grills at the island campsites may be used during the day.

CAMPING—30 single-unit campsites and five group (up to 15 people) campsites are scattered across the flowage; all are free, first-come, first-served, and have a fire ring, a picnic table, and latrine. Some sites can be reached by foot: one is just a short walk in on the nature trail, while a few others can be accessed via the hiking trails. Get directions for the latter from the office since they are well off the marked trail. The private Cedar Falls Campground, 6051 Cedar Falls Rd., (715) 356-4953, at the north end has 42 RV sites and tent campers are allowed.

ENTRY—Open year-round. Free.

CONTACT—DNR, Woodruff Service Center, 8770 County J, Woodruff, WI 54568. Phone (715) 356-5211. Wilderness Cruises, 4973 Willow Dam Rd., Hazelhurst, WI 54531. Phone (715) 453-3310 and (800) 472-1516.

Northern Highland-American
Legion State Forest

WHEN THE GLACIERS retreated from what would become Vilas and Oneida counties, some 10,000 years ago, they left behind one of the world's densest concentrations of lakes, and the Northern Highland-American Legion State Forest encompasses 930 of them. Although 40,000 acres were set aside way back in 1904, the adjacent Northern Highland and American Legion state forests were officially established in 1925 and 1929, respectively, to protect the streamflow at the headwaters of the Wisconsin, Flambeau, and Manitowish rivers. Management efforts were combined in 1968, though by statute they remain separate forests; the American Legion State Forest lies in Oneida County while the Northern Highland is in Vilas and Iron counties. Today the combined state forest spreads out over nearly 224,000 acres, the largest property in state ownership and almost two and a half times larger than the next largest, the Flambeau River State Forest.

The Manitowish River Wilderness Area in the west end of the forest covers 5,460 acres. There are also three designated Wild Areas (Frank Lake, Indian Creek, and Partridge Lake) covering 27,900 acres. These are managed for scenic values, but are not as well protected as actual Wilderness Areas, and some logging is allowed. Sixty of the lakes have been given official Wilderness and Wild protection.

WILDLIFE—Sightings of bald eagle, osprey, and common loon are anything but rare in the forest. Vilas and Oneida counties have one of the largest concentrations of these splendid birds in Wisconsin; 65 percent of all bald eagles in the state and 70 percent of the common loons live in these two counties. The Rainbow Flowage on the Wisconsin River, northeast of Lake Tomahawk in Oneida County, is a great place to look for them, though they can be seen just about anywhere. Some of the other nearly 250 species that can be seen here throughout the course of the year include great blue heron, ruffed and spruce grouse, red-shouldered and Cooper's hawks, northern goshawk, pine siskin, evening grosbeak, red crossbill, hermit thrush, yellow-bellied flycatcher, and Connecticut, Canada, Pine, and black-throated blue warblers.

Mammals of the forest include otter, beaver, mink, porcupine, fisher, fox, coyote, bear, deer, moose, bobcat, mountain lion, pine marten, and timber wolf, though you would have to be extremely lucky to see any of the last five forest dwellers.

HIKING—There are close to 75 miles of dedicated hiking trails in the forest—not to mention hundreds of miles of snowmobile trails and forest access roads open to foot travel—and many of them are excellent. Unless noted otherwise, the trails below are located in Vilas County.

Each of the short nature trails is very scenic, especially the Fallison Lake Nature Trail, 4.5 miles west of Sayner on County N across from the Crystal Lake Campground. This hilly trail leads around the lake through a mixed coniferous-deciduous forest and passes several tamarack bogs along the way. A boardwalk crosses a bog at the far end. Three different interpretive brochures about flora, fauna, and history are available at the trailhead and this is a good place to see bald eagle, osprey, and loons. The main path around the lake is two-and-a-half miles long with additional half-mile loops around the bogs at the north and east ends.

The mostly flat Star Lake Nature Trail, on County K right at the village of Star Lake, loops along a narrow peninsula on its namesake lake—do not miss the short boardwalk at the south end that leads to scenic Black Lagoon; it is one of several bogwalks along the 2.5-mile route. The trail starts out through the Star Lake Forestry Plantation, a 23-acre experimental forestry management area. The trees were sown in 1913 to show that forest trees could be planted, and this spelled the beginning of reforestation in northern Wisconsin. A one-mile loop with interpretive panels discussing the forest offers a shortcut to the main trail.

The mile-long North Trout Nature Trail, three miles south of Boulder Junction on County M, right next to the North Trout Lake Campground, is the easiest trail in the forest and an excellent spring wildflower destination. The mostly level trail loops around a spruce-tamarack bog with two boardwalks crossing through it. The west end leads along a high bank above Trout Lake. Interpretive panels discuss the numerous forest types found along the trail.

The Raven Trail is a hilly eight-mile hiking trail with a 1.5-mile nature trail along one of its many loops. A boardwalk crosses a bog on the east side of the nature trail loop—this is a good place to spot insectivorous plants like sundew and pitcher plant—and passes scenic Hemlock Lake at the north end. Interpretive panels discuss the plants, animals, and history of the forest. The Raven's outer loop is 4.5 miles, but there are numerous inner loops and cut-offs offering a variety of hiking options. The narrow hiking-only section between Inkpot and Clear lakes (known as the Bucktrack Trail, though for some reason few maps identify it by name) is especially scenic. The trailhead is two miles south of the Woodruff forest office on Woodruff Road in Oneida County.

The hilly 11-mile Escanaba Trail, which begins 3.5 miles east of County M on Nebish Road near Boulder Junction, is arguably the most scenic hiking option in the forest. The outer loop past all five lakes is 8.5 miles, though shorter options leading around or alongside just some of the lakes are available, including a fairly easy two-mile loop between Pallette and Escanaba lakes. A 1.5-mile path connects the Escanaba Trail with the Lumberjack Trail (see below). The four lakes encircled by the Escanaba Trail are part of Northern Highland Fishery Research Area, the only detailed research area of its kind in the nation. Fishing on the lakes is allowed only with a permit, available free at the Escanaba Lake Research Station at the trailhead.

The 10-mile McNaughton Trail in Oneida County is generally level, with only a few gently rolling hills. The five-mile loop around McNaughton Lake at the back end is the most scenic section, though the entire trail is quite nice. The trailhead is 13 miles south of Woodruff on Highway 47, then a quarter mile west on Kildare Road.

While the trails detailed above are all highly recommended, the following five are less interesting due to recent logging along much of their routes. Despite this, each still has at least something to make it worth at least considering.

The first mile of the somewhat hilly Lumberjack Trail is very worthwhile. The trail leads to a bridge over White Sand Creek that offers great views of the surrounding wetlands and, quite likely, some wildlife. This trailhead is one mile southeast of Boulder Junction on Old K Road at Concora Road. The trail can also be picked up at its eastern end along County K. There has been recent logging on about half of the trail's 12.5 miles.

The best hiking along the hilly, seven-mile Shannon Trail is at the south end on a two-mile loop around the namesake lake. This loop may be directly accessed at the end of Found Lake Road, three miles north of St. Germain. Another trailhead is off County G farther to the north.

The southern end of the 9.5-mile Madeline Trail has some giant pines, making this section somewhat scenic. The trail is mostly level, though there are a few rolling hills. The trail begins two miles north on Rudolph Road to the northwest of the Woodruff forest office.

The first two loops, each about 1.25 miles, of the 8.5-mile Powell Trail are largely through older forest and provide nice walking. Powell Springs Lake in the middle of the trail is also a scenic destination. The back part of the trail is a ruffed grouse management area and will be of little interest to most. The mostly level trail is in Iron County, four miles south of Manitowish on Highway 47, then half a mile east on Powell Road.

Though not designated hiking trails, there are two other good places to hike in Iron County. The Powell Marsh Wildlife Area is a 4,096-acre expanse of wetlands with many dikes crossing through the open marsh. The best access is from the overlook on Powell Road, east of the Powell Trail. The 192-acre Frog Lake and Pines State Natural Area, one of many natural areas in the forest, is one mile south of Manitowish off Highway 47/182; a sign clearly marks the spot. A level access road leads for half a mile through old-growth forest and then continues beyond the natural area. A few hundred yards into the natural area, a short path turns south to the undeveloped shore of Frog Lake.

PADDLING—Paddlers have their pick of hundreds of lakes, many with canoe-in campsites along their shores. Ask staff at either of the offices to direct you to the some of the 19 Wilderness Lakes and 41 Wild Lakes, all of which have protected shorelines and are reserved for non-motorized recreation.

There are also canoe campsites along the Manitowish River which flows for 44 miles through the forest from its headwaters at Fishtrap and High lakes, before emptying into the Turtle-Flambeau Flowage (p. 37). It is an easy, slow-moving river that is fun for a few hours or a few days.

Another good paddling option is to start at White Sand Lake on County K, southeast of Boulder Junction, and follow the maintained portages to Lost Canoe and Pallette lakes, then take Stephenson Creek to Trout Lake (the forest's largest lake at 4,000 acres), and follow the Trout River through several smaller lakes, eventually joining the Manitowish River, a 19-mile trip. Some paddlers shorten the trip by starting at Trout Lake, thus avoiding the portages.

The Wisconsin River passes through the southern end of the forest in Oneida County and is also an easy trip. The Rainbow Flowage, a reservoir on the Wisconsin, is a prime wildlife viewing spot.

BIKING—Off-road bikes are allowed on all park trails and roads with the exception of the nature trails. The McNaughton, Madeline, Shannon, and Lumberjack trails are the most popular. Also, a paved trail hugs County N and County M for 13.5 miles between the Crystal Lake Campground to the town of Boulder Junction, though it primarily offers convenience rather than scenery.

WINTER—The Escanaba, McNaughton, Raven, Madeline, and Shannon trails offer more than 40 miles of expertly groomed cross-country ski trails. Skate skiing is available on the five-mile loop around the lake on the Mc-Naughton Trail. The Powell and Lumberjack trails are cleared for skiing, but not groomed, though they are both popular, so you might find a decent track along them. Shelters with fire rings are found in the middle of each of the groomed trails except the Shannon.

Parking lots at the trailheads of the Lumberjack, Powell, Fallison, North Trout, and Star Lake trails are kept clear for snowshoers.

There are about 400 miles of snowmobile trails across the forest.

AUTO TOUR—County K between Boulder Junction and Star Lake is officially Rustic Road #60 and is a very scenic drive.

OTHER—The Arthur A. Oehmcke Fish Hatchery, located across from the Woodruff forest office, is one of the largest muskie producers in the world and is open to the public year-round. Guided tours are offered from Memorial Day to Labor Day.

COUNTIES—Vilas, Oneida, and Iron.

DIRECTIONS—Forest offices are located six miles south of Boulder Junction on County M and two miles east of Woodruff on County J.

FACILITIES—Water, toilets, boat launch, nature center, nature programs, picnic area, grills, picnic shelter, beach.

CAMPING—18 campgrounds, 871 sites, 75 walk-in sites, 13 wilderness sites, 118 canoe campsites (free, one night limit), open year-round, reservations accepted, showers, group camp, backpacking permitted throughout forest with free permit.

ENTRY—Open year-round. State park sticker or daily fee required. State trail pass required for off-road biking on the Lumberjack, Madeline, and Mc-Naughton trails and also for cross-country skiing on all groomed trails.

ON THE WEB—www.wiparks.net

CONTACT—Northern Highland-American Legion State Forest, 8770 County J, Woodruff, WI 54568. Phone (715) 356-5211.

Catherine Wolter
Wilderness Area

THE LARGEST SINGLE acquisition ever by the Nature Conservancy's Wisconsin Chapter is a true gem. This 2,189-acre block of northern hardwoods-hemlock forest surrounds 15 unspoiled lakes and ponds and offers a wonderful wilderness getaway far away from the crowds. Besides the beauty and solitude, the property also serves as a vital link and wildlife travel corridor between the Northern Highland-American Legion State Forest (p. 126) to the south and the million-acre Ottawa National Forest in Michigan's Upper Peninsula.

As the proliferation of vacation homes continues to spoil Wisconsin's North Woods this vast preserve at the heart of the Border Lakes region is an increasingly rare commodity, and that is exactly why Catherine Wolter sold it to The Nature Conservancy instead of taking a bigger check from developers. Thanks to these partners, nearly seven miles of undeveloped shoreline is off the real estate market forever. The Wolters acquired their property in 1942 and they limited fishing, development, motor vehicles, and logging. Though some areas fell to the saw to help pay the property taxes, as stewards of the land they were well ahead of their time and all the components of natural forests remain intact.

WILDLIFE—Most mammals associated with the North Woods can be found here, including otter, beaver, pine marten, fisher, porcupine, deer, bear, and timber wolf. There are also occasional visits from moose, bobcat, and lynx. Common birds include ruffed grouse, sharp-shinned hawk, bald eagle, osprey, and common loon. It is also a vital haven for Neotropical migrant songbirds such as magnolia, Blackburnian, black-throated blue, and golden-winged warblers, all of which are in serious decline because of forest fragmentation.

The preserve's most remarkable animals are its fish. The Wolter family and their friends were the only anglers on the property since the mid-20th century, and unlike practically every Wisconsin lake, these waters have had only limited fish stocking. The bass and panfish in these natural aquatic

131

communities have evolved with little human interference and are shorter and skinnier, due to the increased competition required for survival. As global reference lakes, these offer a baseline for future studies. For the time being, catch-and-release fishing with artificial bait is allowed only on Lower Aimer, Knife, and Bug lakes.

HIKING—An 18-mile web of trails following old access roads and fire breaks winds around the lakes. They offer some very scenic routes, frequently passing within sight of the lakes and leading right up to their shores in several places. There are few hills, and none is very steep or long, so hiking is easy, though your feet might get a bit wet at spots, particularly near Upper Aimer Lake. If you have got the time, it would be worth exploring every last mile of trail, though a logical route is what amounts to an outer loop. It passes seven of the largest lakes, a pair of bogs, and covers about seven miles—add the spur along Battine Lake if you have got the time. The shortest possible loop passes three lakes and is about 3.5 miles long. A box with maps is posted at the entrance, though even with a map it is possible to get twisted around, so bring a compass.

PADDLING—You can carry in any non-motorized boat, although because of the distances involved few people do so. The nearest landing is on the southeast shore of Knife Lake, well over a mile from the parking area.

WINTER—Though not groomed, the trails are open to cross-country skiing, and if you are the adventurous sort—and competent in outdoor skills—this would be an excellent place to explore on snowshoes.

COUNTY—Vilas.

DIRECTIONS—The entrance is three miles southeast of Presque Isle on County B, then half a mile north on East Bay Road.

FACILITIES—None.

CAMPING—None.

ENTRY—Open year-round. Free.

ON THE WEB—http://nature.org/wisconsin

CONTACT—The Nature Conservancy. Phone (608) 251-8140. E-mail: wmail@tnc.org

Chequamegon-Nicolet
National Forest

THE NICOLET SIDE of Wisconsin's only national forest is named for Jean Nicolet, who in 1634 was the first European to reach Wisconsin. The federal government purchased the first forestlands in 1928, about the

time the last of Wisconsin's vast North Woods forests were cut down. The national forest was officially established in 1933, and initially included what is now the Chequamegon side before the pair was separated later that year. To save money, the forests were administratively rejoined in 1998, though most people still think of the two individually, and for convenience sake they are discussed separately in this book.

More than 1,200 glacial lakes are scattered across the 661,000-acre forest. Three blocks of land in the northern part of the forest totaling over 30,000 acres are designated as wilderness. The 18,188-acre Headwaters Wilderness Area is by far the largest wilderness area in the state, and features some of the largest and oldest trees in the forest. The Pine River is among the many waterways originating here. The Whisker Lake Wilderness Area covers 7,428 acres. The lake was named after the large pines, called chin whiskers by "old timers," that escaped the lumberjacks saws and the fires that swept through the logged-over land. At 5,886 acres the Blackjack Springs Wilderness Area is the smallest but it is just as beautiful and peaceful as the others.

WILDLIFE—The forest is a great place to see wildlife, especially birds—the American Bird Conservancy has even named it a Globally Important Bird Area. Common loon, wood duck, spotted sandpiper, sandhill crane, osprey, northern harrier, red-shouldered hawk, black-backed woodpecker, ruffed grouse, gray jay, Blackburnian and pine warblers, alder flycatcher, red-breasted nuthatch, white-throated sparrow, and boreal chickadee are representative of the 220-plus species recorded here. Mammalian residents include deer, coyote, fox, pine marten, fisher, porcupine, bear, bobcat, and timber wolf.

Naturally, there are countless good places in the Nicolet to view wildlife, but the forest has several recommended wildlife viewing spots. The 170-acre Knowles Creek Impoundment features a 0.65-mile wheelchair-accessible trail with interpretive signs and a viewing deck. This is a great site for waterfowl, shorebirds, and raptors. The trailhead is nine miles east of Wabeno on County C, in Forest County.

A short ways north of Knowles Creek is the Halley Creek Bird Trail. Constructed in cooperation with the Northeastern Wisconsin Audubon Society specifically for bird-watchers, the level one-mile loop crosses four separate habitats, from grasslands to mature northern forest. A guide brochure is available at the trailhead, which is 5.5 miles southeast of Laona on County H, then five miles east on Forest Road 2136.

In the far north of Forest County, just to the southeast of Alvin along Highway 70, is the West Allen Creek Watchable Wildlife Area. The shallow, 90-acre impoundment is a waterfowl mecca, especially during the fall migration. A wheelchair-accessible observation deck with interpretive signs offers excellent viewing.

The Cathedral Pines, a 20-acre stand of old-growth white pine and hemlock forest in Oconto County, is worth a visit for both the fauna and the flora. The towering trees feature a great blue heron rookery (which should be observed from a distance during the summer to avoid disturbing the nesting birds) as well as nesting eagles and warblers. You might also see a pine marten or a fisher. From Highway 32, one mile west of Lakewood, take Archibald Lake Road to Cathedral Drive. The rookery is visible from the road about one mile to the north.

Also making their watchable wildlife list are the Anvil National Recreation Trail, a good place for sighting warblers and salamanders, and the Brule River, both detailed below.

HIKING—There are over 130 miles of trails for non-motorized use in the forest, and those described here are among the most interesting and scenic. Two other short trails are described above with the Wildlife section.

The Franklin Nature Trail is probably the most popular trail in the forest, and with good reason. Along the one-mile loop are many 400-year-old white pines and hemlocks as well as a boardwalk that goes through a tamarack bog. To top it all off, bald eagles nest nearby, and the forest floor is carpeted with wildflowers in the spring. An interpretive brochure available at the trailhead discusses the life of this forest. There are only a few small hills on the trail, and a short loop at the beginning is wheelchair accessible. The trailhead is at the Franklin Lake Campground (eight miles east of Eagle River on Highway 70, then three miles south on Military Road, and five miles east on Butternut Lake Road) in Forest County, where there are interpretive programs and a nature center open during the summer. The campground buildings are on the National Register of Historic Places.

The Hidden Lakes Trail is a mostly level 13-mile loop that passes many small, undeveloped lakes and links the Franklin Nature Trail, Anvil National Recreation Trail, Nicolet North Trail, and Luna-White Deer Trail—all worthy hikes. There is no bridge over the Pine River on the east side of the trail, but the river is usually only about eight inches deep. Hidden Lakes can be accessed at several places, including the Franklin Lake Campground and a parking area on Forest Road 2008 at the southernmost point of the trail. The four-mile Luna-White Deer Trail, which starts at the Luna-White Deer Campground, has a pair of two-mile loops around undeveloped Luna and White Deer lakes, both home to nesting loons. There are only a few small hills along the gorgeous paths. The fairly hilly Nicolet North Trail is a 15-mile web of loops offering a wide variety of hiking options through the forest. The southern end along Pat Shay Lake is the most scenic destination. The trailhead is west of the Franklin Lake Campground on Forest Road 2460, just north of Butternut Lake Road.

The 12-mile Anvil National Recreation Trail, to the east of the Nicolet North Trail, features six interconnected loops, many of which are hilly, going through a northern hardwood and hemlock forest. This popular trail was constructed in the 1930s, one of the forest's first trails, and today is one of the best places in the forest to view wildlife, especially warblers. Trailheads are located at the Anvil Lake Campground, nine miles east of Eagle River on Highway 70, as well as Military Road and Forest Road 2460 to the south.

Another popular destination in Forest County is the Ed's Lake National Recreation Trail on County W, eight miles west of Wabeno in the southern part of the county. The six-mile trail has four loops with several hilly sections. A shelter overlooking Ed's Lake at the far end of the trail is a great place to relax.

Also in the southern part of Forest County, the two-mile Michigan Rapids Trail follows the Peshtigo River past many rock outcroppings to the namesake rapids, which are one mile from the trailhead. It is a moderately easy trail, though there are some rough spots and it can be a bit wet. The trail is three miles north of Laona on Highway 8, then 12 miles east on Forest Road 2131, and half a mile south on Forest Road 2134. On the way to the Michigan Rapids Trail, where Forest Road 2131 spans the Peshtigo River, you will pass the 0.7-mile Dendro-Eco Trail (AKA Peshtigo River Trail), an easy walk through a northern hardwood and hemlock forest with interpretive panels discussing the area's ecology.

In Florence County, another extensive trail complex is anchored by the Lauterman National Recreation Trail and includes the Ridge, Perch Lake, and Assessor's trails. The fairly hilly Lauterman Trail stretches nine miles with three loops. The five walk-in campsites located on Lauterman Lake are easy to reach and are popular. The northern trailhead is 12 miles west of Florence on Highway 70, then a quarter mile south on Forest Road 2154. The southern trailhead is on Forest Road 2156, just north of the Chipmunk Rapids Campground. The rolling 1.3-mile Perch Lake Trail at the north end of the Lauterman Trail loops around its namesake lake and features five wonderfully situated walk-in campsites. The Ridge and Assessor's trails are at the south end of the Lauterman Trail and may be accessed from the Chipmunk Rapids and Lost Lake campgrounds. The Ridge Trail is a hilly 3.3-mile loop passing through a wide variety of forest types and overlooking the scenic Pine River at its northern end. The Assessor's Trail is a mostly level one-mile loop through a stand of 150-year-old hemlocks. Interpretive signs discuss the natural and human history of the area, including the story of the Assessor White Pine. Part of this trail is wheelchair accessible.

Some of the forest's best long-distance views are found in Oconto County along the Chute Pond Overlook and Quartz Hill trails. Both have some steep climbs, but are absolutely worthwhile. The Chute Pond Overlook Trail is only 0.7-mile long, but has five scenic vistas; three overlooking peaceful Chute Pond. The trailhead is 3.5 miles south of Mountain on Highway 32, then a few hundred yards west on Parkway Drive. The eastern section of the Quartz Hill Trail climbs 0.6-mile to the top of McCaslin Mountain. Along the way, the trail passes a quartz crystal deposit with a sign detailing how Native Americans used it. The western section climbs 0.75-mile to the site of an old fire tower. Both halves of the trail begin on Highway 32, just a mile south of Carter.

The forest's three wilderness areas are all fantastic destinations and, as with the rest of the forest, many old roads and railroad grades remain: these can be hiked in addition to the trails detailed here. The forest offices have wilderness area maps. An 11-mile trail crosses the Whisker Lake Wilderness Area in the northeast corner of the forest. This hilly trail has several different paths winding through the area, connecting three different trailheads, each leading into the area from Forest Road 2150 (ten miles west of Florence on Highway 70) which forms the western border of this wilderness area. Because the northern two trailheads are only half a mile apart, they can be combined into a scenic loop.

A trail leads through the northern part of the Blackjack Springs Wilderness in Vilas County, northeast of Eagle River. Starting either at Forest Road 2178 to the east, or Forest Road 2523 to the west, the hilly trail goes south for four miles to Blackjack Springs. A 1.5-mile loop around Whispering Lake at the north end of the trail is a good shorter hike.

The only developed trail through the Headwaters Wilderness in Forest County is the Giant Pine Trail in the southern portion. Starting on Forest Road 2414, 1.5 miles northwest of the Scott and Shelp Lake trails described below, the two-mile trail loops through an area of old-growth hemlocks and white pines, including the 30-acre Giant Pine Grove State Natural Area. The half-mile Scott Lake Trail, right at the southwest corner of the Headwaters Wilderness, leads through an old-growth forest and bog in the 272-acre Scott Lake-Shelp Lake State Natural Area. The main branch heads south past Scott Lake, and a very short boardwalk leads north to Shelp Lake. The trailhead is five miles east of Three Lakes on Highway 32, then four miles east on Scott Lake Road.

PADDLING—The Brule, Peshtigo, Oconto, Pine, and Popple rivers all provide excellent canoeing and wonderful wildlife viewing. The Brule River offers one of the most scenic trips in the forest, and can be run throughout the season; the others have low summer water levels. The Brule runs for 30 miles along the edge of the forest (it forms the Wisconsin-Michigan border) and is an excellent option for beginners. The first 22 miles between the Brule River

Campground at Highway 55 and the Forest Road 2152 Landing offer quiet paddling, and the few rapids below the landing are just Class I. Two Foot Falls near the end can be run by experienced paddlers, though there is a portage for everyone else. The last takeout in the forest is at Forest Road 2150.

The Pine and Popple rivers, which both begin in the forest, are state-designated wild rivers featuring many Class I and II rapids. The best starting point on the Pine is on Highway 55 just below the confluence with the North Branch Pine River. This offers a 30-mile run through the forest to Goodman Grade Road. Meyer's Falls, near the end of this stretch, is a mandatory portage. A lovely 16-mile trip on the Popple begins at Highway 139 and ends at Forest Road 2159. Intermediate landings on both rivers allow shorter trips. See Pine And Popple Wild Rivers (p. 139) for more information.

Seven miles of the Peshtigo River, from the Big Joe Landing on Highway 139 (one mile north of its junction with Highway 8) to the CCC Bridge at Forest Road 2131, offer easy paddling and one of the best places in the forest to view wildlife—bald eagle and otters are common river residents. The next 10 miles to Burnt Bridge at Forest Road 2134 has some Class I and II rapids, though they are not especially daunting when the waters are not running high. Through the rest of the forest there are several Class III rapids, and this stretch should be run only by people who really know what they are doing. The last take-out in the forest is at the Burton Wells Bridge along Forest Road 2136, though most canoeists continue on for another five miles to Goodman County Park in Marinette County.

The narrow North Branch Oconto River, with many blind turns and Class III rapids, is for experts only. It can be run only during high water, and downed trees are a common hazard. A recommended 10-mile trip begins at the Tar Dam Road Bridge and ends at the Bagley Rapids Campground.

Hundreds of lakes in the forest provide quiet paddling and good wildlife viewing; ask at the forest office for some recommendations in your area. They can also inform you of current water levels on the above rivers.

BIKING—Off-road bikes are allowed on 75 miles of trails, including the Anvil, Ed's Lake, Nicolet North, and Lauterman (plus most of those that adjoin it) trails all described above, in addition to the 11-mile Nicolet Nordic and 14-mile Lakewood trails in Oconto County in the southern part of the forest.

Besides these maintained trails, bikes are allowed on any road or trail that does not run through a wilderness area and is not posted against bikes.

WINTER—Eighty-five miles of trail are groomed for cross-country skiing, including the Anvil, Lauterman (and most of those that adjoin it), Ed's Lake, and Nicolet North trails described above. Skiing is also allowed on the one-mile Phelps Trail in the far northwestern corner of the forest, and the

11-mile Nicolet Nordic, 12-mile Lakewood, 11-mile Jones Spring Area, and four-mile Maranatha trails in the far south. The very popular Anvil Trail is the easiest overall, though its Devil's Backbone Loop is the most challenging run in the entire forest. The Jones Spring Area and Lauterman trails are considered the most difficult systems overall.

The Anvil, Nicolet North, and Lakewood trails can accommodate skate skiers, and the Anvil, Lauterman, Ed's Lake, and Jones Spring Area trails have warming shelters.

There are also some 500 miles of snowmobile trails running throughout the forest.

AUTO TOUR—The Lakewood Auto Tour is a 65-mile loop starting at the Lakewood Ranger Station, where you should pick up a tour brochure. The 17 stops along the route highlight forest management and history, and encompass many scenic locales. You can climb the Mountain Fire Lookout Tower at one of them.

The 21-mile Heritage Drive National Forest Scenic Byway encompasses Military Road, constructed along a former Native American trade route to supply Fort Howard during the Civil War, and Butternut Lake Road between Highways 70 and 32, east of Eagle River. The 80-mile Eagle River Natural History Auto Tour generally follows the same route as the Heritage Drive; it starts in Eagle River and ends in Three Lakes, and brochures may be picked up at the Eagle River Ranger Station. Both drives feature many scenic and historic stops.

Rustic Road #34 follows Fisher Road, Carey Dam Road, and Lakeview Drive west of the village of Alvin. This was the first road built in the Town of Alvin. Rustic Road #74 forms a figure eight on several gravel roads between Highways 101 and 139 in the southwest corner of Florence County. At 32.5 miles, it is the state's longest Rustic Road.

OTHER—Horses are allowed on the 15-mile Nicolet North Trail (described with Hiking above), on the hilly four-mile Maranatha Trail near Lakewood, and on the easy 12-mile Bailey Lake Equestrian Trail near Three Lakes.

COUNTIES—Vilas, Oneida, Forest, Florence, Oconto, and Langlade.

DIRECTIONS—Ranger stations are located in Rhinelander, Lakewood, Laona, Florence, and Eagle River.

FACILITIES—Water, toilets, boat launch, nature center, nature programs, picnic area, grills, picnic shelter, beach.

CAMPING—25 campgrounds, 654 sites, 20 walk-in sites, 8 cabins; most campgrounds are open May through October, though you are welcome to walk or ski into them the rest of the year; reservations accepted, group camp, backpacking permitted throughout forest.

ENTRY—Open year-round. Some developed facilities are free, though most require a $3 daily or $10 annual parking permit—only the daily permits are available at the specific sites; you must purchase annual permits at Forest Service offices or area businesses.

ON THE WEB—www.fs.fed.us/r9/cnnf

CONTACT—Forest Supervisor's Office, 68 S. Stevens St., Rhinelander, WI 54501. Phone (715) 362-1300 or (715) 362-1383 (TTY).

Pine and Popple Wild Rivers

THESE TWO RIVERS in northeast Wisconsin have been officially designated as Wild Rivers by the state of Wisconsin. The DNR, along with the U.S. Forest Service and Florence County, are hard at work to protect the rivers from development and preserve their wilderness character.

Both the 89-mile Pine and 62-mile Popple, a major tributary of the Pine, originate in the swamplands of the Chequamegon-Nicolet National Forest (p. 132) in Forest County, and the state owns well over 5,000 acres along the lower stretches of the two rivers. In total, 30 miles of the Pine and 13 miles of the Popple are protected by the state. Very few buildings stand on their banks. In fact, these are among the least developed rivers in all of Wisconsin, and new development on state-owned land is limited to river access and portage trails. Easements and cooperative management agreements have been arranged to protect the rivers where lands have not yet been acquired. Management efforts are also aimed at protecting nearby lakes and the streams that flow into the rivers to maintain their exceptional water purity.

There are many waterfalls and high cliffs along the pair, including LaSalle Falls on the Pine, which drops 22 feet into a large gorge. In other places, mainly on the upper stretches, both rivers widen as they pass through wetlands, and these are especially good places to see wildlife. There is one dam on the Pine, creating the 130-acre Pine River Flowage 12 miles upstream from where it joins the Menominee River.

WILDLIFE—The undeveloped lands along the river are home to an abundance and variety of wildlife. Look for deer, bear, bobcat, fox, coyote, fisher, porcupine, beaver, otter, mink, ruffed grouse, woodcock, ducks, bald eagle, and many songbirds. Threatened and endangered species include pine marten, timber wolf, and osprey.

HIKING—There is a wonderful mile-long trail to LaSalle Falls (p. 141).

PADDLING—The state section of the Pine River (see p. 137 for canoeing details in the national forest) is a good river for beginning whitewater paddlers, since all of the large rapids, including some Class III, are easily portaged except

LaSalle Falls which takes some effort. Most people running the state portion of the Pine start at the Chipmunk Rapids Campground in the national forest. From there it is 19 miles to the Highway 101 Bridge, the last exit before LaSalle Falls, though there are several take-outs between these points, allowing shorter trips. Below the Pine River Dam, it is easy paddling all the way. The Popple throws up some of the most challenging whitewater in the region and is for experts only.

Spring is the best time for running both rivers, though the Pine below the dam can be run for most of the summer. The upper reaches of the Pine can often be run in the summer, too, but you can not count on it since water levels are apt to drop. Normal water levels on the Popple, on the other hand, are usually too low by mid-May, and only heavy rains change things. Call the Florence Natural Resources Center for water levels or other information.

COUNTIES—Florence and Forest.

DIRECTIONS—Canoes can be launched at many points along the rivers; see Paddling above for some of them.

FACILITIES—Water, toilets, boat launch, picnic area; grills are found at the Wisconsin Electric Power Company campgrounds on the Pine and at the Highway 101 wayside on the Popple.

CAMPING—Camping is available at three Wisconsin Electric Power Company recreation sites on the Pine River, two at the east end of the Pine River Flowage and one just before the river's end; camping is also available in the Chequamegon-Nicolet National Forest and county forestlands. Check with the Florence Natural Resources Center for full camping details.

Pine River pooling below LaSalle Falls.

ENTRY—Open year-round. Free.

CONTACT—Florence Natural Resources Center, Rt. 1, Box 83, Florence, WI 54121. Phone (715) 528-5377.

LaSalle Falls Trail

L aSALLE FALLS is a truly spectacular sight. While not exactly remote, it is out of the way and so does not get crowded—I have been there on gorgeous summer weekend days and had the place all to myself. After the Pine River drops 22 feet, it churns through a narrow half-mile long gorge with vertical cliffs up to a hundred feet high. The rapids actually begin above the falls, as the river narrows before making its plunge.

WILDLIFE—Wildlife abounds in the vast stretches of undeveloped land surrounding the falls. Among the animals that may be seen along the trail or the river are bear, bobcat, fox, coyote, beaver, fisher, deer, bald eagle, and a multitude of songbirds. Lucky visitors might even spot an osprey, timber wolf, or pine marten, all threatened and endangered species.

HIKING—The narrow, mile-long trail to the falls is thickly wooded, featuring large white pines on rolling hills and is a nice walk, even without the gorge and waterfall as destinations. A bridge crosses Spring Creek at about the midpoint of the trail, and just before the river where the falls become audible, the trail splits. The path to the left goes to the falls, while the path to the right almost immediately forks again with both of these paths leading to the river below the falls. No matter which path hikers choose, caution must be taken along the river as the rocks are slippery.

The path that leads to the falls is, of course, the favorite. It ends at a rock overhang leaning out over the middle of the falls, some 50 feet above the bottom. Follow the river upstream above the falls, or climb down below for more views. It is a steep climb to get below the falls, but not too difficult. The river bank here provides the best views of the falls and the sheer canyon walls.

Taking the far-right fork leads to where LaSalle Gorge ends. To the east, the Pine flows away wide and calm, while you get great views of the gorge and rapids to the west. It is possible to walk along the river's edge into the gorge, but it is not as easy as walking along the river near the falls. The middle branch of the trail ends on a ridge above the river, just to the west of the previously mentioned trail, but offers only limited views. Because the river takes a sharp turn when entering the gorge, the falls are not visible from either of these two paths.

PADDLING—The Pine is a state-designated wild river and is popular with paddlers. See Pine And Popple Wild Rivers (p. 139) for more details. For those who wish to visit the falls by water, but do not want a long trip, the nearest boat launch is just two miles below it on the Pine River Flowage; take Power Dam Road west of County N and paddle upstream.

COUNTY—Florence.

DIRECTIONS—10 miles south of Florence on County N, then a quarter mile south on County U, then two miles west on County C, and 2.5 miles north on LaSalle Falls Rd.; parking area is on the north side of the road.

FACILITIES—None.

CAMPING—None.

ENTRY—Open year-round. Free.

CONTACT—Florence Natural Resources Center, Rt. 1, Box 83, Florence, WI 54121. Phone (715) 528-5377.

Cave Point.

143

SOUTHWEST

WHOOPING CRANE

Southwest

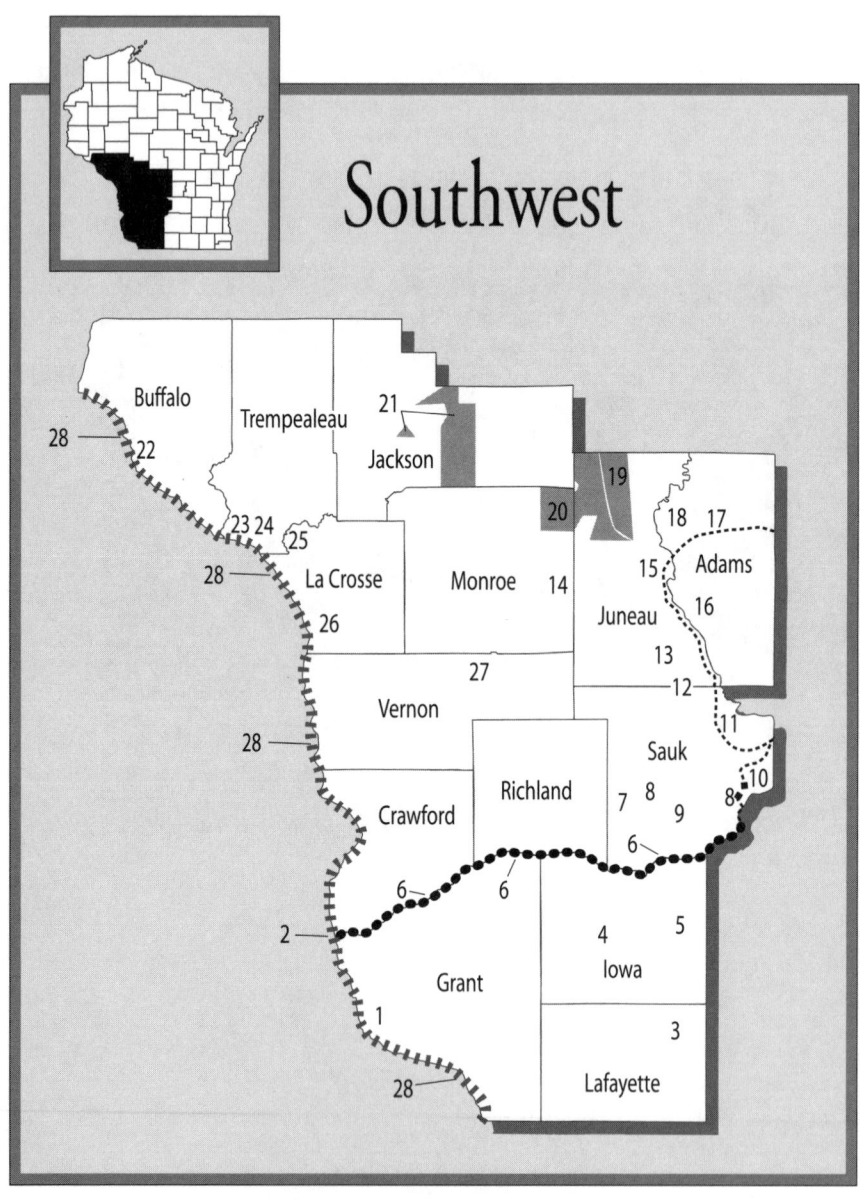

···················· *Proposed* Ice Age National Scenic Trail

■■■■■■■■■■■■■■ *Existing* Ice Age National Scenic Trail

1. Nelson Dewey State Park
2. Wyalusing State Park
3. Yellowstone Lake State Park and Yellowstone Wildlife Area
4. Governor Dodge State Park
5. Blue Mound State Park
6. Lower Wisconsin State Riverway
7. White Mound County Park
8. Baraboo Hills Preserves
9. Natural Bridge State Park
10. Devil's Lake State Park
11. Mirror Lake State Park
12. Rocky Arbor State Park
13. Bass Hollow County Park
14. Mill Bluff State Park
15. Buckhorn State Park
16. Quincy Bluff and Wetlands Preserve
17. Roche-A-Cri State Park
18. Wisconsin River Power Company Recreation Areas
19. Necedah National Wildlife Refuge
20. Central Wisconsin Conservation Area
21. Black River State Forest and Dike 17 Wildlife Area
22. Merrick State Park and Whitman Dam Wildlife Area
23. Trempealeau National Wildlife Refuge
24. Perrot State Park
25. Van Loon State Wildlife Area
26. Hixon Forest and La Crosse River Marsh
27. Wildcat Mountain State Park and Kickapoo Valley Reserve
28. Upper Mississippi River National Wildlife and Fish Refuge

Nelson Dewey State Park

THE SOARING BLUFFS overlooking the Mississippi River are Nelson Dewey's main attraction, and though not as large as its better known neighbor, Wyalusing, it features equally spectacular scenery without the crowds. The park was named for Wisconsin's first governor, whose 2,000-acre Stonefield estate encompassed what is now the park.

Though most of the park's 756 acres of hill and dale are thickly wooded, the most interesting natural feature is the prairie. The Dewey Heights Prairie State Natural Area, one of the first officially designated natural areas in Wisconsin (on the recommendation of pioneering Wisconsin botanist John Curtis) sits atop the bluffs at the end of the park road. Its seven acres of native dry lime prairie is the largest patch of this kind of grassland remaining in the region.

Also clinging to the bluff tops are more than two dozen linear and conical Native American burial mounds. In a rare design, many are connected to each other, forming a chain of sorts. Most of the mounds are found along the main park road and in the campground. They were likely built during the Late Woodland period, between AD 600 and 1300. The same people likely built a similar mound group just across the river in Iowa's Turkey River State Monument. Archaeological surveys have also discovered the remains of three villages along the Mississippi near the park.

WILDLIFE—Bald eagle viewing is one of the park's most popular winter activities. Hundreds of these majestic birds arrive at this stretch of the Mississippi River each December, January, and February, because the local power plant just upstream keeps the water from freezing in even the coldest winters, making fishing easy, and the wooded valleys provide ideal roosts. During January, the park, in cooperation with the nearby village of Cassville, hosts Bald Eagle Days. There are presentations on eagles and spotting scopes set up for easy viewing.

Bald eagles can also be spotted here the rest of the year—one pair even nests in the park—and many other raptors also soar along the ridges and are frequently seen from the bluff-top overlooks. Wild turkey, deer, fox, coyote, and badger all inhabit the park's wooded hills and valleys.

HIKING—Short but scenic best describes the park's six trails. None is more than half a mile long, yet the fantastic views of the river, its islands, and backwaters (as long as you do not look south at the power plant) makes them highly recommended. The Cedar and Prairie trails, each less than a quarter mile long, lead through the natural area, with the latter passing right through the prairie. These narrow trails include some fun rocky climbs.

The 0.3-mile Woodbine Nature Trail starts at the campground and leads through the woods to arguably the most scenic overlook in the park. Interpretive signs along the wheelchair-accessible loop offer information on a variety of topics, including the burial mounds.

The Mound Point Trail leads for about half a mile along the wooded bluff tops past several of the burial mounds. The narrow trail, with some steep hills and scattered benches, lets you watch soaring birds in comfort. The Oakwood Trail and a newly constructed path (tentatively named the Ron Ron Trail) connected to it lead for half a mile on the other side of the park road, and these are the only trails without river views. Plans call for making them wheelchair-accessible.

Though not an official hiking trail, the snowmobile trail running over the steep, forested hills between the group and family campgrounds affords a very scenic hike and is a good place for watching wildlife.

BIKING—Bikers can ride the snowmobile trail between the campgrounds.

WINTER—None of the park's trails are groomed for cross-country skiing, but this is a good time for hikers and snowshoers to explore some of the park's hidden valleys.

OTHER—The Wisconsin Historical Society's Stonefield historic site adjoins the park. Named after the Dewey estate, Stonefield combines a re-created turn-of-the-century village, the State Agricultural Museum, and the governor's restored house.

COUNTY—Grant.

DIRECTIONS—1.5 miles north of Cassville on County VV.

FACILITIES—Water, toilets, picnic area, grills, picnic shelter, playground.

CAMPING—48 sites, 18 electric, four spectacularly located walk-in sites overlooking the river (pushcarts are available for heavy loads), open year-round, reservations accepted, showers, group camp.

ENTRY—Open year-round. State park sticker or daily fee required. Stonefield (separate admission) is open late-May through October.

ON THE WEB—www.wiparks.net

CONTACT—Nelson Dewey State Park, PO Box 658, Cassville, WI 53806. Phone (608) 725-5374.

Wyalusing State Park

WYALUSING, where the Wisconsin River joins the Mississippi, is one of Wisconsin's most beautiful state parks. The panoramic vista of the river's confluence from atop the 500-foot bluffs is among the most scenic sights in the state. If you are lucky, you will witness rivers of fog flowing down the valleys in the early morning, a sight even more spectacular than the famous sunsets. While nearly all visitors gaze out over the valleys from the accessible Point Lookout or one of several other overlooks, many do not take the time to adequately explore the rest of the 2,674-acre park. Between the forests and meadows atop the bluffs and the riverine bottomlands, are rugged hills and narrow valleys with several small caves and waterfalls.

The effort to preserve this area began at the turn of the 20th century when the Glenn family which owned most of the land—and whose home stood at what is now the Homestead Picnic Area—promoted the area as a state park. The state purchased 1,500 acres in 1912 and Wisconsin's fourth state park opened five years later. Originally named in honor of Nelson Dewey, the name was changed when the current Nelson Dewey State Park opened on the former estate of the state's first governor. Wyalusing is a Native American (Munsee-Delaware) word meaning "home of the warrior" and was taken from the village just to the south of the park whose settlers came from Wyalusing, Pennsylvania.

The myriad Native American burial mounds found throughout the park and elsewhere along the confluence of the two rivers were first built beginning about 500 BC. Wyalusing contains examples of all types of mounds created in the area during the next roughly 2,000 years from the earliest conical mounds to the elaborate animal-shaped effigy mounds. Wyalusing's effigy mounds are found along the Sentinel Ridge Nature Trail and in the Spook Hill Mound Group just south of the Homestead Picnic Area, though the best examples are a short distance north of the park in Iowa, at the Effigy Mounds National Monument. The 31 effigy mounds there include the 137-foot long Great Bear Mound. The Ho-Chunk lived in the park when the first Europeans arrived, and more than a dozen other cultures visited the confluence region, which was considered a neutral trading area. Many sites in Wyalusing were named for Native Americans who lived in the park, including the Green Cloud Picnic Area, where in 1882 the last Native Americans, led by Ho-Chunk Chief Green Cloud, camped, and Signal Point, where signal fires were lit.

Famous French missionaries and explorers Marquette and Joliet traveled down the Wisconsin River in 1673, arriving at the Mississippi on June 17. They climbed the bluffs in what is now the park to view the rivers. They are widely regarded as the first Europeans to arrive here, but French explorers Raddison and Grossielliers likely passed through 14 years earlier. French voyageurs came a short while later in search of furs, and ran a lucrative trade for 200 years. Lead mining brought the first large-scale European settlement to this corner of the state in the 1820s and 1830s. Some mining took place in the park, but prospectors had no success.

Most of the forest on the Wisconsin River bluffs is included in state natural areas. At the east end of the park is the 186-acre Wyalusing Hardwood Forest

Wisconsin's most famous scenic overlook—Wyalusing State Park.

State Natural Area. Dedicated to famed botanist John Curtis, it contains four major types of southern forest which illustrate "Curtis's classic concept of vegetational continuum." This was one of the state's first natural areas and is also a National Natural Landmark. Below the Wisconsin Ridge Campground and Point Lookout is the 140-acre Wyalusing Walnut Forest State Natural Area. Like the other natural area, it contains a continuum of southern forest types, plus an unusually large number of black walnut trees near the bottom of the bluff.

There are several noteworthy monuments in the park, including one to the now-extinct passenger pigeon made famous in Aldo Leopold's essay, "On a Monument to the Pigeon," from *A Sand County Almanac*. It overlooks the Mississippi along the Sentinel Ridge Trail next to the Green Cloud Picnic Area. A monument to John Curtis is found at Knob Point. While not really a monument, the marker at the boat launch showing water levels from past floods will likely shock you.

WILDLIFE—Because of the variety of habitats, there is a great abundance of wildlife at this, one of the premier birding spots on the Upper Mississippi River. More than 280 species of birds have been recorded in the park, with nearly a hundred known to nest here—100-species days are not rare for bird-watchers. Look for wood duck, great egret, green-backed heron, belted kingfisher, ring-billed gull, and, in the winter, bald eagle along the rivers. Red-shouldered hawk, American kestrel, and turkey vulture are commonly seen soaring along the bluffs. Common forest dwellers include wild turkey, American woodcock, ruffed grouse, pileated woodpecker, least flycatcher, winter wren, and scarlet tanager. Ten species of warbler including worm-eating, blue-winged, and Kentucky nest in or near the park, and another 21 have been sighted during the spring migration.

Park mammals include mink, beaver, fox, coyote, and some surprisingly tame deer.

HIKING—Hiking in Wyalusing is excellent, and with 20 miles of trails there is something for everybody. The narrow Bluff and Flint Ledge trails parallel the steep wooded bluffs above the river's confluence; both offer excellent valley views. The 0.9-mile Bluff Trail is generally level and easy. It passes Treasure Cave, a small limestone cavern named after a legend of gold having been buried somewhere in the park. The 0.8-mile Flint Ledge Trail, named for the veins of flint used by Native Americans to carve arrowheads, leads along the middle of the bluff where it follows the base of the exposed rock face most of the way, making it the more scenic of the two. It has several steep hills and is rough in spots.

The narrow half-mile Indian Trail winds down the bluff along a path once used by Native Americans. Below the bluff, the mostly level 1.3-mile Old Immigrant Trail follows the Wisconsin River and its wooded backwaters. Once used by settlers going west, it lead to a ferry across the Mississippi.

The Old Wagon Road, Sand Cave, and Walnut Springs trails all run through the quiet east end of the park and have some hills along their paths. The wooded 0.8-mile Old Wagon Road Trail was once a road that led down to the town of Walnut Eddy on the river. There was a ferry in the 1830s, but the town is now long gone. The 1.7-mile Sand Cave Trail is named for a colorful rock overhang, not really a cave, over which flows a small waterfall. The wooded trail passes another small waterfall as well. The lesser-used 2.6-mile Walnut Springs Trail crosses a small stream several times and is a good wildlife-watching destination. It is level at both ends and the top portion leads through open field.

The Sugar Maple Nature Trail is a fairly easy 1.5-mile loop through a wooded valley on the Mississippi River side of the park. Pictured Rock Cave along the trail also has a small waterfall and interpretive panels along the route explain the park's ecology.

The wooded 1.6-mile Sentinel Ridge Trail, following the top of the bluffs along the Mississippi River, has many great views. The ends are hilly, particularly the south end that climbs up the bluff. Branching off of it at the Green Cloud Picnic Area is the Sentinel Ridge Nature Trail, a wheelchair-accessible 0.4-mile loop around a row of burial mounds; interpretive panels discuss the park's human history. In the far south end of the park, the wooded Mississippi Ridge

Trail also runs above the Mississippi, although it has few river views. The 1.7-mile trail has a few gentle hills, but is overall an easy hike.

The Whitetail Meadow Trail passes through open field, while the Turkey Hollow Trail crosses a mix of wooded and open terrain. Both are 3.2-mile loops with no large hills; the White Tail Meadow Trail also has a 1.7-mile inner loop. Both have abundant edge habitats and are good bird-watching destinations.

An eight-mile loop around the park can be formed by combining the Sentinel Ridge, Sugar Maple, Turkey Hollow, Walnut Springs, Old Immigrant, and Indian trails. This route offers walkers a little of everything Wyalusing has to offer.

PADDLING—A six-mile canoe trail leads through the adjacent Upper Mississippi River National Wildlife and Fish Refuge (p. 210). The marked trail passes through the river's backwater sloughs and out along the main channel, which can be rough. The trail is best at the northern end, where a rewarding experience may be had in lazily exploring the many side channels that branch off it. This also avoids the frequent boat traffic on the main channel. The canoe trail is a great place to see waterfowl and wading birds, especially great blue heron, which are very common, while water flowers are especially abundant in July and August. If you do not mind crossing the channel, Wyalusing's trail can be combined with another marked trail (6.5 miles long) on the Iowa side of the river to form a loop of roughly 11 miles.

Although there is no direct access from the park to the Wisconsin River, this smaller river is nonetheless an excellent canoeing option. Paddlers can start upstream—putting in at Wauzeka makes a pleasant 17-mile trip—and return to the park via the Mississippi; just follow the marked canoe trail back to the boat landing. See the Lower Wisconsin State Riverway (p. 161) for details. Canoes may be rented from the park's concessionaire.

BIKING—Bikes are allowed on the Mississippi Ridge and Whitetail Meadows trails, as well as the section of the Walnut Springs Trail along the park road, 5.5 miles total.

WINTER—The Mississippi Ridge and Whitetail Meadows trails are groomed for cross-country skiing. The Mississippi Ridge Trail returns along the park road to form a 3.5-mile loop. Ice waterfalls form at Pictured Rock and Sand Caves and thus these make excellent hiking or snowshoeing destinations.

COUNTY—Grant.

DIRECTIONS—Six miles east of Prairie du Chien on Highway 18/35, then four miles southwest on County C.

FACILITIES—Water, toilets, boat launch, nature center, nature programs, observatory, picnic area, grills, picnic shelter, playground, volleyball, ball field, tennis court.

CAMPING—Two campgrounds, 109 sites, 34 electric, open year-round, reservations accepted, showers, group camp.

ENTRY—Open year-round. State park sticker or daily fee required.

ON THE WEB—www.wiparks.net and www.wyalusing.org

CONTACT—Wyalusing State Park, 13081 State Park Ln., Bagley, WI 53081. Phone (608) 996-2261.

Yellowstone Lake State Park
and Yellowstone Wildlife Area

BEAUTIFUL Yellowstone Lake, the park's main attraction, features high wooded banks and accounts for almost half of the 968-acre park sitting on its northern shore. Wisconsin's Driftless Region has no natural lakes, so many are drawn to Yellowstone to boat, fish, and swim; this narrow body of water, stretching 2.5 miles from the dam in the east to the marsh at the west, is large enough to accommodate the weekend masses. Relatively few people hike the scenic trails through the rest of the park.

To the south and west of the park is the 4,050-acre Yellowstone Wildlife Area, which is a nearly equal mix of forest and grassland. It also includes the marsh at the end of the lake, which is a designated waterfowl area. It is not especially scenic, but it teems with wildlife and offers good bird-watching.

WILDLIFE—More than 170 species of birds have been recorded here, including ducks, Canada goose, sandhill crane, and herons, which are here in large numbers during the fall migration and are most likely to be seen in the marsh at the east end of the lake. The hills and valleys of the park are home to wild turkey, pheasant, ruffed grouse, many songbirds, deer, fox, and coyote.

HIKING—The park's 12 miles of trails feature varied scenery and a lot of hills. The 3.5-mile Blue Ridge Trail runs the length of the park over rolling hills, encompassing most of the park's habitats—prairie, oak forest, and wetland—and connects to each of the other trails along the way. At its far west end is the easy, mile-long Wildlife Loop which follows the dike through the shallow back bay and marsh at the end of the lake, a great place to see wildlife. There is a prairie restoration on the east side.

Several trails loop inside the Blue Ridge Trail and they can be combined to make loops of various lengths. The 2.1-mile Oak Grove Trail passes through small wooded valleys, typical of this region, with many rock outcroppings not worn down during the last Ice Age; some of the hills are steep. The 0.3-mile Shortcut and 0.8-mile Timber trails are similar, though they are generally just used to complete loops rather than be followed on their own. The hilly Windy

Ridge Trail and Savannah Loop take hikers through two and a half miles of wide-open prairie and oak savanna.

Perched atop the ridge on the other side of the park are the adjoining 1.3-mile Oak Ridge Trail and the 0.8-mile Prairie Loop, both of which follow the wooded perimeter of large prairie restorations; the Prairie Loop's restoration is much older and thus more beautiful right now. After you make the long climb up the gully, there are just rolling hills along the twin trails. Neither is difficult, but the latter is hillier.

Access to the wildlife area is along County F and English Hollow Road to the west, and County G to the south. Hikers and bird-watchers can follow the handful of service roads leading through the area.

PADDLING—The western end of the lake is a no-motor zone, making this a quiet place to paddle and avoid the boats on the rest of the lake. Canoes, rowboats, and fishing boats are available for rent at the park.

BIKING—The challenging Windy Ridge Trail and Savannah Loop, and the northern half of the Oak Grove Trail, are open to off-road bikes, 3.5 miles total.

WINTER—The Oak Grove Trail, Oak Ridge Trail, and Prairie Loop offer four groomed miles for cross-country skiing ranging from easy to challenging. The Blue Ridge Trail, which runs very near the ski trails and connects to the county trail system, is used by snowmobilers.

OTHER—A rifle range is located in the wildlife area on County F.

COUNTY—Lafayette.

DIRECTIONS—11 miles northeast of Darlington on County F, then a quarter mile south on Lake Rd.

FACILITIES—Water, toilets, boat launch, nature programs, picnic area, grills, picnic shelter, beach, playground, horseshoes.

CAMPING—128 sites, 38 electric, 14 walk-in, open year-round, reservations accepted, showers, group camp.

ENTRY—Open year-round. State park sticker or daily fee required.

ON THE WEB—www.wiparks.net

CONTACT—Yellowstone Lake State Park, 8495 Lake Rd., Blanchardville, WI 53516. Phone (608) 523-4427.

Governor Dodge State Park

WITH ITS STEEP hills, deep valleys, and spectacular sandstone bluffs, Wisconsin's second largest state park epitomizes the state's Driftless Region. Lakes being a rarity in the Driftless Region, the man-made pair here are recreation magnets, but also add significantly to the park's beauty. This is

Wisconsin's fourth most-visited state park, but with 5,270 acres to explore it is easy to escape the crowds.

Small remnants of the vast prairies that once dominated southern Wisconsin may be found in the park, and a sign at the park office identifies some of the more common prairie grasses and flowers. The surviving prairies harbor many rare plants, as do the cooler microclimates on many of the cliffs. Also hugging the cliffs are native stands of pines, which are quite rare this far south. The 20-acre Pine Cliff State Natural Area, on the southeast end of Cox Hollow Lake, harbors all three species of pine native to Wisconsin—white, red, and jack.

Wind and rain have also carved two caves and several rock shelters which Native Americans lived in as many as 8,000 years ago. The Fox, Sauk, and Ho-Chunk were among the early inhabitants of the area, the first European settlers joining the Ho-Chunk when lead mines were established here. General Henry Dodge, who arrived in 1827, was one of the first miners, followed by many more who heard of his success. They increasingly moved on to Ho-Chunk land without obtaining permission or paying compensation. The U.S. government ordered the miners off the property, but when the settlers refused and threatened to fight, the government purchased the Ho-Chunk's land to diffuse the conflict. Dodge personally signed the treaty in 1829. He later became Wisconsin's first territorial governor, and served in the U.S. Senate.

WILDLIFE—Forest covers half of the park; most of the rest was farmland not too long ago, but is now returning to its natural splendor. The mix of forest, grassland, and lake habitats—along with its vast size—make this an excellent bird-watching destination. Hawks and turkey vultures routinely soar along the hills and bluffs, while bald eagle and osprey may be sighted during the winter. Wild turkey, ruffed grouse, pileated woodpecker, winter wren, Eastern and Western meadowlark, common tern, blue-winged teal, common loon, great blue heron, and sandhill crane are a few of the other 182 species that have been recorded at Governor Dodge. Birders are especially excited about the nearly 20 species of warbler that nest in the park; these include Blackburnian, Cerulean, black-throated green, hooded, Canada, and prothonotary.

Deer, fox, coyote, badger, beaver, otter, mink, and even the rare bobcat are some of the many park mammals.

HIKING—There are nearly 40 miles of trails crossing all parts of Governor Dodge, and with few exceptions the trails are very hilly. The White Oak, Pine Cliff, Stephens Falls, Lakeview, and sections of the Lost Canyon trails lead through the park's most scenic areas and are reserved for hiking only.

If you are going to hike only one part of the park, it should probably be the south shore of Cox Hollow Lake. The mostly wooded White Oak Trail leads for 2.5 miles (3.5 miles if you make a loop of it along the park road) around the lake with great views from atop the bluffs. It crosses a small wetland at the south end of the lake and passes through the Pine Cliff State Natural Area to the east, where a rock shelter is visible in the cliff. The wooded Pine Cliff Nature Trail branches off the west end of the White Oak Trail and heads up the high bluff on the peninsula between the two branches of the lake and returns along its shore. It features interpretive panels and a small seasonal waterfall near the trailhead. While it does not actually pass through the natural area, as the name suggests, there are also pine relics (native pine trees remaining from the time of the last Ice Age) along its path. A much less interesting but still worthy offshoot is the oddly-named Lakeview Trail—it does have a nice lake view, but only where it shares its path with the White Oak Trail. The 1.25-mile trail, also almost all wooded, follows a small valley back through the forest. The Mill Creek Trail provides views of both lakes, with an especially picturesque view of Twin Valley Lake and its surrounding bluffs. The 3.3-mile trail, which crosses an equal mix of forest and grassland, is a good bird-watching destination.

Both ends of the 8.1-mile Lost Canyon Trail are open only to hiking. A 0.75-mile loop at the east end leads around a long, narrow bluff and along Twin Valley Lake. A rough path at the top of the bluff leads up to a cave with a narrow passage that opens into a rather large chamber. The 1.5-mile west end of the trail leads past the many exposed rock faces in Lost Canyon. The Lost Canyon Trail connects to the quarter-mile Stephens Falls Trail, which should not be missed. The falls are small, but the level, wooded trail follows the stream through a beautiful, rock-strewn valley. A set of stairs leads above the falls to an 1850s-era springhouse. The falls may also be reached directly from the park road by a short trail.

The rest of the Lost Canyon Trail shares its path with the 6.8-mile Meadow Valley Trail and the 2.5-mile Gold Mine Trail, both of which have more field than forest. The Gold Mine Trail has many hills, but they are not as steep as those along most of the other trails. The western end of the Meadow Valley and Gold Mine trails lead above Lost Canyon and have two good vista points plus pass an interesting springhouse not shown on the park map. At the northern end of the Meadow Valley and Lost Canyon trails, near the Twin Valley campground, a short narrow path leads to a small cave also not shown on the park map. Approaching from the west, the trail passes near the bottom of the long steep hill where a set of steps leads to the cave. The trail is not marked, but it is easy to find if you are looking for it.

Two horse trails are also open to hiking. A 15.3-mile exterior loop encircles the park. Much of the western end of the loop passes right next to the park road, but the rest provides good scenery. The most scenic section is in the north, where it leads atop the bluffs. A 6.7-mile interior loop lets you create a variety of shorter paths within the exterior loop.

Two short and very scenic paths in the southern end of the park are not shown on park maps, but are worth a visit. At the Box Canyon Picnic Area, a short paved path leads up a steep bluff called Enee Point. The other, at the Deer Cove Picnic Area, leads to a rock shelter below a long and picturesque bluff.

PADDLING—Both of Governor Dodge's lakes, 96-acre Cox Hollow and 152-acre Twin Valley, provide scenic paddling. Only electric motors are allowed, and canoe rentals are available.

BIKING—Off-road bikes are allowed on the Mill Creek, Meadow Valley, and Gold Mine trails, offering 10.6 miles of challenging terrain. The 39.6-mile Military Ridge State Trail, following a former railroad right-of-way between Verona and Mineral Point, now surfaced with crushed limestone, passes along the southern end of the park and is connected to Cox Hollow Beach by a paved two-mile trail.

WINTER—There are about 15 miles of trails groomed for cross-country skiing, including the Gold Mine, Mill Creek, Meadow Valley, Lakeview, and Lost Canyon trails. The 15.3-mile trail around the outside of the park is used by snowmobilers and connects to the Military Ridge State Trail. A skating rink is cleared on Cox Hollow Lake.

OTHER—Two trails, totaling 22 miles and described in the Hiking section, are open to horseback riders. Rentals and guided trips are available from Doby Stables, (608) 935-5205, just across from the park entrance. They can make arrangements for disabled riders.

COUNTY—Iowa.

DIRECTIONS—Three miles north of Dodgeville on Highway 23.

FACILITIES—Water, toilets, boat launch, nature center, nature programs, picnic area, grills, picnic shelter, beach, playground, horseshoes.

CAMPING—Two campgrounds, 269 sites, 77 electric, eight walk-in sites, six backpack sites, 12 horseback rider sites, open year-round, reservations accepted, showers, group camp.

ENTRY—Open year-round. State park sticker or daily fee required. State trail pass required for off-road bikers and horseback riders.

ON THE WEB—www.wiparks.net

CONTACT—Governor Dodge State Park, 4175 Highway 23, Dodgeville, WI 53533. Phone (608) 935-2315.

Blue Mound State Park

WEEHAUKAJA is the Ho-Chunk name for the tall mound at the heart of this 1,153-acre park. It means "a high place with a wonderful view," and the name is certainly appropriate. At 1,716 feet above sea level, Blue Mound, as the settlers called it, is the highest point in southern Wisconsin. The mound rises 415 feet above the surrounding plain, and from the two 40-foot observation towers (or one of the wheelchair-accessible vista points) several distant landmarks are visible on clear days, including the bluffs at Devil's Lake State Park, the Wisconsin River Valley, and the State Capitol dome in Madison. The hill earned its modern name because from a distance it has a bluish-gray cast on hazy days. As the name of the nearby village of Blue Mounds suggests, the park's Blue Mound has a twin. The smaller sibling sits a mile to the east and, at 1,490 feet above sea level, it is not nearly as prominent a landmark. The other mound is the site of Dane County's Brigham Park, named after Ebenezer Brigham, who in 1828 became the area's first European settler. The wooded 112-acre park features picnic grounds, camping, a half-mile nature trail, and more good views.

Before settlers arrived in southwestern Wisconsin, prairie and oak savanna dominated the landscape; yet even back then, as today, the mound was blanketed by forest, probably because the abundant rocks here restricted the fires that kept the prairie free of trees. Extensive prairie and oak savanna restorations blanket the lower east end of the park. The top of the mound is a large, open field, ideal for picnics, flying kites, playing catch, and similar summer pastimes. The oval road around the top was a horseracing track in the 19th century.

Historic Native American tribes who lived here included the Fox, Illinois, Iowa, Ho-Chunk, and Sauk. The mound was long an important spot to the last group, which figured it must be the home of the nature spirit *Manotou*. They believed the spring on the eastern side (near what is now the swimming pool) was sacred to this spirit, and the blue haze came from *Wakanda*, the "Earth Maker." The early Military Road between Green Bay and Prairie du Chien passed by the mound, and today forms the park's southern border. The road, built following a foot trail long used by Native Americans, later became a railway, and the portion near the park is now the popular Military Ridge State Trail.

WILDLIFE—More than 150 species of birds have been observed in Blue Mound's forest and prairie, with half of those nesting here. Turkey vulture and hawks are commonly seen soaring along the mound, while wild turkey, ruffed grouse, pileated woodpecker, great crested and least flycatchers, Eastern wood-pewee, yellow-billed cuckoos, indigo bunting, scarlet tanager, red-eyed vireo, and chestnut-sided warbler are some of the other species you might encounter. Park mammals include deer, fox, coyote, weasel, and badger.

HIKING—Nine miles of hiking trails wrap around Blue Mound. The narrow, half-mile Indian Marker Tree Trail winds gently up the north end of the mound past many large boulders. It is named after a 140-year-old oak at the top of the trail that was bent to point toward the spring at the trail's other end. Both Native Americans and early settlers used trees such as this to help find water. It is the only one remaining in the park.

Also on the north side of the mound are the one-mile John Minix Trail, named after the previous owner of the mound who operated a private park here, the two-mile Willow Spring Trail, and the one-mile Flint Rock Nature Trail. All three are mostly wooded and hilly, though none is too difficult. The trails cross many small streams that flow down the mound during the spring or after a rain. The Flint Rock Nature Trail has interpretive signs discussing the geology of the mound. The narrow end leading to the West Tower is a little rough.

The two-mile Pleasure Valley Trail has two separate loops. The main loop circles the park's prairie restoration and has a few small hills, but the real gem is the shorter loop that drops down into a steep, wooded valley; the narrow north end follows a small stream.

The mile-long Ridgeview Trail parallels the park's southern edge. The west side of the hilly trail leads out of the woods into the open field on the east side. Branching off the trail at the east end is the quarter-mile Walnut Hollow Trail, which is also half-wooded, half-open.

The three wooded trails leading up the mound, one from the swimming pool area, the others from the campground, all are less than a half-mile long and very steep.

BIKING—Off-road bikes are allowed on over ten miles of trail, including the Willow Spring, John Minix, and the main loop of the Pleasure Valley Trail, though riders tend to gravitate toward the park's new and as-of-yet unnamed single track trail—currently four miles have been constructed and more is coming—starting at the pool parking area. Some sections are quite steep, though there are bypasses around the most challenging runs.

Blue Mound lies near the middle of the 40-mile Military Ridge State Trail which connects Verona and Dodgeville along a former railbed now surfaced with crushed limestone. A paved access trail connects the Military Ridge Trail to the park.

WINTER—Cross-country skiing is the most popular winter activity, and all of the park's trails, except those leading up the mound, are groomed; in fact, some local skiers say that these are the best groomed trails for miles around. The trails form five interconnecting loops, ranging from easy to difficult, for a total of nine miles. A warming shelter is available.

OTHER—Blue Mound is the only state park with a swimming pool. It has a chair lift to help disabled users get in and out of the water, and is open daily between the Memorial Day and Labor Day weekends.

COUNTIES—Iowa and Dane.

DIRECTIONS—A quarter-mile north of the village Blue Mounds, on Mounds Park Rd.

FACILITIES—Water, toilets, nature center, nature programs, picnic area, grills, picnic shelter, swimming pool, playground, horseshoes.

CAMPING—78 sites, 16 electric, barrier-free cabin, open year-round, reservations accepted, showers. Camping also available at Brigham County Park.

ENTRY—Open year-round. State park sticker or daily fee required. State trail pass required for Military Ridge and off-road bike trails. Fee also required for swimming pool.

ON THE WEB—www.wiparks.net

CONTACT—Blue Mound State Park, 4350 Mounds Park Rd., PO Box 98, Blue Mounds, WI 53517. Phone (608) 437-5711.

Lower Wisconsin State Riverway
Includes FERRY BLUFF and AVOCA PRAIRIE-SAVANNA STATE NATURAL AREAS

BELOW ITS LAST dam in Prairie du Sac, the Wisconsin River flows freely for 92.3 miles to its confluence with the Mississippi—the longest stretch of undammed river in the eastern United States. This distinction is all the more impressive considering that upriver are 26 hydroelectric dams and 21 storage reservoirs, a greater density of dams than any other river in the U.S., earning the Wisconsin its reputation as the "Hardest Working River in the Nation."

The Lower Wisconsin runs through one of the most scenic areas in the state, flowing entirely through a great gorge with towering bluffs rising 300 to 500 feet. More than four miles wide at Prairie du Sac, where most of the hills are comprised of easily eroded sandstone, the gorge gradually narrows to less than a mile at Bridgeport, near the end, where limestone is predominant. The bluffs, hundreds of millions of years old, are within the state's Driftless Region and thus were never worn away by the glaciers, though the Ice Age did have an effect on the valley. Water from the melting glaciers, the last of which stopped just a few miles to the northeast, poured through, depositing countless tons of sand across the river valley; the river still moves many tons of sediment a day. The river's countless sandbars are constantly moving downstream, some drifting hundreds of feet each year.

DON DAVENPORT

Spectacular scenes such as this are typical along the Lower Wisconsin State Riverway.

Many upland areas have become sand barrens. These, as well as the steep cliffs, protect many rare plants, some found nowhere else in the world. Currently, 62 rare, threatened, or endangered plant and animal species have been found here. The most surprising find in the sand barrens is the state-threatened prickly pear cactus, the only cactus native to Wisconsin. The 130-acre Blue River Sand Barrens State Natural Area, located four miles west of Muscoda on Highway 133, and then a quarter mile north on Wightman Road, features the largest and best example of sand barrens in Wisconsin. The Mazomanie Oak Barrens State Natural Area in Dane County is best seen along County Y; a historical marker discussing the area is located three-quarters of a mile west of Highway 78.

Many other plant communities are found in the riverway. Wetlands and bottomland forests dominate the shore, while upland forests and some prairie remnants blanket the hills. The Avoca Prairie-Savanna State Natural Area, north of the village of Avoca, designated a National Natural Landmark, is one of the most significant prairies in the eastern United States. Both it and the Ferry Bluff State Natural Area are described in detail below in the hiking section. In total there are 17 state natural areas covering 6,000 acres in the riverway.

Luckily, because of flooding in the lowlands and high building costs on the bluffs, development has remained limited over the years. The state, recognizing the importance of protecting the river's natural character, began actively purchasing land for conservation purposes in the late-1940s, but in 1989 efforts were put into high gear with the establishment of the Lower Wisconsin State Riverway, the first such state-owned project. Currently, over 43,000 acres are publicly owned, and eventually the state hopes to nearly double its holdings. The Lower Wisconsin State Riverway Board, an independent state agency, regulates activities on private lands within the riverway to ensure future protection.

Archaeological evidence shows that Native Americans first came to the Wisconsin River Valley as many as 10,000 years ago. Among the more recent groups were the Ho-Chunk, Sauk, Fox, and Ojibwe. Earlier groups built burial mounds on the blufftops all along the Lower Wisconsin. The easiest ones to see are at Wyalusing State Park, though a self-guided driving tour of mounds in southwestern Wisconsin, most of which are in the Lower Wisconsin River valley, should be completed by the time this book goes to press. The Wisconsin River, along with the Fox, formed an important trade route between the Mississippi and the Great Lakes that began over 3,000 years ago. Two thousand years ago a trade network reached across the length of North America and footpaths maintained along the river allowed year-round travel.

One of the most significant historical events to occur in the valley was the Battle of Wisconsin Heights during the Black Hawk War. Though greatly outnumbered, Chief Black Hawk and his band held off the American troops until nightfall and then slipped across the river in hastily assembled rafts. It is widely regarded as one of the most skilled battle strategies of the era. Despite this victory, most of Black Hawk's followers were later slaughtered by the American troops. There is a historical marker on Highway 78, about two miles south of Sauk City, and a short hiking trail with interpretive panels leads visitors through the battle site.

French explorers Raddison and Grossielliers, who traveled from Green Bay to the Mississippi via the Fox and Wisconsin Rivers in 1659, were likely the first Europeans to pass through here, though the credit usually goes to the more famous Marquette and Joliet. They, along with five others, came through in 1673 and were the first to record their journey, thus securing their place in history. The Lower Wisconsin was used by fur traders, missionaries, loggers, miners, military personnel, settlers, naturalists, and tourists, among others. Most early river communities were based around shipping, with steamboats and flatboats regularly moving up and down the river. Lumber rafts from northern Wisconsin, headed toward Mississippi River ports such as St. Louis, were common in the mid-1800s, as many as 150 passing through every day in peak years. By century's end, the railroad had come and life on the river changed. With shipping all but gone, river towns vanished as new towns sprang up along the rail lines.

WILDLIFE—Wildlife is abundant due to the diversity of habitats; over 45 mammal and nearly 300 bird species (over a hundred nesting) have been found in the riverway. Some of the more notable mammals are deer, fox, coyote, beaver, mink, and otter. Even bear and bobcat have been seen on rare occasions. The wavy lines that may be seen crossing sandbars are clam tracks; 31 species live in the river.

Common birds along the river include great blue and green-backed herons, great egrets, hooded mergansers, wood duck, belted kingfisher, pheasant, wild turkey, ruffed grouse, turkey vulture, pileated woodpecker, red-shouldered hawk, osprey, Acadian flycatcher, winter wren, tufted titmouse, and scarlet tanager. Cerulean, Kentucky, prothonotary, and worm-eating are some of the dozen or so warblers nesting in the valley.

The steep wooded bluffs provide a winter haven for bald eagles and from mid-December to mid-February hundreds congregate in the valley. One of the most impressive wildlife displays in the state takes place below the Prairie du Sac dam, where many of these eagles come to fish—they are most active in the morning. A wheelchair-accessible viewing platform with spotting scopes and informational kiosks is located at 540 Water Street in Prairie du Sac. The eagles may also be viewed from the base of the dam or at Veterans Park; the latter is generally the best spot. Both are north of town along Highway 78. Bald Eagle Watching Days, with special events and presentations, are held each January.

HIKING—With more than 20 miles of trails, Wyalusing State Park (p. 149) is the most popular place to hike, and there are also a few miles of trail at Tower Hill State Park. Though there are few designated trails elsewhere on the riverway, service roads through the various units can be hiked. They are seldom used, and while often overgrown can provide nice hikes and great wildlife watching. The two detailed here are some of the most accessible.

The 159-acre Ferry Bluff State Natural Area is one of the most prominent landmarks on the river. The only trail is less than half a mile long, but it offers stunning views of the Wisconsin River Valley. There are, in fact, three bluffs right next to each other. Ferry Bluff, named for a ferry landing located here during the Civil War, is the northernmost. The trail follows the river a short way before heading up to the top of Cactus Bluff, the middle one, where interpretive panels have been installed. The National Wildlife Federation bought the property in 1975 and 1976 as a refuge for the bald eagles that roost here each winter, and later donated the land to the state. The area is closed to entry November 15 to March 31 to protect the eagles and the many other raptors that congregate here.

The 1,885-acre Avoca Prairie-Savanna State Natural Area is one of the most important sites along the river. The 970-acre native tallgrass prairie is the largest east of the Mississippi River and one of the few places in the eastern United States where one can look out and see only natural savanna features in all directions. It formed along a huge outwash plain along the river's banks, and flooding has created small narrow wetlands across the prairie. Sedge meadow and forest make up most of the rest of the area. From the end of Hay Lane Road, one mile east of Avoca, a mile-long gravel service road leading north into the natural area and ending along the river offers a good hike. The path can be quite wet, and some streams must be crossed. A few seldom used, and generally overgrown, paths branch off and provide additional hiking opportunities.

PADDLING—Canoes are the best way to see the area. Paddlers can head straight down the river, take narrower side passages around large islands, or explore hidden backwater channels and sloughs. With no rapids, the Lower Wisconsin offers quiet-water canoeing at its best, though do not let the placidity fool you, as there are sudden drop-offs and localized strong currents, so wearing a personal floatation device is still highly recommended. The riverway office keeps a list of rental and shuttle companies.

Though the scenery is consistently wonderful, when planning your trip keep in mind that two-thirds of all river users stick to the stretch between Prairie du Sac and Spring Green. The middle section between Spring Green and Boscobel offers considerably more solitude, and very few head downstream of Boscobel, even though it is the most primitive part of the river. The last landing on the river before it meets the Mississippi is the Bridgeport Landing at the Highway 18 bridge, but canoeists can easily paddle the last five miles to the Mississippi and take out at Wyalusing State Park by following the park's marked canoe trail to the boat landing; watch for signs about a mile down river.

The Prairie du Sac dam, a run of the river dam, has little effect on water levels downstream, but heavy rains can cause a two-to-three-foot rise overnight, so keep this in mind when setting up camp. Also remember that sandbars often have sudden drop-offs on the downstream side. Finally, people on the water must have a waterproof refuse container on board, and glass containers are prohibited.

OTHER—Horseback riders can use the trails at the Muscoda Unit between Muscoda and Blue River, Millville Town Park near Bridgeport, and the Black Hawk Unit near Sauk City.

COUNTIES—Sauk, Columbia, Dane, Iowa, Richland, Grant, and Crawford.

DIRECTIONS—Directions to specific areas are given above.

FACILITIES—Boat landings line the river, and many have toilets and picnic facilities; parks along the river have many other facilities.

CAMPING—Free camping is allowed on all state-owned islands and sandbars—camping is prohibited on shore lands. Parks along the river with campgrounds are Tower Hill and Wyalusing (p. 149) state parks, Veterans Park in Prairie du Sac, Riverside Park in Muscoda, and Boscobel Recreation Area in Boscobel.

ENTRY—Open year-round, except Ferry Bluff is closed November 15 to April 1. Free.

ON THE WEB—http://lwr.state.wi.us

CONTACT—Tower Hill State Park, 5808 County Rd. C, Spring Green, WI 53588. Phone (608) 588-2116.

White Mound County Park

WHITE MOUND contains the steep hills and narrow valleys typical of the Driftless Region. The park's 1,092 acres are owned by the state and managed as a wildlife area, though the county operates all park facilities. At the heart of the park is 110-acre White Mound Lake. Because there are no natural lakes in the unglaciated region of the state, this is a very popular recreation destination for fishing and swimming. Although most of the parkland is wooded, there are many open areas, including some prairie restorations and wetlands; the latter primarily at the north end of the lake along Honey Creek which feeds it. The park is named for the former village of White Mound, a thriving stagecoach stop in the mid-1800s, which was located about a mile southeast of the park.

WILDLIFE—More than 120 bird species have been recorded in the park, including herons, ducks, hawks, turkey vulture, ruffed grouse, wild turkey, and a variety of warblers. Deer and beaver are also likely to be seen here.

HIKING—Nearly 18 miles of trails wind along the lake and through the forest. Except where noted, the trails are hilly and many of the climbs are quite steep. The two shortest trails are the half-mile Camp Trail (also called the Scenic View Nature Trail) located across from the campground, and the 1.7-mile Kiln Trail south of the main use area. The recommended Camp Trail loops through oak savanna and prairie restorations. The Kiln Trail—named for a restored lime kiln built in the mid-1800s that it passes—heads up a long, steep hill before looping around. Except for a small patch of prairie, the trail is entirely wooded.

Two longer trails circle the lake and wind through the hills to the east. The Lake Trail follows the shore for 2.75 miles through mostly open field, and while not completely flat, it is the park's most level trail. The Ridge Trail is the best for wildlife watchers or those looking for solitude. It follows the lake's quieter east shore and then veers off into the wooded hills completing a scenic 1.9-mile loop. Another good option is the seven-plus mile Horse Trail which roughly follows the park's border through both wooded and open terrain. The east end is the most scenic part, though the loop in the northernmost section of the park is also a nice hike.

PADDLING—Some people enjoy a lazy paddle around the lake. Only electric motors are allowed.

WINTER—The Lake and Ridge trails are groomed for cross-country skiing, offering almost five miles of scenic paths.

OTHER—The scenic, seven-mile horse trail, described above under hiking, is rightly popular with local riders.

COUNTY—Sauk.

DIRECTIONS—Five miles north of Plain on Highway 23, then two miles west on County GG.

FACILITIES—Water, toilets, boat launch, picnic area, grills, picnic shelter, beach, playground, volleyball, ball field.

CAMPING—72 sites, 30 electric, 15 walk-in sites, 10 horseback rider sites, open mid-April to late November, reservations accepted, showers, group camp.

ENTRY—Open year-round. Daily fee or annual sticker required.

ON THE WEB—www.baraboonow.com/parks/whitemound.asp

CONTACT—White Mound Park, S7995 White Mound Dr., Hillpoint, WI 53937. Phone (608) 546-5011.

Baraboo Hills Preserves
Hemlock Draw, Baxter's Hollow, and Honey Creek

THE BARABOO HILLS, extending for 25 miles across the middle of Sauk County, are the eroded remains of an ancient mountain range. The area is unique for its natural diversity, geological features, and, most importantly, its undisturbed environment. The Nature Conservancy has designated the hills as a Last Great Place, identifying this as one of the western hemisphere's most significant ecosystems. It has also been designated a National Natural Landmark. Baxter's Hollow and Honey Creek are just two of a dozen state natural areas scattered across the Baraboo Hills. Several others are found in Devil's Lake (p. 171) and Natural Bridge (p. 170) state parks, which also lie within the Baraboo Hills.

The one-and-a-half-billion-year-old quartzite hills are among the oldest visible physical features on the earth. A north and south range are separated by a narrow valley through which the Baraboo River flows. The three properties highlighted here are in the Driftless Region, but the last glacier to enter Wisconsin did cover the east end of the Baraboo Hills, including that half of Devil's Lake State Park. The numerous cliffs, deep gorges, and expansive forests make this one of the most beautiful spots in the state. It is also of particular interest to botanists, biologists, geologists, and archaeologists. The gorges support relic northern plant communities left over from the last Ice Age, and thus a variety of birds not commonly found in the southern half of the state live here. Many other species found here require large undisturbed tracts of forest, which are also rare in the south.

Hemlock Draw was one of the first Nature Conservancy projects in the Baraboo Hills, with land purchases beginning in 1964. This wooded preserve covers 724 acres and is a real gem. It features many cliffs and exposed rock outcroppings along a small spring-fed stream.

The Wisconsin Society for Ornithology (WSO) began protecting land around Honey Creek as a bird sanctuary in the 1950s. Today the society owns over 300 acres and works cooperatively with The Nature Conservancy, which also owns an additional 178 acres here. Like Hemlock Draw, this mostly wooded gorge features steep rocky cliffs along a small creek. Though the WSO is here mainly for the birds, the variety of plant life is incredible: there are more than 500 known flora species.

Baxter's Hollow covers 4,138 acres. It is not as strikingly scenic as the other two, but it contains southern Wisconsin's only undeveloped watershed and is the largest intact contiguous southern forest in Wisconsin. Since the large gorge surrounding Otter Creek is almost completely undisturbed, much ecological research takes place here. The Baraboo Hills are one of the most important nesting areas for forest birds in southern Wisconsin, and Baxter's Hollow is the most important nesting site in the Baraboo Hills. Some of the earliest Native Americans to occupy Wisconsin lived in rock shelters at Baxter's Hollow, as well as Natural Bridge State Park and other nearby spots, as early as 10,000 BC.

Interest in preserving these hills dates back to the turn of the 20th century. At one time there was a proposal to establish a 20,000-acre state forest here. The Nature Conservancy currently owns 7,000 acres in the Baraboo Hills, and they work closely with local landowners to manage and protect private land. Several other groups are also acquiring land and conservation easements here to ensure preservation.

WILDLIFE—The Baraboo Hills is nesting territory to more than a hundred species, including the threatened and endangered Kentucky, hooded, and worm-eating warblers. Other avifauna you might spot are wood duck, green and great blue heron, wild turkey, ruffed grouse, pileated woodpecker, American kestrel, northern saw-whet owl, turkey vulture, horned lark, brown creeper, winter wren, and scarlet tanager.

Mammals include deer, fox, coyote, and on very rare occasions bear or bobcat. Many of the streams harbor diverse aquatic insect species; Otter Creek in Baxter's Hollow features at least 78 species of caddisflies.

HIKING—Hiking in each of these areas offers wonderful scenery and solitude. The 1.5-mile trail at Hemlock Draw starts out heading north along an old road. You will have to cross two small streams, but these can be impassible during high water. The trail is not very interesting at first, but then it turns east and the scenery becomes progressively more beautiful. After half a mile, a narrow path branches off the road and continues east, passing below 100-foot-high cliffs and ending along an intermittent stream at the edge of the property. The old road continues north and climbs a long hill, ending at an old field along Buck Fever Road.

The main trail at Baxter's Hollow enters from the south. It starts where the pavement ends on Stone's Pocket Road and heads west along Otter Creek through a narrow open area. This part of the trail is generally level. After a mile, it turns north through the forested hills, crossing to Forest Drive at the north end of the preserve.

A small sign on Skyview Road marks the trail at the Honey Creek Preserve; there is no parking lot. The narrow, unmarked trail leads north for about a mile along the creek and the cliffs. It loops around the north end before reconnecting with itself where it crosses the creek. There are boardwalks along the wettest areas, but some wet spots must be crossed on rocks. The trail is not used very often, but is easy to follow.

COUNTY—Sauk.

DIRECTIONS—Hemlock Draw, one mile north of Leland on Reich Dr. Park on the shoulder, south of the mailbox. Baxter's Hollow, eight miles north of Sauk City on Highway 12, then 1.5 miles west on County C, and two miles north on Stone's Pocket Rd. Honey Creek, 2.5 miles north of Leland on County PF, then half a mile west on Skyview (Lins) Rd.

FACILITIES—None.

CAMPING—None.

ENTRY—Open year-round. Free.

ON THE WEB—http://nature.org/wisconsin and www.uwgb.edu/birds/wso

CONTACT—The Nature Conservancy. Phone (608) 251-8140. E-mail: wmail@tnc.org

Wisconsin Society for Ornithology, W330 N8275 West Shore Dr., Hartland, WI 53029.

Natural Bridge State Park

THE 35-FOOT ARCH at the heart of this quiet park is the largest natural bridge in the state. The opening, worn into the sandstone by wind and rain, is 25 feet wide and 15 feet high. A large rock shelter below the bridge is one of the oldest sites of human occupation uncovered in the Midwest. Archaeological surveys show that nomadic Paleo-Indians, who followed the melting glaciers north hunting large game such as mastodon, musk ox, giant beaver, and giant sloth, resided here 12,000 years ago. An old log cabin and smokehouse just west of the picnic area are reminders of more recent inhabitants. The 60-acre area around the bridge is designated the Natural Bridge and Rockshelter State Natural Area. Of interest, in addition to the geological features, are several rare plants that grow on the surrounding cliffs. Both the cliffs and the plants survived because this spot lies just inside the Driftless Region, hence the glaciers never carved them away.

The 530-acre park was established in 1973, but this was a popular picnic location as far back as the late 1800s, the site of many social events held by local communities. Today it is a great place to find solitude, as it is, astonishingly, one of Wisconsin's least visited state parks. The steep hills are mostly covered by an oak forest, though some small prairie remnants are scattered about.

RJ & LINDA MILER

Natural Bridge State Park's namesake.

WILDLIFE—The park is home to deer, fox, ruffed grouse, hawks, wild turkey, turkey vulture, pileated woodpecker, many songbirds, and, in the winter, bald eagles.

HIKING—There are two trails in the park. The bridge and rock shelter are just a quarter-mile north of the picnic area along the Indian Moccasin Nature Trail. This wooded and hilly, mile-long trail loops around the rocky cliffs and features a scenic overlook east of the bridge. Interpretive signs discuss the many uses Native Americans had for the various plants found along the trail, and a branch of the trail also leads from the bridge to the log cabin. There are benches along the path and stairs at the steepest points, making it a pretty easy walk.

The 2.5-mile Whitetail Hiking Trail loops around the park south of County C, a good place to spot wildlife. After passing through a farm field, the trail climbs several hundred feet up into the wooded hills. A shortcut about halfway up the hill bypasses the steepest climb.

COUNTY—Sauk.

DIRECTIONS—One mile east of Leland on County C.

FACILITIES—Water, toilets, picnic area, grills.

CAMPING—None.

ENTRY—Open year-round. State park sticker or daily fee required.

ON THE WEB—www.wiparks.net

CONTACT—Natural Bridge State Park, S5975 Park Rd., Baraboo, WI 59313. Phone (608) 356-8301.

Devil's Lake State Park

NESTLED BETWEEN three 500-foot bluffs, Devil's Lake is nearly as iconic to Wisconsin as cheese, badgers, and the Green Bay Packers. The crown jewel of the state park system is best known for the spectacular views and remarkable geology, but there is much more to this natural gem than just its famous core. Unfortunately it is no secret, and around 1.3 million people visit annually. While it is nearly impossible to avoid crowds in the heart of the park during the summer, at 9,117 acres this is far and away Wisconsin's largest state park, and if you get beyond the bluffs it is easy to escape the masses.

Devil's Lake is located in the Baraboo Hills, an ancient eroded mountain range; the quartzite forming the bluffs is 1.6 billion years old. An ancient river, possibly an older and larger Wisconsin or Baraboo river whose course was altered during the last Ice Age, carved the valley. The glacier ended its advance in what is now the park, and the terminal moraine blocked off both ends of the valley, creating the spring-fed lake. While the lake was formed very slowly, many early visitors assumed a violent creation because of the extensive talus (rock piles) at the base of the bluffs. One Ho-Chunk legend says a meteor formed the lake, while early settlers suspected a volcano. In fact, most of the boulders were sliced off the slopes by the action of ice and tree roots.

This has long been a sacred spot for Native Americans, who built many ancient effigy and burial mounds along the lake. The Indian Mounds Nature Tour (pick up the brochure at the office or nature center) winds around the north shore past many of them. The Ho-Chunk, who lived here in the 1840s when the first European settlers arrived, had dubbed this Spirit Lake, and the settlers slightly mistranslated the name. Several resorts operated on the lake from the mid-1800s to the early 1900s before the state acquired the land.

Below the bluffs, where cold air accumulates, northern plant species, including white pine, are prevalent—many white pines have taken root on the talus slopes. Southern plants, including scattered prairie remnants, are common atop the bluffs and in the rest of the park. At the far east end (on County DL four miles east of the lake) is the 480-acre Parfrey's Glen State Natural Area. This narrow gorge, up to a hundred feet deep around the waterfall at its far end, is one of the most beautiful spots in the state, and was designated the first state natural area both because of its singular beauty and because it hosts many rare plants that normally are found at more northern latitudes. It is well known and can be crowded on summer weekends, but should not be missed.

WILDLIFE—Devil's Lake harbors a great variety and abundance of wildlife. Bird-watchers looking to add forest dwellers to their life lists can not do much better than this site, since they will encounter an impressive mix of both northern and southern species. Wood duck, green heron, turkey vulture, red-tailed hawk, pileated woodpecker, ruffed grouse, wild turkey, willow flycatcher, winter wren, and scarlet tanager are among the more common of the 240 species of birds that have been recorded in the park—and all are among the 110 or so species which nest here. American kestrel, northern saw-whet owl, horned lark, brown creeper, and Henslow's sparrow are some rare summer residents. The 18 nesting warblers include Cerulean, worm-eating, Blackburnian, blue-winged, and chestnut-sided. If you are lucky you will spot a red-throated loon, green-winged teal, solitary sandpiper, Caspian tern, yellow-bellied sapsucker, osprey, or pine siskin migrating through in the spring or fall. Exciting winter visitors include pine grosbeak, snow bunting, and Townsend's solitaire.

Park mammals include otter, beaver, mink, badger, porcupine, fox, coyote, and deer. Even bobcat and bear have been seen on rare occasions.

Though they are very shy, and there is almost no chance of seeing one, timber rattlesnakes do live in the park. Even if you do encounter one, they are harmless if left alone.

JULIA HERTEL

Incomparable Devil's Lake.

HIKING—The park's 23 miles of hiking trails are some of the best in southern Wisconsin. The narrow twisting paths up the bluffs offer truly spectacular views of the lake and beyond (the tops of the bluffs lining the Wisconsin River and even Blue Mounds State Park are sometimes visible far to the south) as well as wonderful up-close scenery, and these trails are naturally the most popular. Most sections of these paths feature stone steps and are surfaced with asphalt in places, though, of course, the steep climbs remain fairly strenuous.

The wooded, 1.5-mile West Bluff Trail climbs to the top of that bluff. A *West Bluff Self-Guiding Tour* brochure, available at the park office and nature center, explains what you see on the trail and discusses the park's complicated geological history. A similar brochure is available for the south face of East Bluff. The level, 0.8-mile Tumbled Rocks Trail parallels the lake through the talus below West Bluff, completing a loop with the West Bluff Trail. Tumbled Rocks is narrow except for the thousand feet at the north end, which has been widened for wheelchair access.

Many more trails lead up and along East Bluff including the 1.3-mile East Bluff Trail that makes the long steep climb from the lake's north shore and winds between the edge of the bluff and the forest. Elephant Rock and the nearby Elephant Cave, which is really just a small opening, sit at the trail's north end. The level, half-mile Devil's Doorway Trail continues from the end of the East Bluff Trail along the top of the bluff's south face. A short section branches off to Devil's Doorway, a massive stone arch.

The Balanced Rock and Potholes trails, both 0.3-mile long, and the 0.6-mile CCC Trail, climb directly up the south face of East Bluff. The first two are named for the rock formations found along them. The improbable Balanced Rock is a four-to-five-ton boulder perched on its narrow end; it is halfway up the trail. There are about a dozen glacially formed potholes near the top of the bluff along the Potholes Trail, which also passes through a massive rock crack.

Below the south face of the East Bluff is the 0.7 mile Grottos Trail, a level, wooded path named for the large depressions of unknown origin (probably running water or ice) found along the base of the bluff. It also passes through the 122-acre Devil's Lake Oak Forest State Natural Area, as do the Potholes and CCC trails. The *Landmark Nature Trail* brochure, available at the South Shore office, points out interesting natural and historical sites in the picnic area and along the Grottos Trail. The two-mile loop formed by combining the Balanced Rock, Devil's Doorway, CCC, and Grottos trails is arguably the most scenic in the park.

There are also many good trails away from the bluffs that, while generally less scenic, are also much less crowded. The Ice Age Trail (p. 1) comes into the park from the southeast, crosses through a pair of farm fields, and then follows a small stream uphill between a gap in the south face of the East Bluff where it joins the mostly wooded Ice Age Loop, a hilly four-mile trail that is most scenic along the south face of East Bluff. Another section of the Ice Age Trail follows the terminal moraine for four miles across the easternmost end of the park to the Parfrey's Glen Natural Area. It is quite hilly, mostly uphill from east to west, and passes through a mix of forest and meadow.

The mostly level Steinke Basin Loop leads through an extinct glacial lakebed within the Ice Age Loop. The-2.5-mile trail is a mix of wooded and open terrain and can be very wet. The 1.3-mile East Bluff Woods Trail is a very long climb up the back side of the bluff. The mostly wooded path forms a loop with the East Bluff Trail, while a short path connecting to the east end of the CCC Trail allows a longer loop. The portion of the East Bluff Woods Loop that leads to the Steinke Basin Loop is also a long climb. The 2.5-mile Johnson Moraine Loop north of County DL follows the rolling terminal moraine through open field and past a few kettle ponds.

Although the blufftop trails around the lake are pretty amazing, the most spectacular walk in the park is the 0.8-mile creekside trail up to Parfrey's Glen. It is a long uphill climb to the glen, and though the trail starts out rather dully, it becomes progressively more beautiful until you enter the otherworldly canyon at the top. Wheelchairs can make it to the edge of the glen for great views, although the interior trail remains wheelchair inaccessible. If you find the lot full, do not park on the road as your car will be ticketed or towed; you will just have to come back later.

For a little variety, try the seldom-used path (formerly the Beaver Pond Nature Trail, though it is no longer maintained) at the southwest end of the lake, which runs for about a quarter of a mile along Messenger Creek to the edge of the 40-acre Koshawago Springs State Natural Area—it is a good bird-watching site. The overgrown trail starts along South Lake Dr. next to the stone pillar.

PADDLING—Canoeing is popular on the 373-acre lake, and only electric motors are allowed. Canoes and rowboats are available for rent.

BIKING—Off-road bikes are allowed on the Ice Age Loop and the mile-long section of the East Bluff Woods Trail that connects it with the north shore.

WINTER—The East Bluff Woods Trail, Ice Age Loop, Steinke Basin Loop, Johnson Moraine Loop, and the 1.5-mile road through the Ice Age Campground are groomed for cross-country skiing, about 15 miles total. The north half of the Johnson Moraine Loop and the path through the Ice Age campground accommodate skating. Devil's Lake is one of the best parks in southern Wisconsin to explore with snowshoes. A warming shelter is available, and a sledding hill is located near the nature center.

OTHER—The bluffs make this one of the Midwest's best places for rock climbing, and the lake's remarkable clarity makes it a popular scuba destination. Snorkels, masks, and fins are available for rent at the park, allowing an easier way to examine its depths. The chateau on the north shore has big-band music and square dancing during the summer.

COUNTY—Sauk.

DIRECTIONS—Two miles south of Baraboo on Highway 123.

FACILITIES—Water, toilets, boat launch, nature center, nature programs, picnic area, grills, picnic shelter, beach (with special wheelchair access), playground, volleyball, horseshoes, basketball.

CAMPING—Three campgrounds, 407 sites, 121 electric, open year-round, reservations accepted, showers, group camp.

ENTRY—Open year-round. State park sticker or daily fee required. State trail pass required for off-road bikers.

ON THE WEB—www.wiparks.net and www.devilslakewisconsin.com

CONTACT—Devil's Lake State Park, S5975 Park Rd., Baraboo, WI 53913. Phone (608) 356-8301.

Mirror Lake State Park

MIRROR LAKE State Park provides a quiet contrast to the Wisconsin Dells, located just to the north. The narrow eastern half of the namesake lake features scenic sandstone bluffs up to 50 feet high. These bluffs help keep the lake calm, allowing beautiful, clear reflections, hence its name. A narrow stretch of the lake between the east and west sections, appropriately called the Narrows, is lined by tall bluffs and is particularly scenic. Forest covers almost all of the park's 2,179-acres, though wetland surrounds the wide western end of the lake and meadow and patches of prairie are scattered about. The cooler microclimates of the cliffs harbor unique pine relic communities.

WILDLIFE—The park's forests are home to deer, fox, coyote, Cooper's hawk, turkey vulture, ruffed grouse, great horned owl, white-breasted nuthatch, and blue-winged warbler, while beaver, mink, ducks, and great blue heron all can be sighted on and around Mirror Lake. The west end of the lake, rimmed by wetlands, is the best place to look for wildlife.

HIKING—There are nearly 20 miles of trails in the park. The most popular is the 0.6-mile Echo Rock Trail, which has great lake views. The trail is generally level with a set of steps leading down to some especially scenic bluffs at the far end. The west side of the trail is wheelchair-accessible.

The four interconnected loops of the 5.5-mile Blue Water Bay Trail provide the best hiking option for both scenery and solitude, particularly the 2.5-mile

Mirror Lake lives up to its name.

DEBORAH PROCTOR

Northwest Loop. This little-used loop features many rock outcroppings and leads past the Narrows of Mirror Lake. It is the park's hilliest hike. The 1.3-mile West and 1.9-mile North loops run along the lakeshore and include several small hills, but are easy routes overall. It is about three miles around the outside of the three loops. The wooded and level one-mile East Loop leading past the campground and along the park road is not nearly as interesting as the others.

Branching off the southern end of the Blue Water Bay Trail is the 0.4-mile Time Warp Trail. This level, open trail begins at the park office and has a guide booklet (available at the trailhead) discussing the ecology of the area and how human activities have changed it. There is also a guide for the 0.7-mile Nature Trail—also known as the Wild Foods and Medicines Trail—which describes past and present uses of some of the plants found along the trail. This wooded path includes some small hills and is a very nice hike overall.

The mostly level Winnebago Trail is not quite as scenic as the Blue Water Trail, but this 10.6-mile path is still worthwhile. All but the half-wooded 1.4-mile Ishnala Loop, the least interesting of the six loops comprising the total trail, are south of Fern Dell Road. The 1.9-mile Hastings, 1.2-mile Pioneer, and 0.7-mile Beaver Pond loops are mostly wooded, while the 2.7-mile Fern Dell Loop includes some large open areas. The Turtleville Loop, also 2.7 miles long, is the most remote and least used. This half-wooded, half-open path leading along the southeast end of the lake and the wetlands surrounding Harrison Creek, is a good wildlife-watching destination.

PADDLING—Canoeing is a popular activity here. Motorboats are allowed, but the entire 137-acre lake is a slow-no-wake zone, offering canoeists peace and quiet most of the time. There are still several private homes on the lake within the park, but most of the shore is undeveloped and lovely. The Narrows, in the center of the lake, is a fantastic destination and a narrow part of the lake with more bluffs extends beyond the north end of the park to the dam at Ishnala Road. The far southeast end of the lake has no bluffs, but also has no development and is a great place to look for wildlife in the surrounding wetlands. There is a boat launch onto the western half of the lake on Lake View Road, off Highway 23. Canoes, kayaks, and fishing boats may be rented at the park.

BIKING—Off-road bikes are allowed on the 9.2 miles of the Winnebago Trail south of Fern Dell Road. There are bikes for rent at the park.

WINTER—The Winnebago and Blue Water Bay trails, over 17 miles total, are groomed for cross-country skiing. The Fern Dell and Turtleville Loops accommodate skate-skiers.

OTHER—The Seth Peterson Cottage overlooking the west end of the lake is one of just two Frank Lloyd Wright-designed houses where guests can spend the night, though it is not cheap and reservations must be made months in advance. The 880-square-foot cottage designed by Wright in 1958 has been described as having "more architecture per square foot than any other building (he) ever designed," and is, of course, listed on the National Register of Historic Places. Named for the man who commissioned it, the building was acquired by the state in 1966 when the park opened. Other homes acquired on the lake were razed when the state bought the land, but park officials spared this one. Time took its toll, but in 1989 a local citizens group refurbished the cottage and built the furniture that Wright had originally designed for it. While not visible from the road (you can get a look if you are out on the lake though), there is an open house the second Sunday of each month from 1–4 p.m.

COUNTY—Sauk.

DIRECTIONS—One half mile south of I-90/94 on Highway 12, then 1.5 miles west on Fern Dell Rd.

FACILITIES—Water, toilets, boat launch, nature programs, picnic area, grills, picnic shelter, beach, playground.

CAMPING—Three campgrounds, 150 sites, 30 electric, barrier-free cabin, open year-round, reservations accepted, showers, group camp. Seth Peterson Cottage (described above).

ENTRY—Open year-round. State park sticker or daily fee required. State trail pass required for off-road bikers.

ON THE WEB—www.wiparks.net

CONTACT—Mirror Lake State Park, E10320 Fern Dell Rd., Baraboo, WI 53913. Phone (608) 254-2333. For Seth Peterson Cottage rentals or information, call (608) 254-6551.

Rocky Arbor State Park

THE CLICHÉ "good things come in small packages" fits Rocky Arbor perfectly. While it is one of the smallest state parks, at just 225 acres, it ranks up there with the most beautiful. The main point of interest is a scenic gorge, lined by 500-million-year-old sandstone ledges, at the southern end of the park. The gorge was carved by the Wisconsin River, which has changed course several times since then and now flows a little over a mile to the east. Today the gorge is filled by a marsh and a tiny creek which, oddly enough, flows in the opposite direction as the Wisconsin did. The gorge has a much cooler microclimate than the surrounding area, and thus supports many plants rarely found this far south—including the giant white pines lining the gorge. Perhaps the best thing about Rocky Arbor is that it provides a quiet escape from the hustle and bustle of the Wisconsin Dells, just a mile away.

WILDLIFE—Because of the park's size and nearby development, wildlife is not especially abundant here, but deer, fox, beaver, wood duck, great-blue heron, pileated woodpecker, wild turkey, Eastern wood pewee, and scarlet tanager might be seen.

HIKING—The mile-long Rocky Arbor Trail leads through the spectacular gorge and then loops back through the forest above. The narrow trail is level except for the steps leading in and out of the gorge. There is an accessible wildlife viewing blind near the start, and interpretive signs discussing the park's ecology are planned.

COUNTIES—Sauk and Juneau.

DIRECTIONS—One mile northwest of Wisconsin Dells on Highway 12/16.

FACILITIES—Water, toilets, picnic area, grills, picnic shelter, playground.

CAMPING—89 sites, 18 electric, open same as park, reservations accepted, showers.

ENTRY—Open Memorial Day weekend through Labor Day weekend. State parks sticker or daily fee required.

ON THE WEB—www.wiparks.net

CONTACT—Rocky Arbor State Park, E10320 Fern Dell Rd., Baraboo, WI 53913. Phone (608) 254-8001.

Bass Hollow County Park

THIS LITTLE-KNOWN park straddles a deep, narrow valley along Sevenmile Creek and is known locally as the "Ozarks of Wisconsin" because of the scenic rock outcroppings. Its 295 acres are undeveloped except for a small picnic area.

WILDLIFE—Deer, fox, ruffed grouse, wild turkey, hawks, pileated woodpecker, and many songbirds can all be found here.

HIKING—A three-mile trail loops through the wooded park, and though mostly level it has steep hills heading in and out of the valley. A bridge at the south end spans the creek, though hikers need to cross on rocks or logs at the north end. Several smaller streams along the trail can easily be stepped over. A spur breaks off the north end of the main loop and continues along the creek. This level trail is used less often and thus it is a little harder to follow, but equally scenic. The trails are often wet in spots.

BIKING—Off-road bikes are allowed on the trail.

WINTER—Cross-country skiing is allowed on the trail, though it is not groomed.

OTHER—Horseback riders often use the trail.

COUNTY—Juneau.

DIRECTIONS—1.5 miles southeast of Mauston of Highway 12/16, then seven miles south on County K.

FACILITIES—Water, toilets, picnic area, grills, picnic shelter, playground, volleyball.

CAMPING—None.

ENTRY—Open year-round. Free.

CONTACT—Juneau County Land, Forestry, and Parks, 650 Prairie St., Mauston, WI 53948. Phone (608) 847-9389.

Mill Bluff State Park

AS YOU DRIVE ALONG Interstate 94, you can not help but notice the towering mesas and buttes rising out of the surrounding plain, but for some reason few people stop to explore them up close. Despite being located in the state's Driftless Region, these 80- to 120-foot-tall mounds were indirectly formed by the glaciers of the last Ice Age. The melting ice filled the expansive Glacial Lake Wisconsin, and while the lake wore away or buried most of the region's hills, these limestone-capped sandstone bluffs survived as islands. Mill Bluff, one of nearly a dozen mounds in the park, is presumed to be named for a sawmill that was once located nearby, but there is no actual evidence that one ever existed here.

The rest of the 1,258-acre park is a mix of forest and field, with some small prairie remnants and wetlands in abandoned cranberry bogs. With the interstate and a rail line cutting right though its heart, Mill Bluff is not one of the state's most peaceful getaways, but the unique beauty offsets the constant highway hum.

WILDLIFE—The park is home to great blue and green-backed herons, wood duck, sandhill crane, Northern harrier, Copper's hawk, turkey vulture, wild turkey, ruffed grouse, pileated woodpecker, yellow-billed cuckoo, great crested flycatcher, white-breasted nuthatch, rose-breasted grosbeak, savannah sparrow, blue-winged warbler, and bobolink. Larger mammals include deer, fox, and coyote.

HIKING—Just about every park visitor climbs the 185 steps to the top of Mill Bluff for the excellent views of the park's other glacial islands. Circling the mound is the easy, half-mile Bluff Nature Trail, which has interpretive panels discussing the park's flora and fauna.

The 1.25-mile Camelback Trail in the northern half of the park runs east from 33rd Lane through forest and open field past Camelback Bluff before looping back. The trail is generally level, with just a few small hills. At the far end of the trail is Devil's Needle, a slender 30-foot rock pinnacle. South of the railroad tracks is the unmarked and seldom used Beaver Pond Trail. The level half-mile path heads west past little Sugar Bowl Bluff and loops around a narrow pond.

COUNTIES—Monroe and Juneau.

DIRECTIONS—Three miles west of Camp Douglas on Highway 12/16.

FACILITIES—Water, toilets, nature programs, picnic area, grills, picnic shelter, beach, playground.

CAMPING—21 sites, 6 electric, open same as park, reservations accepted.

ENTRY—Open Memorial Day weekend through mid-October. State park sticker or daily fee required.

ON THE WEB—www.wiparks.net

CONTACT—Mill Bluff State Park, 15819 Funnel Rd. Camp Douglas, WI 54618. Phone (608) 427-6692 or (608) 337-4775 (off-season).

Buckhorn State Park

BUCKHORN STATE PARK sits at the end of a large peninsula on the Castle Rock Flowage. The park's wilderness aspect is, for many, the main draw. The 6,990-acre park and wildlife area remains almost completely undeveloped, which was the plan when the state purchased its first land in 1974. In keeping with the wilderness aspect of the park, most camping is limited to shoreline sites, and these can be reached by boat or trail. The lake is another major draw. The 26-square-mile reservoir, the fifth largest in Wisconsin, lies behind one of more than two dozen dams on the "hardest working river in the nation." The flowage holds back both the Wisconsin River and the Yellow River with the parkland covering the peninsula in between. Most park facilities are found on the west side of the park along the Yellow River, leaving the rest of the park peaceful and unspoiled.

While the flowage is large, it pales in size compared to Glacial Lake Wisconsin which once covered this area and deposited the sand still found throughout the region. Remains of the lake bottom can be seen at the Sandblow Vista, just south of the park entrance, where a short, accessible boardwalk leads to a desert-like opening. There is also a short, accessible path along the edge of the park's large savanna restoration.

WILDLIFE—Buckhorn is a good destination for wildlife watchers. Deer, fox, coyote, bear, pileated woodpecker, wild turkey, and many warblers may all be seen in the forest. On the water, look for sandhill crane, great blue heron, geese, and ducks, as well beaver, otter, and mink. Two of the more thrilling sightings, neither of which is rare, are osprey, which nests in the park, and bald eagle. The latter congregate just north of the park near the Petenwell Dam each winter (see Wisconsin River Power Company Recreation Areas, (p. 186) though they may be seen near the park anytime during the year. Three accessible wildlife observation blinds are located on the property.

HIKING—Three level trails, totaling 3.5 miles, wind through the forest past scattered wetlands and prairies (both remnant and restored) near the end of the peninsula. The Nature Trail, a 1.4-mile loop, has signs along its path discussing the sandy environment of the former Glacial Lake Wisconsin. The Turkey Hollow Segment is a 0.75-mile extension to the Nature Trail, though there are no interpretive signs, while the 1.2-mile Partridge Trail joins the other two. A loop around the perimeter of the three trails is about a three-mile hike.

East of the Sandblow Vista, an unmarked trail leads through the forest to a bi-level wildlife observation/hunting blind with a wheelchair-accessible lower level. The trail is not surfaced, but is wide and flat, and people with disabilities are allowed to drive out here.

PADDLING—The peninsula has several narrow sloughs, backwater areas that are excellent spots to explore from the seat of a canoe. An easy, marked canoe trail on the east side of the park loops for about a mile through a narrow channel between a large island and the mainland. The trail is marked with numbered posts that correspond to a guide booklet, available at the landing, that describes the abundant wildlife found in the area.

A small island east of the peninsula is a popular stop for canoeists and other boaters. There are no facilities, but many go there to picnic and swim. It is just about a mile and a half from the canoe launch. Canoeists should be aware that waves can be quite high on the open flowage when it is windy.

WINTER—All three main trails are groomed for cross-country skiing.

COUNTY—Juneau.

DIRECTIONS—Three miles south of Necedah on Highway 80, then three miles south on Highway 58, and four miles east on County G.

FACILITIES—Water, toilets, boat launch, nature programs, picnic area, grills, picnic shelter, beach, playground, volleyball, horseshoes.

CAMPING—Seven regular sites, 26 walk-in and backpack sites (pushcarts available), barrier-free cabin, open year-round, reservations accepted, group camp.

ENTRY—Open year-round. State park sticker or daily fee required.

ON THE WEB—www.wiparks.net

CONTACT—Buckhorn State Park, W8450 Buckhorn Park Ave., Necedah, WI 54646. Phone (608) 565-2789.

Quincy Bluff
and Wetlands Preserve

THIS UNIQUE AREA of virtually untouched wilderness is a joint project between The Nature Conservancy, owners of the southern half, and the Wisconsin Department of Natural Resources, who own the northern half. Together more than 4,700 acres have been protected, and the goal is to more than double that total eventually. Most state natural areas are small and represent only one or two natural communities, but Quincy Bluff is one of the few natural areas protecting an entire ecosystem. In all, nine Central Sands communities are protected here, as is a multitude of rare plants.

Quincy Bluff, the property's most prominent landmark, stretches north to south for two miles and rises 200 feet above the surrounding plain. Northeast of Quincy Bluff is the smaller Lone Rock, and to the east is Rattlesnake Mound, which will eventually be included in the preserve. These sandstone mounds and others across the region were formerly islands in Glacial Lake Wisconsin, which once covered this area. The land surrounding the bluffs consists mostly of wetlands and oak and pine forest, with some pine barrens in the north and small sand prairie remnants scattered about.

WILDLIFE—Turkey vultures and hawks are frequently seen soaring above the mounds. Other inhabitants include herons, sandhill crane, wild turkey, many warblers, deer, beaver, and even bobcat.

HIKING—There are over 20 miles of unmarked trails throughout both sections of the property, and except where they head up the mounds they are completely flat.

In the southern (Nature Conservancy) section, a trail leads east from the main parking area right over the middle of Quincy Bluff. At the top, a narrow spur path leads north to two overlooks at exposed rock faces, one to the east and one to the west, where almost nothing manmade is visible for as far as the eye can see. On the other side of the bluff, the trail splits, following the base of the bluff and the wetlands which lie to the east—a short loop leads right into the wetlands. The path to the south leads back over the bluff, and you can either return to the parking area or back to where the trail first starts up the bluff. Heading north along the bluff's east face, the trail continues past the bluff and leads to the corner of 16th Drive and Edgewood Avenue, a half mile north of the parking area. An old fire tower sits on the northern edge of the bluff, and though a trail leads up to it, there are no views as the area is heavily wooded. A seldom-used trail heads east from 16th Drive at Ember Avenue through open field and into the forest at the south end of the mound.

In the state-owned section, a three-mile trail leads from the parking area up

183

to and around Lone Rock. This trail largely passes through narrow fingers of upland forest surrounded by wetlands and is an excellent wildlife watching route. No trail leads to the top of Lone Rock, which has steep cliffs around its top edge, but many people do climb to the top for the views. From Lone Rock, a few other trails branch out in several directions through the surrounding forest.

Eventually, the northern and southern portions of the preserve will be connected by a trail, but currently private property blocks this path. The future also probably includes a segment of the Ice Age Trail (p. 1).

WINTER—Though not groomed the trails are available for cross-country skiing.

COUNTY—Adams.

DIRECTIONS—The Nature Conservancy section is 8.5 miles south of Adams on Highway 13, then 2.5 miles west on County H, half a mile north on 16th Ave., half a mile west on Evergreen Ave., and finally 2.25 miles north on 16th Dr. There is an informational kiosk at the parking area. The DNR section is 3.5 miles south of Adams on Highway 13, then 1.5 miles west on Dyke Dr., and half a mile north on 14th Dr.

FACILITIES—None.

CAMPING—None.

ENTRY—Open year-round. Free.

ON THE WEB—http://nature.org/wisconsin

CONTACT—The Nature Conservancy. Phone (608) 251-8140. E-mail: wmail@tnc.org; DNR, PO Box 100, Friendship, WI 53934. Phone (608) 339-3385.

Roche-A-Cri State Park

Spectacular Roche-A-Cri Mound at the heart of this 604-acre park towers 300 feet above the surrounding plain. The narrow sandstone mesa, like most of the mounds in the area, was formerly an island in Glacial Lake Wisconsin, which covered central Wisconsin at the end of the last Ice Age. The state acquired Roche-A-Cri as well as several other nearby mounds to ensure their preservation, making this a state park in 1948 while highway waysides opened at several others.

This unique hill is as significant historically as it is geologically, since it features numerous ancient petroglyphs (carvings) and pictographs (paintings), one of the few places in the U.S. where the two can be seen side by side. The significance of these markings, some of which date back thousands of years, is unknown. The abundance of the art likely means this mound was an impor-

DOUG ALFT

Roche-A-Cri mound.

tant spiritual site, though it is also possible that it had no special significance whatsoever. It is also unclear just who created the art. A barrier-free observation deck on the south end of the mound allows up-close viewing and interpretive panels reveal what is known about the markings and some of the theories surrounding them. In addition to the ancient art, several more recent carvings date back to 1845 and include the signatures of some of Adams County's earliest European settlers.

Previously visitors could scramble to the top of the mound at will, but to protect it from erosion climbing was banned in the 1970s. Today, the Top of the Rock Trail, a 303-step stairway, leads to an observation deck at the top of the mound. The path is steep, but worth every gasp as the views are fantastic. Several other mounds, including Quincy Bluff (p. 183) to the south, rise above the forest in the distance. On a clear day it is possible to see 60 miles and ten counties. There are benches on the way up for those who need a rest.

WILDLIFE—Turkey vultures commonly soar above Roche-A-Cri Mound and the nearby Friendship Mound. For the best views of the vultures, head south on the Turkey Vulture Trail toward the winter parking lot. Deer, wild turkey, and ruffed grouse are also common park residents.

HIKING—Six miles of virtually flat hiking trails wind through the park and, because this is one of the least visited of Wisconsin's state parks, this is an excellent place to avoid the crowds. The wooded 3.5-mile Acorn Trail, the park's longest, circles the park and offers hikers a little of everything Roche-A-Cri has to offer. It passes the base of the mound to the east and leads to Chick-

185

adee Rock, an interesting 30-foot-tall rock formation north of Roche-A-Cri Mound. The 0.3-mile Mound Trail branches off the Acorn Trail and offers up close views of the north side of the mound.

The other trails, each less than a mile long, connect with the Acorn Trail. The wooded, 0.4-mile Chickadee Rock Trail is the shortest route to its name-sake rock formation. It is wheelchair-accessible and has interpretive panels along it. The 0.6-mile Spring Peeper Trail, also wooded, roughly follows Carter Creek, connecting the park office and the rock art site. The Turkey Vulture Trail leads through the woods, crosses a bridge over Carter Creek, and ends in an open field at the south end of the park, where there is a small prairie restoration. The south end of this trail is wheelchair-accessible.

WINTER—The main entrance is closed in the winter, but visitors are still welcome; there is a winter parking area on Czech Avenue at the south end of the park. The trails are groomed for cross-country skiing when snow conditions are good.

COUNTY—Adams.

DIRECTIONS—Two miles north of Friendship on Highway 13.

FACILITIES—Water, toilets, nature programs, picnic area, grills, picnic shelter, playground.

CAMPING—41 sites, open May 1 to October 20, reservations accepted.

ENTRY—Open year-round. State park sticker or daily fee required.

ON THE WEB—www.wiparks.net

CONTACT—Roche-A-Cri State Park, 1767 Highway 13, Friendship, WI 53934. Phone (608) 339-6881 or (608) 565-2789 (off-season).

Wisconsin River Power Company
Recreation Areas—Petenwell Wildlife Area, Van Kuren Trail, and Castle Rock Trails

THE WISCONSIN RIVER Power Company has more than 10,000 acres along the Wisconsin River in central Wisconsin open to public recreation, and these three public-use areas centered on the Petenwell Dam have the most to offer. The 800 acres of marsh, swamp, forest, and a few small prairie remnants comprising the Petenwell Wildlife Area preserve the landscape much as it was before the dam was built. The land around the Van Kuren Trail features wooded hills interspersed with marsh; native prairie plants can be found under the power lines running through the area. The Castle Rock Trails, covering a thousand acres, are the largest area and feature extensive river frontage.

The Petenwell Dam, which created the third largest lake in Wisconsin (Castle

Rock Flowage downstream is the sixth largest), was the first of its kind in the United States. Built on sand, it features a "floating type construction." The sandy soils found here, which ruined many farmers, are the remains of Glacial Lake Wisconsin.

WILDLIFE—The Wisconsin River and its backwaters provide a winter refuge for bald eagles because the river stays open, allowing them to fish. The eagles usually gather here between November and March. Many roost on Petenwell Rock, the large bluff south of the dam on the west side of the river. The 30-foot observation tower near here is the ideal spot for eagle viewing. The best time is generally in the morning, when the eagles are most likely to be feeding. Other animals that may be seen in the area include osprey (which nest here), wild turkey, sandhill crane, herons, ducks, otter, mink, beaver, fox, coyote, and deer. The Petenwell Wildlife Area is a premier wildlife-viewing site.

HIKING—A 2.7-mile trail leads through the Petenwell Wildlife Area. The first half runs along East Dike, providing a wide overview of the area, and then it returns through the area you have just surveyed from above on a service road, eventually breaking away and leading along a sand ridge. At the western end of the trail there is an observation blind overlooking one of the large ponds, although the trail leading to the blind can be hard to find. Interpretive signs are found at several points along both this and the Van Kuren Trail.

The Van Kuren Trail's two segments total 2.7 miles; the main segment, the White Pine Run, is 1.8 miles long and the Red Fox Run adds about a mile more. The short Shoreline Trail Loop, as the name suggests, leads to the flowage. Most of the trail is forested, with scattered marsh along the way. There are some hills along the trail, but none are very large.

The Castle Rock Trails have seven interconnected paths totaling about 35 miles. They are flat and very wet in many places, particularly the Black and White Trail, which has the most frontage along the river and its backwaters and is thus the most scenic. Much of the area is pine plantation, but there is enough natural scenery to make these trails worthwhile. They can be accessed at several points along 20th, 21st, 22nd, and Cumberland avenues.

PADDLING—The Petenwell Flowage is not a very scenic area for paddlers, and motorboats and occasional large waves are also deterrents. The best canoeing is below the Petenwell Dam on the Castle Rock Flowage, alongside the Castle Rock Trails, where there are many back channels to explore. Also, between July 8 and September 1, canoeists can portage into the shallow ponds in the Petenwell Wildlife Area for some up-close wildlife watching.

WINTER—The Van Kuren Trail is groomed for cross-country skiing and has a warming shelter along the White Pine Loop. Skiing is also allowed on the Castle Rock Trails though they are not groomed.

OTHER—The Castle Rock Trails were developed as horse trails in cooperation with the Glacial Drumlin Horse Trails Association; horseback riding is still the principal use.

COUNTY—Adams.

DIRECTIONS—To reach all locations, you must first head three to seven miles east of Necedah on Highway 21. The viewing platform is one mile north on 18th Ave. in Juneau County. The Castle Rock Trails are 0.75 mile south on 22nd Ave. The Petenwell Wildlife Area is 1.25 miles north on 21st Ave. The Van Kuren Trail is two miles north on 20th Ave. and then 200 yards east on Chicago Ave.

FACILITIES—Water, toilets, boat launch, picnic area, grills.

CAMPING—The private Ukarydee Equestrian Campground, (608) 564-2233, lies adjacent to the Castle Rock Trails on Cumberland Ave. It is open year-round.

ENTRY—Van Kuren and Castle Rock trails open year-round. Petenwell Wildlife Area open May 1 to September 31. All are free.

CONTACT—Wisconsin River Power Company, PO Box 19001, Green Bay, WI 54307. Phone (715) 422-3927 or (800) 53-WATCH.

Necedah National
Wildlife Refuge

BETWEEN THIS 44,000-acre wildlife refuge and the adjacent DNR-managed Central Wisconsin Conservation Area (p. 190) there are over 200 square miles of wilderness. Like Wisconsin's other national wildlife refuges, Necedah is managed primarily for migratory birds, but unlike the rest Necedah does not consist mostly of wetlands, though it once did. A part of Glacial Lake Wisconsin thousands of years ago, Necedah was primarily a vast, open peat bog with numerous wooded islands when settlers arrived in the 1800s. The wetlands were drained, but attempts at farming were unsuccessful and most of the land had been abandoned by 1939, when it was set aside as a wildlife refuge. Since then, many wetlands have been restored and now cover about a quarter of the area. Forest covers half of the property, while many of the open areas have been restored to oak barrens and prairie, two plant communities which were once very common in Wisconsin but are now nearly gone. Necedah means "land of yellow waters" in the Ho-Chunk language. The water gets its color from its high iron and mineral content.

WILDLIFE—Over 220 species of birds have been recorded at Necedah, with at least a hundred nesting here, including common loon, wood duck, sandhill crane, bald eagle, northern saw-whet owl, pileated woodpecker, wild turkey, willow flycatcher, white-breasted nuthatch, sedge wren, and bobolink. Peak populations of migratory waterfowl occur in late April and mid-October, and some 25,000 ducks and Canada geese, plus hundreds of sandhill cranes, during the fall migration. Because of its expansive uplands, Necedah is also an important spring stopover for Neotropical migrant songbirds.

The trumpeter swan was returned here as a part of a program to re-establish the species in Wisconsin. Twenty-five cygnets were released in 1994 and were acclimated to the area by people floating around in waders attached to inner tubes covered by swan decoys—a unique but successful approach. Swans are most likely to be seen on Rynearson Pool #1, which has an observation tower and a photography blind. The blind is half a mile north of the headquarters down a marked path.

This is the southernmost extent of timber wolf range in Wisconsin, with two packs roaming Necedah. Other mammals on the refuge include deer, coyote, fox, badger, porcupine, bear, mink, beaver, and otter. The endangered Karner blue butterfly may be seen throughout the oak barrens where lupine, the only food the larvae eat, grows. The endangered eastern massasauga rattlesnake is also found in the area, though encountering one is highly unlikely and not a danger if you leave it alone.

HIKING—All three of the refuge's easy, level hiking trails lie along the Hot Spots auto tour (see below). The 0.75-mile wooded Nature Trail at Stop B leads through forest and out to a narrow peninsula extending into Rynearson Pool #1, offering great views and a good chance to see trumpeter swans. The 1.3-mile Pair Ponds Trail at Stop C leads through oak barrens and passes along some small flowages; it can be a little wet at times. Stop F is the Lupine Loop, a 0.8-mile trail which follows the shore of Goose Pool before passing through oak savanna where you might see the Karner blue butterfly. The last trail is closed September 15 to December 15 to avoid bothering waterfowl.

Hiking is allowed only on these trails or township roads, except between July 1 and August 15 when the entire refuge is open for berry picking. Blueberries are the most coveted.

BIKING—Bikes are allowed only on township roads, and they offer the best way to follow the Hot Spots auto tour.

WINTER—Cross-country skiing and snowshoeing are permitted throughout the refuge from December 15 to March 31 though no trails are groomed.

AUTO TOUR—The Wildlife Viewing "Hot Spots" auto tour follows an 11-mile route through the refuge on township roads. Each of the six lettered stops has an informational display, and most also have observation decks and/or hiking trails. The tour (brochures are available) starts at an information area on Headquarters Road just off Highway 21.

The Wetlands Observation Deck at stop A is wheelchair-accessible. Stop B is the Rynearson Wetlands Observation Tower, which looks out over Rynearson Pool #1, where trumpeter swans are likely to be seen. There is also a hiking trail beginning here. Stop C is named Pair Ponds, after the small ponds used by mating pairs of ducks. It has a trail and wheelchair-accessible observation deck. There are no trails or observation decks at stops D and E, but they are still worth a visit. Stop D is an area of open field where bluebirds can commonly be found, while eagles and waterfowl are frequently seen along Sprague Pool at Stop E. Stop F, the Lupine Loop, has a trail through an oak savanna where the endangered Karner blue butterfly resides.

COUNTIES—Juneau, with a small segment extending into Wood.

DIRECTIONS—The headquarters is four miles west of Necedah on Highway 21, then two miles north on Headquarters Rd.

FACILITIES—Water, toilets, nature center. A picnic area with grills is located alongside the refuge at the wayside on Highway 80, just south of Sprague.

CAMPING—None.

ENTRY—Open year-round. Free.

ON THE WEB—http://midwest.fws.gov/necedah

CONTACT—Necedah National Wildlife Refuge, W7996 20th St. W, Necedah, WI 54646. Phone (608) 565-2551. E-mail: necedah@fws.gov

Central Wisconsin
Conservation Area
Sandhill, Meadow Valley, and Wood County Wildlife Areas

B Y FAR THE MOST significant feature of this remote preserve is its size; at 150 square miles it is the largest block of state-managed wildlife land in Wisconsin. Though it covers nearly 9,500 acres, the Sandhill Wildlife Area is the smallest of the three principal units, but it has the most to offer and receives the most visitors. While Sandhill is never crowded, true solitude can be found in the 58,327-acre Meadow Valley Wildlife Area or the Wood County Wildlife Area, which covers over 19,000 acres.

Formerly covered by Glacial Lake Wisconsin, the area is virtually flat, except for a few scattered quartzite bluffs that were once islands. After the forests were cleared in the mid-1800s, settlers moved in and tried, unsuccessfully, to farm the area. Agriculture failed for many reasons, including poor soil and drainage, a short growing season, and frequent wildfires that scorched hundreds of square miles. Extensive drainage ditches were constructed in the early part of the 20th century to "improve" the land, but by the 1930s most farmers had given up. Today the ditches have been plugged, bringing back the wetlands that now cover half the area and are intermingled with dry, sandy ridges. These uplands are dominated by forest, but some small, scattered prairies and barrens provide variety.

Sandhill Wildlife Area is encircled by a tall fence and serves as a wildlife demonstration area and outdoor laboratory where management methods can be studied and evaluated. Sandhill got its start with Wallace Grange, a contemporary of Aldo Leopold, who purchased the devastated land in 1937. He constructed a deer-proof fence around the property and worked to restore the natural communities. For 24 years, he operated the Sandhill Game Farm, conducting research and sending deer and grouse to eastern states for reintroduction programs, as well as selling deer, grouse, and waterfowl to fancy restaurants in New York, Chicago, and other cities. When he retired, he sold the land to the state with the stipulation that it continue to operate as a wildlife demonstration area.

Public programs and classes ranging from tracking and bird-watching to winter camping and orienteering are held throughout the year at the Outdoor Skills Center.

WILDLIFE—Because this is such a vast, undeveloped area, it is one of the most bounteous wildlife-watching places in the state. By 1930, only 15 pair of sandhill cranes were left in Wisconsin. Today, Gallagher Marsh in the Sandhill Wildlife Area has one of the largest concentrations of staging sandhill cranes in the state, with an average of 3,000 congregating each fall to prepare ("stage") for their migration south; a handful now nest here, also. Some of the other 120-plus species of birds that may be seen here during the summer months include herons, geese, ducks, bald eagle, pileated woodpecker, ruffed and sharp-tailed grouse, woodcock, wild turkey, Eastern meadowlark, great-crested flycatcher, American bittern, sora rail, and black tern. Also look for osprey, great egret, and trumpeter swan; all threatened or endangered species. Other endangered and threatened species that have been seen here include the Karner blue butterfly, Blanding's turtle, and massasauga rattlesnake; the last two are extremely timid and there is no reason to be worried about them.

This is the southernmost range for the state's timber wolves, and while there is little chance of actually spotting one, if you are lucky you might hear their howls. Beaver, otter, mink, fisher, coyote, bear, badger, and deer—Sandhill is known for its older, larger bucks—are among the other mammals residing here.

One of the most popular sights at Sandhill are the bison. The herd of about a dozen, descendants of the bison Grange acquired in the late 1940s, roam freely within a 260-acre enclosed oak savanna restoration.

HIKING—The most popular way to see Sandhill is along the auto tour (see below), but there are many opportunities to get out of the car and see less-visited areas. The best hike is the 3.5-mile Swamp Buck Hiking Trail. This level path leads through wetlands on dikes and boardwalks, and also has some forested areas. It begins between the third and fourth stops of the auto tour, just half a mile from the entrance, and ends at the observation tower atop North Bluff. There are also countless dikes and service roads that can be hiked, many of which are shown on the brochure map available at the entrance.

There are no formal hiking trails in either Meadow Valley or Wood County wildlife areas, but many miles of service roads and dikes offer easy access to remote areas. In Meadow Valley, several paths lead along the Meadow Valley Flowage from Flowage Road (3rd Street). The dike along Beaver Flowage, in the center of the property, is also a nice walk. Sprague Mather Road (9th Street) has several good wooded paths branching off from it.

In Wood County, many good paths lead north from Ball Road through the extensive wetlands. Several wooded paths cross the forest around South Bluff; you can reach them from Stout Marsh and South Bluff roads. One leads to a fire tower at the top of the bluff, and even though there are only limited views from here because of the trees, it is a still a pleasant hike.

PADDLING—Canoeing on one of the many large flowages, many of which are easily accessible from adjacent roads, is a good way to explore the area, especially for bird-watchers.

BIKING—There are no bike trails, but many cyclists follow Sandhill's Trumpeter Trail Auto Tour.

WINTER—While the auto tour route is not open to cars in winter, three cross-country ski trails follow it. The easy, groomed trails begin along the same path and branch off from each other. They range from 2.5 to five miles in length. The middle trail, 3.5 miles in length, leads past North Bluff. The trailhead is on Ball Road, two miles west of the headquarters.

AUTO TOUR—Most people see Sandhill from the 14-mile Trumpeter Trail auto tour, which is open, weather permitting, mid-April through November. Fifteen interpretive stops correspond to a guide booklet that you may pick up at the start. The route consists of two loops, and skipping the second one cuts the trip down by half. Three observation towers are found along the route, and the spectacular panoramas from the tower atop North Bluff, which rises 200 feet above the otherwise flat plain, should not be missed. The Bison Tower overlooks the bison range, while the Marsh Tower overlooks Gallagher Marsh, Sandhill's largest.

COUNTIES—Wood, Juneau, Monroe, and a small section in Jackson.

DIRECTIONS—The headquarters and entrance to Sandhill is half a mile west of Babcock on Highway 80/73, then half a mile north on County X.

FACILITIES—Water, toilets, nature programs, picnic area, grills.

CAMPING—14 designated camping sites with no facilities at Meadow Valley and Wood County wildlife areas (free), but visitors are allowed there only for a wildlife-related activity (e.g., hunting, bird-watching, photography), and they are open only September 1 to December 31.

ENTRY—Open year-round. Free.

ON THE WEB—www.dnr.state.wi.us/org/land/wildlife/reclands/sandhill

CONTACT—Sandhill Wildlife Area, County Highway X, PO Box 156, Babcock, WI 54413. Phone (715) 884-2437.

Black River State Forest
and Dike 17 Wildlife Area

IT IS NOT THE trees or the namesake river but the unique topography that sets the 67,070-acre Black River State Forest apart from other natural areas. Towering sandstone mounds rising out of the otherwise flat landscape, visible from miles away, dot the landscape. One of the most prominent is the 180-foot Castle Mound in the small detached section of the forest south of Black River Falls. A narrow spine with vertical cliffs up to 30 feet high tops the 400-million-year-old butte.

Logging began here in 1850 and by the end of the century the forest was cleared. Settlers moved in soon afterward and tried to make a living farming the land, but were quickly bankrupted due to the infertile sandy soil and early frosts. An old cemetery dating back to the late 1800s on Smrekar Road, and a root cellar and well along the adjacent hiking trails are reminders of this era. In the early 1900s, the U.S. Resettlement Administration bought the "useless" land from the settlers and moved them elsewhere in Jackson County. The Civilian Conservation Corps came in to reforest the area shortly after this and in 1955 the federal government turned the land over to the state.

Centuries before the loggers or farmers arrived, the area was a meeting ground for the Ho-Chunk; it was also the scene of many clashes with invading tribes. The river's name is more recent, having been given by early French traders due to its dark color caused by a combination of tannic acid leaching in from pine needles and the high iron content of the soil.

Differing significantly from the rest of the forest are the grasslands, marsh, and flowages of the Dike 17 Wildlife Area in the northeast corner of the forest.

This 3,700-acre refuge is managed primarily for waterfowl and can easily be seen from an observation tower off North Settlement Road.

WILDLIFE—The most exciting animals in the forest are the timber wolves; five packs roam within the forest boundaries—two north of Highway 54 and three to the south. Although there is little chance of seeing one, you might just hear their howl during the early evening hours. Other resident mammals include bear, deer, fox, coyote, porcupine, northern flying squirrel, mink, otter, and beaver. Many bird species usually found much further north, such as red-breasted nuthatch, solitary vireo, and Canada, pine, and black-throated green warblers nest in the forest, while bald eagle, northern goshawk, broad-winged hawk, pileated woodpecker, wild turkey, and ruffed grouse are some of the other avifauna residing here. During the spring and fall migrations, the duck and geese populations swell into the thousands, and as many as 400 sandhill cranes gather here. The Dike 17 Wildlife Area is the best place to view these travelers—its open grasslands also support sharp-tailed grouse.

Many threatened and endangered species can be seen here, including osprey, red-shouldered hawk, Karner blue butterfly, Eastern massasauga rattlesnake, and Blanding's turtle.

HIKING—There are many hiking opportunities in the forest. Short nature trails are found at each of the three campgrounds. The best of these is the hilly, 1.5-mile Castle Mound Nature Trail. It loops around the mound through the 80-acre Castle Mound Pine Forest State Natural Area which encompasses similar but distinct forest communities: northern dry on the north side and northern dry-mesic on the south. An interior path leads along the top of the mound and passes a small observation tower in the middle. This section is narrow and a little rough, but it is well worth it for the great views. It is just a quarter mile from the trailhead to the tower. The 1.5-mile Pigeon Creek Nature Trail begins along the Pigeon Creek Flowage, a good place to look for wildlife, and then turns into the woods. The forested part loops over and along a small hill, but the rest is level. Finally, the beautiful East Fork Nature Trail is a level half-mile path along the East Fork Black River which has many rapids at this point.

The hilly Wildcat and Smrekar trails are the best options for serious hikers. There are a few pine plantations along the trails' interconnected loops, but for the most part they lead through a scenic hardwood forest and the steep hills provide several overlooks with great forest views. Both trails can be accessed from the Wildcat trailhead three miles north of the Pigeon Creek Campground on North Settlement Road. The Wildcat Trail has three loops totaling nine miles; the four-mile Wildcat Loop which goes up the prominent Wildcat Mound is arguably the most scenic route. The 11.5-mile Smrekar Trail has four loops ranging from just over a mile to the seven-mile Ridge Loop, which has the largest hills and the best scenery. An old root cellar and well are found on the Central Loop just half a mile north of the main trailhead.

Two other long trails, the 4.7-mile Pigeon Creek and 4.5-mile Perry Creek trails, are less scenic overall, but still make worthy hikes and are nearly level. They can be accessed at the Pigeon Creek and Castle Mound campgrounds, respectively.

The northwest corner of the forest, where scenic bluffs line the Black River, is another good area for hikers. While there are no designated trails, several service roads can be hiked. An especially good one starts at the end of Palm Road. There are also over 10 miles of dikes and service roads around the flowages at the Dike 17 Wildlife Area that provide good hiking, particularly those around Seventeen Flowage. Several wooded routes lead off Battle Point Road.

PADDLING—The Black River flows for 24 miles along the northwest edge of the forest from Lake Arbutus to the Hoffman Wayside on Highway 54. There are a few rapids, one rated Class III in high water, above Halls Creek (midway between the lake and Black River Falls), though the river is nearly calm below this. Four canoe landings within the forest, allowing trips of various lengths through the sandstone and granite bluffs, make the 15-mile, eight-hour stretch between the lake and Black River Falls a highly recommended paddle. Downstream from the forest it is another 40 miles to New Amsterdam, just before the Black empties into the Mississippi River. This stretch provides calm, easy canoeing, and the last few miles of river pass through the Van Loon Wildlife Area (p. 203).

Other canoeing options include the scenic East Fork Black River, which forms the forest's northern border for its last two miles; the rest is through county forest. There are several small rapids along the 10 miles (five hours) between the Pray Road canoe landing and the East Fork Campground, a recommended half-day route. Rock-strewn Morrison Creek can also be run in high water, and many of the flowages in and around the Dike 17 Wildlife Area offer relaxed paddling with easy access from forest or township roads.

Water levels can drop quite low on the East Fork from mid-summer on, and heavy water releases from the Black River Falls Dam can affect canoeing below the city, so check on conditions with the forest office before setting out. Canoe rental and shuttle service are available in Black River Falls.

BIKING—Off-road bikes are currently allowed on the Wildcat and Smrekar trails, though this is likely to change soon because of severe erosion. That decision will leave the easy Pigeon Creek and Perry Creek trails—plus any forest road not posted against riding—to mountain bikers. The auto tour routes are paved and make for nice road rides.

WINTER—The main cross-country ski trails, the Wildcat and Smrekar trails, are among the area's best. They are groomed and have warming shelters. The Castle Mound Nature Trail is also groomed, and skate skiers can use the Perry Creek Trail.

Over 50 miles of snowmobile trails wind through the forest; many of them are also open to ATVs.

AUTO TRAIL—The forest's 17-mile Mound View auto tour begins and ends at the Pigeon Creek Campground. The route goes as far north as the Dike 17 Wildlife Area and has nine numbered stops which correspond to a guide booklet available at the main park office or the campground.

Jackson County's 62-mile Wazee Trail auto tour through the eastern end of the county also passes Dike 17. Both of these tour routes follow North Settlement Road, which is officially Rustic Road #54. This bucolic road stretches 12 miles between Highway 54 and County O and is entirely within the forest.

OTHER—There are 34 miles of trails for horseback riders and 33 for ATV and motorcycle riders.

COUNTIES—Jackson and a small section in Clark.

DIRECTIONS—The Castle Mound section of the forest is a mile east of Black River Falls on Highway 12, while the main forest area begins four miles east of Black River Falls on Highway 54.

FACILITIES—Water, toilets, boat launch, picnic area, grills, picnic shelter, beach, playground, horseshoes.

CAMPING—Three campgrounds, 98 sites, five electric, two canoe sites, 12 horseback rider sites, open year-round, reservations accepted, showers, group camp, backpacking permitted throughout forest with free permit, canoe camping permitted on rivers.

ENTRY—Open year-round. State park sticker or daily fee required. State trail pass required for off-road bike, horse, and cross-country ski trails.

ON THE WEB—www.wiparks.net

CONTACT—Black River State Forest, 910 Highway 54 E, Black River Falls, WI 54615. Phone (715) 284-1400.

Merrick State Park
and Whitman Dam Wildlife Area

YOU ARE NEVER FAR From the water at Merrick State Park. The park's 320 acres are stretched out for two miles along the Mississippi River while the adjoining Whitman Dam Wildlife Area forms a 2,493-acre maze of backwater bays, sloughs, and islands. Though not within the park, the 500-

foot bluffs lining the Mississippi River Valley provide a striking scenic backdrop.

Merrick opened in 1932 on land donated by John Latsch of Winona, Minnesota, who loved to paddle the river's backwaters. One day an incoming storm forced Latsch to leave the water and take shelter under his overturned canoe. The land was generally considered public property at the time, but a local farmer bucked convention and ordered Latsch to leave. To prevent such actions for future generations, Latsch not only purchased the land he had been ejected from, but over the rest of his lifetime bought more than 18,000 acres of Mississippi River bottomland in both Wisconsin and Minnesota, then donated it for parks and wildlife conservation. Perrot State Park (p. 200) to the south also benefited from his generosity. At Latsch's request, the park was named for George Merrick, a steamboat pilot from Prescott, Wisconsin, and noted historian of that bygone era.

WILDLIFE—Deer, fox, coyote, beaver, otter, great blue heron, great egret, many ducks, Canada goose, hawks, bald eagle, and prothonotary warbler may all be spotted here. Waterfowl are especially abundant during migration.

HIKING—While the park is best experienced on the water, two mostly level trails provide easy hiking. A short but scenic half-mile trail loops around a small wooded peninsula jutting into Fountain City Bay. The pair of small mounds near the trailhead are probably Native American burial mounds, though since they have not been excavated no one is completely certain.

The other trail runs for 2.5 miles around the northern half of the park through both wooded and open areas. It is not as interesting as the shorter trail because it never gets very far away from the bustle of park activity.

PADDLING—Canoeists are naturally drawn to the Mississippi's scenic backwaters. You can follow the park's marked canoe trail (it currently runs for a couple of miles, but will likely be expanded in the near future) or explore at will. Canoeists will want to avoid the main river channel, which is often crowded with motorboats and large commercial barges.

Canoes and boats may be moored at many of the sites in the South Campground, which lies on a narrow stretch of land jutting out into Fountain City Bay. There is also a mooring site located near the North Campground. Canoes are available for rent at the park.

WINTER—An ungroomed three-mile trail is open for cross-country skiing and snowshoeing.

COUNTY—Buffalo.

DIRECTIONS—Three miles north of Fountain City on Highway 35.

FACILITIES—Water, toilets, boat launch, nature center, nature programs, picnic area, grills, picnic shelter.

197

CAMPING—Two campgrounds, 64 sites, 22 electric, five walk-in sites, reservations accepted, showers, group camp.

ENTRY—Open year-round. State park sticker or daily fee required.

ON THE WEB—www.wiparks.net

CONTACT—Merrick State Park, S2965 Highway 35, PO Box 127, Fountain City, WI 54629. Phone (608) 687-4936.

Trempealeau National
Wildlife Refuge

THIS SPECTACULAR wildlife watching spot along the Mississippi River is one of Wisconsin's best kept secrets. Established in 1936 by President Franklin Roosevelt as a refuge for migratory waterfowl, the refuge has grown from its original 706 acres to over 6,200, most of which are wetlands. Trempealeau is unique because a series of dikes constructed for railroads walls off the refuge from the Mississippi and Trempealeau Rivers, protecting it from silt and pollution. While the refuge is best known for its wetlands, it also encompasses 350 acres of prairie, one of the largest contiguous prairie habitats in the state. Much of this prairie has undergone intensive restoration, but there are also some undisturbed remnants and several areas that have returned on their own. Prairie flowers are in bloom from spring through fall, though the fields are especially beautiful in the fall when the colors of the little blue stem (reddish purple stems and white fluffy seeds) and Indian grass (golden) provide magnificent color.

WILDLIFE—A barrier-free observation deck with a mounted spotting scope overlooks the bay near the refuge headquarters, and it is often staffed by knowledgeable volunteers on weekends. This is the best place to view the refuge's abundant bird life—the American Bird Conservancy has designated the refuge as a Globally Important Bird Area. More than 250 bird species have been recorded here, including bald eagle, osprey, red-shouldered hawk, sandhill crane, great blue heron, great egret, Canada goose, ducks, black tern, pileated woodpecker, Eastern bluebird, indigo bunting, scarlet tanager, marsh wren, American redstart, and blue-winged warbler—all of which nest on or near the refuge. Also look for American white pelican, which first started arriving in the early 1990s and are now fairly common. In the spring (and to a lesser degree in fall) the woods are filled with migrating songbirds such as Canada, palm, and blackpoll warblers, while various duck species including American wigeon, green-winged teal, and ruddy duck rest on the water. Deer, fox, coyote, mink, beaver, and otter are also common residents while Blanding's, painted, and snapping turtles are commonly seen laying their eggs in the late spring and early summer.

HIKING—There are two easy half-mile interpretive trails on the refuge. The wheelchair-accessible Prairie View Trail has interpretive panels explaining the prairie community it passes through. The partly wooded Wetlands and More Trail begins at the observation deck and has interpretive panels explaining the other refuge environments.

Hikers also have some 10 miles of dikes and service roads that are closed to motorized travel and thus great for hiking. The Pine Creek Dike, leading west from the observation deck through wooded wetlands for three-quarters of a mile, no longer has a viewing blind at the end, although it might be replaced. Dike Road can be followed for over two miles along the refuge's eastern border towards Trempealeau Mountain and Perrot State Park, while a short service road leads out to wooded Kiep's Island from the boat launch. Two miles west of the main entrance on Highway 54/35 is the Marshland entrance—used only when the main entrance is flooded—which provides easy access to less frequently visited parts of the refuge. Marshland Road, which is usually closed to motorized traffic, leads southeast for a little over a mile to the main part of the refuge, while a more interesting trail heads south, also for a little more than a mile, along the dike known as Delta Road which passes through marsh. Two miles west of the Marshland entrance, the seldom-used River Bottoms Road leads for 1.25-miles south into the refuge past some old river oxbows that have been cut off from the Mississippi by railroad construction.

PADDLING—Canoeing is a great way to see the area up close. A boat launch is southeast of the refuge headquarters, and only electric motors are allowed.

BIKING—The Prairie's Edge Wildlife Drive is great for biking; in fact, it is a part of the Great River State Trail's 24-mile-long biking route along the Mississippi River between Marshland and Onalaska. Most of the rest of the trail follows an abandoned railroad right-of-way surfaced with crushed limestone. Bikes are also allowed on the dikes and service roads that are closed to cars.

WINTER—Cross-country skiing is permitted throughout the refuge, but no trails are groomed. On occasion, a two-mile stretch of the Great River State Trail between the refuge and Perrot State Park is groomed for skate skiers.

AUTO TOUR—The easiest and most common way to see the refuge is along the 4.5-mile Prairie's Edge Wildlife Drive which does pass through large patches of prairie, but also features the abundant wetland areas and some forest. Pick up the guide booklet at the main entrance.

COUNTY—Trempealeau.

DIRECTIONS—3.5 miles west of Centerville on Highway 54/35, then one mile south on West Prairie Rd.

FACILITIES—Toilets, boat launch.

CAMPING—None.

ENTRY—Open year-round. Free.

ON THE WEB—http://midwest.fws.gov/Trempealeau and www.umesc. usgs.gov/umr_refuge/umrtre/umrtre.html

CONTACT—Trempealeau National Wildlife Refuge, W28488 Refuge Rd., Trempealeau, WI 54661. Phone (608) 539-2311.

Perrot State Park

WITH ITS MANY spectacular bluffs, Perrot State Park preserves some of the most beautiful land along the Mississippi River. Trempealeau Mountain, which rises out of the bay in the southwest corner of the 1,270-acre park, was a prominent landmark for early travelers on the river. At 384 feet it is not as tall as most of the other bluffs in the park, many of which exceed 500 feet, but it is the tallest "island-mountain" on the entire Mississippi. Its name, bestowed by French voyageurs, means "mountain with its foot in the water." The park itself was named for Nicholas Perrot, one of the earliest French traders in the area—he built a winter camp here in 1685. Later, in 1731, the French erected a small fort, though it was occupied for only six years. The first Native Americans lived here as much as 7,000 years before the French, and burial mounds built by the early Hopewellian dwellers can still be found in the park, though most have been destroyed.

WILDLIFE—Bird-watchers tend to focus on the nearby Trempealeau National Wildlife Refuge (p. 198), though with about a hundred species of birds known to nest in the park and another hundred or so passing through at some point in the year, Perrot can also be very productive. Look for bald eagle, osprey, sandhill crane, great egret, blue-winged teal, black tern, ruffed grouse, American woodcock, pileated woodpecker, yellow-bellied sapsucker, great-crested flycatcher, scarlet tanager, marsh wren, and a large number of warblers. Park mammals include deer, fox, mink, beaver, and the occasional otter. Timber rattlesnakes also live in the park, but are rarely seen and are harmless if left alone.

HIKING—Twelve miles of trails wind over and around the wooded bluffs and alongside the Mississippi River and its backwaters. Many of the trails have steep, rough climbs, but the effort is always rewarded with fantastic scenery. Brady's Bluff, the highest point in the park, has three trails leading to a log shelter at the top—the Brady's Bluff North, East, and West trails. The West Trail is the most popular. At just a half mile it is the shortest route to the top and also

Looking out over the Mississippi from atop Perrot State Park.

the easiest because it has a long set of wooden stairs at the steepest part. It is also the most scenic route with numerous rock outcroppings and several vista points along the way. It is 1.75-miles to the top along the less frequently followed North Trail. The 0.75-mile East Trail passes through the 10 acres of native prairie comprising the Brady Bluff Prairie State Natural Area. This dry bluff prairie has never been plowed or grazed and is a wonderful example of just how rich and diverse prairie communities can be. The small preserve contains more than a hundred species of plants, many of which are rare. It was recommended for natural area designation by famed Wisconsin botanist John Curtis.

The 1.75-mile Perrot Ridge Trail starts along the park road at the east entrance parking lot and picnic area and climbs nearly 500 feet to the top of its namesake bluff before looping back through the forest. Overall it is not as beautiful as the Brady's Bluff trails, but it's still recommended.

The two-mile Riverview Trail runs from the campground along the Mississippi River and Trempealeau Bay for the length of the park. The level trail passes through several picnic and parking areas, but overall is very beautiful and a fine choice for bird-watching. A short spur near the middle of the trail leads to Horseshoe Falls. The falls is only "on" during the spring and after rains, but the arching rock face that it drops over is beautiful at all times. If you do not want to hike to the falls, there is direct access from the parking area between the scenic vista and the boat launch.

The park's easiest trail is the Black Walnut Nature Trail, which displays interpretive signs discussing the many uses the Ho-Chunk once had for the forest products found along its wooded half-mile path. It is generally level, with just one short climb.

The park's two bike/ski trails are also worthy hikes. The west end of the easy, 1.25-mile Bay Trail leads along Trempealeau Bay, and so has views of Trempealeau Mountain, and is good for bird-watching. The main branch of the five-mile trail though the quiet eastern half of the park begins at the office and heads east for a half mile before separating into three loops. At one mile in length, the generally level Wilber's Trail is the shortest and also the least interesting loop. The longest is the 2.25-mile Cedar Glade Trail that extends out to the bluffs in the easternmost end of the park, with many steep hills. The hilly 1.25-mile Prairie Trail looping around Perrot Ridge connects the other two.

PADDLING—There is a well-marked canoe trail around Trempealeau Bay, and since there is no river current the route is very easy to follow—perfect for families. The 3.4-mile loop starts at the nature center and passes along Trempealeau Mountain before continuing through a marsh. There is also direct access to the Mississippi River for those who want to explore a little more. Canoes can be rented at the park office.

BIKING—Off-road bikes are allowed on the trails, through the hilly east end of the park and near the campground, over six miles total. The Great River State Trail, which runs for 24 miles from Marshland to Onalaska, much of the way on an abandoned railroad right-of-way surfaced with crushed stone, passes along the northern boundary of the park. A short spur from this trail leads into the campground. Taking the Great River State Trail west through the nearby Trempealeau National Wildlife Refuge is an excellent day-trip.

WINTER—The same trails open to off-road bikes are groomed for cross-country skiing; a skate lane is sometimes groomed from the park over to the Trempealeau National Wildlife Refuge, a four-mile roundtrip.

COUNTY—Trempealeau.

DIRECTIONS—One mile west of Trempealeau on Park Rd.

FACILITIES - Water, toilets, boat launch, nature center, nature programs, picnic area, grills, picnic shelter, volleyball, horseshoes.

CAMPING—98 sites, 37 electric, open year-round, reservations accepted, showers, group camp.

ENTRY—Open year-round. State park sticker or daily fee required. State trail pass required for off-road biking in Perrot and biking on the Great River State Trail.

ON THE WEB—www.wiparks.net

CONTACT—Perrot State Park, PO Box 407, Trempealeau, WI 54661. Phone (608) 534-6409.

Van Loon Wildlife Area

FOR A FIVE-MILE stretch between Hunter's Bridge on Highway 53/93 and New Amsterdam, the Black River splits and most of this low, 3,981-acre wildlife area lies between the two channels. Van Loon is one of the largest remaining tracts of bottomland forest in the state, and its scattered streams, sloughs, marshes, small lakes, and the occasional wooded and open uplands add variety.

The state acquired the first land in 1957 when it purchased 758 acres from the estate of William Van Loon, hence the name. Locally, though, the area is known as McGilvray Bottoms after one of the first settlers in the area, Alexander McGilvray, who arrived in 1853. He soon built a ferry to transport people and goods between La Crosse and Trempealeau counties. Logjams, from lumber being floated down to sawmills on the Mississippi, were common, and since they often blocked ferry operations La Crosse County laid McGilvray Road through the bottoms in 1892. Frequent floods spelled a short life for the wooden bridges, and between 1905 and 1908 five steel bridges with a unique bowstring arch truss design replaced most of the original spans. Instead of rivets and bolts, the patented process of these bridges used hooks to increase strength. Around 1920, a wooden kingpost bridge was added, and along with the original steel bridge across the Black River the route earned the local name Seven Bridges Road. This road, which once bustled with cars and horse-drawn carriages, was abandoned in 1948 because of constant flooding, but today it forms a wonderful hiking trail.

The five steel bridges are among only eight remaining of this design in Wisconsin; another is found in Amnicon Falls State Park (p. 12). Because so few of these bridges remain, these five have been added to the National Register of Historic Places. A local non-profit group, the Friends of McGilvray Road, works to improve the trail and maintain the bridges.

WILDLIFE—More than 170 species of birds have been recorded at Van Loon, with waterfowl naturally being among the most common ones sighted. Also look for herons, bald eagle, pileated woodpecker, ruffed grouse, and wild turkey. Deer, fox, coyote, mink, beaver, and otter are some of the mammals that call Van Loon home. Threatened and endangered species include osprey, red-shouldered hawk, wood turtle, and the massasauga rattlesnake, though the last is extremely timid and very unlikely to be seen. If you do encounter one just give it a wide berth and there is nothing to worry about.

HIKING—McGilvray Road (now a hiking trail) leads through the scenic Black River bottoms. The main channel bridge at the end of the road has been removed, and the wooden bridge burned years ago, but the five steel bowstring bridges remain. Until just recently, the trail extended only to where the fifth bridge, the wooden one, once stood, but a new iron truss bridge has been added, allowing access all the way to the main channel of the river; it is about a two-mile hike. The level trail starts out wide, but soon narrows. There are several wet areas, but these can easily be crossed on rock paths. A small picnic area and water pump are located at the beginning of the trail.

PADDLING—While McGilvray Road allows good viewing of the area, the best way to see it is by canoe. A 100-foot-wide scenic zone with no development is maintained along all waterways. The west channel of the Black River is wide and easy to canoe, while the narrower east channel offers more backwater areas to explore. Blow-downs are frequent and water levels are highly variable, however, so it would be wise to check with the DNR before heading down the west side. Boat launches are located by Hunter's Bridge (Highway 53) at the north end of the wildlife area and to the south along Highway 35.

WINTER—Cross-country skiers sometimes use McGilvray Road though it is not groomed.

COUNTIES—La Crosse and Trempealeau.

DIRECTIONS—One mile north of New Amsterdam on County XX, then 1.5 miles north on Amsterdam Prairie Rd.

FACILITIES—Water, boat launch, picnic area.

CAMPING—None.

ENTRY—Open year-round. Free.

ON THE WEB—www.7bridgesrd.org

CONTACT—DNR, 3550 Mormon Coulee Rd., La Crosse, WI 54601. Phone (608) 785-9000. Friends of McGilvray Road, PO Box 2976, La Crosse, WI 54602.

Hixon Forest
and La Crosse River Marsh

TOGETHER, the 630-acre Hixon Forest and the adjoining 500-acre La Crosse River Marsh form an impressive natural oasis. Hixon Forest climbs the bluffs just west of La Crosse. The area was logged in 1909 and quarrying was set to begin the next year. Luckily, it did not. To stop the destruction of this prominent landmark, Mrs. Ellen Hixon bought the land and donated it to the City of La Crosse for a park. Many mockingly called it Hixon Hill at the time, because the logging had left the area virtually bare. Surely they would be pleased with what a little time can do. Many of the forest's steep bluffs harbor remnant prairies, known as goat prairies. Formerly there were vast stretches of prairie in the La Crosse area and throughout southern Wisconsin, but these small patches are all that remain around here. In the southwest corner of the forest is Grand-dad Bluff, one of La Crosse's most popular attractions. At 600 feet, it offers expansive views of the city and the Mississippi River Valley.

The La Crosse River Marsh extends right through the heart of the city and, with many buildings and roads hugging the edge and power lines running through the middle, you will never forget that this is an urban park, but it still offers good up-close viewing of wetlands and an abundance of wildlife.

The Hixon Forest Nature Center, operated by a non-profit group in conjunction with the La Crosse City Parks Department, lies between the marsh and the forest. Displays focus on the plants and animals found here, and center staff offer frequent programs for school groups and the general public.

WILDLIFE—The forest and marsh provide a haven for wildlife. Herons, egrets, ducks, geese, beaver, and mink make the marsh home, while fox, coyote, deer, turkey vulture, and hawks are all found in the forest. In the marsh, it is nearly impossible not to see shorebirds and waterfowl. In addition, grassland species inhabit the prairie restoration atop the hill. Peregrine falcon, an endangered species, are sometimes sighted here, and bald eagle are common winter visitors. A spotting scope in Myrick Park offers easy viewing of the marsh. A butterfly house is located next to the nature center.

HIKING—The marsh and forest are connected by a single trail, marked by green posts, that runs for five miles from Riverside Park on the Mississippi River up to County FA at the top of the forest's bluffs; it is appropriately called the River-to-Bluff Trail. Another dozen, mostly narrow trails, totaling around eight miles, lie in a deep valley between two bluffs, which rise about 400 feet above the valley floor. The setting makes the trails scenic, but also very hilly in most cases. If you want to start your hike from above, there are connections along Bliss Road to the south and County FA to the east.

The Sumac Trail leads in for three quarters of a mile from the main entrance to a small picnic area at the heart of the trail system. The Bicentennial and Lookout trails, which wind up the bluff to the east, are the steepest trails in the forest—two vistas at the top overlook the valley. Together, the two trails form a roughly 2.5-mile loop from the picnic area. You can combine the quarter-mile Moss Pass Trail with the Bicentennial Trail to make a short, fairly level loop out of the picnic area. Both the 0.75-mile Hickory and quarter-mile Gully trails climb only about a third of the way up the bluff, making an easier loop. The Gully Trail follows an intermittent stream down a small valley and has a historic rock shelter, probably used as a brick kiln in the late 1800s, at its base.

Heading south from the picnic area are the hilly Log and Fern trails, the loops totaling one mile and a half-mile, respectively. At the top of the Log Trail is the Oak Trail, which leads along a relatively level path to a parking area on Bliss Road, a mile away. The short Aspen Trail connects the Log Trail with the Alpine Inn, a bar and grill with a large deck where you can re-energize for the hike back down. If you are starting your trip here, note that you have to follow the gravel road to reach the trailhead. Also starting above the valley, over on County FA by the National Weather Service station, is the Prairie Trail Loop, a moderately hilly path through a large prairie restoration. On its north side, the trail skirts the forest edge and some paths branch off right through it. The Prairie Trail is connected to the Bicentennial Trail, so you could just add it as part of a longer loop.

Starting next to the nature center is the easy 0.6-mile Nature's Edge Trail. A corresponding booklet discusses the various forest and prairie plants found along this trail's two loops. While the trail is informative, it is not very scenic or peaceful, as it passes many buildings and the highway.

In the marsh there are another 3.5 miles of level trails, with access from all three of the adjacent city parks: Riverside, Red Cloud, and Myrick. The River-to-Bluff Trail crosses the marsh east to west, while the Old Rail Trail running north to south connects Myrick Park and St. James Street. The east end of the marsh is the largest, least developed, and most scenic portion. Naturally this is where you are most likely to see wildlife, but you really could see it anywhere.

PADDLING—Canoes can be launched onto the La Crosse River from County B at the north end of the marsh.

BIKING—The trails through the marsh are surfaced with crushed stone and are popular with bikers.

WINTER—Four and a half miles of trails, including the challenging hills of the Log Trail, are groomed for cross-country skiing. The trails in the marsh are also open to skiing but are not groomed. A warming shelter is available in the forest.

COUNTY—La Crosse.

DIRECTIONS—The nature center is located on Highway 16, east of downtown, at the edge of La Crosse.

FACILITIES—Water, toilets, nature center, nature programs, picnic area. Many other recreational facilities are available in the adjoining parks.

CAMPING—None.

ENTRY—Open year-round. Free.

ON THE WEB—www.geocities.com/Yosemite/Forest/8488

CONTACT—Hixon Forest Nature Center, 2702 Quarry Rd., La Crosse, WI 54601. Phone (608) 784-0303. E-mail: hfnc@bigfoot.org

Wildcat Mountain State Park
and Kickapoo Valley Reserve

W ISCONSIN IS NOT a mountain state, but it sure seems like it around this beautiful park. Wildcat Mountain lies at the heart of the unglaciated Kickapoo Valley and encompasses 3,643 acres of the forested bluffs and valleys and wide-open grasslands typical of the area. The Kickapoo River flows through the west end of the park. Translated from the Algonquin language, Kickapoo literally means "he who goes there, then here" or, less poetically, "crooked." It was aptly named. The Kickapoo travels 125 river miles to cover the 65-mile straight-line distance from its origin, north of the park in Monroe County, to where it empties into the Wisconsin River at Wauzeka.

The park began in 1948 when Amos Theodore Saunders donated 40 acres to the state so that the land he loved could be enjoyed by future generations. A recent expansion of Saunders' vision is the 8,569-acre Kickapoo Valley Reserve, stretching south from the park for seven miles. The U.S. Army Corps of Engineers initially acquired the land for a reservoir. Nearly a hundred farm families were removed, the highway was relocated, and half the dam was erected by 1975 when the project was halted because of numerous issues, including water quality, environmental concern, and, most of all, cost. Most of the land was transferred to the state in 2000, and after a sometimes bitter debate about the area's

Typical Kickapoo River scenery.

PHILIP G. OLSON

future, it was decided to preserve it in a natural state and to promote recreation.

WILDLIFE—In the forest you might see pheasant, ruffed grouse, wild turkey, northern saw-whet owl, pileated woodpecker, white-breasted nuthatch, scarlet tanager, fox, coyote, or deer. Look for beaver, mink, otter, great blue and green-backed herons, wood duck, spotted sandpiper, and belted kingfisher along the Kickapoo or one of its tributaries. Turkey vulture and sharp-shinned hawks are routinely spotted soaring in the updrafts along the hills, and occasionally bald eagle, osprey, and merlin can be seen. In total, 170 species of birds have been recorded here.

HIKING—The park has four short but steep hiking-only trails totaling about four miles; they lead through forest for the most part. The excellent, 2.5-mile Old Settler's Trail loops above and below Wildcat Mountain. A part of the trail, as the name implies, was used by early settlers. A half-mile wheelchair-accessible section leads from the park office to the Taylor Hollow Overlook. Also atop Wildcat Mountain is the quarter-mile Prairie Trail, which runs through a prairie restoration (this portion is wheelchair-accessible) and a bit of forest, though it parallels the park road and is thus usually not very peaceful.

The Hemlock Nature Trail, a 1.3 mile loop, follows the river through the 65-acre Mt. Pisgah Hemlock-Hardwoods State Natural Area before climbing to an overlook atop Mt. Pisgah. This northern forest relic was protected as a natural area because it is relatively undisturbed, and the cool bluffs harbor several rare plants. Interpretive panels along the trail explain the ecology of this unique area.

The Ice Cave Trail is a short path going from a secluded picnic area to a shallow sandstone depression that looks like a cave from a distance. A spring flows over the top, forming a small waterfall in the warmer months and a giant icicle in winter. Spring wildflowers bloom here, even before the ice completely melts away. If you ask at the park office, they can direct to you some other large ice caves in the area.

There are another 60-some miles of trails in the Kickapoo Valley Reserve, all of which can be hiked, though only two short, unnamed paths are set aside for hikers only. The mile-long loop through the meadow in the south end has little to recommend other than the dam tower at the end, and you can see that by driving out along the road that parallels the trail. The roughly three-mile trail in the north end, however, follows the sandstone cliffs along Billings Creek and the Kickapoo River, and is a very beautiful and seldom-used hike. The trail is not for everyone, since there are some steep hills and the route is rough and wet in a few places. There is no bridge across the creek, though it may easily be waded. Because this trail is a bit remote and passes a variety of habitats—wetland, forest, meadow—it is a good place to spot wildlife. Locals in the know are quick to point out that the reserve is an excellent place to explore off-trail, and you can find scenic cliffs all over the place; in winter there are many ice caves. The office staff knows this area very well and is eager to assist visitors looking to explore.

PADDLING—The slow-flowing Kickapoo offers easy paddling and, due to the many exposed cliffs, the section within the park and reserve is the most scenic part of the river. It is about a 20-mile (nine-hour) run from Highway 33 in Ontario to Highway 82 at La Farge, and the trip can easily be broken up with a stay at one of the plentiful riverside campsites within the park and reserve. The last six and a half miles starting at County P (known as Bridge 14) is the least traveled section of the river and makes a great three-hour trip. Canoe rental and shuttle service is available upstream from the park, in the village of Ontario.

BIKING—Bikes are not allowed on any of the trails in Wildcat Mountain, though the 14 miles of trail open to off-road bikes in the Kickapoo Valley Reserve offer some fairly challenging rides. An easy, paved, seven-mile trail runs between Rockton and La Farge.

WINTER—The park grooms a seven-mile cross-country ski trail with bypasses of the hilly sections, making it suitable for beginners. The trail loops along the top of Wildcat Mountain, connecting five scenic overlooks. Snowshoes are the perfect way to explore the Kickapoo Valley Reserve in winter; at the moment there are no designated cross-country skiing trails.

OTHER—The Kickapoo Valley has long been a favorite of horseback riders. The park's 15 miles of horse trails are laid out in four connected loops, allowing riders to choose the length and difficulty of their ride. The trails are a mix of open and wooded terrain and have many hills. The 45 miles of trail open to horses in the Kickapoo Valley Reserve are rugged and brushy, with many steep hills; perfect for riders looking for a challenge.

COUNTY—Vernon.

DIRECTIONS—Wildcat Mountain is three miles south of Ontario on Highway 33. Kickapoo Valley Reserve lands start just south of the park, and a new visitor center along Highway 131 could be open by the time this book is published.

FACILITIES—Water, toilets, nature programs, picnic area, grills, picnic shelter, playground.

CAMPING—Wildcat Mountain's family campground has 30 sites; the horse-trail campground has 24 sites, one canoe campsite, family camp open year-round, horse camp open May 1–November 15, reservations accepted, showers, group camp. Twenty-one primitive campsites are spread out along the Kickapoo and its tributaries in the Kickapoo Valley Reserve, ten with vehicle access; register at the office or one of the self-registration stations.

ENTRY—Open year-round. Wildcat Mountain: state park sticker or daily fee required, and state trail pass required for horseback riders. Kickapoo Valley: day-use or annual permit required, though canoeists, anglers, hunters, trappers, and snowmobilers are exempt.

ON THE WEB—www.wiparks.net and http://kvr.state.wi.us

CONTACT—Wildcat Mountain State Park, PO Box 99, Ontario, WI 54651. Phone (608) 337-4775. Kickapoo Valley Reserve, 505 N. Mill St., La Farge, WI 54639. Phone (608) 625-2960. E-mail: kickapoo.reserve@krm.state.wi.us

Upper Mississippi River
National Wildlife and Fish Refuge

"WE MOVE through the river—always through enchanting scenery, there being no other kind on the Upper Mississippi." Mark Twain's words from over a century ago still hold true today. The Mississippi, forming much of Wisconsin's western border, is one of the world's great rivers, stretching 2,552 miles with tributaries snaking in from 33 states and two Canadian provinces. The Upper Mississippi River National Wildlife and Fish Refuge, established in 1924, follows the river for 261 miles from the mouth of the Chippewa River in Wisconsin south to Rock Island, Illinois. Along the way, the longest wildlife refuge in the lower 48 states encompasses almost 200,000 acres of river, wooded islands, bottomland forest, marshes, sloughs, backwater lakes, sandbars, and scattered prairie remnants. The river ranges from two to five miles wide and is lined by towering bluffs, many rising more than 500 feet above the river. While refuge lands are confined almost exclusively to the floodplain, the bluffs are mostly undeveloped, adding greatly to the scenery. Despite the fact that this is one of the country's most visited national wildlife refuges, solitude remains easy to find.

Streams which would become the Mississippi began carving this valley millions of years ago. Water from the melting glaciers deposited countless tons of sand and gravel and formed the wide, level Mississippi River floodplain. Today, during high water periods, the river deposits nutrient-filled silt across the valley, creating an area rich in flora and fauna. High water occurs every spring as the region's snow melts, but major summer floods are not uncommon, as recent history has shown. The waters are constantly changing the surrounding landscape; islands and sandbars appear and disappear with floods and backwater areas slowly become dry land, progressing from marsh to bottomland forest, as they are filled in by silt.

Before the 1840s, steamboats had a hard time navigating the Upper Mississippi because of sandbars, low water, and snags. In 1845, grain producers formed the Mississippi River Improvement Company to improve navigation by removing the snags and wrecks. In 1878, a channel was dug and dams were constructed to maintain it, and over time the channel was expanded to its current nine-foot depth. Between 1930 and 1938 a series of locks and dams were constructed by the U.S. Army Corps of Engineers. There are 11 such locks and dams in the refuge, with the pools in between ranging from 10 to 30 miles long. Originally the river had several winding channels with many rapids and sandbars, but in the process of improving navigation, the Corps created a lake habitat rather than that of a river. The current was slowed by both the main dams and the smaller wing dams (underwater rock piles) that help maintain the channel. This increased the amount of silt deposited in the backwater areas. These changes hurt many wildlife species, fish in particular, but some benefited. Excessive sedimentation is now a serious threat to the river.

The Mississippi, meaning "Big River" or "Father of Waters," was of great importance to Native Americans. Some considered the river to be the center of the universe; this is one reason for the abundance of burial and effigy mounds built along it. Mounds are found in each of Wisconsin's state parks within the refuge boundaries—Nelson Dewey, Perrot, Merrick, and Wyalusing. Effigy Mounds National Monument, three miles north of Marquette, Iowa, on Highway 76, has nearly 200 mounds including the 137-foot long, 70-foot wide Great Bear Mound.

More than a dozen Native American cultures are known to have lived or traded along the river, including the early Red Ochre, Hopewell, and Woodland cultures, and later the Fox, Ojibwe, Sauk, Ho-Chunk, and Dakota. In fact, they laid the foundation for modern life on the river; cities such as Prairie du Chien and La Crosse were the sites of Native American villages, and many of today's highways follow early footpaths. In 1832, Chief Black Hawk was captured after fleeing across Wisconsin and most of his followers were massacred near Black Hawk Park in Vernon County.

The fur trade brought the first Europeans to the region and later loggers floated their lumber to sawmills along the river. Commercial clamming, which still continues on a small scale today, was another significant river industry. Shipping was also very important, and for many the steamboat is synonymous with the Mississippi. While the paddleboat era is long gone, a few still ply these waters, serving as casinos and tour boats. Today, commercial transport on the Upper Mississippi is less important than it once was; still, millions of tons of goods are transported on the river each year, mainly grain, coal, and oil. A typical 15-barge tow stretches for a quarter mile and carries the equivalent of 990 semi-trucks or 225 train cars.

WILDLIFE—The refuge was established primarily to protect smallmouth bass spawning areas on the river, but birds have been the biggest winners—

nearly 300 species have been recorded—because the Mississippi River is one of the continent's major migration corridors. Geese and ducks are especially abundant. Each fall up to 75 percent of the North American population of canvasback ducks may be seen on river Pools 7 and 8 near La Crosse. As many as 10,000 tundra swans pass through during the fall migration, and are best seen at the northern end of the refuge. Rieck's Lake Park in Alma has an observation platform and is staffed by volunteers during peak viewing times in late October and early November. The magnificent assembly of warblers and other Neotropical migrants in the spring and fall is one reason behind the American Bird Conservancy's decision to designate the refuge as a Globally Important Bird Area.

Bald eagles are year-round residents, though they are most impressive in winter when they congregate below dams and at the mouths of tributaries where the water does not freeze over. Over 200 eagles can be seen each winter around Cassville. Eagle-viewing activities with spotting scopes and educational programs are held every Saturday during January at Riverside Park in Cassville and at nearby Nelson Dewey State Park (p. 148). Eagles also gather around Riverside Park in La Crosse.

Heron and egret rookeries, often with hundreds of nests, are found in the more remote areas. The 154-acre Whitman Bottoms Floodplain Forest State Natural Area north of Merrick State Park (p. 196) has one of the largest rookeries in the state, with some 500 nesting pairs.

Other birds found in the refuge include sandhill crane, turkey vulture, ruffed grouse, wild turkey, and American white pelicans, which are becoming increasingly common. Osprey, peregrine falcon, red-shouldered hawk, great egret, and yellow-crowned night heron are endangered and threatened species residing along the river.

Among the 57 species of mammals found here are deer, coyote, fox, beaver, otter, and mink. There are also 53 reptile and amphibian species, including the endangered Blanding's and wood turtles, and 118 species of fish ranging from the smallest minnows to the giant lake sturgeon.

HIKING—Hiking is best at Wisconsin's state parks, particularly Perrot and Wyalusing—both are detailed earlier in this chapter. There are also two short, easy trails at Goose Island County Park south of La Crosse. The Great River State Trail is another option for hiking; see specifics in the Biking section below.

PADDLING—Canoeing is fantastic in the quiet backwaters where countless side channels and sloughs wind through wooded islands, marsh, bottomland forest, and small backwater lakes forming expansive mazes to explore. In addition to the rich flora and fauna found in the backwaters, they offer adventure and solitude; motorboats have a hard time going there. In the summer, acres of flowering water plants such as lotuses and water lilies come into bloom. These backwater areas are most abundant in the upper sections of each pool, where the construction of the locks and dams has had less effect on the river. Because of heavy boat traffic, the main river channel is not a good place to canoe, and even just crossing it can be difficult or dangerous. Boat launches and rentals are found all along the river.

Several marked canoe trails wind through the backwaters. Wyalusing, Merrick, and Perrot (each detailed earlier in this chapter) state parks all have marked trails, and two others are maintained by the refuge. The 4.5-mile Long Lake Canoe Trail starts and ends at the Long Lake boat landing south of the village of Trempealeau on Fremont Street. Another marked trail circles Goose Island County Park south of La Crosse. A part of this six-mile trail passes through an area that is voluntarily closed from October 1 to November 15 to protect migrating birds. Canoeists should take time to explore beyond each of the marked trails, especially around Goose Island. Because it is easy to get lost, a map is highly recommended whether you are following a trail or not.

BIKING—The best biking option is the Great River State Trail, which hugs the Mississippi for 24 miles between Onalaska and Marshland along an abandoned railroad right-of-way surfaced with crushed stone. The best river scenery along the trail is found on the 5.4-mile section between the village of Trempealeau and Lytle's Landing at the end of County Z.

WINTER—Wyalusing and Perrot state parks, both detailed earlier in this chapter, have groomed cross-country ski trails. There are also six miles of level groomed trails at Goose Island County Park. Skiing on the frozen backwaters is becoming increasingly popular, though care must be taken as currents can cause ice conditions to be unstable in places.

AUTO TOUR—The Great River Road, marked with green pilot wheels, is a scenic drive along both sides of the river from Canada to the Gulf of Mexico. In Wisconsin, the route mostly follows Highway 35 and generally borders the river, only occasionally drifting away. Historic sites are found in almost every city or village on the river, and there are scenic overlooks and interpretive markers in many of them. Three of the best scenic overlooks are at Wyalusing State Park (p. 149) with its famous view of the Wisconsin River's confluence with the Mississippi, Granddad Bluff in La Crosse (see Hixon Forest and La Crosse River Marsh, p. 204), and Buena Vista Park in Alma; all are perched more than 500 feet above the river.

OTHER—Houseboats, which may be rented in La Crosse and Trempeleau, are a popular way to travel the Mississippi. Boats can be moored on refuge islands for picnics or camping. All boaters need to be aware of stump fields, areas logged before the dams were built, which are shown on the pool maps.

COUNTIES—Grant, Crawford, Buffalo, La Crosse, Vernon, and Trempealeau

DIRECTIONS—Access is available all along the river. Visitor contact stations are located in Onalaska, Wisconsin; McGregor, Iowa; Winona, Minnesota; and Tomson, Illinois. Goose Island County Park is five miles south of La Crosse on Highway 35.

FACILITIES—A full range of facilities are found in parks and rest stops along the river.

CAMPING—Camping is allowed on refuge islands, though during the waterfowl hunting season (generally the end of September through the end of November) camping is allowed only outside closed areas and on sites visible from the main channel. Parks with campgrounds are found all along the river, including in Nelson Dewey, Wyalusing, Perrot, and Merrick state parks, the U.S. Army Corps of Engineers-operated Grant River Recreation area near Potosi, Black Hawk Park near De Soto, and the enormous Goose Island County Park where, with more than 400 campsites, room is always available, even on the busiest weekends.

ENTRY—Open year-round. Refuge is free, though the state parks require entrance fees.

ON THE WEB—www.umesc.usgs.gov/umr_refuge.html

CONTACT—U.S. Fish and Wildlife Service, 51 E. 4th St., Winona, MN 55987. Phone (507) 452-4232.

Parfrey's Glen.

SOUTHEAST

AMERICAN BADGER

Southeast

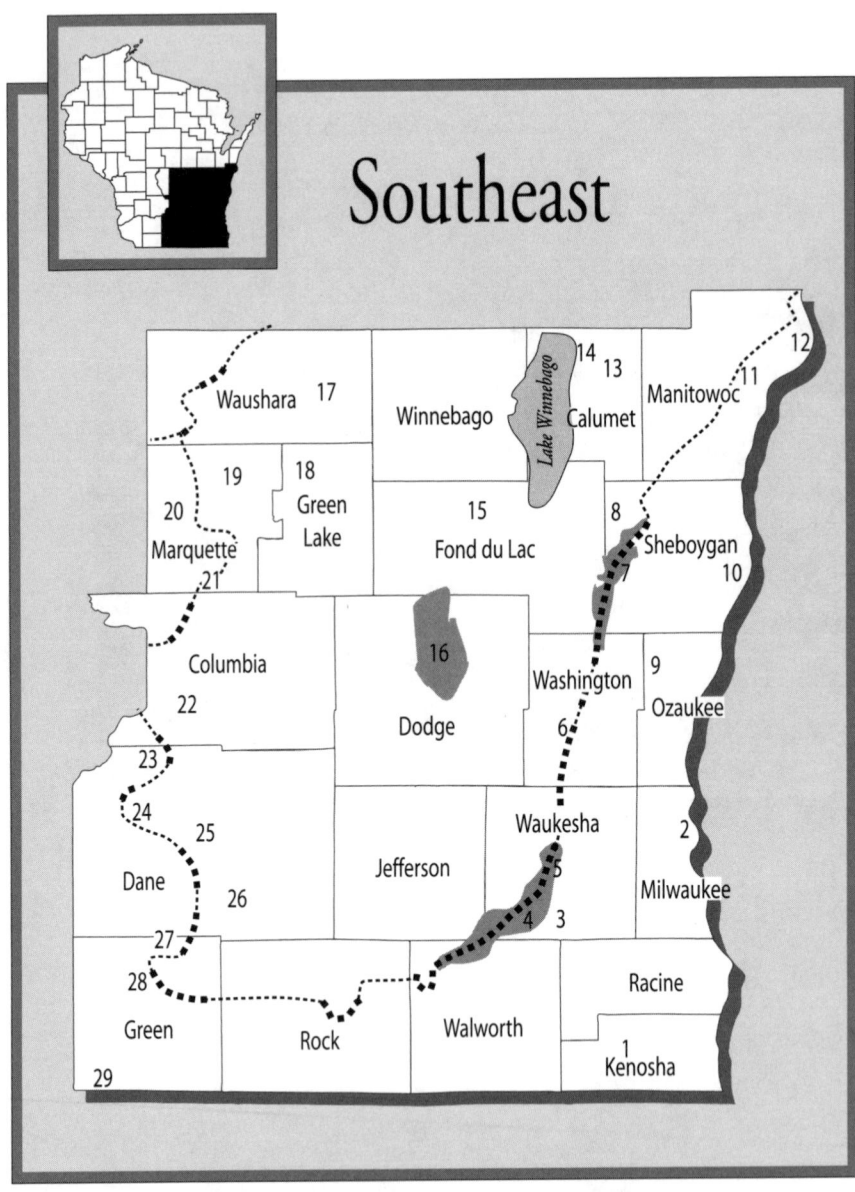

Waushara 17

Winnebago

Lake Winnebago

14 13

Calumet

Manitowoc 11

12

19 18

Green Lake

15

Fond du Lac

8

Sheboygan

10

20

Marquette

21

7

Columbia

22

16

Dodge

Washington

6

9

Ozaukee

23

24

25

Jefferson

Waukesha

5

2

Dane

26

4 3

Milwaukee

27

28

Green

Rock

Walworth

Racine

1

Kenosha

29

- - - - - - - - - - - *Proposed* Ice Age National Scenic Trail
■■■■■■■■■■■■■ *Existing* Ice Age National Scenic Trail

1. Richard Bong State Recreation Area
2. Schlitz Audubon Center
3. Vernon Marsh Wildlife Area
4. Kettle Moraine State Forest – Southern Unit
5. Kettle Moraine State Forest – Lapham Peak Unit
6. Kettle Moraine State Forest – Pike Lake Unit
7. Kettle Moraine State Forest – Northern Unit
8. Broughton Sheboygan Marsh Park and Wildlife Area
9. Riveredge Nature Center
10. Kohler-Andrae State Park
11. Woodland Dunes Nature Center
12. Point Beach State Forest
13. Brillion Wildlife Area
14. High Cliff State Park
15. Eldorado Marsh Wildlife Area
16. Horicon National Wildlife Refuge, Horicon Marsh State Wildlife Area, and Marsh Haven Nature Center
17. Poygan Marsh Wildlife Area
18. White River Marsh Wildlife Area
19. Germania Marsh Wildlife Area
20. Page Creek Marsh
21. John Muir Memorial Park
22. Rowan Creek Fisheries Area
23. Lodi Marsh Wildlife Area
24. Indian Lake County Park
25. Governor Nelson State Park
26. Lake Kegonsa State Park
27. Brooklyn Wildlife Area
28. New Glarus Woods State Park
29. Browntown-Cadiz Springs State Recreation Area

Richard Bong
State Recreation Area

BONG WAS Wisconsin's first State Recreation Area and it is unique because of the wide variety of nontraditional activities, from hang gliding to landsailing, offered here. More traditional pursuits such as camping, swimming, and hiking are also popular. Despite the many activities available, with 4,515 acres to explore there is plenty of space to enjoy nature and escape the crowds. Before European settlement in the mid-1800s, the Potawatomi spent summers in the prairie here, and today, thanks to an extensive restoration project, this is southeastern Wisconsin's largest managed prairie. There are also extensive wooded areas and many lakes and ponds on the property. Since the main management objective is to restore and preserve the natural aspects of the area, only a small portion of the park has been developed.

Bong's origin as a recreation area is an interesting story. In 1954, the federal government purchased 5,540 acres for an Air Force base that was to protect the Chicago-Milwaukee area. It was to be named for Wisconsin native Richard Ira Bong, America's most accomplished World War II fighter pilot, who in two years of service downed 40 enemy aircraft. Construction of the base began in 1958, but from the start many deemed the project unnecessary, and a year later—three days prior to the scheduled paving of the 2.5-mile runway—the base was cancelled. Topsoil had already been removed from nearly half the land, however, ruling out a return to agriculture, and after two years of discussion it was decided that residential and industrial development was the best use. The plan then called for a small portion of the land to be set aside for recreational purposes, but many local residents wanted the entire area used for recreation and conservation. The battle between development and conservation eventually reached the Wisconsin Supreme Court, where the conservationists won.

WILDLIFE—Today this undeveloped land is an important wildlife haven in the most populated and developed corner of the state. More than 210 species of birds have been recorded here. Look for sandhill cranes, great blue and green-backed herons, ducks, Forster's tern, pheasant, American kestrel, white-breasted nuthatch, plus bald eagle, and osprey, which have been known to stop here during their migrations. Because of habitat loss across the state, Bong is especially important for grassland species such as bobolink, that migrate to Central and South America each winter. Park mammals include beaver, mink, fox, coyote, and deer.

HIKING—Almost 17 miles of trails cover the eastern half of the property. The eight trails, all loops, pass almost entirely through prairie, though they also all cross some wooded and wetland areas. The trails are more or less flat, with just a few scattered steep hills. The trails start near the nature center, though most can be accessed at other places as well. All trails are interconnected loops, allowing a variety of possible routes. In several places there are blinds built for hunters, and these make good bird-watching spots out of hunting season.

The South Trails (Highway 142 divides the trails) begin on a boardwalk through a pond and lead around the main use area. The 1.8-mile Green Trail winds along the north edge of Wolf Lake, while the 4.2-mile Blue Trail encircles the entire lake, passing the beach area and joining the Visitor Center Nature Trail along the way.

The North Trails provide a more intimate setting, winding through an area with no facilities other than a small, wooded picnic area on County BB. At 8.3 miles the Red Trail is the longest, the northern part crossing land unaltered by the original Air Force plan. Both it and the 6.4-mile Orange Trail pass the small picnic area. The 4.4-mile Yellow Trail follows an artificial ridge, created with topsoil removed during base construction, for half a mile. There are distant views of the surrounding landscape as the trail exits the ridge. The Gray Trail is the shortest of the hiking trails at 1.7 miles.

Two short nature trails are lined with detailed interpretive signs. The 0.75-mile Visitor Center Nature Trail is an excellent place to learn about prairie habitats, and a hundred-yard boardwalk leads into the wetlands around East Lake. The mile-long Vista Nature Trail's interpretive panels discuss woodland environments. The Vista Trail begins two miles west of the main use area at the overlook on County B—Bong's highest point. Because of its location away from the main visitor area, this trail is lightly used.

PADDLING—Canoeists may paddle around 150-acre Wolf Lake. Only electric motors are allowed.

BIKING—The North Trails, 11 miles total, are open to off-road bikes. A paved road (closed to traffic) heads north across from the park entrance in the same area as the North Trails and makes a good, short bike path.

WINTER—The hiking trails are all groomed for cross-country skiing, with the North Trails facilitating skate skiers. There is a sledding hill next to the visitor center, and a warming shelter for between runs. The trails in the Special Use Zone, open for snowmobiles and ATVs, are connected to the county snowmobile trail system.

AUTO TOUR—County B, which is Rustic Road #43, begins in the north end of the park and continues north for 3.7 miles into Racine County.

OTHER—Bong's nontraditional activities take place in a 1,200-acre Special Use Zone centered around the 2.5-mile gravel runway. Activities allowed in this zone include hang gliding, paraplane flying, hot air ballooning, model airplane flying, model boat driving, skydiving, landsailing, ATV and dirt bike riding, dog sledding, dog training, falconry, and stargazing—telescopes are set up each Saturday night if the skies are clear. Events are scheduled to avoid conflict, so check with the park office for details. Interested park visitors may observe most activities.

A 13-mile horse trail circles the southern half of the park.

COUNTY—Kenosha.

DIRECTIONS—Three miles south of Union Grove on Highway 45, then four miles west on Highway 142.

FACILITIES—Water, toilets, boat launch, nature center, nature programs, picnic area, grills, picnic shelter, beach, playground, volleyball, ball field, horseshoes.

CAMPING—Two campgrounds, 217 sites, 53 electric, 15 horseback rider sites, open year-round, reservations accepted, showers, group camp.

ENTRY—Open year-round. State park sticker or daily fee required. State trail pass required for off-road bikers and horseback riders.

ON THE WEB—www.wiparks.net

CONTACT—Richard Bong State Recreation Area, 26313 Burlington Rd., Kansasville, WI 53139. Phone (262) 878-5600.

Schlitz Audubon Center

ONCE YOU SET FOOT on the trails or peer out over Lake Michigan, it is easy to forget that this popular nature center lies deep in an urban setting. Schlitz packs five different natural communities—lakeshore, pond, woodland, open field (including some prairie), and bluff/ravine—into the 185 lakeshore acres. There is more wildlife here than you might expect.

Originally this land was the Uihlein Nine Mile Farm, so named because it was nine miles from the Uihlein family's Schlitz Brewery in Milwaukee, and served as a resting site for the draft horses that pulled the beer wagons. With that purpose long gone, the Schlitz Foundation defied pressure to develop the area and donated the land to the National Audubon Society in 1971. The center opened three years later and is run by a dynamic local group. With environmental education the principal focus, programs are provided to tens of thousands of people annually. The interpretive building with its numerous hands-on displays and excellent natural science bookstore complements their mission.

WILDLIFE—Despite the center's small size and urban setting, a large number of animals can be seen here, especially birds: more than 250 species have been recorded. This abundance is due largely to its Lake Michigan location, the shoreline being a major migration route. Wood duck, great blue heron, sharp-shinned hawk, downy woodpecker, great-crested flycatcher, and ovenbird are all fairly common, while tundra swan, sandhill crane, bald eagle, osprey, red-shouldered hawk, peregrine falcon, willet sandpiper, snow bunting, and hooded warbler are rare, but have been spotted. The last three are threatened and endangered species. Deer, fox, and mink might also be seen roaming the woods.

HIKING—There are six miles of mostly level trail here. The only steep parts are the hills leading down to the beach, one of which is paved, and a set of stairs that cross a deep ravine.

Three loop trails, the 2.2-mile Grassland Trail, 0.8-mile Ravine Trail, and 0.7 mile Beach Trail, cover most of the property, together encompassing all of the plant communities found here. Most of the trails pass through the meadows. Reflecting its past, old farm equipment is displayed along these paths. While each of the segments may be hiked individually, most people follow a 2.5-mile interpretive route (pick up a guide booklet in the building) that combines the three. The beach loop allows access to Lake Michigan, and the half mile of lakeshore is a nice place to walk, though swimming is not allowed.

The other main trail is the two-mile Woodland Trail, which is indeed mostly wooded. The northern segment leads past Mystery Pond, across Boardwalk Pond, and through a deep and narrow ravine. A guide booklet is also available for this trail. Just south of the interpretive building is the Green Tree Trail, a paved 0.35-mile featuring a small wildflower garden and the Tree Top Classroom, a 60-foot observation tower.

WINTER—Two and a half miles of level trails are open to cross-country skiing and snowshoeing, though they are not groomed. There is a warming shelter.

COUNTY—Milwaukee.

DIRECTIONS—1.5 miles east of I-43 on Brown Deer Rd.

FACILITIES—Water, toilets, nature center, nature programs.

CAMPING—None.

ENTRY—Open year-round Tuesday through Sunday 9 a.m.-5 p.m. Admission fee.

ON THE WEB—www.schlitzauduboncenter.com

CONTACT—Schlitz Audubon Center, 1111 E. Brown Deer Rd., Milwaukee, WI 53217. Phone (414) 352-2880.

Vernon Marsh Wildlife Area

THIS 4,114-ACRE wildlife area in southern Waukesha County lies at the edge of a sprawling metropolitan Milwaukee. With the vast majority of southeast Wisconsin's wetlands lost to farming and development, Vernon

Marsh is vitally important to wildlife, especially migratory birds. Due to its proximity to large numbers of people, its abundant wildlife, and its ease of access, many locals visit Vernon Marsh though visitors will never feel crowded.

The roughly six by 1.5-mile marsh straddles the Fox River and is surrounded by wooded uplands. Vernon was once a shallow lake (then called Mud Lake) that over time has filled in with silt and decaying vegetation, much of which came from the rapid development upstream. There were once many Potawatomi villages nearby, and the residents hunted and gathered wild rice here. They also supplied furs to a French trader named Elmore, who set up a trading post in 1804 and is the first known European to settle the area. Attempts to farm around the marsh in the early 20th century were largely unsuccessful because of poor drainage. The state began acquiring land here in 1951, primarily for waterfowl management, and today, despite the encroaching suburbs, many hunters consider it one of the best preserves in the entire state.

WILDLIFE—Bird-watchers are mostly attracted by shorebirds and migrating warblers, although the spring waterfowl migration (generally during April) is considered the best viewing time by most casual wildlife watchers. Among the animals that can be seen in the marsh are sandhill crane, tundra swan, black tern, beaver, and mink, while deer, fox, coyote, pheasant, and many hawks reside in the preserve's uplands. Great egret, osprey, and Blanding's turtle, all threatened species in Wisconsin, and the state-endangered Forster's tern are also found here.

HIKING—There are several paths, providing easy, up-close marsh viewing. To the east, at the end of Benson Avenue, a path leads to the edge of the marsh and then splits. The branch to the right follows a dike northwest between the Fox River and a flowage for about a mile out toward a great blue heron rookery. The other winds south for two miles, ending at the railroad tracks that form most of the eastern border of the marsh. This path also starts out between the river and a flowage before passing through wooded and open uplands and ending along more marsh.

Two trails on the west side of the marsh start at the end of Frog Alley Road. The parking area here is on a hill, offering good views of the marsh. Heading north, a series of dikes leads for over two miles into the heart of the marsh and right up to the river. Another two-mile path follows a dike through the marsh to the south. Beyond the marsh, it veers west and continues through wooded uplands, ending at a parking area on County NN. Just before the end, a narrow trail leads to an open area with several springs bubbling up though the sand.

There is also foot access from Highway 83 and County I, though these paths are less interesting overall.

PADDLING—The Fox River provides easy canoeing through the marsh.

Canoes can easily be put in at County I at the north end of the marsh and taken out at County ES just beyond the south end. Canoeists can also paddle around the area's flowages. There is a boat launch at the end of Frog Alley Road. A better place to put in is at the end of Benson Avenue, but canoes must be carried in about a hundred yards. Only electric motors of 5 hp or less are allowed on the flowages.

COUNTY—Waukesha.

DIRECTIONS—3.5 miles north of Mukwonago on County ES, then two miles north on County XX, and half a mile west on Benson Ave. to parking area.

FACILITIES—Boat launch.

CAMPING—None.

ENTRY—Open year-round. Free.

CONTACT—DNR, Wildlife Management, S91 W39091 Highway 59, Eagle, WI 53119. Phone (262) 594-6208.

Kettle Moraine State Forest

THE KETTLE MORAINE is a world-famous geological wonder. When the last glacier retreated across Wisconsin some 11,000 years ago, it left behind a dense concentration of glacial landforms, unequalled anywhere else in the world. The Kettle Interlobate Moraine, as it is actually called, stretches for over a hundred miles from northern Manitowoc County down to Walworth County. The remarkable line of hills spreads one to ten miles wide and rises 100 to 300 feet above the surrounding land. The Kettle Moraine marks the spot where the glacier's Green Bay Lobe joined the Lake Michigan Lobe during the last ice advance. The glacier picked up billions of tons of sand and gravel, and as the two lobes alternated melting and advancing, the gaps that formed were filled with the debris creating these hills.

Besides protecting the abundant kames, eskers, drumlins, outwash plains, and, of course, kettles and moraines, these four diverse units contain half of Wisconsin's 30 plant communities. In-depth explanations of all aspects of the Kettle Moraine's unique natural history are available at the Northern and Southern units' excellent nature centers.

A 1924 flood of the Milwaukee River caused major damage in the city of Milwaukee, and officials realized that protecting the river's headwaters (in what is now the Northern Unit) could prevent future floods; it was also decided that this would also be an ideal location for a park. Land purchases began in 1926 when the Izaak Walton League bought 842 acres around Mauthe (then called Moon) Lake. The state got involved a decade later, and the Northern and

Southern units were created. Early plans called for the forest to stretch continuously across the whole of the Kettle Moraine, though the state never appropriated enough money to implement to plan. Today, about half of the 40-mile gap between the two principal units is owned by the state or private conservation groups, and though plans still call for acquiring more land, it is a very slow process; there is already so much development that it will never be an intact preserve.

The Potawatomi were the dominant group in the area when European settlers arrived, and the Ho-Chunk and Menominee were other recent inhabitants. Sauk Chief Black Hawk twice eluded the U.S. Army (a young Abraham Lincoln was one of the soldiers) in the hills of the Southern Unit as they pursued him across Wisconsin.

The Kettle Moraine Scenic Drive is a 125-mile route (marked with green acorn signs) connecting all four units, as well as most major forest facilities in the large Northern and Southern units. Brochures with maps and information are available at each of the units. Many cyclists also follow this route, but do be aware that there is no shoulder in some places, and many drivers fly over the hills going way too fast.

I. Southern Unit

AT 21,300 ACRES, the southern forest is the smaller of the two principal units, though it receives far more visitors—summer weekends can actually be uncomfortably crowded—though unless you are here to mountain bike, you will generally find the trails offer a pleasant getaway.

What most sets the Southern Unit apart from its northern sibling is the abundance of prairie and savanna. Currently there are about 5,000 acres of these rare habitats here, although more funds are needed to manage them better and keep invasive brush and trees in check. Several state natural areas protect some of the least disturbed examples of each habitat in the entire state. The 185-acre Scuppernong Prairie State Natural Area was one of the first state natural areas. The prairie and adjacent 3,000-acre Scuppernong Marsh are best viewed from County N northwest of Eagle. Also significant is the Clifford F. Messinger Dry Prairie and Savanna Preserve State Natural Area, which encompasses 16 separate areas ranging from one to 120 acres scattered across the forest.

WILDLIFE—The Southern Unit's bird count exceeds 230 species, though it is the grassland dwellers such as bobolink, Western meadowlark, upland sandpiper, loggerhead shrike, dickcissel, lark sparrow, northern bobwhite, and merlin that most excite bird-watchers. Though birders generally come for the grasslands, they can also do quite well in the woods. Twenty species of warbler nest in or near the forest, and you can expect to see Nashville, Kentucky, pine, hooded, and Cerulean warblers, in addition to yellow-breasted chat and Louisiana waterthrush. Other forest dwellers include Acadian flycatcher, tufted titmouse, golden-crowned kinglet, scarlet tanager, pine siskin, pileated woodpecker, saw-whet owl, an increasing number of wild turkey, and one of the Midwest's largest concentrations of Cooper's hawks. American black duck, wood duck, king rail, black tern, belted kingfisher, sandhill crane, and mute swan reside on the lakes and in the marshes.

Mammals of the Southern Unit include deer, fox, coyote, badger, mink, beaver, and otter. There have been rare wolf sightings, though these were just lone wolves wandering far out of their usual range.

HIKING—There are 54 miles of hiking-only trails here. Because of the glacial terrain, most trails are quite hilly and offer scenic views. There are many pine plantations along the trails but mixed hardwood forest dominates.

The Southern Unit's portion of the Ice Age Trail (p. 1) stretches for 31 miles across the forest, and though the path is mostly wooded, it passes through many prairies and meadows as well. There are numerous scenic overlooks along the trail, and a few rock formations that are recommended destinations for short hikes. Most famous is the Stone Elephant, a giant granite boulder 39 feet in circumference that was carried here by the glaciers and is thought to have been sacred to the Potawatomi. It lies along the trail between County H and Tamarack Road, south of Palmyra. The shortest route to it is a mile-long hike from the end of Dahlin Road. North of Eagle is Brady's Rock, one of the most unique spots in the forest. About a mile west of Highway 67 (there is no parking area here, but there is room enough to pull completely off the road), a rough and narrow spur trail follows a ridge of Niagara Dolomite (part of the same massive escarpment that Niagara Falls drops over) for half a mile. Not only are the jagged rock outcroppings beautiful, but the trail looks down upon a marsh.

The two other long hiking-only trails are a set of interconnected loops that allow you to set your own agenda. The mostly-wooded 7.5-mile Scuppernong Trail has three hilly loops ranging from 2.3 to five miles. The west end of the trail is the hilliest, and there is an especially good overlook at the north end of the Red Loop. The trail can be accessed one mile east of the Ottawa Lake Recreation Area on County ZZ or at the Pine Woods Campground. The 12-mile Nordic Trail has five loops ranging from 2.5 miles to the 9.2-mile Blue Loop that winds around the outside, and which has some very long and steep hills. The trail is a mixture of open and wooded terrain, passing several small kettle ponds along the scenic Green Loop. The trailhead is 1.5 miles north of La Grange on County H.

The forest's seven short nature trails offer some excellent scenery. All but Stony Ridge have detailed guide booklets, available at the trailheads. The mostly level Scuppernong Springs Trail, across County ZZ from the Ottawa Lake Recreation Area, is a fascinating 1.5-mile loop. The mostly wooded trail passes many springs and has several wetland boardwalks—look for the other-worldly Red Algae (which is actually more purplish than red) in the ponds during the colder months. The trail brochure details the history of the area which includes Native Americans, fur traders, marl production, trout farming, and a hotel. There is a shortcut, but the long route is by far most interesting. Unfortunately the trail is quite popular and is also close to the highway, but it should not be missed.

The wooded Paradise Springs Nature Trail also focuses on the human history of the area, including a former resort that once operated here. The level half-mile trail has been designed to accommodate disabled users. It has a guide-cable along its paved path and a tape-recorded version of the brochure is available at the visitor center. An old, elaborate spring house sits over Paradise Spring from which 500 gallons of water flow each minute. There is a trout stream and pond here, as well, and display panels to explain fish habitat improvement. Across the street is the Gotten log cabin built here by settlers in the 1850s. Paradise Springs is one mile northwest of Eagle on County N.

The Stony Ridge Trail is a hilly, half-mile loop behind the visitor center, with interpretive panels discussing glacial geology. The trail climbs a ridge high above a large, gorgeous kettle pond near the beginning.

Just around the corner from the visitor center, the Stute Springs and Homestead Nature Trail passes through the remains of a farmstead settled in the 1850s, and while the guide booklet only discusses this aspect of the trail, it is, in fact, one of the best places in the forest to experience Kettle Moraine's unique geology. Beyond the few restored farm buildings, the path loops over two tall ridges and has a spur to a fantastic overlook at the top of the Big Hill which, despite the resemblance, is not a kame.

The Bald Bluff Nature Trail, two miles south of Palmyra on County H, climbs for half a mile up one of Jefferson County's highest points, offering a great view—the Ice Age Trail also crosses the hill. The trail passes through a mix of forest and field, the human and natural history of which is discussed in the guide booklet. Originally this hill was covered by prairie, hence its name, but now trees have taken over. The Potawatomi used it as a signal hill and council grounds, and held ceremonial dances on the summit. For a look at some of the area's settler history, pick up the *Skoponong Pioneer Settlement* brochure at the visitor center; it guides you to several spots in this part of the forest.

The Lone Tree Bluff Nature Trail offers great views of the forest to the south.

The quarter-mile, mostly-wooded path climbs straight to the top of this steep hill which was named for a large, solitary tree at the top that, unfortunately, is no longer there. The guide booklet discusses glacial formations and the oak openings common in the forest. Lone Tree Bluff is at the southernmost end of the forest, two miles northeast of the Whitewater Lake Campground on Hi-Lo Road, then a quarter mile southeast on Esterly Road.

The half-mile Rice Lake Nature Trail, at the Whitewater Lake Recreation Area in the southernmost end of the forest, is a narrow shoreline path following a small bay that is almost completely cut off from Rice Lake. The wooded trail has some small hills and an elevated viewing platform, and the trail brochure discusses wetland ecology.

Though not within the forest boundaries, the 78-acre Beulah Bog State Natural Area is administered by the forest staff, and is absolutely worth a quick detour. Many of the plants found in this remarkably pristine environment are more typical of the far north, including half a dozen insectivorous species. The bog is about ten miles east of the forest, or two miles north of East Troy, on Stringers Bridge Road, just north of Lake Beulah. Follow the unmarked but obvious trail about a quarter mile west over the hills to the bog where a boardwalk cuts right through to its heart. This is a very ecologically fragile area so do not step off the boardwalk.

With all the other great trails in the forest, there is no need to hike the two off-road bike trails; they are so busy at times that it would not be a good idea, anyway. If you do hike them, you will find scenery similar to that along the Scuppernong and Nordic trails.

PADDLING—There is no place wild to canoe in the Southern Unit, but the Ottawa Lake Canoe Trail is easy and informative. Eight marked buoys around the perimeter of this 27-acre lake correspond to a pamphlet available at the visitor center that discusses the lake's ecology. There is a popular beach on the lake so the trail is most peaceful in the morning or evening. Some canoeists also paddle around Rice Lake on the southern border, though much of the shoreline is developed and can be busy with motorboats.

BIKING—The John Muir and Emma F. Carlin trails, plus a five-mile trail that connects them—22 miles total—are some of the busiest and best-known mountain-bike trails in the country. While they can be maddeningly crowded on summer weekends, a large number of riders stick to the easier routes so the traffic jam in the parking lot should not necessarily scare you off. Both sets of interconnected loops are hilly and mostly wooded, and are as scenic as they are challenging. Although some riders hate the erosion mats on parts of the trail, without them there would be no riding here.

The 12.5-mile John Muir Trail has five loops ranging from 1.5 to 10 miles.

The Red and White loops are the easiest—the latter passes the Leather Leaf Bog, the forest's largest—while riding the Blue Loop and the connector trail is about a 25-mile round-trip with both technical and long climbs—and there are relatively few people. The trailhead is 1.5 miles north of La Grange on County H.

The 4.7-mile Emma F. Carlin Trail's three loops range from 1.9 to four miles; all are challenging. There are three small kettle ponds and an overlook with limited views of the Scuppernong Marsh along the Red Loop, and on clear days you can see Holy Hill from the far end of the Green Loop. The trailhead is one mile west of the visitor center on Highway 59, then 0.75 mile south on County Z.

WINTER—The Scuppernong and Nordic trails, along with the nine-mile McMiller Ski Trail, a challenging trail starting at the McMiller Sports Center and open only in the winter, offer nearly 30 miles of groomed cross-country ski trails. The Nordic and McMiller trails can accommodate skate skiers and have warming shelters. Those of limited ability prefer the Nordic Trail, the White Loop in particular.

The forest is an excellent place to give snowshoeing a try, with the Ice Age Trail being a natural destination. Also, the horse trails become part of a 56-mile snowmobile trail system.

OTHER—Over 50 miles of horse trail cross most of the forest from north to south. Like the other trails in the forest, they offer a little of everything, from open to wooded terrain and from flat paths to steep hills. Three sets of loops, the Eagle, Palmyra, and Blackhawk, are all linked to the horseriders' campground. The Blackhawk Trails off Highway 12 are the least used, and are a part of the system that follow old roads that nearly became a subdivision. The Ottawa Trails at the forest's northern end are not yet connected to the others, but many consider them the most scenic of the forest's four horse trails. Several stables in the area offer rentals and guided trips.

One and a half miles south of Eagle, on Highway 67, is Old World Wisconsin (262) 594-6300, an outstanding 600-acre state historic site featuring restored buildings from settlers of the various nationalities that came to Wisconsin in the early days, along with historical reenactments of pioneer life. The site is open May 1 to October 31, with special Christmas events in December.

The McMiller Sports Center shooting range near Eagle offers a wide range of gun and bow-shooting opportunities, and a biathlon course is planned.

COUNTIES—Waukesha, Jefferson, and Walworth.

DIRECTIONS—Headquarters and visitor center is two miles west of Eagle on Highway 59.

FACILITIES—Water, toilets, boat launch, nature center – nature programs, picnic area, grills, beach, picnic shelter, playground, volleyball, soccer, horseshoes.

CAMPING—Three campgrounds, 265 sites, 49 electric, 75 horseback-rider sites, three Adirondack-style backpacking shelters, barrier-free cabin, open year-round, reservations accepted, showers, group camp.

ENTRY—Open year-round. State park sticker or daily fee required. State trail pass required for off-road bikers and horseback riders. Separate fees for Old World Wisconsin and McMiller Shooting Range.

ON THE WEB—www.wiparks.net

CONTACT—Kettle Moraine State Forest-Southern Unit, S91 W39091 Highway 59, Eagle, WI 53119. Phone (262) 594-6200.

II. Lapham Peak Unit

AT 1,233 FEET above sea level, Lapham Peak is the highest point in Waukesha County. The eastern section of this 1,006-acre preserve, including Lapham Peak itself, is almost entirely wooded, while most of the old farm field in the western half has become meadow and some patches are being restored to prairie and oak savanna; there is even a small marsh. The prominent hill has been a popular vacation destination since the mid-1800s, when Charles Hanson built a 20-foot-tall observation tower atop it and charged people a fee to picnic there. A restaurant opened soon after. The foundation of the Hanson home may still be seen at the Homestead Hollow Picnic Area. Today the observation tower on the peak rises 45 feet; both Holy Hill and Milwaukee's First Wisconsin building are visible on clear days.

Some of the peak's early names were Stoney Hill, Prospect Hill, and Government Hill. Its final name came in honor of Increase A. Lapham, a prominent scientist and conservationist who founded the U.S. Weather Bureau. In 1870, Lapham had the Signal Corps of the U.S. Army set up a series of signal stations between here and Pike's Peak in Colorado to transmit weather data from the west, which was then relayed to Great Lakes ports. In 1907 the state purchased the land around the peak for use as a sanitarium. It was transferred to the Wisconsin Conservation Department in 1939.

WILDLIFE—More than 135 species of birds have been recorded at Lapham Peak with about 80 of those nesting here, including wood duck, green-backed heron, belted kingfisher, Cooper's hawk, wild turkey, scarlet tanager, grasshopper sparrow, bobolink, and Eastern meadowlark. Cerulean, pine, prothonotary, and northern parula are a few of the nearly 30 species of warblers that have been spotted over the years during the spring migration when the forest is filled with their songs. Deer, fox, and coyote are some of the mammalian residents, and there is a butterfly garden along the trails behind the nature center.

HIKING—Four miles of the Ice Age Trail (p. 1) cuts through the park, passing the observation tower along the way. Near where it crosses County C, the trail passes a couple of kettle ponds—an observation deck overlooking the largest one can be reached directly by a short path from the Evergreen Grove parking lot—and spans a small marsh along a boardwalk; otherwise the route boils down to forest to the east and grasslands to the west. South of the park the trail follows an outwash plain for 1.5 miles before joining the Glacial Drumlin State Trail, a long-distance trail that follows an abandoned railroad right-of-way from Waukesha all the way to Cottage Grove.

Another 18 miles of extra-wide, color-coded trails weave a web across the forest and are, with few exceptions, quite hilly. The Prairie Path (red), which is also open to bikes and horses, winds for 4.8 miles through the prairie, meadow, and savanna in the western portion of the park and, for the most part, has just medium-sized hills. The five trails east of County C intersect and overlap as they twist around the peak. The main trail, and the one with the longest and steepest hills, is the seven-mile Moraine Ridge Trail (black) while the 5.8-mile Kettle View Trail (blue) follows pretty much the same route but bypasses the steepest parts; both offer a mix of open and wooded terrain. The very steep northeastern corner of the Moraine Ridge is one of the least used sections of the trail system and arguably the most scenic. The two-mile Meadow Trail (green) to the west of the peak has only small hills and, as the name implies, is mostly through open terrain—you will pass two marker trees used by the Potawatomi at the trail's east end. The two-mile Kame Terrace Trail (purple) through the forest east of the peak is also relatively level. The 1.5-mile Plantation Path is not the most scenic, but it is the most varied. The paved path runs uphill through meadow and prairie restoration and then loops through a mature pine plantation. It passes the nature center and butterfly garden.

BIKING—Off-road bikes are allowed on the five-mile Prairie Path.

WINTER—This is one of southern Wisconsin's most popular cross-country ski areas. All trails (excluding the Ice Age Trail, which makes a good snowshoeing path, and the Prairie and Plantation) are groomed for both classical and skate skiers, and the Meadow Trail and two short loops branching from it (2.6 miles total) are lit for night skiing Monday through Saturday until 10 p.m. Ski rentals are available on weekends and some evenings. Call (262) 646-4421 for information or trail updates. The Prairie Path is a multi-use trail open for skiing, snowshoeing, and even dogsledding, and there is talk of clearing the Plantation Path for winter hiking. Homestead Hollow Pond is kept clear for ice-skating and two warming shelters are available for winter visitors.

OTHER—Horses are allowed on the Prairie Path.

COUNTY—Waukesha.

DIRECTIONS—Two miles south of Delafield on County C.

FACILITIES—Water, toilets, nature center, nature programs, picnic area, grills, picnic shelter.

CAMPING—One backpack site along the Ice Age Trail, open year-round, reservations accepted.

ENTRY—Open year-round. State park sticker or daily fee required. State trail pass required for cross-country skiing, off-road biking, and horseback riding.

ON THE WEB—www.wiparks.net

CONTACT—Kettle Moraine State Forest-Lapham Peak Unit, W329 N846 County Highway C, Delafield, WI 53018. Phone (262) 646-3025.

III. Pike Lake Unit

PIKE LAKE, a 522-acre kettle lake forming the western border of the property , lent its name to this 678-acre unit, though Powder Hill is the dominant natural feature. The steep kame rising above the lake is the second highest point in southeast Wisconsin—at 1,350 feet above sea level it is even taller than nearby Holy Hill. An observation tower perched atop the grassy summit offers great views of the surrounding landscape. The unit is half wooded and half meadow, though forest is slowly claiming much of the open area. There are also wetlands near the lake, scattered prairie remnants, and several spring-fed ponds. Visitors are drawn more for fishing, swimming, and boating than for the natural scenery.

WILDLIFE—Though Pike Lake is not quite as productive for birding as the other units, well over a hundred species visit during the course of the year. Wood duck, Canada goose, Caspian and common terns, belted kingfisher, northern goshawk, ruffed grouse, indigo bunting, white-breasted nuthatch, rose-breasted grosbeak, scarlet tanager, chestnut-sided warbler, winter wren, bobolink, and Eastern meadowlark all nest in or near the park. The best bird-watching spots are the open fields and wetlands north and south of the beach area. Deer, fox, coyote, badger, and mink also make their homes here.

HIKING—Two roads, Kettle Moraine Drive and Powder Hill Road, divide the forest into three sections, and each is quite different from the others. Along the lake the land is mostly open and level and has some wetlands; the middle section is mostly wooded and has the best examples of the glacial hills, including Powder Hill; and there is a good mix of forest and field in the generally level eastern section. Eight miles of trail cross all three sections, and the many benches along them allow relaxing viewing of the area. Most of the trails begin at the beach/picnic area—though they can also be accessed at many other places, including a parking area on Powder Hill Road—and continue north through the meadow along the lake before continuing into the rest of the unit. They share the same path at the beginning and end, but branch off at different places, making four progressively longer loops. Because all the trails connect, a variety of hiking routes is possible. One excellent route starts at the parking area on Powder Hill Road and combines the Black Forest Nature Trail with the Green and Orange trails, and the trail up Powder Hill, making a hilly but very scenic 2.5-mile hike.

The following descriptions of each trail loop tells about the portion that breaks off from the others. The hilly and wooded Green Trail, the shortest of the four, at two miles, passes many small kettle ponds and has the best examples of glacial terrain. The 2.4-mile Orange Trail also crosses some wooded hills; to the south of the trail is the steep quarter-mile path leading up to the observation tower atop Powder Hill. The Black Forest Nature Trail, a 0.8-mile mostly wooded and hilly loop with detailed interpretive panels discussing Pike Lake's southern mesic forest, branches off the Orange Trail. This highly recommended trail goes through many glacial hills and kettles. Hikers can also start this trail at the Powder Hill Road parking area. The 3.75-mile Blue Trail and 4.2-mile Brown Trail lead past the campground into mix of forest and field in the eastern end of the unit.

Two other short paths starting by the beach circle wetlands and should not be overlooked. The 0.7-mile Red Trail is mostly open, while the quarter-mile Lions Accessible Trail (named in honor of the local Lions club that donated time and money to build it) has a paved trail and a pair of boardwalks through forest, and passes along the edge of the lake. Despite their proximity to the park's busiest and noisiest space, these are good bird-watching destinations.

The Ice Age Trail (p. 1) also passes through Pike Lake, following a 2.6-mile path along the unit's trail; it loops from the northeast corner across to the southwest corner. The trail continues another seven miles beyond Pike Lake's southern border to the wooded grounds of Holy Hill with its spectacular church perched on the summit. The church, listed on the National Register of Historic Places, was built in 1931 and replaced several other churches that had stood there since a wooden cross was first erected at the spot in 1858. The trail to Holy Hill leads through a mix of open field and forest over many rolling hills, ending at Donegal Road. Because of hikers' littering and straying from the trail, a short section between Highway 167 and Shannon Road has been closed by the landowner. A road-route around it is marked, but do check with the office about the status of this section.

BIKING—A three-quarter-mile bike trail, surfaced with crushed limestone, connects the beach area to the Hartford Bike Trail that follows Highway 60 into town.

WINTER—The trails are groomed for cross-country skiing and can accommodate skate skiers. A warming shelter is available.

OTHER—Starting in the campground is the "Stroll thru the Solar System." This unique path has signs (taken down during the winter) discussing each of the planets, spaced so as to illustrate their distance from the sun. Monthly evening star-gazing programs are held near the campground entrance.

COUNTY—Washington.

DIRECTIONS—2.5 miles west of Hartford on Highway 60.

FACILITIES—Water, toilets, nature programs, beach, picnic area, grills, picnic shelter, playground.

CAMPING—32 sites, open late April to mid-October, reservations accepted, showers.

ENTRY—Open year-round. State park sticker or daily fee required.

ON THE WEB—www.wiparks.net

CONTACT—Kettle Moraine State Forest-Pike Lake Unit, 3544 Kettle Moraine Rd., Hartford, WI 53027. Phone (262) 670-3400.

IV. Northern Unit

THE 29,268-ACRE Northern Unit is a part of the Ice Age National Scientific Reserve (p. 1) and encompasses the Kettle Moraine's most striking glacial landforms including the famous Parnell Esker, Greenbush Kettle, and Dundee Kame. Each of these is described in detail in the Hiking section below. Also not to be missed is what forest staff call the Kame Field, where you can see half a dozen earthen cones that arise out of the surrounding farms. Best viewing is from the corner of County V and Deer Road. You can also see the rocky interior of Garriety Hill, about a mile to the north of Deer Road at Scenic Drive.

A dozen state natural areas protect a remarkable number of rare plants and animals. Two in particular are worth visits, especially if you are a bird-watcher. Several narrow, unmarked trails wind over the steep hills of the Haskell Noyes Memorial Woods State Natural Area, a 67-acre stand of old-growth forest purchased in 1947 to prevent it from being logged. A historical marker and parking area are located just north of the Mauthe Lake Recreation Area on County GGG at the corner of County SS. A short boardwalk leads through a pristine bog out to Spruce Lake, at the center of the 117-acre Spruce Lake Bog State Natural Area; the bog has been designated a National Natural

Landmark. From Dundee take Vista Drive 1.3 miles north, then follow Airport Road west for 0.4 mile to a parking area.

WILDLIFE—The Northern Unit is an excellent bird-watching destination. Nearly 250 species have been documented here, and because it lies along the state's ecological "tension zone" there are both northern and southern species present in large numbers. While the Northern Unit has little prairie habitat, the 200-acre Jersey Flats prairie restoration at the corner of County G and County SS, just west of New Prospect, is a very beautiful and productive birding site, with Henslow's and grasshopper sparrow, bobolink, Eastern meadowlark, and northern harrier, all nesting. Every spring you will see a good variety of ducks and several common loons on the lakes, plus maybe even an osprey, green heron, pied-billed or horned grebe, black tern, or solitary sandpiper, if you are lucky.

While the prairie and lakes add variety, the forest-dwellers are naturally the dominant avifauna. Cooper's and red-shouldered hawks, pileated and red-bellied woodpeckers, black-billed cuckoo, Eastern wood pewee, great-crested flycatcher, wood thrush, blue-gray gnatcatcher, red-eyed vireo, indigo bunting, and scarlet tanager are all relatively common, and the wild turkey population has exploded in recent years. The Spruce Lake Bog, detailed above, is probably the best place in the forest to seek out one of the 32 warblers documented in the forest, including Nashville, magnolia, and Canada. Other species with northern affinities nesting in the bog include northern waterthrush and white-throated sparrow.

Mammals of the Northern Unit include deer, fox, coyote, badger, mink,

GARY KNOWLES

Hiking the hills of the Kettle Moraine.

beaver, otter, and possibly bear. There is also a butterfly garden at the Ice Age Center.

HIKING—Close to 50 miles of hiking-only trails cross the Northern Unit. The highlight is a 31-mile segment of the Ice Age Trail (p. 1) that stretches the length of the forest and offers a little of everything there is to see here; it is especially hilly and scenic at the north end. Near that north end of the trail, just south of the Greenbush Recreation Area, it passes the large Greenbush Kettle, an ideal example of this type of glacial landform. The kettle can also be seen from an observation deck along Kettle Moraine Road. In the middle of the forest, the Ice Age Trail follows the Parnell Esker, an absolute must-see for forest visitors. The narrow, winding gravel ridge stretches four miles and is from five to 35 feet tall. The easiest place to see it is at Butler Lake, three miles east of the Long Lake Recreation Area. The scenic Butler Lake Trail starts here and shares the Ice Age Trail's path along the esker before branching off and completing a 3.1-mile loop. The mostly wooded trail has some small hills, but is not too tough.

The eight-mile Zillmer Trail, named for Ray Zillmer, who inspired both the Ice Age Trail and Ice Age National Scientific Reserve, has four connected loops ranging from 1.2 to 5.4 miles. The shortest loop is generally level while the rest have many rolling hills. The trail is mostly through open land, and the Brown Loop at the south end is primarily through a pine plantation. The main trailhead is 2.5 miles south of Dundee on County G, then a quarter-mile mile west on County SS, though it can also be accessed at the Henry S. Reuss Ice Age Visitor Center, where it joins the Moraine Nature Trail. This wooded loop has some small hills along its 0.75-mile path. A guide booklet discusses many of the trees found along the trail.

The Parnell Tower Trail starts at the Parnell Tower, one of the most popular stops in the forest. Situated at the Northern Unit's highest point, the 60-foot tower offers great views, especially of the glacial hills to the southwest. The trail is a mostly wooded 3.5-mile loop that joins the Ice Age Trail along the southwest end. The trail has many hills, including the short path from the parking lot to the tower.

The steep 0.75-mile Summit Nature Trail leads through open field up a 270-foot kame known as Dundee Mountain. Views from the top are wonderful—you can see the Campbellsport Drumlins Unit of the Ice Age National Scientific Reserve (p. 1) to the west—and interpretive panels along the trail discuss glacial geology. The trail may be accessed near site 944 of the Long Lake Campground. The Dundee Kame, a nearly perfect cone frequently featured in geology textbooks, is located southwest of Dundee Mountain and may be clearly observed from the unmarked parking area off County F.

The two-mile Tamarack Nature Trail leads around Mauthe Lake and can be started at the Mauthe Lake Recreation Area or the forest headquarters on the lake's opposite shore. The mostly level trail is a good bird-watching area. There is a guide booklet explaining the human and natural forces that have shaped this area.

The trails open to off-road biking are popular, but not as crowded as those in the Southern Unit, so you might consider hiking them though stay to the side and keep your eyes peeled at all times if you choose to do so.

PADDLING—The Milwaukee River is easiest to canoe between Long and Mauthe lakes; it is quite shallow in most places below Mauthe in the summer and fall. Many people also paddle each of the lakes, though Long Lake is heavily developed. Just below Mauthe Lake is the 230-acre Milwaukee River and Swamp State Natural Area, which features an unusual combination of southern and northern wet-mesic forests; the river cuts through the heart of the area.

BIKING—The nine-mile Greenbush and 5.5-mile New Fane trails are designated as off-road bike trails. The mostly forested Greenbush Trail has some serious single-track, with four difficult loops ranging from 1.2 to 5.4 miles. It is the most challenging of the two and thus the most popular—most riders consider it an equal to the more famous trails in the Southern Kettle Moraine, and when you consider the smaller crowds here, it is even a notch above them. The less popular New Fane Trail, with four loops ranging from 0.7 to 3.1 miles, offers some easy-to-moderate rides through a mix of open and wooded terrain.

WINTER—The Zillmer and Greenbush trails, almost 20 miles total, are groomed for both traditional and skate skiing. Both offer skiers a challenge, though there are also routes for beginners. Though not groomed, the New Fane Trail is still popular with skiers. The Greenbush Trail area has a warming shelter as well as a sledding hill. The forest is also a fantastic place to snowshoe. Snowmobilers have 58 miles of trails across the forest.

AUTO TOUR—County S, running 2.4 miles between Glenbeulah and Highway 23, is Rustic Road #63.

OTHER—Horseback riders have 39 miles of trails set aside for their use. A 33-mile horse trail stretches the length of the forest, and in the middle it joins two loops totaling six miles.

The Wade House State Historic Site (920) 526-3271 in Greenbush recreates the era when stagecoaches ruled the road. Tours of the restored 1860s inn show visitors what life was like during those bygone days, while the on-site carriage museum houses the state's largest collection of hand and horse-drawn wagons and carriages. The site is open May through October.

COUNTIES—Sheboygan, Fond du Lac, and Washington.

DIRECTIONS—Henry S. Reuss Ice Age Visitor Center is half a mile southwest of Dundee on Highway 67.

FACILITIES—Water, toilets, boat launch, nature center, nature programs, picnic area, grills, picnic shelter, beach, playground, volleyball, ball field.

CAMPING—Two campgrounds, 367 sites, 52 electric, 12 walk-in sites, 15 horseback rider sites, tipi rental, six Adirondack-style backpacking shelters, open year-round, reservations accepted, showers, group camp.

ENTRY—Open year-round. State park sticker or daily fee required. State trail pass required for off-road bikers and horseback riders. Fee for Wade House and carriage museum.

ON THE WEB—www.wiparks.net

CONTACT—Kettle Moraine State Forest-Northern Unit, N1765 County Highway G, Campbellsport, WI 53010. Phone (262) 626-2116.

Broughton Sheboygan Marsh
Park and Wildlife Area

THE KETTLE MORAINE region is best known for its rolling hills, but the melting glaciers left behind extensive wetlands, as well. The 14,000-acre Sheboygan Marsh, of which over 8,000 acres are owned by the county and state, is a remnant of the former Glacial Lake Sheboygan that was once 50 feet deep. While wetlands comprise the majority of the area, there are also extensive upland and lowland forests, plus cedar swamps and tamarack bogs which are more typical of northern Wisconsin. Broughton Sheboygan Marsh Park (30 acres) sits at the northeast end of the marsh.

As in most other large marshes in Wisconsin, attempts were once made to drain this land to open it up to farming. Two major efforts failed, and in 1937 more than 6,000 acres were purchased by the county, which then built a small dam and reflooded the marsh. Since then, the state and county have continued to expand the wildlife area, and it is now known far and wide as one of the most productive hunting grounds in the state. Sheboygan businessman and conservationist Charles Broughton was one of the leaders in the effort to conserve this area.

Besides being a natural wonder, with nearly a hundred prehistoric sites identified so far, this is one of the most significant archaeological sites in the country. Because the finds "encompass virtually the entire spectrum of prehistoric occupation in Wisconsin" and the potential for major future discoveries is high, the marsh has been recommended for inclusion as a National Archaeological District on the National Register of Historic Places.

WILDLIFE—Bird-watchers will likely find a visit to the marsh very produc-

239

tive. Among the many species they might spot are sandhill crane, green-backed heron, wood duck, sora rail, black tern, pheasant, ruffed grouse, northern harrier, prothonotary warbler, Cerulean warbler, Acadian flycatcher, yellow-headed blackbird, pileated woodpecker, and the state-threatened osprey and red-shouldered hawk. Mammalian residents include deer, fox, coyote, beaver, otter, and mink.

HIKING—Plans call for the Ice Age Trail (p. 1) to pass through the marsh eventually, but right now the only options are three seldom-used paths in the southern part of the marsh. One starts at the end of School Road and another begins at the end of Hulls Crossing Drive; both lead past farm fields before entering into the marsh. The path from Hulls Crossing winds for 1.5 miles before ending near the Sheboygan River. The School Road trail leads for three-quarters of a mile east and then north, where it splits; one path heads east, the other west, and both dead-end after half a mile. The School Road paths are within a waterfowl refuge and access is restricted in fall.

The other option is a former railroad grade that cuts through a large tamarack bog along the south edge of the property; it can be accessed off County C just northwest of Glenbeulah. Though used primarily as a snowmobile trail, the mile-long hike (beyond this the land is currently still private property) is very scenic, and makes a good bird-watching destination. If you do not mind getting muddy, several "cut lines" (narrow, unofficial trails used by hunters) lead right into the bog. Even though some of these are marked, do not head into the bog without a compass; it is very easy to get lost in there.

PADDLING—The only way to really see the preserve is to get out onto the water. There are 675 acres of open water here, including Sheboygan Lake, the Sheboygan River, several smaller streams, and over 20 miles of ditches left from past drainage efforts. The best place to launch a canoe is at the park, where maps are available and canoes or rowboats may be rented. Keller's Landing, at the west end of the marsh on River Lane, is a private boat landing at a farm, and the owner allows the public to use it for a small donation. If, while paddling you happen to notice an island floating across your path, you do not have to worry about your sanity. High winds send these floating cattail bogs downstream with some regularity, so keep your eyes peeled.

COUNTY—Sheboygan.

DIRECTIONS—The park is located 1.5 miles northwest of Elkhart Lake on County J.

FACILITIES—Water, toilets, boat launch, picnic area, grills, picnic shelter, playground, volleyball.

CAMPING—64 sites, all electric, open year-round, reservations accepted, one wilderness site (free, first come-first served) at the western intersection of the Sheboygan River and the main ditch.

ENTRY—Open year-round. Free.

CONTACT—Sheboygan County Planning Dept., 508 New York Ave., She-boygan, WI 53081. Phone (920) 459-3060. DNR, PO Box 408, W5750 Wood-chuck Ln., Plymouth, WI 53073. Phone (920) 892-8756.

Riveredge Nature Center

RIVEREDGE, southeast Wisconsin's first nature center, was founded in 1968 with the dual mission of preservation and education. The center consists of 351 acres of forest, marsh, meadow, and prairie along the large Milwaukee River and small Riveredge Creek. Classes and special events are held throughout the year for school groups and the public, while the educa-tion and visitors center features many hands-on displays. Because of their abundance, wildflower-identification is popular here, and the variety of habi-tats also makes for productive bird-watching.

WILDLIFE—Nearly 190 species of birds have been recorded here, includ-ing wood duck, great blue heron, Cooper's hawk, the state-threatened red-shouldered hawk, bluebird, and many songbirds. Mammals include deer, fox, and coyote. The 67-acre Riveredge Creek and Ephemeral Pond State Natural Area in the southeast portion of the property features an exceptionally diverse invertebrate population.

HIKING—Fifteen mostly level trails totaling 8.5 miles lead through the property, and the short intersecting trails branch off each other, allowing a wide variety of hiking combinations. Over a mile of trails around the nature center and along the river in the southwest are wheelchair-accessible. The cen-ter also has a "trail trekker" (golf cart) available for disabled visitors.

The trails to the east of Hawthorne Drive, which bisects the property, offer a mix of all the center's habitat types, and contain most of the many board-walks and viewing platforms. The main trails of interest include the 0.9-mile Ecology Trail, which crosses Riveredge Creek and has a viewing blind and a viewing platform overlooking small ponds. The quiet Bluebird Trail leads for a mile out to the far end of the reserve. Two other short trails also pass small ponds—the 0.3-mile Swamp Walk Trail has a floating boardwalk, and there is another viewing blind along the Outlook Trail. The Milwaukee River lies in the wooded area west of Hawthorne Drive, and the Marsh and Oak trails, both 0.6-mile long, pass along the river, as does the half-mile River Trail. A boardwalk crosses the small wetlands along the Marsh Trail.

The 1.4-mile Big Oak Trail on the west side of the river cannot be reached directly from the center's main area, so it is used much less frequently. The often-wet path loops through the lowland forest and up to the river. It can be accessed three-quarters of a mile northeast on Hickory Road, just across the bridge in Newburg. Turn south on the gravel drive and continue to the parking area where the road is once again paved.

PADDLING—A canoe launch provides access to the 1.5 miles of Milwaukee River within the reserve.

WINTER—The 6.5 miles of trail east of the river are groomed for cross-country skiing. This includes an extra mile through the natural area that is open only in the winter, in order to protect this fragile environment. There is a warming shelter.

COUNTY—Ozaukee.

DIRECTIONS—One mile north of Newburg on County Y.

FACILITIES—Water, toilets, nature center, nature programs.

CAMPING—None.

ENTRY—Open year-round. Admission fee.

ON THE WEB—www.riveredgenc.org

CONTACT—Riveredge Nature Center, 4458 W. Hawthorne Dr., Newburg, WI 53060. Phone (262) 375-2715. E-mail: info@riveredge.us

Kohler-Andrae State Parks

THE EXPANSIVE sand dunes along Kohler-Andrae's two miles of Lake Michigan shoreline are the park's most striking feature and are reason enough to visit. The largest dunes, some still active, and small interdunal wetlands, Wisconsin's rarest natural community, comprise the 135-acre Kohler Park Dunes State Natural Area. The preserve harbors many rare plants, including dune thistle and possibly the state's last population of prairie moonwort, though this tiny fern has not actually been seen by botanists since 1985. In addition to the shifting sands, the 988-acre park consists of forest, meadow, and a marsh along the Black River.

While managed as a single unit, Kohler-Andrae is actually two state parks. In 1927, the widow of Frank "Terry" Andrae donated 122 acres of lakeshore to the state in his memory, thus making possible Terry Andrae State Park. The Kohler Company donated 280 acres to the state in 1966 in honor of the company's founder, and this parcel was named John Michael Kohler State Park.

WILDLIFE—Look for beaver, otter, mink, belted kingfisher, common tern, wood duck, great blue and green-backed herons, and sandhill crane in the wetlands, and deer, fox, coyote, badger, turkey vulture, red-shouldered hawk, pheasant, pileated warbler, Eastern meadowlark, chestnut-sided warbler, oven-bird, and scarlet tanager in the wooded and open uplands. Each fall thousands of monarch butterflies congregate here during their migration south.

HIKING—The fantastic 2.5-mile-long Kohler Dunes Cordwalk, consisting of boards roped together to make a trail, leads through the natural area right over some of the dunes allowing excellent up-close viewing of this unique environment. The portion of the cordwalk immediately south of the nature center is the Creeping Juniper Nature Trail, which features interpretive panels along the easy half-mile loop. You can learn more about the park's natural and human history at the adjacent Sanderling Nature Center.

Neither of the other three easy trails in the park is as interesting as the cordwalk, but each is worthwhile. The mile-long Woodland Dunes Nature Trail loops through the wooded southern end of the park, and the first quarter-mile of the trail is wheelchair-accessible. Interpretive panels discuss several of the northern and southern tree species growing in the forest. The quarter-mile Black River Marsh Boardwalk is an accessible loop with several benches along it, and is a good place to look for birds. Hidden away in the northern end of the park is the 2.5-mile Black River Trail with several short loops through a mix of forest and open field. There is a parking area at the trailhead on County V, but there is no direct access from the main entrance.

DONALD S. ABRAMS

The Kohler Dunes Cordwalk.

BIKING—Off-road bikes are permitted on the Black River Trail.

WINTER—In winter, a groomed, level, two-mile, cross-country ski trail circles the southern end of the park through the campground, picnic area, and along a portion of the Woodland Dunes Nature Trail. A warming shelter is available.

OTHER—Horseback riders may use the Black River Trail.

COUNTY—Sheboygan.

DIRECTIONS—Four miles south of Sheboygan on County KK, then one mile east on Old Park Rd.

FACILITIES—Water, toilets, nature center, nature programs, picnic area, grills, picnic shelter, beach (a beach wheelchair is available for disabled access to the beach), playground, volleyball, ball field.

CAMPING—106 sites, 49 electric, tipi rental, open year-round, reservations accepted, showers, group camp.

ENTRY—Open year-round. State park sticker or daily fee required.

ON THE WEB—www.wiparks.net

CONTACT—Kohler-Andrae State Parks, 1020 Beach Park Ln., Sheboygan, WI 53081. Phone (920) 451-4080.

Woodland Dunes Nature Center

THIS LARGE, undeveloped area between Two Rivers and Manitowoc was first used as a bird-banding center by researchers studying migration. Bird-watchers and others were drawn to the area and eventually local citizens got together to ensure that this important migratory stopover would be preserved. From their initial purchase of 40 acres in 1974, Woodland Dunes has been expanded to nearly 1,200 acres. Bird-banding programs continue.

The area encompasses marsh, upland, and lowland forest, meadow, swamp, and a small prairie restoration. Much of the area is covered by beach ridges formed thousands of years ago by a much-higher Lake Michigan. Unlike other beach ridges in the area, such as nearby Point Beach State Forest (p. 246), where the dunes formed parallel to Lake Michigan, these lie in a unique fan-shaped pattern.

WILDLIFE—The area lies in the ecological "tension zone" between northern and southern habitats, and thus birds from both commonly nest here; more than 130 species have been recorded in summer surveys, including green-backed heron, Canada goose, hawks, saw-whet owl, ruffed grouse, pheasant, Eastern meadowlark, white-eyed vireo, and a dozen or so warblers. Many more birds pass through during migration, including all species of raptor common to Wisconsin. Birds are not the only airborne animals to congregate here during migration; monarch butterflies and dragonflies also are abundant in the fall. There is a butterfly garden by the Rahmlow Marsh Haus, an old brick farmhouse that now serves as the headquarters and nature center. Area mammals include deer, fox, coyote, badger, mink, and weasel.

HIKING—The preserve's seven trails total about six miles and are all very easy walks. Three trails begin at the nature center. The half-mile Cattail Trail is a wheelchair-accessible boardwalk through the swamp and marsh, with benches at the end for resting or observation. The 0.75-mile Goldenrod Trail passes through open meadow and loops around a small pond at the end, though you should continue along the 1.4-mile Horsetail Trail. The Horsetail passes through meadow, an alder thicket, and along an old tree farm, but is most interesting at its back end, where it loops through a unique (and wholly unnatural—this is what resulted from the heavy disturbance here in the past) plot that vaguely resembles a tamarack bog, but with cedars instead of tamaracks. There are also numerous flowering plants and some other unusual vegetation, including several species of horsetails. It also passes Manitowoc County's largest tree, a plains cottonwood with an 18-foot girth. Pick up the interpretive guide booklets for these trails at the nature center.

Three other trails start at the end of Goodwin Road and are almost entirely wooded. The Yellow Birch Trail, a wheelchair-accessible boardwalk, is a little less than half a mile. The 0.75-mile Black Cherry Trail and the 1.5-mile Trillium Trail are narrow, but easy to follow; the latter crosses numerous ridges and swales, and boardwalks lead over wet sections of both. The Conifer Trail is a three-quarter-mile loop that follows two beach ridges past 11 different species of conifer.

COUNTY—Manitowoc.

DIRECTIONS—Just west of Two Rivers on Highway 310.

FACILITIES—Water, toilets, nature center, nature programs.

CAMPING—None.

ENTRY—Open year-round. Free.

ON THE WEB—www.woodlanddunes.com

CONTACT—Woodland Dunes Nature Center, PO Box 2108, Manitowoc, WI 54221. Phone (920) 793-4007. E-mail: woodlanddunes@lsol.net

Point Beach State Forest

THIS SIX-MILE-LONG stretch of forest and dunes tucked up against Lake Michigan was once considered for a national park. When nothing came of those plans, local citizens convinced the Wisconsin state legislature to establish a state forest instead, and the first land was acquired in 1937. Today the Point Beach State Forest covers 2,903 acres and the dune ridges within the forest have been designated a National Natural Landmark. While it is managed like a state park, the land was acquired under the state forestry law, and the name continues today, even though no commercial logging takes place.

Throughout the 19th century, this was an important area for commercial fishing, and camps operated in what is now the state forest. Native Americans had found the area to be fertile fishing grounds long before the first Europeans arrived, and early Copper Culture groups as well as the later Ho-Chunk, Fox, and probably Sauk, all lived here at one time. The National Register of Historic Places listed Rawley Point Lighthouse, near the park office, one of the largest and brightest on the Great Lakes—its two-million-candle-power beacon is visible 19 miles out from shore. Though closed to the public, it may be viewed from the beach. Dozens of ships sank nearby before the lighthouse began operation, and the hull of one of them is displayed near the park office; scuba divers can explore some of the others.

WILDLIFE—Among the many common residents at Point Beach are green-backed heron, wild turkey, northern harrier, pileated woodpecker, great-crested flycatcher, white-breasted nuthatch, pine warbler, indigo bunting, white-throated sparrow, deer, fox, coyote, weasel, and mink. Many other birds such as wood duck, blue-winged teal, sandhill crane, spotted sandpiper, Caspian tern, and many other warblers stop here as they migrate down the Lake Michigan shoreline.

HIKING—The ten miles of trails at Point Beach are almost completely level and do not get nearly as much use as you might expect when seeing the beach crowds. The Ridges Trail runs north to south from the nature center down to Molash Creek in the middle of the forest, its three colored loops totaling about 7.25 miles. The trail is mostly wooded, following the many beach ridges, and the eastern half leads up to the beach at several points. There are many swales—periodically dry wetlands—between the ridges. Just south of the main entrance road, the Red Loop crosses through the T-shaped Wilderness Ridge State Natural Area, which protects an eight-acre cross-section of the unique beach-ridge topography. The Blue Loop leads to the group camp road, which is a good place to access the trails as it is away from the crowds and has several boardwalks over the swales at the southern end. The Yellow Loop at the southernmost end leads right up to Molash Creek before turning back north, and is the least used part of the trail, though arguably the most beautiful.

The Swales Nature Trail, a level 0.75-mile loop with interpretive panels discussing the park's ridge-swale topography, winds through the forest west of the nature center. The four-mile Red Pine Trail looping through the woods across the highway is scenic, but does not feature the beautiful ridges and swales of the other trails.

In addition to the trails, there are six miles of beach for scenic strolls, and walking the entire way to Neshota Park in Two Rivers makes for a great couple of hours—both Molash and Silver creeks are shallow at their mouths and can be waded with ease. Swimming is allowed anywhere along the shore, but most people gather near one of the three picnic areas north of the office so hikers heading south will have the sand largely to themselves.

BIKING—The four-mile Red Pine Trail is open to off-road bikes, while the new Rawley Point Trail, surfaced with crushed limestone, connects the nature center to Two Rivers.

WINTER—The hiking trails are groomed for cross-country skiing, and a warming shelter is available on weekends.

AUTO TOUR—Sandy Bay Road (County O), which runs the length of the forest, is Rustic Road #16.

COUNTY—Manitowoc.

DIRECTIONS—Four miles north of Two Rivers on County O.

FACILITIES—Water, toilets, nature center, nature programs, picnic area, grills, picnic shelter, beach, playground, volleyball.

CAMPING—127 sites, 70 electric, open year-round, reservations accepted, showers, group camp.

ENTRY—Open year-round. State park sticker or daily fee required.

ON THE WEB—www.wiparks.net

CONTACT—Point Beach State Forest, 9400 County Highway O, Two Rivers, WI 54241. Phone (920) 794-7480.

Brillion Wildlife Area

DO NOT LET the junkyard by the entrance fool you; the Brillion Wildlife Area is a beautiful spot. Brillion Marsh, centered on the junction of Spring Creek and the North Branch Manitowoc River, covers much of this 5,159-acre wildlife area, which also features extensive bottomland forest and is surrounded by wooded and open uplands. A small nature center run by a private group, but used mostly by local schools, opened in 1987 on the site of a for-

mer farm, and is surrounded by a large prairie restoration. Public nature programs are offered occasionally.

WILDLIFE—Wildlife in the marsh and surrounding uplands includes
deer, coyote, fox, weasel, mink, pheasant, ruffed grouse, northern harrier, great
blue and green-backed herons, sandhill crane, Canada goose, and many ducks.
Grassland songbirds such as savannah sparrow, Eastern meadowlark, and
bobolink are also common. Osprey may be seen on nesting platforms from the
marsh platform or from the observation mounds along Conservation Flowage
Road. Tundra swans often stop during migration, and bald eagle are occasionally seen.

HIKING—About six miles of easy trails are maintained by the nature center.
There are a few interpretive signs along them, though for a more detailed look
at the ecology and history pick up the guide brochure at the nature center. Five
interconnected trails lead through the forest around the nature center. The
1.25-mile White Oak Trail, as well and the half-mile Red Oak and 0.7-mile
Hickory trails looping within it, cut through a scenic hardwood forest. The
0.75-mile Cottonwood Trail, with a mix of the same forest plus prairie and
even a tiny stand of conifers, is the reserve's most varied trail. The half-mile
Marsh Platform Trail leads to an elevated, wheelchair-accessible viewing platform that juts out into the cattail marsh; it is an excellent wildlife watching
spot, Brillion's one must-see. To the south, starting at the parking area on
Deerview Rd., is the Sugar Maple Trail. It cuts through a mix of forest and field
and passes an old log cabin and lime kiln along its 1.25-mile path. The 1.25-
mile Sugar Maple Link leads through more open field connecting the Sugar
Maple Trail to the others. Only the White Oak Trail has any hills along its route,
and these are not very large.

PADDLING—Canoeists can paddle up the North Branch Manitowoc
River from the County PP Bridge in the village of Potter.

WINTER—The trails are open for cross-country skiing and snowshoeing
though none are groomed.

COUNTY—Calumet.

DIRECTIONS—One mile south of Brillion on County PP, then one mile
west on Deerview Rd.

FACILITIES—Water, toilets, nature center, nature programs, picnic area.

CAMPING—Group camp.

ENTRY—Open year-round. Free. The nature center is open weekdays by
appointment.

ON THE WEB—www.brillion.k12.wi.us/bnc/bnchome.htm

CONTACT—DNR, 3369 W. Brewster St., Appleton, WI 54914. Phone
(920) 832-1804. Brillion Nature Center, c/o Brillion Public Schools, 315 S.

Main St., Brillion, WI 54110. E-mail: brillionnaturecenter@juno.com
Phone (920) 756-3591.

High Cliff State Park

B USY HIGH CLIFF State Park lies on the northeast shore of Lake Winnebago, the largest lake in Wisconsin. The high cliff of the name is a long
limestone ledge rising more than 200 feet above the shore, with vertical cliffs as
high as 25 feet. It is part of the Niagara Escarpment which stretches north
through Door County, across Michigan and Canada, and creates Niagara Falls
at the other end of the arc. The 125-acre High Cliff Escarpment State Natural
Area stretches along the lake for over a mile, protecting the cliffs themselves
and the many rare plants, such as the northern fragile fern, that grow on them.
There are many cliff-dwelling species here, and the many springs flowing down
the ledge create another rich environment on the forest floor below. Atop the
ledge, north of the campground, are a dozen burial mounds, constructed 1,500
years ago. Of particular interest is a 285-foot-long panther mound.

The 1,147-acre park includes the former Western Lime and Cement Company quarry, which operated from 1895 to 1956. The kilns, which separated the
lime from the stone, were heated to 2,200°F, originally by wood fire and later by
coal. Once the process began, the kilns would stay in continual operation from
six months to a year, turning out a thousand pounds of lime an hour. Both the
quarry and the kilns are still visible today, and a general store which was part of
the company town is open weekends during the summer.

WILDLIFE—High Cliff is not exactly teeming with wildlife, but deer, fox,
weasel, mink, hawks, red-eyed vireo, ovenbird, Eastern meadowlark, and
white-breasted nuthatch all make the park their home. Many waterfowl and
shorebirds can be seen along the lake, and this is a good spot for birders to
observe the spring warbler migration.

HIKING—There are 7.5 miles of hiking trails in the park. By far the most
scenic is the 2.3-mile Lime-Kiln Trail, which starts south of the old lime kiln
and loops through the northern half of the natural area. The portion of the
trail along the lake is generally level, while the section along the ledge has steep
hills. A cut-off about halfway along the trail allows a shorter and easier hike.

The Red Bird Trail is named for the former Ho-Chunk chief who fre-
quented this area—a 12-foot-tall bronze statue of the chief at the main picnic
area, near the trailhead, overlooks the lake. The mostly level and wooded trail
loops for 3.7 miles through the quarry and around the wooded campground.
The southern section of the trail lies along the top of the ledge, and actually

offers better views of the cliffs than does the Lime-Kiln Trail; a set of stairs west of the campground connects these two trails.

There are two easy self-guided nature trails, the 0.3-mile Indian Mound Trail and the 1.3-mile Forest Management Trail. The wooded Indian Mound Trail, as the name suggests, leads along the park's mounds. The wheelchair-accessible path connects to the Red Bird Trail. The Forest Management Trail is of particular interest to landowners. It loops through the 49-acre High Cliff Stewardship Forest which consists of both a managed woodlot and one that is natural, letting you compare the two.

PADDLING—You could paddle around Lake Winnebago, though with large waves and heavy use by motorboats and sailboats there is really no point.

BIKING—Off-road bikes are allowed on the 8.5-mile Horse Trail and the 1.5 miles of the Red Bird Trail along the top of the cliff. Neither is very challenging.

WINTER—An extended Red Bird Trail provides 4.2 miles of groomed cross-country skiing.

OTHER—An 8.5-mile horse trail leads along the eastern edge of the park. It is mostly level, going through open field, though the southern segment has some rolling hills.

COUNTY—Calumet.

DIRECTIONS—Six miles east of Menasha on Hwy. 114, then 2.5 miles south on State Park Rd.

FACILITIES—Water, toilets, boat launch, marina, nature center, nature programs, picnic area, grills, picnic shelter, beach, playground, volleyball, ball field.

CAMPING—112 sites, 32 electric, open March to Nov., reservations accepted, showers, group camp, overnight stays allowed on boats moored in the marina.

ENTRY—Open year-round. State park sticker or daily fee required.

ON THE WEB—www.wiparks.net

CONTACT—High Cliff State Park, N7630 State Park Rd., Sherwood, WI 54952. Phone (920) 989-1106.

Eldorado Marsh Wildlife Area

THE LARGE MARSH that comprises most of this 6,371-acre wildlife area was originally a lake formed at the end of the last Ice Age. Like many of Wisconsin's marshes, it was created when a glacial lake filled with silt and decaying vegetation. Another similarity was an unsuccessful attempt to drain it for agriculture before the land was acquired by the state for conservation purposes. A 1,500-acre flowage in the center of the marsh, fed by the West Branch of the Fond du Lac River and several smaller streams and kept in place by a three-quarter-mile dike, provides favorable habitat for waterfowl and numerous other wetland birds.

WILDLIFE—Ducks and geese are among the area's most common residents, especially in spring and fall, since the area lies on a major waterfowl migration route. Sandhill cranes, black-crowned night heron, great egret (a state-threatened species), black tern, marsh hawk, beaver, otter, and mink are also found in or near the marsh, while deer, fox, badger, and pheasant inhabit the wooded and open uplands. The area's extensive grasslands, some of which are slowly being returned to prairie, provide an important haven for Neotropical songbirds that migrate between Wisconsin and Central and South America, including bobolink and more than a dozen warblers.

HIKING—There are two primary hiking trails at Eldorado. Dike Road bisects the property between Highway 23 and County I. The middle mile and a half of this gravel road, including the dike, is closed to traffic and affords an easy, scenic walk along the flowage and marsh. It is great for wildlife viewing. An abandoned railroad grade, now forming the Mascoutin Valley State Trail, defines most of Eldorado's southern border, and allows some good views from its elevated gravel path. Though still a work in progress, when completed, the trail will stretch 31 miles between Fond du Lac and Berlin; currently the nine-mile completed section crossing the Eldorado Marsh links Fond du Lac with Rosendale. Access to the east end of the trail along the marsh is at Ridge Road, and to the west at Rose-Eld Road; it can also be accessed from Highway 23 at two points in the trail's middle—Hageman Road and Heinrich Road.

There are other hiking opportunities here, too. Several access roads lead into the area—from the east on Marsh Road and County I, from the west on Town Hall Road and Rose-Eld Road, and from the north on County N. Most of these are mowed trails through open fields and will be overgrown at times. The two best for hikers are a gravel road leading west from County I at Brenner Road and a mowed trail on Town Hall Road, a quarter-mile south of County N.

Between Highway 23 and the Mascoutin Valley State Trail, just beyond Rose-Eld Rd., is the Eldorado Outdoor Education Center, used by area school groups. There are about half a mile of unmarked trails here, leading mostly through open field. A pond with a small pier is found in the northeast corner.

PADDLING—Canoeing on the flowage is a good way to see things up close. Abundant vegetation means that wildlife could show itself around any turn. A boat launch directly onto the flowage is located in the east at the southernmost parking area, on Marsh Road. Another is located to the west at the end of School Road; from here you can follow a ditch to reach the flowage.

BIKING—Bikers can easily follow Dike Road and, of course, the Mascoutin Valley State Trail.

COUNTY—Fond du Lac.

DIRECTIONS—Five miles west of Fond du Lac on Hwy. 23.

FACILITIES—Boat launch.

CAMPING—None.

ENTRY—Open year-round. Free.

CONTACT—DNR, 625 E County Road Y, Suite 700, Oshkosh, WI 54901. Phone (920) 424-3050.

Horicon National
Wildlife Refuge, Horicon Marsh State Wildlife Area, and Marsh Haven Nature Center

FEW NATURAL EVENTS are more beloved than the annual migration of Canada geese, and nowhere is this migration as impressive as Horicon Marsh. Each fall, as many as 300,000 honkers stop here on their way to their southern winter homes, and nearly twice as many people come to witness the world's largest population of migrating geese. Though the annual fall spectacle is far and away the most popular time to visit, there is much to see and do at other times of the year, and with far fewer people around.

Often called the "Everglades of the North"—a description that somewhat applies visually, but has absolutely no scientific relevance—Horicon is the largest freshwater cattail marsh in the United States. It stretches roughly 14 miles long by 5 miles wide, and has been designated a Wetland of International Importance, a Globally Important Bird Area, and the southern, state-owned portion is a unit of the Ice Age National Scientific Reserve (p. 1). The marsh is a remnant of Glacial Lake Horicon, formed by the retreating glaciers, while the narrow islands scattered throughout are the tops of drumlins, formed during the glacier's advance.

Archaeological remains have been found at the marsh from all major Native American cultures of the Upper Midwest, starting with the first nomadic hunters who came through 12,000 years ago. Many Native American trails passed by the marsh as they crossed the state, and both Highway 26 and County Z follow their former routes. The first Europeans on the marsh settled near Ho-Chunk villages; in fact, Horicon was first known as The Great Marsh of the Winnebagos, though the name Horicon is an Algonquin word for "land of clean, pure water." An 1850 survey of burial and effigy mounds surrounding the marsh located more than 500; while most have since been destroyed, at least 200 still remain, all on private lands. Conical and panther mounds along County Z (just north of Ledge Road) in Dodge County are marked by a sign and may be seen from the road.

In 1846 a dam was built in the City of Horicon, the area's first modern town, which raised the water level of the marsh by nine feet, creating Lake Horicon, then the largest man-made lake in the world. The dam was removed after 23 years due to land disputes, and the marsh again became a haven for wildlife. Then, early in the 20th century, miles of ditches were dug to drain the marsh for agriculture but these efforts were a spectacular failure. Not only was farming unsuccessful, but wildfires routinely ripped through the dried peat and what had been prime wildlife habitat became a barren wasteland. Conservationists did not give up on the land, however, and in 1921 they began to push for restoration. Seven years later, the Horicon Marsh Wildlife Refuge Bill was passed and the state began acquiring and restoring the land, building a low dam to restore water levels to original levels. When the state ran out of funds, the U.S. Fish and Wildlife Service stepped in, and today the northern two-thirds of the marsh (21,000 acres) comprise the Horicon National Wildlife Refuge, while the southern third (11,000 acres) is the Horicon Marsh State Wildlife Area.

The Marsh Haven Nature Center is a privately-run, 47-acre facility on the northwest end of the marsh right along Highway 49. The main building hosts displays about the marsh's natural and human history, educational programs, and a wildlife art gallery. The best part of Marsh Haven is the 30-foot

FOND DU LAC CONVENTION AND VISITORS BUREAU

Horicon Marsh's most famous residents.

observation tower; it offers great views of geese flying into the marsh in the late afternoon.

WILDLIFE—The honkers that stop at Horicon each year are from the Mississippi Valley population of Canada geese, a subspecies that nests on the southwestern end of Hudson Bay in Canada. The 850-mile flight from Canada to Horicon takes as little as 15 hours, depending on the winds; the youngest members of the flock are less than six months old when they make their first trip. After stopping at Horicon to feed and rest, the geese continue on to their wintering grounds in Missouri, Kentucky, Tennessee, and southern Illinois, another 450 miles away. Geese were not always here in such large numbers; in 1948 only 2,000 stopped at Horicon but more and more discovered the marsh, and through restoration and good management at Horicon the entire Mississippi Valley population has thrived. By the 1970s, geese were so plentiful at Horicon that other nearby marshes were restored to accommodate them, though Horicon is still far and away their most important staging area. Each year, up to 80 percent of the Mississippi Valley population stops in east central Wisconsin, and as many as 700,000 are in the vicinity at any one time during the fall.

The best goose-viewing occurs just after sunrise, when they leave the marsh to feed in surrounding fields, and just before sunset when they return to spend the night. In fall, the geese begin arriving in mid-September, and most are gone by the end of December—the peak is mid to late October. In spring, the geese are at the marsh from early March to mid-April, though there are far fewer at this time since the flocks are more widely distributed as they gain weight for the northerly migration.

The geese are the stars at Horicon, and rightfully so, but they are not the only spectacular wildlife display. Horicon was originally established for ducks, and 100,000 still use the marsh each year. This is the largest nesting area for redhead ducks east of the Mississippi with more than 3,000 residing here. Also impressive are the thousands of wading birds that nest here. For many years Fourmile Island was home to as many as a thousand pairs of great blue heron, black-crowned night heron, great egret, and double-crested cormorant. However, a severe storm in 1998 toppled many of the trees, and over the years the abundance of birds has led to a loss of nesting trees because of accumulating guano. Many birds still nest on this 15-acre island, but others have found new sites on the marsh and in surrounding areas. The island, designated the Fourmile Island Rookery State Natural Area, is easily visible from the DNR Field Office on Quick's Point, just north of the city of Horicon, or from the DNR Service Center/International Education Center on Highway 28; canoeing on the East Branch Rock River offers a closer look.

Altogether, more than 275 species of birds have been sighted on the Horicon Marsh over the years, with some of the best bird-watching occurring during April and May. The Horicon Marsh Bird Festival is held annually on the second weekend of May, which is usually the peak of the spring bird migration. In addition to those birds listed above, sandhill crane, American white pelican, pied-billed grebe, Virginia and sora rails, least bittern, black and Forster's tern, and marsh wren nest on the marsh. Horicon has limited uplands, but great horned owl, yellow-bellied sapsucker, willow flycatcher, black-capped chickadee, Tennessee warbler, scarlet tanager, and rose-breasted grosbeaks can be seen in the scattered forests. Bobolink, Eastern (and on rare occasions, Western) meadowlark and savannah sparrow may be found in the small prairie restorations—you will find some prairie at Quick's Point in the state section and around the hiking trails in the federal area. Horicon regularly attracts some of Wisconsin's rarest birds. If you are very lucky, you might just add a black-bellied whistling duck, white-winger scoter, Eurasian wigeon, brant, Ross' goose, black-necked stilt, snowy egret, tricolored heron, glossy ibis, or a buff-breasted sandpiper to your life list. Photo blinds may be reserved on both ends of the marsh.

Mammals at Horicon include deer, coyote, fox, mink, and muskrat, whose houses are found all across the marsh. Beaver are uncommon, and while the otter population is strong they are rarely seen.

HIKING—In the northwest corner of the federal refuge, off Highway 49, three hiking trails are interwoven with the TernPike auto tour (see below), which is itself a nice walk when it is closed to traffic. The level Egret Nature Trail is the shortest and also the most popular of the three, since about half of its 0.4-mile route is a floating boardwalk going right through the marsh; it returns through a small woodlot. The 2.5-mile Redhead Trail and the half-mile Red Fox Nature Trail pass along the marsh in some places, but both are mostly through prairie and meadow. The Redhead Trail leads along the Rock River for part of its length. Both trails have only short, rolling hills and are very easy walks. Across the marsh is the Bud Cook Hiking Area, where a pair of trails loop through some meadow, a small prairie restoration, and some bottomland forest. The main path is the nearly two-mile Two Hawks Trail, which makes a long but gradual descent down to a wildlife observation blind overlooking a small pond, while the 0.3-mile Deer Track Trail stays close to the parking area and though it is not surfaced, the route is level enough to accommodate wheelchairs.

The 1.5-mile Horicon Habitat Trail, starting by the DNR Service Center/ International Educational Center, loops around Quick's Point along the edge of the marsh and has interpretive signs explaining the various habitats it passes and the wildlife that live in them. Like the federal hiking trails, this one is mostly open, with scattered woods and only small hills. Connected to the Horicon

Habitat Trail, though usually accessed at the DNR Service Center/International Education Center, is the completely level Bachhuber Flowage Trail which circles a 200-acre wetland, a very good spot for watching wildlife. Hunting is prohibited in the areas around both the state and federal designated hiking trails, allowing worry-free, year-round use for both humans and other species.

There are also a number of dikes open to hiking in the state-owned portion. One of the best begins at One Mile Island and leads out along the Rock River for about a mile. Though not marked or maintained, it is a popular hiking destination. It begins at the end of Nebraska Street in the city of Horicon. Another popular and scenic destination is the service road that branches off the Bachhuber Flowage Trail and leads around wooded Indemuhle Island. In the northeast corner of the state area, south of Dike Road, a three-mile series of dikes and service roads circles the Greenhead Impoundment. These little-used, somewhat overgrown paths are a good place to view wildlife. Another three miles of dikes lead into the marsh on the west end of the state area off Swan Road.

Finally, if you still need more options, there are two 0.75-mile trails at the Marsh Haven Nature Center, although these level trails are much less interesting than those in the marsh. The Woodland Discovery Trail loops through a small prairie restoration and then a small forest before leading out to a 30-foot tall observation tower; a few detailed interpretive signs along the trail discuss forest ecology. The Vander Woude Wetland Trail leads around a pond with several boardwalks and bridges; it connects to the Wild Goose State Trail (see the Biking section below) which is an additional hiking option.

PADDLING—Almost all visitors see the Horicon Marsh from the perimeter, but naturally the best way to experience it is out on the water. Paddling is allowed only in the state portions, where the East and West Branches of the Rock River and numerous other ditches and channels may be explored. The East Branch Rock River, which passes the Fourmile Island heron rookery (it is about a one-hour paddle to reach it), is the most common destination. The old branch of the Rock River through Miescke Bay is another good route. There are two boat launches onto the Rock River at the southern tip of the marsh on Nebraska and Chestnut streets. Two others are located on the East Branch Rock River at the end of Greenhead Road, and onto Burnett Ditch to the west from Burnett Ditch Road. To make a longer trip, launch onto the Rock at the village of Kekoskee and paddle down to the marsh.

Paddlers should heed all signed restrictions and take care to avoid disturbing nesting birds in the spring; also note that you will not see many birds on hot and windy days. You might also want to avoid paddling during the opening weekend of waterfowl hunting—around the end of September—though this is an issue of serenity rather than a safety. Blue Heron Landing, (920) 485-

4663, in the city of Horicon has canoe rentals and guided canoe trips.

BIKING—Biking is limited within the marsh. In the federal refuge, bikers can ride the TernPike auto tour, even when cars aren't allowed. Bikers can also enter the marsh on the two roads open to cars—Ledge Road (open year round) and Main Dike Road (open from April 15 to September 15).

There is also good biking around the marsh. Just to the west of the marsh, passing alongside it at the very north end, is the Wild Goose State Trail, which follows an abandoned railroad right-of-way—a spur trail leads to the federal Auto Tour route. The Horicon Marsh Parkway, a 36-mile marked road route around the marsh, is detailed under the Auto Tour section.

WINTER—While no trails are groomed, cross-country skiing is permitted on the state and federal hiking trails and the federal Auto Tour route.

AUTO TOUR—The federal refuge's 3.2-mile Horicon TernPike auto tour is open to motor vehicles April 15 through September 15. There are many interpretive stops along the way. Other areas accessible by car include the three-mile Main Dike Road (also open April 15 to September 15) that leads into the heart of the marsh near the dividing line between the state and federal areas, and Ledge Road to the north, which remains open to cars all year long.

The Horicon Marsh Parkway is a marked route around the marsh on public roads that connect all the major access points; there are several excellent viewing sites along the way. Highway 49 leads right through the north end of the marsh, and has an extra wide shoulder for those wishing to pull over and stop. The best spot to see geese is along Highway 49 just west of County Z, where you will find a scenic overlook with information panels. The National Wildlife Refuge headquarters has a viewing deck with a spotting scope and displays about the marsh. There is another good viewing point atop a hill on Rockvale Road, just to the south of the headquarters. The best views in the state portion are from the DNR Service Center/International Education Center, located on Highway 28, and the DNR Field Office just north of the city of Horicon on Palmatory Road. Both offer a few picnic tables.

OTHER—Boat tours of the marsh are available from Blue Heron Landing, (920) 485-4663, and if you can not get out on the water on your own, you should seriously consider going for a ride on one of these pontoon boats.

COUNTIES—Dodge and Fond du Lac.

DIRECTIONS—State headquarters, two miles northeast of Horicon on Highway 28. Federal headquarters, 2.5 miles north of Mayville on County Y, then three miles northwest on County Z. Marsh Haven, 2.5 miles east of Waupun on Highway 49.

FACILITIES—Water, toilets, nature center, nature programs, picnic area, picnic shelter.

CAMPING—Marsh Haven has a group camp.

ENTRY—Federal and state lands open year-round. Marsh Haven open April through November. State and federal areas are free. Nominal admission fee for hiking at Marsh Haven.

ON THE WEB—www.dnr.state.wi.us/org/land/wildlife/reclands/horicon, http://midwest.fws.gov/Horicon, and www.horiconmarshbirdclub.com

CONTACT—DNR Headquarters, N7725 Highway 28, Horicon, WI 53032. Phone (920) 387-7860. Horicon National Wildlife Refuge, W4279 Headquarters Rd., Mayville, WI 53050. Phone (920) 387-2658. Marsh Haven Nature Center, W10145 Highway 49 E., Waupun, WI 53963. Phone (920) 324-5818.

Poygan Marsh Wildlife Area

POYGAN MARSH is an important waterfowl haven along the west shore of Lake Poygan. Nearly all of its 3,282 acres are wetlands, with a large area of wooded uplands along the Pine River. Land acquisition began in 1958 and continues today; eventually, another thousand acres will be added. The Pine River, Pumpkinseed and Willow creeks, and many smaller streams, flow through the property before emptying into Lake Poygan along the marsh's six miles of shoreline. Archaeological surveys have found two prehistoric Native American camps on the property and, considering that wild rice grows here, there were probably many more.

WILDLIFE—Among the animals that can be seen at Poygan Marsh are deer, fox, mink, otter, beaver, marsh hawk, saw-whet owl, ruffed grouse, woodcock, wild turkey, marsh wren, ducks, sandhill crane, green-backed heron, and the endangered Forster's tern.

HIKING—The many miles of dikes offer easy hiking and up-close wildlife viewing. To the north, a series of dikes leads in from the end of Beaver Road to parking areas along Badger Road. A narrower, seldom-used path leads south from the Beaver Road parking area and follows a winding stream through bottomland forest before joining the main dike after less than a mile. More dikes lead through the southern end of the marsh from the end of Blackhawk Avenue. Bighorn Drive leads into the forested middle section of the wildlife area, but there are no trails here.

PADDLING—There is a boat launch onto Willow Creek, the largest of the waterways leading through the property, just north of County D. Paddlers can also travel up the Pine River and Pumpkinseed Creek. There are numerous boat launches directly onto Lake Poygan; the one nearest to the wildlife area is at the end of Badger Road.

COUNTY—Waushara.

DIRECTIONS—1.5 miles east of Poy Sippi on County H, then two miles southeast on Beaver Rd.

FACILITIES—Boat launch.

CAMPING—None.

ENTRY—Open year-round. Free.

CONTACT—DNR, 905 Bayshore Dr., PO Box 2565, Oshkosh, WI 54903. Phone (920) 424-3050.

White River Marsh Wildlife Area

THE VAST White River Marsh lies in a glacially-formed basin bordered by the Fox River on the south, while its smaller namesake waterway bisects the marsh from the northwest to the southeast. A mixture of wooded and open uplands surrounds the marsh creating ideal habitat for a variety of wildlife. Aldo Leopold first recommended state acquisition of the property after surveying it in the 1940s, but the state did not begin land purchases until 1962. Today the wildlife area covers nearly 11,100 acres and will eventually be expanded by another 5,500. Many people are drawn here by the abundant wildlife, but there are never crowds.

WILDLIFE—Within the wildlife area's varied habitats you may spot deer, fox, coyote, mink, or beaver. More than 200 species of birds have been seen here, including wild turkey, ruffed grouse, pheasant, woodcock, herons, hawks, and a multitude of songbirds. Sandhill cranes and ducks in particular thrive at White River. Green Lake and Marquette counties are home to almost half of Wisconsin's sandhills.

HIKING—Foot access into the marsh is limited. A few service roads and unmaintained trails branch off the public roads through the area, though they are generally overgrown and do not lead very far. County D west of Marsh Road is the best place to look for a path. Directly north from Princeton, the highway takes a sharp turn west; continuing straight onto the gravel road past the large wildlife area sign leads to two of the easiest paths to follow. White River Road also has some hikeable paths leading away from it.

PADDLING—The Fox River offers leisurely canoeing. A boat launch onto the Fox is located four miles north of Princeton on Huckleberry Road. The White River is shallow and often blocked by downed trees.

AUTO TOUR—The most popular way to experience the area by car is along Rustic Road #22, the White River Road. This scenic route runs for 5.5 miles right through the heart of the marsh.

COUNTIES—Green Lake and Marquette.
DIRECTIONS—Three miles north of Princeton on County D.
FACILITIES—Boat launch.
CAMPING—None.
ENTRY—Open year-round. Free.
CONTACT—DNR, Box 343, Berlin, WI 54923. Phone (920) 361-3149.

Germania Marsh Wildlife Area

THE SCENIC Germania Marsh lies in a shallow basin carved during the last Ice Age. The nearly 2,400-acre wildlife area consists mostly of marsh, but also encompasses much of the surrounding uplands. The winding Mecan River which bisects the marsh was dammed for a mill in 1867, creating Germania Lake, which became a major wildlife haven. The dam was removed in the early 1900s to allow farmers to harvest marsh hay. When the area was purchased by the state in 1955, a new dam and several dikes were constructed to again attract waterfowl and other wildlife.

WILDLIFE—Germania Marsh, ranking among the best waterfowl habitats in the region, is an important stop for migrating birds of all kinds. Ducks, geese, tundra swan, and herons are all found in the marsh, and sandhill cranes are very likely to be spotted because Marquette County has the largest nesting population of these birds in the nation. Deer, fox, coyote, mink, beaver, osprey, pheasant, ruffed grouse, and wild turkey inhabit the wooded uplands and open fields around the marsh.

HIKING—Germania offers easy access for hikers. A 1.5-mile gravel road passes right through the heart of the marsh between Eagle and Duck Creek roads. Both this unnamed gravel road and Duck Creek Road itself, which runs through the northeast portion of the property, can be nice hikes on their own. They are sometimes gated and even when not closed to traffic they are never busy.

The best hiking option is just south of the river, at the end of a short, unnamed road heading west from the gravel road that cuts through the property. Here a series of dikes leads for more than a mile through a very scenic section, passing two small impoundments along the way. Another three-quarters of a mile of dikes start at a parking area on Duck Creek Road, a quarter mile west of County N. These dikes can also be hiked, though they may be a little overgrown.

Additional parking areas along Eagle Road to the west and south, and County N to the east, provide limited access.

PADDLING—Canoeing on the Mecan River is a good way to see the area, especially since motorboats are prohibited. Boat landings are found at several different places on the river within the wildlife area.

COUNTY—Marquette.

DIRECTIONS—Seven miles north of Montello on Highway 22, then half a mile east on Dyke Rd., and two miles southeast on Eagle Rd.

FACILITIES—Boat launch.

CAMPING—None.

ENTRY—Open year-round. Free.

CONTACT—DNR, Box 343, Berlin, WI 54923. Phone (920) 361-3149.

Page Creek Marsh

THE WETLANDS along slow-moving Page Creek are virtually undisturbed, making this an important area for migrating birds. In addition to the marsh, this diverse property includes sedge meadow, tamarack bog, oak barrens, upland forest, and small prairie and savanna remnants. An extensive prairie restoration is underway in the northern end of this preserve. The area previously served as an outdoor education center called Camp Corbin, and though most buildings have been removed, you might still see some camp remains. The first 69 acres of the preserve were donated to The Nature Conservancy in 1986, and today over 6500 acres have been protected—the goal is to expand to over a thousand. While access can be difficult, the solitude, abundance of wildlife, and wetland boardwalks make this a worthy destination.

WILDLIFE—The marsh is an important staging area for sandhill cranes during migration, though they are likely to be seen at other times, as well. Many other animals make the marsh their home, including ducks, geese, green-backed herons, wild turkey, willow flycatchers, deer, coyote, fox, and beaver.

HIKING—Miles of trails wind through the area, though because they are seldom used, most are overgrown and hard to follow; in some stretches there is no remaining trail at all. This makes spring the ideal time to visit, because the trails are easier to find. Benches offering superb marsh views are strategically placed around the property.

A narrow trail leads east into the marsh from the parking area in the southwest corner. Small stumps with their tops painted white help to lead the way, but even these can be hard to find. A few hundred feet beyond the parking area, the trail crosses Page Creek and passes through a tamarack bog on a narrow boardwalk. Some interpretive signs are located along this part of the trail.

Past the bog, the trail joins an old dirt road that is still very easy to follow. This old road leads through the center of the property to the mostly-wooded eastern end. The road ends just north of Bright Lake, the largest of three lakes on the property. On the eastern edge of the lake, more boardwalks pass through the marsh and bog. Many other trails, both wide and narrow, branch off in all directions from the road.

COUNTY—Marquette.

DIRECTIONS—Two miles east of Packwaukee on County D, then half a mile north on County K.

FACILITIES—None.

CAMPING—None.

ENTRY—Open year-round. Free.

ON THE WEB—http://nature.org/wisconsin

CONTACT—The Nature Conservancy. Phone (608) 251-8140. E-mail: wmail@tnc.org

John Muir Memorial Park

I T IS ONLY appropriate that the land that inspired John Muir, one of the United States' earliest and most important conservationists, be preserved to inspire future generations. Founder of the Sierra Club and "Father of the National Parks," his enduring legacy benefits us all. Muir was born in Scotland but raised in southern Marquette County after his family emigrated to the United States in 1849, when John was 11 years old. Muir's travels later took him all over the world, but his deep respect for nature can be traced back to his southern Wisconsin home. Some of the land that had been the Muir family's Fountain Lake Farm is now protected in this park, and though the buildings are gone, this is also a National Historic Landmark. The very idea of nature conservation was born here when Muir tried to buy 40 acres from his brother. "I want to keep it untrampled for the sake of its ferns and flowers," Muir explained. His brother refused, but nearly a century later John's wish came true. A granite monument in honor of Muir, erected at the park's dedication in 1957, is located just north of the picnic area and long-range plans call for an interpretive center.

The most prominent feature is 30-acre spring-fed Ennis Lake, known as Fountain Lake when Muir swam and fished in it. The rest of the park is a mix of forest, wetland, and prairie communities containing more than 300 plant species. Because of its numerous interrelated plant and aquatic communities, the park is a part of (Muir's) Ennis Lake-Muir Park State Natural Area. Though at 125 acres the park is rather small, it is still a wonderful place to visit, since the undeveloped surroundings, including the 640-acre Fox River Unit of the Horicon Marsh National Wildlife Refuge (not open to the public) to the west, makes this unspoiled park feel much larger than it really is.

WILDLIFE—Wildlife is abundant in the park. The sandhill cranes that delighted Muir in his day may still be seen regularly, along with geese, ducks, wild turkey, pheasant, hawks, deer, coyote, and fox.

HIKING—A level, two-mile trail circles the lake. It is mostly wooded to the south and passes through a mix of wetland and prairie to the north. Boardwalks span the wettest parts of the trail, but it can still be a little muddy at times. The Ice Age Trail (p. 1) will likely pass through here in the future.

PADDLING—The lake is small, but some people enjoy a quiet paddle around it. Only electric motors are allowed.

COUNTY—Marquette.

DIRECTIONS—Eight miles south of Montello on County F.

FACILITIES—Toilets, boat launch, picnic area.

CAMPING—With prior approval.

ENTRY—Open year-round, but the entry road is not plowed. Free.

CONTACT—Marquette County Clerk's Office, PO Box 186, Montello, WI 53949. Phone (608) 297-9136.

Rowan Creek Fishery Area

ESTABLISHED TO protect Rowan Creek, one of southern Wisconsin's best trout streams, this 629-acre reserve stretches for seven miles along Rowan Creek toward its junction with the Wisconsin River. The village of Poynette lies near the middle of the area. To the west of the village the land is mostly marsh and forest, while to the east it is mostly open field. Jamieson Park, operated by the Village of Poynette, adjoins the western half.

WILDLIFE—Among the 150 species of birds that might be seen here are wild turkey, pheasant, ruffed grouse, ducks, sandhill crane, and herons. Deer, fox, and mink are common mammals. Threatened and endangered species include ornate box and Blanding's turtles and the legless, slender glass lizard.

HIKING—The two-mile Rowan Creek Trail leads through the wooded western section of the preserve. The level path consists of four loops plus a narrow section that leads to Mill Street in Poynette. Three floating boardwalks passing through cattail marsh between the loops are a highlight of the trail; interpretive signs discuss the area. The loop around Pine Island, consisting of pine plantation and brushy forest openings, is the least scenic part of the trail, though it is a good place to pick berries. The quarter-mile path connecting the loop around Oak Island with Poynette leads right along Rowan Creek, mostly through marsh. There are several bridges and wood-chip-covered sections along this part of the trail, helping to keep it dry. At the end is the foundation of an old mill, built in 1860, that produced Dole's Best Flour for half a century.

WINTER—The Rowan Creek Trail is usually groomed for cross-country skiing.

COUNTY—Columbia.

DIRECTIONS—The trailhead is half a mile west of Poynette on County CS.

FACILITIES—Jamieson Park has water, toilets, picnic area, grills, picnic shelter.

CAMPING—Camping allowed in Jamieson Park (free), 15 sites, open Memorial Day to Labor Day.

ENTRY—Open year-round. Free.

ON THE WEB—www.rowancreek.org

CONTACT—DNR, N3344 Stebbins Rd., Poynette, WI 53955. Phone (608) 275-3242.

Lodi Marsh Wildlife Area

T HE ICE AGE TRAIL (p. 1) crosses the Dane-Columbia county line through this 1,070-acre wildlife area. It follows a line of hills and bluffs covered by both forest and field, including a large and still expanding oak savanna restoration at the southern end. According to the DNR, "the least disturbed dry-mesic prairie in the state" sits at the base of the prominent Hawk Hill, part of the 545-acre Lodi Marsh State Natural Area. The landscape will remind visitors of Wisconsin's Driftless Region which is, in fact, several miles to the west. Spring Creek, a popular trout stream surrounded by marsh, winds through the western half of the property.

WILDLIFE—Look for deer, fox, coyote, mink, wild turkey, pheasant, sandhill crane, great blue heron, ducks, hawks, willow and alder flycatcher, sedge wren, and blue-winged warbler. The area is noted for its diverse and bountiful population of butterflies and moths including the rare ottoe skipper and net-veined leafhopper.

HIKING—The Lodi Marsh segment of the Ice Age Trail is a short but scenic hike. The three-mile section of trail within the wildlife area has two distinct parts, separated by Lodi-Springfield Road at the area's southern end, where there is a parking lot offering maps and other posted information.

West of the road the trail leads for a mile to a prairie overlook near Center Bluff, Lodi Marsh's most prominent landmark. This part of the trail traverses an oak savanna restoration. A set of steps leads down to Spring Creek, about a quarter-mile in from the road. This area has only small hills and little forest.

Across the road, the trail leads two and a half miles north over the bluffs, creating a more strenuous hike. This area is mostly wooded, though there are some open spots. A few rock outcroppings are scattered about the forest toward the north end, and Devil's Lake State Park and the Baraboo Hills are visible to the northwest from the trail's higher points. Beyond the north end of the wildlife area, the trail cuts east and follows Highway 13 into Lodi, where it passes the Ice Age Trail office on Main Street.

COUNTIES—Dane and Columbia.

DIRECTIONS—A quarter-mile southwest of Lodi on Highway 60, then a quarter-mile south on Lodi-Springfield Rd.

FACILITIES—None.

CAMPING—None.

ENTRY—Open year-round. Free.

CONTACT—DNR, 3911 Fish Hatchery Road, Fitchburg, WI 53711. Phone (608) 275-3292. Ice Age Park & Trail Foundation, Dane County Chapter, 2302 Lakeland Ave., Madison, WI 53704. Phone (608) 249-7870.

Indian Lake County Park

T HIS MOSTLY undeveloped 442-acre park lies right at the edge of the last glacial advance. While the ice did not completely carve away the steep slopes, a narrow finger of ice did reach into the park, forming the shallow kettle lake. Indian Lake received its name because Native Americans lived at the southwest edge into the mid-1800s, well after the first European settlers arrived in the area. Today the park is mostly wooded, but originally this area was dominated by prairie, and a few scattered remnants remain.

Many people come here to see the St. Mary of the Oaks chapel. The tiny stone shrine was built in 1857 by John Endres, reportedly fulfilling a vow to do so if his family was spared from a diphtheria epidemic. According to the property's deed, the chapel is to be maintained forever.

WILDLIFE—As many as 180 species of birds can be seen throughout the year, including wild turkey, ruffed grouse, turkey vulture, pileated woodpecker, ducks, great blue and green-backed herons, sandhill crane, the state-threatened great egret, Eastern meadowlark, scarlet tanager, and red-eyed vireo. Park mammals include deer, badger, and coyote.

HIKING—There are eight miles of trails winding through the park's wooded hills. The 4.5-mile Red Loop leads past the lake and around the perimeter of the park. Three shorter loops circle within the Red, and all connect, allowing various hiking options. While all paths are hilly, the 1.8-

mile Yellow Loop is the most level, sharing much of its path with the two-mile Green Loop. The Orange Loop is the shortest at 1.3 miles, but is also the hilliest. Branching off the Orange Loop, a trail leads around the lake, crossing the east end along a 900-foot floating boardwalk. The Ice Age Trail (p. 1) follows these trails through the park. The modest chapel is not all that interesting, though the 0.75-mile path up the steep, wooded hill is worthwhile for the views of the lake and surrounding valley. Also along this path are several interpretive signs that discuss many of the plants found here. Steps at the steepest parts make it a fairly easy climb.

PADDLING—Canoeists can paddle around Indian Lake if they want to, though it is just 66 acres and abuts the highway. Only electric motors are allowed.

WINTER—The trails are groomed for cross-country skiing and there is a log cabin warming house. These are some of the most popular winter trails in the Madison area.

COUNTY—Dane.

DIRECTIONS—Nine miles west of Waunakee on Highway 19.

FACILITIES—Water, toilets, boat launch, picnic area, picnic shelter.

CAMPING—Group camp.

ENTRY—Open year-round. Free. County trail pass or daily fee for cross-country skiing.

ON THE WEB—www.co.dane.wi.us/parks

CONTACT—Dane County Park Commission, 4318 Robertson Rd., Madison, WI 53714. Phone (608) 246-3896. E-mail: dane-parks@co.dane.wi.us

Governor Nelson State Park

GOVERNOR NELSON is located on the northwestern edge of Lake Mendota, just outside Madison. The State Capitol is clearly visible across the lake. When the land for the park was acquired, over half of it was farmland, though in a positive reversal of tradition, wildflowers have replaced wheat and the extensive prairie and oak savanna restoration is a highlight of the 422-acre park. Come between mid-July and mid-August to see it in full bloom. While the prairie dominates the landscape, the southern end of the park is forested, and marsh borders Six Mile Creek to the north.

Governor Nelson is also a major archaeological site. Numerous effigy mounds are found in the southern end, the most prominent being a 358-foot-long panther mound. While park facilities were being constructed, a 244-foot section of a stockaded village, roughly a thousand years old, was uncovered.

Villages of this sort were rare in the state. The oval stockade was built by the effigy mound builders, not the group that lived to the east at Aztalan, though that famous village may have been the inspiration for this smaller one.

WILDLIFE—Deer, fox, beaver, trumpeter swan, sandhill crane, green and great blue heron, wood duck, Cooper's hawk, wild turkey, pheasant, and indigo bunting can all be found in the park's varied environments. The birdhouses scattered around the park are part of a successful bluebird restoration project.

HIKING—There is a lot to see along the park's trails, especially the 1.8-mile Woodland Trail which loops through the southern part of the park. Naturally, forest is the dominant habitat, though you will catch a glimpse of the prairie from the north end and along the west side. The trail is mostly flat, with just a few moderate hills. These hills, as well as Lake Mendota, were formed by the last glacier to sweep across Wisconsin, which stopped its advance just ten miles beyond the park. One of the hills along the western side of the trail provides a wonderful scenic overlook of the lake. It is situated in such a way that the lake appears to be untouched by human hands, when in fact the shoreline is almost completely developed. Also along the Woodland Trail are many of the park's burial mounds, including the large panther effigy mound. A short spur path at the southern end leads to the Wakanda Picnic Area on Lake Mendota. Lakeshore homes surround this small plot, but it is much quieter than the primary picnic areas. The remaining part of what had been a 282-foot-long panther mound can be seen here as well. A trail pamphlet discusses the past uses by Native Americans and settlers of some of the plants you will find growing along the trail.

The 3.5-mile Morningside Trail, circling the northern end of the park, is the best destination for wildlife watchers. The virtually level path crosses through prairie and oak savanna, and passes alongside an extensive marsh on the back end. There is a wheelchair-accessible wildlife-viewing platform overlooking Dorn Creek on the northern loop. The mile-long Redtail Hawk Trail and the 2.1-mile Oak Savanna Trail offer a wonderful up-close look at the park's prairie. Both loops cross some moderate hills in the south, but are overall easy hikes. The latter path runs right by the park office, where there is another accessible viewing platform.

PADDLING—Paddling lazily around Six Mile Creek is a good way to look for wildlife, though park staff request that you avoid the smaller Dorn Creek to protect the large number of birds nesting on its banks. It is possible to travel south through Lakes Mendota, Monona, Waubesa, and Kegonsa via the Yahara River to Lake Kegonsa State Park (p. 1), a trip of about ten miles. Development is extensive, so do not expect a great deal of natural scenery, but the mix of urban and rural life can be fun. A much better trip is to head north up the

267

Yahara River through the Cherokee Marsh, which is about two miles away from the park. Lake Mendota can be crowded with motorboats in summer, and on windy days the waves can become large, making canoeing undesirable at times.

WINTER—The park's trails are all groomed for cross-country skiing, and the Oak Savanna and Woodland trails can accommodate skate skiers. A snow-shoeing path is maintained next to the Morningside's groomed ski track.

COUNTY—Dane.

DIRECTIONS—Three miles northeast of Middleton on County M.

FACILITIES—Water, toilets, boat launch, nature programs, grills, picnic area, picnic shelter, beach (with a separate pet swim area), playground (accessible).

CAMPING—None.

ENTRY—Open year-round. State park sticker or daily fee required.

ON THE WEB—www.wiparks.net

CONTACT—Governor Nelson State Park, 5140 County Road M, Waunakee, WI 53597. Phone (608) 831-3005.

Lake Kegonsa State Park

AT 343 ACRES, Lake Kegonsa is one of Wisconsin's smallest state parks, and yet, even with extensive development within its borders, a visit is still worthwhile for nature lovers. The primary attraction is a 60-acre tall-grass prairie restoration begun in the mid-1970s. Restoration of the adjacent oak woods to pre-settlement savanna began about twenty years later, and for a little natural variety there is also some marsh along the small creek that empties into the lake.

The namesake lake, on whose shores the park sits, was known by early settlers as First Lake because it was the first of four they encountered along the Yahara River. Kegonsa, meaning "Lake of Many Fishes," was the Ho-Chunk's name for this 3,209-acre body of water, and anglers will still find this be an apt name. Glacial meltwater played a significant role in shaping Kegonsa and the other three lakes in the chain—Waubesa, Monona, and Mendota. The last glacier to creep down across Wisconsin stopped only a few miles south of the park.

WILDLIFE—At least a hundred species of birds can be seen throughout the year including ducks, geese, herons, red-tailed hawk, great horned owl, pheasant, wild turkey, spotted sandpiper, bobolink, and nearly three dozen species of warbler during the spring migration. Also look for deer, fox, and the state-threatened Blanding's turtle.

HIKING—Five level trails totaling 4.4 miles loop through the park, though due to its small size, none carries visitors very far from park facilities or roads. The best way to enjoy the paths is to take your time and examine the little things. The 1.2-mile White Oak Nature Trail loops through an 80-acre oak forest, part of which is being restored to oak savanna. Two linear burial mounds lie along the trail, and a guidebook available at the trailhead, discusses forest ecology. The nature trail shares a trailhead with the Prairie Trail, which has three short loops, each about half a mile long, leading around and through the prairie restoration.

Two other short loop trails are found within the park, the 0.3-mile Bluebird Trail and the 0.6-mile Oak Knoll Trail. The Bluebird Trail is entirely through open field and is surrounded by park roads. The Oak Knoll Trail has two short loops; the longer leads through a small oak woods and open field, while the shorter is all open. At its southern end, it connects to an old roadbed that leads to a bridge; this is the best place to view the marsh and the birds that live in it. Finally, the 0.6-mile Beach Trail crosses an open field, connecting the campground and the beach.

PADDLING—Lake Kegonsa is not a great canoeing option because of the many motorboats and large waves on windy days, but that does not mean people do not canoe here. For a unique mix of urban and rural scenery, paddle the Yahara River between Governor Nelson (p. 266), and Lake Kegonsa state parks, a ten-mile trip that passes through all four lakes in the chain.

WINTER—The park has over five miles of groomed cross-country ski trails, including all the hiking trails (except the Oak Knoll Trail, which is left open for winter hiking) plus the road through the campground. Skate-skiing is allowed on the Blue Trail. A sledding hill is located down near the lake.

COUNTY—Dane.

DIRECTIONS—3.5 miles north of Stoughton on Williams Dr., then half a mile west on Williams Point Dr., and a few hundred yards north on Door Creek Rd.

FACILITIES—Water, toilets, boat launch, nature programs, picnic area, grills, picnic shelter, beach, playground, volleyball, horseshoes, ball field.

CAMPING—80 sites, open May 1 to October 31, reservations accepted, showers, group camp.

ENTRY—Open year-round. State park sticker or daily fee required.

ON THE WEB—www.wiparks.net

CONTACT—Lake Kegonsa State Park, 2405 Door Creek Rd., Stoughton, WI 53589. Phone (608) 873-9695.

Brooklyn Wildlife Area

T HE HIGHLIGHT of this 2,537-acre wildlife area is the Ice Age Trail (p. 1) which winds through a mix of meadow, prairie, and oak woodlands along the western edge of the property. Story Creek, an excellent trout stream, and its associated wetlands dominate Brooklyn's eastern half. The mix of habitats makes this a good bird-watching area. There are also abundant wildflowers, including bird's foot violet, puccoon, and three varieties of gentians.

The distinct line of hills visible just a few miles to the east marks the terminal moraine of the last glacier to cross Wisconsin. Though the landscape, most notably the rock outcroppings of St. Peter's Sandstone (some 450 million years old) found along some of Brooklyn's rolling hills, reminds one of the state's Driftless Region, earlier glaciers did scour this land. The flat landscapes just west of the trail are glacial outwash plains.

WILDLIFE—Among the animals found here are deer, fox, coyote, beaver, blue-winged teal, wood duck, sandhill crane, wild turkey, pheasant, ruffed grouse, bobolink, dickcissel, Eastern meadowlark, grasshopper sparrow, Bell's vireo, and a good number of warblers including the yellow-breasted chat.

HIKING—The Brooklyn segment of the Ice Age Trail stretches for 5.5 miles though the property. The southern end of the trail is at Hughes Road, half a mile east of Green County D. It leads north for 3.8 miles, where it crosses the highway and heads up a wooded hill to a large prairie restoration. The southern portion passes several beautiful rock outcroppings, has a pair of wetland overlooks, and is overall more scenic than the northern segment. Several DNR trails and service roads branch off the main Ice Age Trail, providing additional hiking opportunities; some of these are shown on the maps posted along the trail. The Ice Age Trail continues north of Brooklyn through private property, so please stay on the trail.

Low maintenance paths also lead into other parts of the property from Highway 92 in the south, Bell Brook Road in the north, and Alpine Road in the east though they are generally overgrown and not as scenic.

WINTER—The Ice Age Trail is popular with cross-country skiers though it is not groomed.

COUNTIES—Dane and Green.

DIRECTIONS—Two miles east of Belleville on County D.

FACILITIES—None.

CAMPING—None.

ENTRY—Open year-round. Free.

CONTACT—DNR, 2514 Morse St., Janesville, WI 53545. Phone (608) 743-4800.

New Glarus Woods State Park

THIS SMALL BUT scenic park is a perfect companion to the Sugar River State Trail, which ends in the nearby village of New Glarus. It is great for a picnic or just some post-ride relaxing. As the name suggests, forest covers most of the park's 411 acres, though a large prairie restoration is found in the southeastern section and another on the northern border. Several intermittent streams cut through property.

WILDLIFE—Park wildlife includes deer, fox, coyote, weasel, mink, hawks, pheasant, ruffed grouse, and wild turkey.

HIKING—Five trails totaling almost six miles wind through the park; all but one have small rolling hills. The longest path is the Havenridge Nature Trail, which winds around the park through mostly wooded terrain, but also passes the park's prairie habitat. Because it passes along the edge of the park, the adjacent farms are frequently visible. A guide booklet available at the park office discusses natural features found along the trail. The half-mile Walnut Trail provides a level, wooded shortcut to the portion of the Havenridge Trail in the southern end of the park. There is an accessible turkey-viewing blind at the north end.

Three all-wooded trails cross the northern part of the park. The 0.4-mile Basswood Nature Trail loop has detailed interpretive signs along it, discussing the ecology of New Glarus Woods. The 0.4-mile Chattermark Trail provides an alternate return path for the Havenridge Trail. The 0.2-mile Great Oak Trail connects the Basswood and Havenridge trails to the Sugar River Trail spur. Though short, these three trails are quite scenic.

BIKING—A 1.6-mile spur trail connects to the north end of the Sugar River State Trail; this converted railroad right-of-way, surfaced with crushed limestone, runs 23 miles from New Glarus southeast to Broadhead. Walk-in campsites are spread out along this trail.

WINTER—Cross-country skiing and snowshoeing are popular though the trails are not groomed.

COUNTY—Green.

DIRECTIONS—Two miles south of New Glarus on Highway 69 at the intersection with County NN.

FACILITIES—Water, toilets, nature programs, picnic area, grills, picnic shelter, playground.

CAMPING—32 sites, 14 walk-in, open year-round, reservations accepted, group camp.

ENTRY—Open year-round. State park sticker or daily fee required.

ON THE WEB—www.wiparks.net

CONTACT—New Glarus Woods State Park, W5446 County Highway NN, PO Box 805, New Glarus, WI 53574. Phone (608) 527-2335.

Browntown-Cadiz Springs
State Recreation Area

BECKMAN AND Zanders lakes are the main draw to this quiet day-use facility. The small, man-made waters attract many anglers, while a picnic area and beach lie on the shore of Beckman Lake, the larger of the two. The rest of the park's nearly 650 acres is an undeveloped wildlife area and public hunting ground, comprised of a mixture of marsh, grassland, and scattered woodlots. The 40-acre Browntown Oak Forest State Natural Area, an excellent example of southern Wisconsin's native forests, sits at the north end of the property.

WILDLIFE—Among the animals found here are deer, fox, mink, ruffed grouse, wild turkey, pheasant, herons, geese, ducks, many songbird species, and the state-threatened Blanding's turtle.

HIKING—Nearly ten miles of easy and peaceful trails wind around the lakes and through the rest of the park. A paved path between the two lakes is part of the easy 0.65-mile Zanders Lake Nature Trail. It loops around Zanders Lake, through some woods, and across a short boardwalk in a marsh. Signs along the trail discuss the varied ecology of the area.

Beckman Lake is circled by a level, open, two-mile trail. At the back end, a set of steps connects it with the Cheese Country Recreation Trail, which follows an abandoned railroad right-of-way and offers some additional hiking. The trail returns via the nature trail to complete the loop, or hikers can continue on to the eastern portion of the park where there are about five miles of lightly-used trails. These trails lead through a mix of wooded and open terrain, over some small rolling hills, and past some farm fields to the north. There are also several direct access points to these trails along Allen Road.

Another little-used trail loops for about half a mile through the forest south of the beach; because of on-going research, the adjacent trails through the natural area are no longer maintained, and entry is discouraged.

PADDLING—Canoeists can paddle around the lakes, where only electric motors are allowed.

BIKING—The Cheese Country Recreation Trail, stretching for 47 miles between Mineral Point and Monroe, forms the park's southern border and is available for bikers, though it is also popular with ATVers.

WINTER—The trails are open for snowshoeing or cross-country skiing but are not groomed.

COUNTY—Green.

DIRECTIONS—Eight miles west of Monroe on Highway 11, then half a mile south on S. Cadiz Springs Rd.

FACILITIES—Water, toilets, boat launch, picnic area, grills, picnic shelter, beach, playground.

CAMPING—None.

ENTRY—Open year-round. State park sticker or daily fee required.

ON THE WEB—www.wiparks.net

CONTACT—Browntown-Cadiz Springs Recreation Area, Box 256, Monroe, WI 53566. Phone (608) 966-3777 or (608) 325-4844.

The Kohler Dunes Cordwalk.

DONALD S. ABRAMS

State and County
Tourism Contacts

STATEWIDE

Wisconsin Department of Tourism
201 W. Washington Ave.
PO Box 7976
Madison, WI 53707
(608) 266-2161
(800) 432-8747
tourinfo@travelwisconsin.com
www.travelwisconsin.com

Department of Natural Resources
101 S. Webster St.
Madison, WI 53703
(608) 266-2621
(608) 267-6897 (TDD)
www.dnr.state.wi.us

COUNTIES

Adams
Adams County Chamber of Commerce
115 S. Main St.
PO Box 576
Adams, WI 53910
(608) 339-6997
adamsccc@mags.net
www.adamscountywi.com

Ashland
Ashland Chamber of Commerce
PO Box 746
Ashland, WI 54806
(715) 682-2500
(800) 284-9484
ashchamb@centurytel.net
www.visitashland.com

Barron
Office of County Clerk
330 E. LaSalle Ave.
Barron, WI 54812
(715) 537-6200
(800) 523-6318
bcclerk@co.barron.wi.us
www.co.barron.wi.us/tourism.htm

Bayfield
Bayfield County Tourism
117 E. 5th St.
Washburn, WI 54891
(715) 373-6125
(800) 472-6338
tourbc@travelbayfieldcounty.com
www.travelbayfieldcounty.com

Brown
Packer Country Regional Tourism Office
PO Box 10596
Green Bay, WI 54307
(920) 494-9507
(888) 867-3342
visitorinfo@packercountry.com
www.packercountry.com

Buffalo
County Clerk's Office
PO Box 58
Alma, WI 54610
(608) 685-6209

Burnett
Burnett County Department of Tourism
7410 County Rd. K #112
Siren, WI 54872
(715) 349-7411
(800) 788-3164
bctour@sirentel.net
www.burnettcounty.com

Calumet
Calumet County Tourism Association
PO Box 24
Chilton, WI 53014
(920) 439-2092
(888) 576-9196
www.calumetcountytourism.com

Chippewa
Chippewa Valley Convention
& Visitors Bureau
3625 Gateway Dr., Suite F
Eau Claire, WI 54701
(715) 831-2345
(888) 523-3866
info@chippewavalley.net
www.eauclaire-info.com

Clark
Clark County Economic
Development Corporation
212 S. Main St., PO Box 236
Greenwood, WI 54437
(715) 267-3205
clarkwi@tds.net
www.clark-cty-wi.org

Columbia
Columbia County Economic
Development Corporation
311 E. Wisconsin St., Suite 108
Portage, WI 53901
(608) 742-6161
(800) 842-2524
ccedc@palacenet.net
www.fun.co.columbia.wi.us

Crawford
UW-Extension Office
111 W. Dunn St.
Prairie du Chien, WI 53821
(608) 326-0223
www.uwex.edu/ces/cty/crawford

Dane
Greater Madison Convention & Visitors Bureau
615 E. Washington Ave.
Madison, WI 53703
(608) 255-2537
(800) 373-6376
gmcvb@visitmadison.com
www.visitmadison.com

Dodge
Dodge County Tourism Association
127 E. Oak St.
Juneau, WI 53039
(920) 386-3705
(800) 414-0101
dplanning@dodgecountywi.com
www.dodgecounty.com

Door
Door County Chamber of Commerce
PO Box 406
Sturgeon Bay, WI 54235
(920) 743-4456
(800) 527-3529
info@doorcountyvacations.com
www.doorcountyvacations.com

Douglas
Superior-Douglas County Convention
& Visitors Bureau
205 Belknap St.
Superior WI 54880
(715) 392-2773
(800) 942-5313
vacation@visitsuperior.com
www.visitsuperior.com

Dunn
Greater Menomonie Area Chamber of
Commerce
700 Wolske Bay Rd., Suite 200
Menomonie, WI 54751
(715) 235-9087
(800) 283-1862
chamber@menomonie.com
www.menomoniechamber.org

Eau Claire
Chippewa Valley Convention
& Visitors Bureau
3625 Gateway Dr., Suite F
Eau Claire, WI 54701
(715) 831-2345
(888) 523-3866
info@chippewavalley.net
www.eauclaire-info.com

Florence
Florence Natural Resources Center
HC 1, Box 83
Florence, WI 54121
(715) 528-5377
(888) 889-0049
info@florencewisconsin.com
www.florencewisconsin.com/visitor

Fond du Lac
Fond du Lac Area Convention
  & Visitors Bureau
171 S. Pioneer Rd.
Fond du Lac, WI 54935
(920) 923-3010
(800) 937-9123 ext. 71
visit@fdl.com
www.fdl.com

Forest
Advertising Committee
200 E. Madison St.
Crandon, WI 54520
(715) 478-2212
(800) 334-3387
information@forestcountywi.com
www.forestcountywi.com

Grant
UW-Extension Office
PO Box 31
Lancaster, WI 53813
(608) 723-2125
www.grantcounty.org/visitor

Green
Welcome Center
N3150 Highway 81 #B
Monroe, WI 53566
(608) 328-1838
(888) 222-9111
tourism@greencounty.org
www.greencounty.org

Green Lake
Green Lake Country Visitor's Bureau
PO Box 305
Ripon, WI 54971
(920) 748-6764
(800) 662-6927
info@glcountry.com
www.glcountry.com

Iowa
Clerk's Office
222 N. Iowa St.
Dodgeville, WI 53533
(608) 935-0399
www.iowacounty.org

Iron
Development Zone Council
PO Box 97
Hurley, WI 54534
(715) 561-2922
ironctyinfo@gogebic.cc.mi.us
www.ironcountywi.com

Jackson
Black River Area Chamber of Commerce
120 N. Water St.
Black River Falls, WI 54615
(715) 284-4658
(800) 404-4008
chamber@blackrivercountry.com
www.blackrivercountry.com

Jefferson
Fort Atkinson Area Chamber of Commerce
244 N. Main St.
Fort Atkinson, WI 53538
(920) 563-3210
(888) SEE-FORT
fortcham@idcnet.com
www.fortchamber.com

Juneau
Juneau County Economic Development
Corporation
119 S. Adams St., Suite III
PO Box 145
New Lisbon, WI 53950
(608) 562-5850
(888) 898-2550
jcedc@mwt.net
www.juneaucounty.com

Kenosha
Kenosha Area Convention
  & Visitors Bureau
812 56th St.
Kenosha, WI 53140
(262) 654-7307
(800) 654-7309
www.kenoshacvb.com

Kewaunee
Promotions and Recreation Board
E 4280 County Rd. E
Kewaunee, WI 54216
(920) 388-0444
www.kewauneeco.org

La Crosse
La Crosse Area Convention
  & Visitors Bureau
410 E. Veterans Memorial Dr.
La Crosse, WI 54601
(608) 782-2366
(800) 658-9424
info@explorelacrosse.com
www.explorelacrosse.com

Lafayette
UW-Extension Office
700 N. Main St., Suite 112A
Darlington, WI 53530
(608) 776-4820
ldc@mhtc.net
http://wicip.uwplatt.edu/lafayette

Langlade
Antigo Area Chamber of Commerce
329 Superior St.
Antigo, WI 54409
(715) 623-4134
(888) 526-4523
antigocc@newnorth.net
www.newnorth.net/antigo.chamber

Lincoln
Lincoln County Economic
  Development Department
1106 E. 8th St.
Merrill, WI 54452
(715) 536-0304
(800) 352-9602
lincolnc@pcpros.net
www.co.lincoln.wi.us/tourism.htm

Manitowoc
Manitowoc Area Visitor & Convention Bureau
PO Box 966
Manitowoc, WI 54221
(920) 684-5575
(800) 627-4896
manitowocvcb@lakefield.net
www.manitowoc.org/tourism

Marathon
Wausau-Central Wisconsin Convention
  & Visitors Bureau
10204 Park Plaza, Suite B
Mosinee, WI 54455
(715) 355-8788
(888) 948-4748
info@wausaucvb.com
www.wausaucvb.com

Marinette
Marinette Area Chamber of Commerce
601 Marinette Ave.
Marinette, WI 54143
(715) 735-6681
(800) 236-6681
marinettechamber@cybrzn.com
www.marinettechamber.com

Marquette
Marquette County Clerk's Office
PO Box 186
Montello, WI 53949
(608) 297-9136
(877) 627-6767
www.co.marquette.wi.us

Menominee
Menominee Indian Tribe
PO Box 910
Keshena, WI 54135
(715) 799-5218
www.menominee.nsn.us

Milwaukee
Greater Milwaukee Convention
  & Visitors Bureau
101 W. Wisconsin Ave., Suite 425
Milwaukee, WI 53203
(414) 273-7222
(800) 554-1448
visitor@milwaukee.org
www.milwaukee.org

Monroe
UW-Extension Office
Courthouse Annex
112 S. Court St., Rm. 107
Sparta, WI 54656
(608) 269-8722

Oconto
Oconto County Tourism
PO Box 43
Oconto, WI 54153
(920) 834-6969
(888) 626-6862
request@ocontocounty.org
www.ocontocounty.org

Oneida
Oneida County Chamber of Commerce
PO Box 795
Rhinelander, WI 54501
(715) 365-7466
(800) 236-3006
www.oneidacounty-wi.org

Outagamie
Fox Cities Convention & Visitors Bureau
3433 W. College Ave.
Appleton, WI 54914
(920) 734-3358
(800) 236-6673
tourism@foxcities.org
www.foxcities.org

Ozaukee
Ozaukee County Tourism Council
PO Box 143
Port Washington, WI 53074
(262) 284-9288
(800) 237-2874
www.co.ozaukee.wi.us/tourism

Pepin
Economic Development Office
PO Box 39
Durand, WI 54736
(715) 672-5709
www.pepinwisconsin.com
info@co.pepin.wi.us

Pierce
Pierce County Partners in Tourism
PO Box 53
Ellsworth, WI 54011
(715) 273-5864
(800) 4-PIERCE
info@travelpiercecounty.com
www.travelpiercecounty.com

Polk
Polk County Information Center
710 Highway 35 S
St. Croix Falls, WI 54024
(715) 483-1410
(800) 222-POLK
polkinfo@lakeland.ws
www.polkcountytourism.com

Portage
Stevens Point Area Convention
   & Visitors Bureau
340 Division St. N
Stevens Point, WI 54481
(715) 344-2556
(800) 236-4636
info@spacvb.com
www.stevenspointarea.com

Price
Tourism Department
126 Cherry St.
Phillips, WI 54555
(715) 339-4505
(800) 269-4505
tourism@co.price.wi.us
www.pricecountywi.net

Racine
Racine County Convention
   & Visitors Bureau
14015 Washington Ave.
Sturtevant, WI 53177
(262) 884-6400
(800) 272-2463
visit@racine.org
www.racine.org

Richland
Richland County Economic
   Development Corporation
174 S. Central Ave.
Richland Center, WI 53581
(608) 647-4310
(800) 422-1318
www.richlandcounty.com

Rock
Rock County Tourism Council
PO Box 8041
Janesville, WI 53547
(608) 757-5587
(866) 376-8767
wifrontporch@co.rock.wi.us
www.rockcounty.org

Rusk
Rusk County Visitor Center
205 W. 9th St. S
Ladysmith, WI 54848
(715) 532-2642
(800) 535-7875
info@ruskcounty.org
www.ruskcounty.org

St. Croix
Hudson Area Chamber of Commerce
502 Second St.
Hudson, WI 54016
(715) 386-8411
(800) 657-6775
info@hudsonwi.org
www.hudsonwi.org

Sauk
Baraboo Area Chamber of Commerce
660 W. Chestnut St.
Baraboo WI 53913
(608) 356-8333
(800) BARABOO
chamber@baraboo.com
www.baraboo.com/chamber

Sawyer
Hayward Area Chamber of Commerce
PO Box 726
Hayward, WI 54843
(715) 634-8662
(800) 724-2992
info@haywardlakes.com
www.haywardlakes.com

Shawano
Shawano Area Chamber of Commerce
213 E. Green Bay St.
Shawano, WI 54166
(715) 524-2139
(800) 235-8528
chamber@shawano.com
www.shawano.com

Sheboygan
Convention & Visitors Bureau
712 Riverfront Dr., #101
Sheboygan, WI 53081
(920) 457-9495
(800) 457-9497
info@sheboygan.org
www.sheboygan.org

Taylor
Medford Area Chamber of Commerce
104 E. Perkins St.
PO Box 172
Medford, WI 54451
(715) 748-4729
(888) 682-9567
chamber@dwave.net
www.medfordwis.com

Trempealeau
Trempealeau County Tourism Council
PO Box 21
Arcadia, WI 54612
(608) 323-7076
(800) 927-5339
vacation@trempealeaucountytourism.com
www.trempealeaucountytourism.com

Vernon
Vernon County Tourism Council
S3535 County Rd. S
Viroqua, WI 54665
(608) 637-2575
vvc.com@visitvernoncounty.com
www.visitvernoncounty.com

Vilas
Advertising and Publicity Department
330 Court St.
Eagle River, WI 54521
(715) 479-3649
(800) 236-3649
vilasadv@co.vilas.wi.us
www.vilas.org

Walworth
Walworth County Visitor's Bureau
109 N. Wisconsin St.
Elkhorn, WI 53121
(262) 723-3980
(800) 395-8687
wctc@elknet.net
www.walworthcountytourism.com

Washburn
Washburn County Tourism Association
122 N. River St.
Spooner, WI 54801
(715) 635-9696
(800) 367-3306
washburncotour@centurytel.net
www.washburncounty.com

Washington
Washington County Convention
& Visitors Bureau
3000 Highway PV
West Bend, WI 53095
(262) 677-5069
(888) 974-8687
info@visitwashingtoncounty.com
www.visitwashingtoncounty.com

Waukesha
Waukesha County Tourism Initiative
2240 N. Grandview Blvd. Suite 2
Waukesha, WI 53188
(262) 695-7903
(800) 366-1961
www.waukeshacountywi.com

Waupaca
Waupaca Area Chamber of Commerce
221 S. Main St.
Waupaca, WI 54981
(715) 258-7343
(888) 417-4040
discoverwaupaca@waupacaareachamber.com
www.waupacaareachamber.com

Waushara
Waushara Area Chamber of Commerce
124 E. Main St.
Wautoma, WI 54982
(920) 787-3488
(877) 928-8662
wacc@voyager.net
www.1wautoma.com/Chamber

Winnebago
Oshkosh Convention & Visitors Bureau
2 N. Main St.
Oshkosh, WI 54901
(920) 303-9200
(877) 303-9200
info@oshkoshcvb.org
www.oshkoshcvb.org

Wood
Heart of Wisconsin Business
and Economic Alliance
1120 Lincoln St.
Wisconsin Rapids, WI 54494
(715) 423-1830
(800) 554-4484
chamber@wctc.net
www.wisconsinrapidsarea.com

Index

More Great Titles
From Trails Books and Prairie Oak Press
Activity Guides

Great Cross-Country Ski Trails: Wisconsin, Minnesota, Michigan & Ontario, Wm. Chad McGrath

Great Minnesota Walks: 49 Strolls, Rambles, Hikes, and Treks, Wm. Chad McGrath

Great Wisconsin Walks: 45 Strolls, Rambles, Hikes, and Treks, Wm. Chad McGrath

Paddling Illinois: 64 Great Trips by Canoe and Kayak, Mike Svob

Paddling Southern Wisconsin: 82 Great Trips by Canoe and Kayak, Mike Svob

Paddling Northern Wisconsin: 82 Great Trips by Canoe and Kayak, Mike Svob

Wisconsin Underground: A Guide to Caves, Mines, and Tunnels in and around the Badger State, Doris Green

Minnesota Underground & the Best of the Black Hills: A Guide to Mines, Sinks, Caves, and Disappearing Streams, Doris Green

Travel Guides

Great Little Museums of the Midwest, Christine des Garennes

Great Minnesota Weekend Adventures, Beth Gauper

The Great Wisconsin Touring Book: 30 Spectacular Auto Tours, Gary Knowles

Tastes of Minnesota: A Food Lover's Tour, Donna Tabbert Long

Wisconsin Lighthouses: A Photographic and Historical Guide, Ken and Barb Wardius

Wisconsin Waterfalls, Patrick Lisi

Wisconsin Family Weekends: 20 Fun Trips for You and the Kids, Susan Lampert Smith

County Parks of Wisconsin, Revised Edition, Jeannette and Chet Bell

Up North Wisconsin: A Region for All Seasons, Sharyn Alden

Great Wisconsin Taverns: 101 Distinctive Badger Bars, Dennis Boyer

Great Weekend Adventures, the Editors of Wisconsin Trails

Eating Well in Wisconsin, Jerry Minnich

Acorn Guide to Northwest Wisconsin, Tim Bewer

Nature Essays

Wild Wisconsin Notebook, James Buchholz

Trout Friends, Bill Stokes

Northern Passages: Reflections from Lake Superior Country, Michael Van Stappen

River Stories: Growing Up on the Wisconsin, Delores Chamberlain

Home & Garden

Wisconsin Country Gourmet, Marge Snyder & Suzanne Breckenridge

Wisconsin Herb Cookbook, Marge Snyder & Suzanne Breckenridge

Creating a Perennial Garden in the Midwest, Joan Severa

Wisconsin Garden Guide, Jerry Minnich

Bountiful Wisconsin: 110 Favorite Recipes, Terese Allen

Wisconsin's Hometown Flavors, Terese Allen

Historical Books

Prairie Whistles: Tales of Midwest Railroading, Dennis Boyer

Barns of Wisconsin, Jerry Apps

Portrait of the Past: A Photographic Journey Through Wisconsin 1865-1920, Howard Mead, Jill Dean, and Susan Smith

Wisconsin: The Story of the Badger State, Norman K. Risjord

Wisconsin At War: 20th Century Conflicts Through the Eyes of Veterans, Dr. James F. McIntosh

Gift Books

The Spirit of Door County: A Photographic Essay, Darryl R. Beers

Milwaukee, Photography by Todd Dacquisto

Duck Hunting on the Fox: Hunting and Decoy-Carving Traditions, Stephen M. Miller

Spirit of the North: A Photographic Journey Through Northern Wisconsin, Richard Hamilton Smith

Ghost Stories

Haunted Wisconsin, Michael Norman and Beth Scott

W-Files: True Reports of Wisconsin's Unexplained Phenomena, Jay Rath

The Beast of Bray Road: Tailing Wisconsin's Werewolf, Linda S. Godfrey

Giants in the Land: Folktales and Legends of Wisconsin, Dennis Boyer

For a free catalog, phone, write, or e-mail us.
Trails Books
P.O. Box 317, Black Earth, WI 53515
(800) 236-8088 • e-mail: trailsbooks@wistrails.com